World War II in Europe

A Concise History

MARVIN PERRY

Baruch College, City University of New York

WADSWORTH
CENGAGE Learning·

Australia · Brazil · Japan · Korea · Mexico · Singapore · Spain · United Kingdom · United States

WADSWORTH
CENGAGE Learning·

World War II in Europe:
A Concise History
Marvin Perry

Senior Publisher: Suzanne Jeans

Acquiring Sponsoring Editor:
Brooke Barbier

Development Editor:
Lauren Floyd

Editorial Assistant:
Katie Coaster

Managing Media Editor:
Lisa Ciccolo

Marketing Program Manager:
Michael Ledesma

Design Direction, Production
Management, and Composition:
PreMediaGlobal

Manufacturing Planner:
Sandee Milewski

Senior Rights Acquisition
Specialist: Jennifer Meyer Dare

Cover Image: © Yevgeny
Khaldei/Corbis

For product information and technology assistance, contact us at
Cengage Learning Customer & Sales Support, 1-800-354-9706

For permission to use material from this text or product, submit all requests online at **www.cengage.com/permissions**. Further permissions questions can be emailed to **permissionrequest@cengage.com**.

Library of Congress Control Number: 2011943696

ISBN-13: 978-1-111-83652-8

ISBN-10: 1-111-83652-3

Wadsworth
20 Channel Center Street
Boston, MA 02210
USA

Cengage Learning is a leading provider of customized learning solutions with office locations around the globe, including Singapore, the United Kingdom, Australia, Mexico, Brazil and Japan. Locate your local office at: **international.cengage.com/region**

Cengage Learning products are represented in Canada by Nelson Education, Ltd.

For your course and learning solutions, visit **www.cengage.com**.

Purchase any of our products at your local college store or at our preferred online store **www.cengagebrain.com**.

Instructors: Please visit **login.cengage.com** and log in to access instructor-specific resources.

Printed in the United States of America
1 2 3 4 5 6 7 16 15 14 13 12

Brief Contents

Contents

✳

Preface

There are numerous books on World War II. However, because many of them are extremely large and detailed, they are often not suitable for college courses. In this relatively concise volume, I have tried to provide a comprehensive and accessible overview of the war in Europe that synthesizes key concepts and incorporates recent scholarship and, where applicable, conflicting interpretations. In treating key military campaigns, I have made a special effort to describe clearly the essential character, course, and importance of the engagements; in the process, I have deliberately avoided inundating the reader with excessive data and complex schemata that tend to overwhelm nonspecialists.

Nazi Germany fought two wars simultaneously, one against the Allies and the other against the Jews. Regarded by the Nazi leadership as an equally important objective as the German domination and exploitation of Europe, the war to liquidate the Jews was waged with a fierce determination. Although the Third Reich was totally defeated by the Soviet Union, Britain, and the United States, in its war against the Jews it achieved almost total victory, killing two-thirds of Europe's Jews. For this reason, I give more attention to the Holocaust than is usually found in a short history of the war, including the involvement of non-Germans in the Final Solution and the responses of the Allies and the Vatican to the Jewish tragedy.

In the concluding chapter, "The Aftermath, Legacy, and Meaning of the War," considerable attention is given to the war's wide effects on European history. Among the topics discussed are population transfers, the treatment of collaborators and war criminals, the ordeal of Jewish survivors, changing German responses to the Nazi era, the emergence of the Cold War, steps toward European integration, and the impact of the war on Western consciousness.

I have tried to produce a coherent narrative that provides in a clear and engaging manner a frame of reference for understanding the most destructive, murderous, and dehumanizing war in world history. To help realize this goal, numerous quotations from relevant primary sources are integrated into the narrative. I have also made a deliberate effort to go beyond the data and, where appropriate, discuss the larger meaning of events within the context of the war, European history, and human experience.

I am grateful to the staff of Wadsworth/Cengage Learning who lent their talents to the project. Nancy Blaine, then senior sponsoring editor, recognized the project's merit and recommended publication. Brooke Barbier, acquiring sponsoring editor, provided useful guidelines. A special thanks to Lauren Floyd, development editor, who conscientiously and efficiently prepared the manuscript for production. I thank also Gunjan Chandola, senior project manager, who skillfully guided the book through production. Also deserving of my gratitude are Margaret Sears, copyeditor, who read the manuscript with a trained eye; Will Moore, proofreader, who demonstrated an extraordinary facility for mastering technical details; Maria Leon Maimone, who managed the difficult task of obtaining text permissions smoothly; Wendy Granger, who oversaw the selection and research of all of the images; and Cathy Richmond Robinson, who managed the design of the cover.

I am also grateful to Retired Brigadier General John W. Mountcastle for his careful reading of the manuscript and for his valuable suggestions regarding military concerns. Also making sound suggestions was my old friend and colleague Howard Negrin. George Bock, another old friend and colleague, proofread the copyedited manuscript and the page proof with his usual skill. Finally, I wish to thank Herbert Brotspies for obtaining for me some hard-to-find books and articles and Bodo Dolch and Herbert Beyenbach for checking some statistics in German sources. And as always I am grateful to my wife, Phyllis Perry, for her encouragement and computer skills, which saved me much aggravation.

M.P.

Chapter 1

✳

Hitler's War

From the early days of his political career, Adolf Hitler dreamed of forging in Central and Eastern Europe a vast German empire that would bring the millions of Germans living there under the rule of his Third Reich. He believed that only by waging a war of conquest against Poland and the Soviet Union could the German nation gain the living space, resources, and security it required and, as a superior race, deserved. War was an essential component of National Socialist racial ideology, which postulated an eternal struggle between races and called for the racial restructuring and cleansing of Europe. War also accorded with Hitler's temperament. Germany's defeat and surrender in World War I tormented the former corporal from the trenches until his dying day. Once in power, he intended to mobilize the German nation for wars of revenge and conquest. He would settle for nothing less than German domination and exploitation of Europe, a mission for which this deranged dreamer was certain that fate had chosen him. Whereas historians may debate the question of responsibility for World War I, few would deny that World War II was Hitler's war. Most would concur with the assessment of French historian Pierre Renouvin:

> It appears to be an almost incontrovertible fact that the Second World War was brought on by the actions of the Hitler government, that these actions were the expression of a policy laid down well in advance in *Mein Kampf*, and that this war could have been averted up until the last moment if the German government had so wished.[1]

Western statesmen had sufficient warning that Hitler was a threat to peace and the essential values of Western civilization. In the 1920s, Hitler had openly proclaimed his commitment to a war of revenge and expansion, and in the 1930s he scrapped the Versailles Treaty and openly rearmed. But Western statesmen, not fully grasping the danger inherent in Hitler's ideological obsession with creating a German racial empire and underestimating his pathological ruthlessness and Machiavellian cunning, failed to rally their people and take a stand until Germany had greatly increased its capacity to wage aggressive war. Those who warned that Nazism was a threat to democracy were often dismissed as warmongers. Opportunities to stop Hitler were lost as a consequence of poor statesmanship.

THE LEGACY OF WORLD WAR I

In many ways, World War II was an extension of World War I. "There will be wars as never before on earth," predicted Friedrich Nietzsche toward the end of the nineteenth century. World War I proved him right. Modern technology enabled the combatants to kill with unprecedented efficiency; modern nationalism infused both soldiers and civilians with the determination to fight until the enemy was totally beaten. Exercising wide control over its citizens, the modern state mobilized its human, material, and spiritual resources to wage total war. As the war hardened into a savage stalemate, statesmen did not press for a compromise peace but rather demanded ever more mobilization, ever more escalation, and ever more sacrifices.

The Great War profoundly altered the course of Western civilization. How could Europeans speak of the inviolability of the individual when the Continent had become a slaughterhouse, or of the primacy of reason when nations permitted the orgy of violence to go unabated for four years? How could they explain students leaving their schoolbooks to become, as one participant said, "nocturnal beasts of prey hunting each other in packs"?[2] With some 9.4 million dead and 21 million wounded, many of them pathetically mutilated and disfigured, the agony touched millions of homes. World War I was a great turning point in the history of the West. It seemed that Western civilization was fragile and perishable, that Western people despite their extraordinary accomplishments were never more than a step or two away from barbarism. And the conditions World War I created led to an even more horrific cataclysm that nearly destroyed Western civilization.

The Germans unanimously denounced the peace treaty drawn up by the victorious Allied powers in 1919. In their minds, the war had ended not in a German defeat but in a stalemate. They regarded the armistice as the prelude to a negotiated settlement among equals, based on President Woodrow Wilson's call for a peace of justice. Instead, the Germans were barred from participating in the negotiations, and they viewed the terms of the Treaty of Versailles as humiliating and vindictive measures designed to keep Germany militarily weak. What standard of justice, they asked, allowed the Allies to strip Germany of its colonies while retaining their own, reduce the German military to a pitiful size without disarming themselves, and saddle the country with impossible reparations? Why should Germany lose approximately one-eighth of its territory and one-tenth of its population? Why should the Allies make Germany solely responsible for the war? And why should they provide for the self-determination of Poles while placing Germans under Polish rule and declaring the German port of Danzig a free city with Poland controlling its import duties and foreign policy? Defenders of the treaty pointed out that if Germany had won the war, it would have imposed a far harsher settlement on the Allies. German war aims called for the annexation of parts of France and Poland and the reduction of Belgium and Romania to satellites. In the Treaty of Brest-Litovsk, which Germany compelled Russia to sign in 1918, an insatiable Germany took huge areas of Russia's most valuable territory. But, for the most part, these arguments fell on deaf German ears.

However, what is most significant about the treaty is that it did not solve the German problem. Germany was left weak but unbroken—its industrial and military power only temporarily contained, and its nationalist fervor not only undiminished but also stoked by a settlement that all political parties viewed as unjust, dictated, and an affront to national pride. The real danger for Europe was German unwillingness to accept defeat or surrender its dream of expansion. And in a little more than two decades, a rearmed Germany would subject much of Europe to its will.

Would France, Britain, and the United States enforce the treaty against a resurgent Germany? The war had demonstrated that an Allied victory depended on American intervention. But in 1920, the U.S. Senate, fearing that membership in the League of Nations would involve America in future wars, refused to ratify the Treaty of Versailles. Britain, feeling somewhat guilty over the treatment of Germany, lacked the will for enforcement and even came to favor treaty revision. The responsibility for preserving the settlement therefore rested primarily with France, which was not encouraging. Germany had greater industrial potential, and with Russia, France's World War I ally, now under Communist rule, France could not count on Russian manpower to balance Germany's larger population. The Paris peace settlement left Germany resentful but potentially powerful—German industrial capacity was considerable, and of Europe's countries, only the Soviet Union had a larger population. To the east lay small and weak states, some of them with a sizable German minority, that could not check a rearmed Germany.

The war produced a generation of young people who had reached their maturity in combat. Violence had become a way of life for millions of battle-hardened soldiers and for millions of civilians aroused by four years of martial propaganda. The fascination with violence and contempt for life persisted in the postwar world, particularly in Germany. Many returned veterans yearned for the excitement of battle and the fellowship of the trenches. These veterans made ideal recruits for extremist political movements that glorified action and brutality, propagated extreme nationalism, and promised to rescue society from a decadent liberalism and a hateful Communism and undo the shame of the Versailles Treaty. Hitler, an ex-soldier imbued with the ferocity of the front, knew how to appeal to them.

Yet while some veterans clung to an aggressive militarism, others aspired to build a more humane world. Such veterans embraced democratic and socialist ideals and resolved that the bloodbath would never be repeated. Tortured by the memories of war, European intellectuals wrote pacifist plays and novels and signed pacifist declarations. Moreover, regarding the war as a great calamity in both human and economic terms, British and French statesmen would go to great lengths to avoid a second world war. Indeed in the 1930s, an attitude of "peace at any price" discouraged resistance to Nazi Germany's bid to dominate Europe.

During World War I, new weapons were introduced that revolutionized the future of warfare, particularly tanks and bombers and fighters. After the war, imaginative military planners recognized that properly deployed planes and tanks could penetrate and smash the enemy's defenses, circumventing the stalemate of trench warfare. Planes also meant terror from the skies, for bombs could pulverize a city, killing thousands of civilians.

The intensified nationalist hatreds following World War I helped fuel the fires of World War II. The Germans vowed to regain lands lost to the Poles. Many Germans, like the embittered Hitler, were consumed by anguish over a defeat that they believed never should have happened and over the humiliating Treaty of Versailles; a desire for revenge festered in their souls.

In many respects, World War I was total war; it encompassed the entire nation and had no limits. States demanded total victory and total commitment from their citizens. They regulated industrial production, developed sophisticated propaganda techniques to strengthen morale, and exercised ever greater control over the lives of their people, organizing and disciplining them like soldiers. This total mobilization of resources and manipulation of public opinion provided a model for Hitler. He also drew a moral lesson from the immense loss of life in the trenches: a desired political end justifies vast human sacrifices.

THE RISE OF THE NAZIS

The New German Republic

In the last days of World War I, a revolution brought down the German government, a semiauthoritarian monarchy, and led to the creation of a democratic republic, soon to be called the Weimar Republic. The new government, led by Social Democrats, signed the armistice agreement ending the war. German generals, knowing that the war was lost, had pressed for an armistice. Early in the war, Germany had won a string of victories, and at the time of the armistice, German troops were deep inside France; German soil had remained inviolate after the Russians had been soundly defeated at the battle of Tannenburg in the opening days of the war. Consequently, the German people had no clear sense of military defeat. Many Germans blamed the new democratic leadership for what they called the "stab in the back"; traitors at home betrayed the invincible German military, they said—a baseless accusation, for the German High Command had sought an end to the war before German troops were overwhelmed by the advancing Allies, aided by a strong American presence, and the fatherland invaded. The Weimar Republic was born in revolution, which most Germans detested, and military defeat, which many attributed to the new government, and it faced an uncertain future. The legend that traitors, principally Jews and Social Democrats, cheated Germany of victory was created and propagated by the conservative Right: generals, high-ranking bureaucrats, university professors, and nationalists who wanted to preserve the army's reputation and bring down the new and hated Weimar Republic.

Dominated by moderate democratic socialists, the infant republic faced internal threats from both the radical Left and the radical Right. In 1919, a revolution by the newly established German Communist Party, or Spartacists, was crushed. The Communists had been easily subdued, but fear of a Communist insurrection remained deeply embedded in the middle and upper classes. This fear drove many of their members into the ranks of the Weimar Republic's right-wing opponents. The following year, staunch German nationalists staged a coup that collapsed when labor unions called a general strike that kept the coup leaders from governing.

In the early 1920s, the Weimar Republic overcame a spiraling inflation that had made the German currency worthless, and by the end of the decade economic conditions had significantly improved. By 1929, iron, steel, coal, and chemical production exceeded prewar levels. The value of German exports also surpassed that of 1913. It appeared that Germany had achieved political stability, as threats from the extremist parties of the Left and the Right subsided. Given time and continued economic stability, democracy might have taken firmer root in Germany. But in October 1929 came the Great Depression, which gave the National Socialist German Workers' Party, led by Adolf Hitler, its opportunity for power.

Adolf Hitler: The Early Years

Adolf Hitler was born in Austria in 1889, the fourth child of a minor civil servant. Hitler's worldview was shaped in part by the years he spent drifting around Vienna just prior to World War I. There he came into contact with the racial, nationalist, anti-Semitic, and pan-German literature that circulated widely in the Austrian capital. This literature introduced Hitler to a bizarre racial mythology: a heroic race of blond, blue-eyed Aryans battling for survival against inferior races. The racist treatises preached the danger posed by mixing races, called for the subjugation of racial inferiors, and marked the Jew as the embodiment of evil and the source of all misfortune. These themes became core Nazi principles.

Battle experience during World War I taught Hitler to prize discipline, regimentation, leadership, authority, struggle, and ruthlessness. The shock of Germany's defeat and of revolution affected him profoundly. Like many returning soldiers, he required vindicating explanations for lost victories. His own explanation was simple and demagogic: Germany's shame was due to the creators of the Weimar Republic in November 1918, the "November criminals"; behind them was a Jewish-Bolshevik world conspiracy.

After the war, Hitler joined a small right-wing extremist group. Displaying fantastic energy and extraordinary ability as an orator, propagandist, and organizer, Hitler quickly became the leader of the National Socialist German

Workers' Party (commonly called Nazi). At mass meetings, Hitler was a spell-binder who gave stunning performances. His pounding fists, throbbing body, wild gesticulations, hypnotic eyes, rage-swollen face, and repeated, frenzied denunciations of the Versailles Treaty, Marxism, the Weimar Republic, and Jews inflamed and mesmerized the audience, as did his intense conviction and great self-confidence.

In November 1923, Hitler tried to seize power in Munich, in the state of Bavaria, as a prelude to toppling the republic, but the putsch failed miserably. However, a judge sympathetic to right-wing nationalism gave Hitler a light sentence: five years' imprisonment with the promise of a quick parole. While in prison, Hitler dictated *Mein Kampf*, which contained the essence of his world-view. Given to excessive daydreaming and never managing to "overcome his youth with its dreams, injuries, and resentments,"[3] Hitler sought to make the world accord with his fantasies—struggles to the death between races, a vast empire ruled by a master race, and a thousand-year Reich.

Hitler's Worldview

Hitler's thought comprised a patchwork of nineteenth-century antidemocratic, anti-Marxist, anti-Semitic, Volkish, and Social Darwinist ideas. Emerging in the late nineteenth century, Volkish thought was an ominous expression of German nationalism. (*Volk* means "folk" or "people"; in the context in which it was used, racial or ethnic is the most apt translation.) Volkish thinkers glorified all things German and denounced the liberal-humanist tradition of the West as alien to the German soul. Transferring Charles Darwin's scientific theories to the social world, Social Darwinists insisted that nations and races were engaged in a struggle for survival in which only the fittest survive and deserve to survive. In their view, war was nature's way of eliminating the unfit. From these ideas, many of which enjoyed wide popularity, Hitler constructed a worldview rooted in myth and fantasy and sought to found a new world order based on racial nationalism. For Hitler, race was the key to understanding world history: "With the conception of race National Socialism will carry its revolution and recast the world."[4] As the Germanic tribes had overwhelmed a disintegrating Roman Empire, a reawakened, racially united Germany led by men of iron will would undo the humiliation of the Versailles Treaty, carve out a vast European empire, and deal a decadent liberal civilization its deathblow. It would conquer European Russia, eradicate Communism, eliminate the Jewish threat, and reduce to serfdom the subhuman Slavs, "a mass of born slaves who feel the need of a master."[5]

Hitler divided the world into superior and inferior races and pitted them against each other in a Social Darwinian struggle for survival. For him, this fight for life—that is, for territory and resources—was a law of nature and history. He saw all history as a pitiless struggle between races in which only the strongest and most ruthless are destined to survive, and exalted war as a great moral enterprise, the supreme test of both the nation and the individual. As a higher race, the Germans were entitled to conquer and subjugate other races. Leading Germany to total victory over its racial enemies, particularly Jews and

Slavs, became his obsession. And in pursuit of this objective Hitler saw himself as the executor of the will of history. From the beginning, he sought German expansion through war, mainly against Russia.

An obsessive and pathological hatred of Jews dominated Hitler's thought and feelings. Austria, Hitler's homeland, and Germany, where his movement was born, were both riddled with anti-Semitism. To be sure, unlike in Russia, Romania, and Poland, German Jews were not subjected to violent attacks. And unlike in France, it was not until after World War I that anti-Semitism had significant political implications. But in Germany and Austria, Jew-hatred developed into a systematic body of beliefs; a rich anti-Semitic literature, some of it written by prominent figures, circulated widely.

In the nineteenth century, with the spread of the liberal ideals of the Enlightenment and the French Revolution, most European states granted Jews citizenship and legal equality. Jews had hitherto been confined to ghettos. Motivated by outsiders' fierce desire to prove their worth and spurred by deeply embedded traditions that valued education and family life, many Jews achieved striking success as entrepreneurs, financiers, lawyers, journalists, physicians, scientists, musicians, performers, and scholars. Nowhere was this success more impressive than in Germany. By the early 1930s, German Jews, amounting to less than 1 percent of the population, accounted for 10.9 percent of the physicians, 10.7 percent of the dentists, 5.1 percent of the authors and editors, and 16.3 percent of the lawyers. They also accounted for 30 percent of Germany's Nobel laureates, principally in science and medicine. (In the 1930s, many German-Jewish scientists and engineers, including internationally prominent experts in nuclear energy, fled Nazi Germany for Britain and the United States, where they performed invaluable service during the war.) The overwhelming majority of German Jews considered themselves loyal Germans and greatly valued German culture, to which they contributed so much. Many Germans, however, reacted negatively to the astounding ascent of German (and Austrian) Jews, arguing that the disproportionate influence on German economic and cultural life by what they perceived as an alien people threatened traditional German ways and values.

In the Middle Ages, Jews had been persecuted and degraded primarily for religious reasons. Christian theology taught that the Jews remained a cursed people for having rejected Jesus. In the nineteenth century, national-racial considerations augmented the traditional biased Christian perception of Jews and Judaism. Racial anti-Semites said that Jews belonged to a different species of the human race, that they were indelibly stained and eternally condemned by their biological makeup, and that their evilness and worthlessness derived from inherited racial characteristics that could not be altered by conversion to Christianity. German racial nationalists saw the Jew as fundamentally materialistic, cowardly, and devious, the very opposite of the creative, idealistic, heroic, and faithful German. These Jewish traits, they argued, were corrupting German society. This was the model of Jew-hatred that Hitler embraced.

Everything Hitler despised—liberalism, intellectualism, pacifism, parliamentarianism, individualism, international finance capitalism, and international Communism—he attributed to Jews. For him, the Jews were an evil people who caused Germany's defeat in World War I* and perverted German culture. Intermarriage with Jews, which was very common in Germany, infected the nation with inferior racial qualities, which diminished its vitality. He often described Jews as dangerous bacteria and vermin that contaminated a healthy German nation. "Two worlds face one another," declared Hitler in language that clearly reveals the mythical character of his thought, "the men of God and the men of Satan! The Jew is the anti-man, the creature of another god. He must have come from another root of the human race. I set the Aryan and the Jew over and against each other."[6]

Hitler combined racism with widely circulated Jewish-conspiracy myths that held that Jews throughout the world conspired to control the state, political parties, the press, and banking in order to dominate the planet. The myth of an international Jewish conspiracy found its culminating expression in the notorious forgery, the *Protocols of the Learned Elders of Zion*, which was written in France by an unknown author in the service of the Russian secret police; a standard version was published in 1905. The forger described an alleged meeting of Jewish elders in the ancient Jewish cemetery of Prague, where they plot to take over the world and reduce non-Jews to slavery. The book became enormously popular, second only to the Bible in worldwide distribution, and it continued to enjoy wide circulation even after it was exposed as a forgery. Utilizing the language of the *Protocols*, Hitler interpreted Communism as a Jewish creation that Jews employed in their pursuit of world domination.

Nazi anti-Semitism served a functional purpose: Hitler intended it as a force for unifying and mobilizing the nation. By concentrating all evil in one enemy, the "conspiratorial," "parasitical," and "demonic" Jew, the "personification of the devil," Hitler provided true believers with a simple all-embracing and emotionally satisfying explanation for their personal and the nation's misfortunes. By defining themselves as the racial and spiritual opposites of Jews, true believers of all classes felt joined together in a Volkish union. By seeing themselves engaged in a heroic battle against a demonic enemy that threatened the fatherland, they strengthened their will. For Hitler, anti-Semitism fostered solidarity and resolve, necessary traits for shaping a powerful country that would excel at war. When the mind accepts an image such as Hitler's image of Jews as vermin, germs, and satanic conspirators out to dominate the world, it has lost all sense of balance and objectivity. Such a disoriented mind is ready to be absorbed into the collective will of the nation; it is ready to believe and to obey, to be manipulated and to be led, to brutalize and to tolerate brutality.

That many people, including intellectuals and members of the elite, believed and propagated Hitler's racial outlook shows the enduring power of mythical thinking and the vulnerability of reason. In 1933, the year Hitler took power, Felix Goldmann, a German-Jewish writer, commented astutely on the irrational character of Nazi anti-Semitism: "The present-day politicized racial anti-Semitism is the embodiment of myth, nothing is discussed, only felt, ... nothing is pondered

---

*Many Germans believed that Jews had shirked fighting in the war. In actuality, Jews served in the German armed forces out of proportion to their numbers, many were highly decorated, and some twelve thousand perished fighting for their country.

critically, logically or reasonably, only inwardly perceived, surmised…. We are apparently the last [heirs] of the Enlightenment."[7]

Hitler understood that in an age of political parties and universal suffrage the successful leader must win the support of the masses. This was to be achieved through propaganda aimed at the emotions. The masses are not moved by objective and abstract knowledge, said Hitler, but by primitive feelings. The most effective means of stirring the masses is through explosive oratory at mass meetings. Elevated to an insidious art form, propaganda would play a crucial role in binding the German people to Hitler after the Nazis gained power.

THE NAZIS IN POWER

When Hitler left prison in December 1924 after serving only nine months, he proceeded to tighten his hold on the Nazi Party. He relentlessly used his genius for propaganda and organization to strengthen the loyalty of his cadres and to instill in them a sense of mission. In 1928, when economic conditions had significantly improved, the National Socialists received only 2.6 percent of the vote. Nevertheless, Hitler never lost faith in his own capacities or his destiny. He continued to build his party and waited for a crisis that would rock the republic and make his movement a force in national politics. The Great Depression that began in the United States at the end of 1929 provided that crisis. With unemployment reaching six million, the German people became more amenable to Hitler's radicalism. The Nazi Party went from 810,000 votes in 1929 to 6,400,000 in 1930, and its representation in the Reichstag soared from 12 to 107. In the election of July 31, 1932, the Nazis received 37.3 percent of the vote and won 230 seats— far more than any other party, but still not a majority. Germany's traditional elite, industrialists and aristocratic landowners, who always hated the democratic Weimar Republic, as did many intensely nationalistic bourgeoisie, maneuvered to have Hitler appointed chancellor. They regarded him as a useful instrument to fight Communism, block social reform, break the backs of organized labor, and rebuild the armament industry.

Never intending to govern within the spirit of the constitution, Hitler, who took office on January 30, 1933, quickly moved to establish dictatorial power and to imbue the German people with Nazi ideology. Hitler interpreted his ascent to political power as a sign of his political genius, unconquerable will, and historical destiny. Now he would unite the German people into a racially pure nation and lead them in their world–historical struggle against their racial enemies. Propaganda had helped the Nazis come to power. Now it was used to shape a "new man," committed to Hitler, race, and Volk. Hitler was a radical revolutionary who desired not only the outward form of power but also control over the inner person, over the individual's thoughts and feelings. The purpose of Nazi propaganda was to condition the mind to revere their *Führer* (leader) and to think and respond as the Party directed; goals that were largely realized.

The Nazi regime won the support of the great majority of German people. Most Germans believed that the new government, the Third Reich, was trying

© Topham/The Image Works

Here, young Nazis are seen burning books in Salzburg, Austria, in 1938. "The age of extreme Jewish intellectualism has now ended," said Joseph Goebbels to cheering students.

to solve Germany's problems in a vigorous and sensible manner, in contrast to the ineffective Weimar Republic. (Just before Hitler took power, Germany was showing signs of coming out of the Depression.) By 1936, the reinvigoration of the economy stimulated largely by rearmament had virtually eliminated unemployment, which had stood at six million when Hitler became chancellor. (The reintroduction of military conscription in 1935 also removed many young men from the unemployment rolls.) After the war, a German soldier who fought on the Russian front recalled his gratitude to Hitler:

> In 1933, when Hitler took power, I was 11 years old. In the Ruhrgebiet where I lived there was abject poverty. I went to school with a small piece of bread, my father was out of work, everyone was out of work, it was a time of great poverty.... I got my first shoes from Adolf Hitler. All of a sudden my father was given work, the neigbours got work.... So of course we all supported Hitler. He had rescued us from a terrible situation.[8]

An equally astounding achievement in German eyes was Hitler's bold repudiation of the humiliating Versailles Treaty, the rebuilding of the military, and the restoration of German power in international affairs, all without war. It seemed to most Germans that Hitler had awakened a sense of self-sacrifice, national pride, and dedication among a people dispirited by military defeat, political weakness, and economic depression. They welcomed the Volkish unity that Hitler offered them; it promised to regenerate and unite a country torn apart by

U.S. Army Center of Military History, Washington, D.C.

In this painting by a German artist, Adolf Hitler is idolized as a heroic medieval knight.

class antagonisms and social distinctions and seemed to assure a splendid future. Rejoicing in Hitler's leadership, they did not regret the loss of political freedom and remained indifferent to the plight of the persecuted, particularly Jews. Viewing Nazism as the victory of idealism over materialism and of dedication to the community over selfish individualism, many intellectuals endorsed the Nazi regime, even supporting the burning of books written by Jews or considered hostile to Nazi ideology and the suppression of political opposition. Workers had jobs, businessmen had profits, and generals had troops; the bonds of community had been greatly strengthened and pride in Germany restored—what could be wrong?

To many Germans, Hitler was exactly as Nazi mythology depicted him, a man of destiny and a savior of the nation who "stands like a statue grown beyond measure of earthly man."[9] Very few Germans realized that they were ruled by evil men driven by an evil ideology and that their country, an advanced industrial society with an impressive tradition of high culture, was passing through a long night of barbarism. Still fewer considered resistance.

During the war, the Hitler mystique would retain its power. In 1941, three months after the invasion of the Soviet Union, a private expressed his belief in Hitler and his ideology in a letter home: "The Führer has grown into the greatest figure of the century, in his hands lies the destiny of the world.... May his pure sword strike down the Satanic monster.... This [battle] is for a new ideology, a new belief, a new life! I am glad that I can participate, even if as a tiny cog, in this war of light against darkness."[10] Propagated by Nazi propaganda, such sentiments had telling effect on the great mass of Germans, both at home and at the front.

The frenzied adoration the German people showed for Hitler both in peacetime and in war and their faith in his mission to regenerate the German nation is an extraordinary phenomenon that continues to intrigue historians and social psychologists and to astonish new generations of Europeans, including Germans. It was considerably different for the other dictators of Hitler's generation. Whatever devotion the Italians felt for Benito Mussolini quickly faded after he brought the country into the war. And the Soviet people's bonds to Stalin, particularly for non-Russian ethnic groups, were often based more on fear than genuine adulation. The German people's hero worship of Hitler and their positive view of his dictatorship were not driven by terror. For many Germans, this attitude persisted for the duration of the war and even afterward. Ordinary Germans did not have to be coerced to support and serve the Nazi state. Rarely in history has a nation been so spellbound by a leader.

THE BREAKDOWN OF PEACE

Hitler's Foreign Policy Aims

After consolidating his power and mobilizing the nation's will, Hitler moved to implement his foreign policy objectives: the destruction of the Versailles Treaty, the conquest and colonization of Eastern Europe, and the domination and exploitation of "racial inferiors." In some respects, Hitler's foreign policy accorded with the goals of Germany's traditional conservative leaders. Like them, Hitler sought to make Germany the preeminent power in Europe. During World War I, German statesmen and generals had sought to conquer extensive regions of Eastern Europe. In the Treaty of Brest-Litovsk imposed on Russia, Germany would dominate Poland, the Ukraine, and the Baltic states which Russia was forced to surrender. But Hitler's racial nationalism—the subjugation and annihilation of inferior races by a master German race—marked a break with the outlook of the old governing class. Traditional conservatives had considered revoking the civil rights of German Jews, but they had not done so. They had also sought to Germanize, not enslave, Poles living under the German flag.

As Hitler had anticipated, the British and the French backed down when faced with his violations of the Treaty of Versailles and threats of war. Haunted by the memory of World War I, Britain and France went to great lengths to avoid another catastrophe—a policy that had the overwhelming support of public opinion. Both British and French policy makers felt that another European war, so soon after the Great War, could do irreparable damage to European civilization. Moreover, woefully unprepared for war from 1933 to 1938 and believing that the Versailles Treaty had treated Germany too severely, Britain was amenable to making concessions to Hitler. Although France had the strongest army on the Continent, it was prepared to fight only a defensive war. France built seemingly impregnable fortifications called the Maginot Line to protect its borders from a German invasion, but it lacked an effective doctrine for employing a mobile striking force that would punish an aggressive Germany. The United States, concerned with the problems of the Great Depression and standing aloof from Europe's troubles, did nothing to strengthen the resolve of France and Britain. Given that both France and Britain feared and mistrusted the Soviet

Established in 1936, the German-American Bund held rallies and parades that displayed Nazi symbols (including the swastika and the Hitler salute), set up three military training camps, and constantly engaged in vicious anti-Semitic tirades. After Pearl Harbor the Bund disintegrated. This picture shows German-American Bundists in October 1937 parading in Yorkville, a German neighborhood, in Manhattan. Violent confrontations between the Bundists and counter-demonstrators were common.

Union, the grand alliance of World War I was not renewed. There was an added factor: suffering from a failure of leadership and political and economic unrest that eroded national unity and still traumatized by the memory of World War I, France was experiencing a decline in morale and a loss of nerve. France constantly turned to Britain for direction.

British statesmen championed a policy of appeasement: giving in to Germany in the hope that a satisfied Hitler would not drag Europe through another war. British policy rested on the disastrous illusion that Hitler, like his Weimar predecessors, sought peaceful revision of the Versailles Treaty and that he could be contained through concessions. This perception was as misguided as the expectations of Weimar conservatives, who had placed Hitler in power, that the responsibility of governing would compel him to abandon his National Socialist radicalism. Some British appeasers swallowed the view cleverly propagated and exploited by Nazi propaganda that Hitler was a defender of European civilization and the capitalist economic order against Soviet Communism, which they saw as a greater threat than German National Socialism.

In *Mein Kampf*, Hitler explicitly laid out his philosophy of racial nationalism and *Lebensraum* (living space) through conquest. As dictator, he established a one-party state, confined political opponents to concentration camps, and persecuted Jews. But the proponents of appeasement did not properly assess these signs. They still believed that Hitler could be reasoned with. British and French statesmen underestimated Hitler's abilities, and Hitler demonstrated an uncanny facility to recognize and exploit his opponents' weaknesses. Appeasement, which in the end was capitulation to blackmail, failed. Germany grew stronger and the German people more devoted to the Führer. Hitler did not moderate his ambitions and the appeasers did not avert war.

Tearing Up the Versailles Treaty

To realize his foreign policy aims, Hitler required a formidable military machine. Germany had to rearm. The Treaty of Versailles limited the size of the German army to one hundred thousand volunteers; restricted the navy's size; forbade the production of military aircraft, heavy artillery, and tanks; and disbanded the general staff. In March 1935, Hitler declared that Germany was no longer bound by the Versailles Treaty. Germany would restore conscription, build an air force (which it had been doing secretly), and strengthen its navy. The German people were ecstatic over Hitler's boldness. France protested but offered no resistance. Britain negotiated a naval agreement with Germany, thus tacitly accepting Hitler's rearmament.

A decisive event in the breakdown of peace was Italy's invasion of Ethiopia in October 1935. Mussolini, the posturing Fascist dictator, sought colonial expansion, revenge for the defeat that the African kingdom had inflicted on Italian troops in 1896, and personal glory. The League of Nations called for economic sanctions against Italy, and most League members restricted trade with the aggressor. But Italy continued to receive oil, particularly from American suppliers. Believing that the conquest of Ethiopia did not affect their vital interests and hoping to keep the Italians friendly in the event of a clash with Germany, neither Britain nor France sought to restrain Italy despite its act of aggression against another member of the League of Nations. The Fascists claimed that they were civilizing a backward nation. In the process, tens of thousands of Ethiopians perished as victims of saturation bombing, poison gas, and mistreatment in the concentration camps into which they were herded. Mussolini's subjugation of Ethiopia discredited the League of Nations, already weakened by its failure to deal effectively with Japan's invasion of the mineral-rich Chinese province of Manchuria in 1931. At that time, the League formed a commission of inquiry and urged nonrecognition of the puppet state of Manchukuo created by the Japanese. The later invasion of Ethiopia, like the invasion of Manchuria, showed the League's reluctance to use force to resist aggression.

On March 7, 1936, Hitler marched troops into the Rhineland, which was the region of Germany that the Versailles Treaty had stipulated would remain a demilitarized zone. German generals had cautioned Hitler that such a move would provoke a French invasion of Germany and reoccupation of the Rhineland[*] that the German army, still in the first stages of rearmament, could not repulse. But Hitler gambled that France and Britain, lacking the will to fight, would take no action. When Hitler announced to the Reichstag that German troops were on the move into the Rhineland, American reporter William L. Shirer recorded that the delegates "spring, yelling and crying, to their feet. The audience in the galleries does the same…. Their hands are raised in slavish salute, their faces now contorted with hysteria, their mouths wide open, shouting, shouting, their eyes burning with fanaticism, glued on the new god, the Messiah."[11]

Hitler had assessed the Anglo-French mood correctly. Britain was not greatly alarmed by the remilitarization of the Rhineland. After all, Hitler was not expanding the borders of Germany but only sending soldiers to Germany's frontier. Such a move, reasoned British officials, did not warrant risking a war. France viewed the remilitarization of the Rhineland as a grave threat. It deprived France of the one tangible advantage that it had obtained from the Treaty of Versailles: a demilitarized buffer area. Now German forces could concentrate in strength on the French frontier, either to invade France or to discourage a French assault if Germany attacked Czechoslovakia or Poland, France's eastern allies. France lost the advantage of retaliatory attack against a demilitarized zone.

Four factors explain why France did not try to expel the twenty-two thousand German troops that occupied the zone. First, France would not act alone, and Britain could not be persuaded to use force. Second, the French general staff overestimated German military strength and thought only of defending French soil from a German attack. Third, with the memory of World War I still weighing heavily, French public opinion showed no enthusiasm for a confrontation with Hitler. Fourth, both military and government leaders feared that full mobilization would be a heavy burden on the French treasury during difficult economic times.

In July 1936, General Francisco Franco, stationed in Spanish Morocco, led a revolt against the democratic Spanish republic. He was supported by army leaders, the church, monarchists, large landowners, industrialists, and the Falange, the newly formed Fascist party. From 1936 to 1939, the Spanish republic was torn by a bloody civil war in which Nazi Germany and Fascist Italy aided Franco and the Soviet Union supplied the Spanish republic. The republic appealed to France for help, but the French government feared that the civil war would expand into a European war. With Britain's approval, France proposed the Nonintervention Agreement. Italy, Germany, and the Soviet Union signed the agreement but continued to supply the warring parties. By October 1937, some sixty thousand Italian "volunteers" were fighting in Spain. Hitler sent between five thousand and six thousand men and hundreds of planes, which proved decisive. By comparison, the Soviet Union's aid to the republic was meager. Viewing the conflict as a struggle between democracy and Fascism, thousands of Europeans and Americans volunteered to fight for the republic.

---

*From 1919 to 1930, French troops occupied the Rhineland in accordance with the Versailles Treaty. Right-wing nationalists were incensed that many were black colonial soldiers, some of whom married German women or had children out of wedlock.

MAP 1.1   German and Italian Aggressions, 1935–1939

German aggression from 1936 to 1939 included the militarization of the Rhineland (1936), *Anschluss* with Austria (1938), and the dismemberment of Czechoslovakia (1938–1939).

Without considerable help from France, the Spanish republic was doomed, but Leon Blum, the French prime minister, continued to support nonintervention. He feared that French intervention would cause Germany and Italy to escalate their involvement, bringing Europe to the edge of a general war. Moreover, supplying the republic would have unsettling consequences at home because French rightists were sympathetic to Franco's conservative–clerical authoritarianism. In 1939, the republic fell, and Franco established a dictatorship, imprisoning or banishing to labor camps more than one million Spaniards and executing another two hundred thousand.

The Spanish Civil War was a victory for Fascism. It also provided Germany with an opportunity to test weapons and pilots and demonstrated that France and Britain lacked the determination to fight Fascism, a fact that Hitler carefully noted for the future. The war also widened the breach between Italy on one side and Britain and France on the other that had opened when Italy invaded Ethiopia, and it drew Mussolini and Hitler closer together. In October 1936, Mussolini sent his foreign minister to meet with Hitler in Berlin. The discussions bore fruit, and on November 1, Mussolini proclaimed the creation of a Rome–Berlin "Axis."

One of Hitler's aims was the incorporation of German–speaking Austria into the Third Reich. The Treaty of Versailles expressly prohibited the union of the two countries, but in *Mein Kampf*, Hitler insisted that an *Anschluss* (union) was necessary for German Lebensraum. In February 1938, under intense pressure from Hitler, Austrian chancellor Kurt von Schuschnigg promised to accept Austrian Nazis in his cabinet and agreed to closer relations with Germany. Austrian independence was slipping away, and increasingly Austrian Nazis undermined Schuschnigg's authority. Seeking to gain his nation's support, Schuschnigg made plans for a plebiscite on the issue of preserving Austrian independence. An enraged Hitler ordered his generals to draw up plans for an invasion of Austria. Hitler then demanded Schuschnigg's resignation and the formation of a new government headed by Arthur Seyss-Inquart, an Austrian Nazi.

Believing that Austria was not worth a war, Britain and France informed the embattled chancellor that they would not help in the event of a German invasion. Schuschnigg then resigned, and Austrian Nazis began to take control of the government. Under the pretext of preventing violence, Hitler ordered his troops to cross into Austria, and on March 13, 1938, Austrian leaders declared that Austria was a province of the German Reich.

Most Austrians were ecstatic about the *Anschluss*. The creation of a "Greater Germany" appealed to their pan-German sentiments, and they hoped that Hitler's magic would produce economic recovery. Moreover, depriving Jews of their rights, property, and occupations had widespread appeal among traditionally anti-Semitic Austrians. The Viennese celebrated by ringing church bells, waving swastika banners, and, in a sadistic orgy, spontaneously beating, robbing, and humiliating Jews, including ripping Torah scrolls, cutting the beards off rabbis, and forcing whole families to scrub sidewalks before a taunting crowd. The Austrians' euphoria over the *Anschluss* and their brutal treatment of helpless Jews, several hundred of whom committed suicide, astonished many foreign observers, including even the Nazi occupiers.

Czechoslovakia: The Apex of Appeasement

Hitler obtained Austria merely by threatening to use force. Another threat would give him the Sudetenland of Czechoslovakia. Ethnic Germans numbering some

3.25 million were dominant in the Sudetenland. The region contained key industries and strong fortifications; because it bordered Germany, it was also vital to Czech security. Deprived of the Sudetenland, Czechoslovakia could not defend itself against a German attack. Encouraged and instructed by Germany, the Sudeten Germans, led by Konrad Henlein, shrilly denounced the Czech government for "persecuting" its German minority and depriving Sudeten Germans of their right to self-determination. The Sudeten Germans agitated for local autonomy and the right to profess the National Socialist ideology. Behind this demand was the goal of German annexation of the Sudetenland and the dismemberment of Czechoslovakia.

While negotiations between the Sudeten Germans and the Czech government proceeded, Hitler's propaganda machine accused the Czechs of hideous crimes against the German minority and warned of retribution. Hitler also ordered his generals to prepare for an invasion of Czechoslovakia and to complete the fortifications along the French border. Fighting between Czechs and Sudeten Germans heightened the tensions. Seeking to preserve peace, British Prime Minister Neville Chamberlain offered to confer with Hitler, who then extended an invitation.

Britain and France held somewhat different positions toward Czechoslovakia, the only democracy in Central and Eastern Europe. In 1924, France and Czechoslovakia had concluded an agreement of mutual assistance in the event that either was attacked by Germany. Czechoslovakia had a similar agreement with the Soviet Union, but with the provision that Soviet assistance depended on France's first fulfilling the terms of its agreement. Britain had no commitment to Czechoslovakia. Some British officials, swallowing Hitler's propaganda, believed that the Sudeten Germans were indeed a suppressed minority entitled to self-determination. They also thought that the Sudetenland, like Austria, was not worth another world war that would leave Europe in ruins. Hitler, they said, only wanted to incorporate Germans living outside of Germany, carrying out the principle of self-determination to its logical conclusion. Completely misjudging Hitler, Chamberlain believed that he was amenable to reason, that once the Sudeten Germans lived under the German flag, a satisfied Hitler would make no other demands. In any case, Britain's failure to rearm adequately between 1933 and 1938 weakened its position. The British chiefs of staff maintained that the nation was not prepared to fight and that it was necessary to sacrifice Czechoslovakia to buy time.

Czechoslovakia's fate was decided at the Munich Conference in September 1938, attended by Chamberlain, Hitler, Mussolini, and Prime Minister Edouard Daladier of France. The Munich Agreement called for the immediate evacuation of Czech troops from the Sudetenland and its occupation by German forces. Britain and France then promised to guarantee the territorial integrity of the truncated Czechoslovakia. Both Chamberlain and Daladier were praised by adoring crowds in their respective countries for keeping the peace, which they believed was worth the price of sacrificing a small country in a distant part of Europe.

Critics of Chamberlain have insisted that the Munich Agreement was a tragic blunder. Chamberlain, they say, was a fool to believe that Hitler could be bought off with the Sudetenland. The German dictator regarded British and

French concessions as signs of weakness that only increased his appetite for more territory. The critics argue further that it would have been better to fight Hitler in 1938 than a year later, when war actually did break out. In the year following the Munich Agreement, Britain increased its military arsenal, but so did Germany, which strengthened western border defenses; built submarines, heavy tanks, and planes; and trained more pilots.

Had Britain and France resisted Hitler at Munich, it is likely that the Führer would have attacked Czechoslovakia. But the Czech border defenses, built on the model of the French Maginot Line, were formidable. The Czechs had a sizable number of good tanks, and the Czech people were willing to fight to preserve their nation's territorial integrity. By itself, the Czech army could not have defeated Germany. But while the main elements of the German army were battling the Czechs, the French, who could mobilize a hundred divisions, could have breached the lightly defended German West Wall; then they could have invaded the Rhineland and devastated German industrial centers in the Ruhr. Such a scenario, of course, depended on the French overcoming their psychological reluctance to taking the offensive. And there was the possibility, although probably a slim one, that the Soviet Union would have fulfilled its agreement and come to Czechoslovakia's aid.

After the annexation of the Sudetenland, Hitler plotted to extinguish Czechoslovakia. He encouraged the Slovak minority in Czechoslovakia led by a Fascist priest, Josef Tiso, to demand complete separation. On the pretext of protecting the Slovak people's right of self-determination, Hitler ordered his troops to enter Prague. In March 1939, Czech independence ended.

The destruction of Czechoslovakia was of a different character than the remilitarization of the Rhineland, the *Anschluss* with Austria, and the annexation of the Sudetenland. In these previous cases, Hitler could claim the right of German self-determination, Woodrow Wilson's grand principle. The occupation of Prague and the end of Czech independence, though, showed that Hitler really sought European hegemony. Outraged statesmen demanded that the Führer be deterred from further aggression.

Poland: The Final Crisis

After Czechoslovakia, Hitler turned to Poland, demanding that Poland return the free city of Danzig to Germany and build railways and roads, over which Germans would enjoy extraterritorial rights, across the Polish Corridor linking East Prussia with the rest of Germany. Poland refused to restore the port of Danzig, which was vital to its economy. The Poles would allow a German highway through the Polish Corridor but would not permit German extraterritorial rights. France informed the German government that it would fulfill its treaty obligations to aid Poland. Chamberlain also warned that Britain would assist Poland if it were attacked.

On May 22, 1939, Hitler and Mussolini entered into the Pact of Steel, promising mutual aid in the event of war. The following day, Hitler told his officers that he wanted more than just the return of the territory lost to Poland in the Treaty of Versailles; his real goal was the destruction of Poland. "Danzig is not the objective. It is a matter of expanding our living space in the east, of making our food supplies secure.... There is therefore no question of sparing Poland, and the decision remains to attack Poland at the first suitable opportunity."[12] In the middle of June, the army presented Hitler with battle plans for an invasion of Poland.

Britain, France, and the Soviet Union had been engaged in negotiations since April. The Soviet Union wanted a mutual-assistance pact, including joint military planning, and demanded bases in Poland and Romania in case of a war with Germany. Britain was reluctant to endorse these demands, fearing that a mutual-assistance pact with Russia might cause Hitler to embark on a mad adventure that would drag Britain into war. Moreover, Poland would not allow Soviet troops on its soil because it feared Russian expansion.

At the same time, the Soviet Union was conducting secret talks with Nazi Germany. Unlike the Allies, Hitler could tempt Stalin with land that would serve as a buffer between Germany and Russia. Moreover, a treaty with Germany would give the Soviet Union time to prepare for what seemed an inevitable war with the aggressive Nazi state. And there was the possibility that Germany and Britain and France would become drawn into a long and bloody war that would exhaust these major capitalist states that yearned for the demise of the Communist state. On August 23, 1939, the two totalitarian states and unrelenting ideological foes signed a nonaggression pact that stunned the world. A secret section of the pact called for the partition of Poland between the two parties and Soviet control over Latvia and Estonia (later the agreement was amended to include Lithuania). By signing such an agreement with his enemy, Hitler had pulled off an extraordinary diplomatic coup: he blocked Russia, Britain, and France from duplicating their World War I alliance against Germany.

The Nazi-Soviet Pact was the green light for an invasion of Poland, and at dawn on September 1, 1939, German troops crossed the frontier. Two days later, when Germany did not respond to their demand for a halt to the invasion, Britain and France, who had done everything they could to avoid a conflict, declared war on Germany. Their concern was less Poland's territorial integrity than the fear of German domination of Europe—the same concern they had in 1914. Britain and France's firm response took Hitler, who at this time only wanted a limited war, by surprise. His experience with the Western powers at Munich had led him to view them as "little worms," too feeble and decadent to wage war.

CHRONOLOGY

March 1935	Hitler announces German rearmament
October 1936	Italy invades Ethiopia
1936–1939	Spanish Civil War
March 7, 1936	Germany remilitarizes the Rhineland

March 13, 1938	*Anschluss* with Austria, which becomes a German province
September 1938	Munich Agreement: Britain and France approve Germany's annexation of the Sudetenland
March 1939	Germany invades Czechoslovakia
April 1939	Italy invades Albania
May 22, 1939	Pact of Steel between Hitler and Mussolini
August 23, 1939	Nonaggression pact between Germany and the Soviet Union
September 1, 1939	Germany invades Poland
September 3, 1939	Britain and France declare war on Germany

NOTES

1. Pierre Renouvin, *World War II and Its Origins*, trans. Douglas Parmee (New York: Harper & Row, 1969), 167.

2. Michael Adas, *Machines as the Measure of Man* (Ithaca, NY: Cornell University Press, 1989), 376.

3. Joachim C. Fest, *Hitler*, trans. Richard and Clara Winston (New York: Harcourt Brace Jovanovich, 1974), 548.

4. Alan Bullock, *Hitler: A Study in Tyranny* (New York: Harper Torchbooks, 1964), 400.

5. *Hitler's Table Talk, 1941–1944*, preface and essay by H. R. Trevor-Roper, trans. Norman Cameron and R. H. Stevens (New York: Enigma Books, 2008), 27.

6. Lucy S. Dawidowicz, *The War Against the Jews, 1933–1945* (New York: Holt, Rinehart and Winston, 1975), 21.

7. Uri Tal, "Consecration of Politics in the Nazi Era," in *Judaism and Christianity Under the Impact of National Socialism*, ed. Otto Dov Kulka and Paul R. Mendes Flohr (Jerusalem: Historical Society of Israel, 1987), 70.

8. Bob Carruthers, *Servants of Evil: New First Hand Accounts of the Second World War from Survivors of Hitler's Armed Forces* (St. Paul, MN: Zenith Press, 2005), xv.

9. Fest, *Hitler*, 532.

10. Omer Bartov, *Hitler's Army: Soldiers, Nazis, and War in the Third Reich* (New York: Oxford University Press, 1992), 166.

11. William L. Shirer, *Berlin Diary: The Journal of a Foreign Correspondent 1934–1941* (New York: Galahad Books, 1995), 53.

12. *Documents on German Foreign Policy, 1918–1946*, vol. 6 (London: Her Majesty's Stationery Office, 1956), series D, no. 433.

Chapter 2

✳

The German Blitzkrieg, 1939–1940

When the war began, the mood in Europe differed markedly from August 1914, the start of World War I. In 1914, crowds gathered in capital cities, demonstrating allegiance to the various fatherlands and willingness to fight. Thomas Mann, a distinguished German writer, saw the war as "purification, liberation … an enormous hope; [it] sets the hearts of poets aflame…. How could the artist, the soldier in the artist," he asked, "not praise God for the collapse of a peaceful world with which he was fed up, so exceedingly fed up."[1] In Paris, men marched down the boulevards singing the stirring words of the French national anthem, the "Marseillaise," while women showered young soldiers with flowers. A participant recollected: "Young and old, civilians and military men burned with the same excitement…. Thousands of men eager to fight would jostle one another outside recruiting offices, waiting to join up…. The word 'duty' had a meaning for them and the word 'country' had regained its splendor."[2] Similarly, a German newspaper editorialized: "It is a joy to be alive. We wished so much for this hour."[3] To the prominent German historian Friedrich Meinecke, August 1914 was "one of the greatest moments of my life which suddenly filled my soul with the profoundest joy."[4]

There was nothing like that in Germany when war broke out on September 1, 1939. There were no processions, no waving flags, no cheering, no women throwing flowers at marching soldiers. The mood was somber, grim and foreboding, even among those who believed Nazi propaganda that Germany was only returning fire after a Polish attack. Some German generals, fearful of intervention by France and Britain, approached the war more with resignation than enthusiasm. With World War I a painful memory, Europeans, including Germans, overwhelmingly were not eager for another conflict of such magnitude. A major reason why Hitler's earlier foreign policy achievements—scrapping of the Versailles Treaty, remilitarization of the Rhineland, *Anschluss* with Austria, Munich and Prague—were so popular with the German people is that they had been attained without war. Aware of the people's lack of appetite for war—except for some extreme nationalists and young people with little or no memory of World War I and indoctrinated for several years with Nazi ideology—Nazi leadership regarded the mobilization of the nation's martial spirit as a prime objective, a task that they rigorously pursued throughout the war.

THE INVASION OF POLAND

Mechanized Warfare: A New Military Tactic

Seeking to conquer Poland before France and Britain could provide meaningful support—if, indeed, they even attacked—Germany struck with speed and power, implementing tactical concepts of a mobile armored offensive worked out by German military planners. These planners were influenced by the works of two British military theorists, Basil H. Liddell-Hart and J. F. C. Fuller, who introduced innovative concepts for modern technological warfare. Later called *Blitzkrieg* (lightning war), this new military tactic was intended to avoid the static and costly trench warfare that produced so little gain in World War I.

The blitzkrieg stressed rapid *Panzer* (tank) assaults supported by mobile artillery and motorized infantry divisions against a weak point in the enemy's line. To achieve maximum concentration of firepower, tanks would be arrayed in massed formations. The blitzkrieg also called for bombers and dive bombers, acting as aerial artillery, to support land operations by blasting enemy defense positions that stood in the way of the advancing panzers and smashing bridges and rail lines to block the movement of enemy reserves. These powerful integrated attacks, implemented without warning and with lightning speed, were intended to shock, disorient, and demoralize the enemy forces, preventing them from effectively reacting to the breakthrough. Exploiting the breach in the enemy's front line, the German spearhead would fan out, secure the flanks, and with great speed penetrate to the enemy's rear, surrounding and trapping him in a "cauldron" or pocket before he could react. In contrast to World War I when senior officers led from miles behind the front, tank commanders would operate in key places in the spearhead giving instructions to their units by radio, with which German tanks were equipped.

Surprise and speed were key principles of the blitzkrieg: the panzers must open up a gap in the enemy's front line and race to its rear before he could counter-attack, employing tanks and antitank guns. Moving rapidly in armored personnel carriers on the heels of the panzers, the infantry would complete the encirclement and destroy the enemy's military capacity. In World War I, tanks were generally subordinate to infantry and simply broke into enemy lines. These new tactics gave tanks the primary role: their mission was to crash through the enemy front like an iron fist and, in the words of General Heinz Guderian, Germany's most prominent panzer theorist and a panzer commander, "to knock out his batteries, his reserves, his staffs, all at the same time."[5] Germans employed these tactics in Poland with great success and would use them elsewhere as well in their march to empire.

The Defeat of Poland

The German army that swept into Poland on September 1, 1939, consisted of highly skilled commanders and soldiers gripped by nationalist sentiments and the Führer mystique. From the outset, Poland was at a disadvantage as it tried to fight the modernized German army with insufficient mechanized armor and planes. Fearful of harming its precarious economy by removing skilled workers from industry, Poland waited too long to mobilize. A second reason for the delay was not to provide Germany with an excuse for launching an attack, a course that Paris and London urged the Poles to take. Poland could only expect assistance from Britain and France if it were obvious that German aggression was unprovoked. France in particular had promised to attack Germany if Poland were invaded. This would compel the Third Reich to move substantial forces to the French frontiers, easing the pressure on Poland.

Because the Poles took the precaution to scatter their aircraft over many airfields, the Germans could not wipe out the Polish air force in one blow as they intended. Nevertheless the *Luftwaffe* (air force) did catch Polish planes on the ground in the first few hours and incapacitated bases and command and control facilities, preventing Polish aircraft from fighting as a cohesive unit. Enjoying considerable superiority in both numbers and quality—German planes were significantly faster—the Luftwaffe virtually eliminated the Polish air force within a few days. Commanding the skies, German planes struck railways, bridges, and roads, hampering Polish mobilization; attacked tanks; blasted defense networks and munitions dumps; bombed and strafed fleeing refugees; and pulverized Warsaw, terrorizing the population. Racing across the flat Polish terrain, panzers opened breaches in the Polish defenses, and mechanized columns overran the foot-marching Polish army, trapping large numbers of troops. Frontline German troops possessed mobile artillery whose firepower prevented Polish divisions, many of them now broken into uncoordinated units, from regrouping. Although Poland had the fourth largest army in Europe, it had few mechanized units and artillery to oppose the German blitzkrieg, and the Polish High Command, unskilled in mobile operations, could not cope with the unnerving speed and coordination of German air and ground attacks. Moreover, Germany's takeover of Czechoslovakia gave it additional invasion routes into Poland.

With an extremely large frontier to defend, the most sensible strategy for Poland was to pull back to the Vistula River. The river was a natural barrier where they could destroy bridge approaches, establish in-depth defensive positions, and wait for France and Britain's promised assistance. But this would mean abandoning the Polish Corridor, the stretch of German land given to Poland by the Treaty of Versailles, and valuable industrial areas and major cities to the west. This blow to national pride was too great for Polish leaders to

In October 1939, Hitler celebrated Germany's defeat of Poland at a parade in Warsaw.

consider. Consequently, Polish forces were strung out over great distances; spread too thin, they could not hold the line everywhere the Germans attacked. In several places, the panzer divisions smashed through the Poles' front positions and maneuvered to their rear, forcing them into a pocket. The Poles put up fierce and valiant resistance, but their situation was soon hopeless.

By September 8, the rapidly moving Germans advanced to the outskirts of Warsaw. The besieged citizens of Warsaw, under German fire, resisted. Men, women, and children labored for hours digging trenches and setting up barricades to stop German tanks. In the approaches to Warsaw, brave Poles dashed into the streets and hurled burning rags under tanks, which caused them to explode. Snipers shooting from windows pinned down German infantry. Seeking to avoid brutal street fighting within the capital, the German High Command decided to bombard the city into submission with round-the-clock bombing raids and artillery barrages that targeted both the city's infrastructure and residential areas. With only a limited number of antiaircraft guns, the Poles had no defense against the German terror attacks from the air that killed thousands. Warsaw, which Poles regarded as the Paris of Eastern Europe, was set ablaze, and its citizens faced serious food and water shortages.

On September 17, Soviet troops invaded Poland from the east to obtain its share of Poland in accordance with the Nazi-Soviet Pact. On September 27, a hapless Poland surrendered. In this brief war, more than 100,000 Polish soldiers and civilians perished. The Germans took 693,000 prisoners; the Soviets, 217,000.

In less than a month, the German army's integration of tanks, aircraft, and motorized infantry to achieve breakthrough and envelopment had vanquished Poland. The German military had successfully tested and honed the new techniques of mechanized mobile warfare, techniques that would soon be applied in France, the Soviet Union, and North Africa. That France had reneged on its pledge to attack Germany in the west if Poland were invaded made it easier for Germany, which did not have to divert forces to the French frontier. Analysts point out that at the time of the Polish invasion, both the German army and air force were ill-prepared to fight on two fronts. German border defenses—the West Wall, hurriedly built, not yet completed, and manned by an inadequately armed second-rate skeleton force—could not have repelled a massive French attack. (Three weeks after the invasion of Poland, the French launched a weak and ineffective offensive in the Saar region of Germany; it was no more than a pathetic gesture.) In this instance, Hitler's intuition was correct. He told his generals that France and Britain lacked the will to fight for Poland. The view of General Heinz Guderian is indicative of how German generals interpreted the French leaders' failure to attack in strength the vulnerable German border. "We were amazed that they had not taken advantage of their favourable situation ... to attack, while the bulk of German forces, including the entire armoured force, was engaged in Poland.... The caution shown by the French leaders led us to believe that our adversaries hoped somehow to avoid a serious clash of arms."[6] In 1940, German generals would exploit the deficiencies of French military leaders.

Escaping across the borders, the Polish government went into exile first in Paris and then in London. More than one hundred thousand Polish troops and airmen escaped, many of whom would fight again, mainly with Britain. Polish pilots in particular would distinguish themselves in the air war over Britain in 1940. Poland, which had only regained its independence after World War I, ceased to exist: the Soviet Union annexed the eastern parts of Poland, and Germany annexed regions in the west and north that had a substantial number of ethnic Germans who were ecstatic over joining the German Reich; the rest of the betrayed and broken country was governed by German occupation authorities.

At the onset of the campaign, senior German generals had agreed that the SS (an elite Nazi force; see footnote on page 103) would be responsible for policing rear areas, with the authority to liquidate intellectuals, aristocrats, and priests, who might lead a resistance movement, as well as Jews, Germany's racial enemy. Operating behind the German lines, three SS Death's Head regiments lost no time in launching a racial war, assisted at times by elements of the regular army. They organized massacres that included machine gunning to death prisoners and Polish civilians at the edge of pits they had been forced to dig and herding Jews into a synagogue and setting it on fire. Joining the Nazis in these murderous rampages were ethnic Germans. At the start of the war, fearing that these Germans were a fifth column in their midst, Polish civilians and retreating troops had murdered some six thousand of them. No doubt seeking vengeance, but also aiming to support the Nazi invaders, these ethnic Germans organized militias that slaughtered thousands of Poles and Jews in the three months following the Nazi triumph. This was only the beginning of the Polish people's ordeal under the Nazi occupation (see Chapter 4).

Most Wehrmacht commanders simply withdrew their troops while the SS engaged in mass executions of civilians, but some did protest that these brutal acts were violations of the military's honor code and potentially harmful to troop morale. General Johannes Blaskowitz sent Hitler a memorandum to this effect. Hitler replied by demanding Blaskowitz's dismissal, adding that the methods of the Salvation Army do not apply to war. The Poles also suffered at the hands of the Soviets, who annexed eastern Poland. The Soviets' behavior paralleled that of the Nazis: imprisonment, torture, and execution of people considered dangerous to the Communist system, particularly professors, intellectuals, priests, and politicians. From February 1940 until the Nazis drove the Soviets out of Poland in June 1941, the Soviets rounded up several hundred thousand Poles, including Jews who had fled the SS, and deported them to distant parts of the Soviet Union. Many deportees did not survive the long trip in subzero weather or the harsh conditions where they were resettled (perhaps as many as half of the deportees perished). The Soviets also engaged in mass executions of 20,000 Polish officers, including 4,100 at Katyn Forest near Smolensk.* Thousands more Polish citizens were sent to prisons run by the Soviet secret police where they were shot in the back of the head.

The success of the blitzkrieg greatly increased the German people's devotion to their leader, as the following description written by an officer in the early days of the war illustrates. The officer is describing Hitler's visit to German troops in Poland a few days after the invasion:

> Meanwhile, we are pressing in ever closer to the Führer—the highest soldier of our nation.... We are delighted beyond words to stand face to face with him.... Our hearts swell in his presence.... We can read in his countenance the inexorable, iron will to see this struggle to win worldwide recognition for the Greater German Reich through to its final objective. From the nearby Plevno, women [ethnic Germans] appeared with their children.... Girls and mothers ... cover the Führer with flowers. Many of the women are quietly sobbing with happiness.... The echo of our "Sieg Heils" is still hanging in the air, the women and girls are still staring as though spell-bound at the spot where the Führer had just stood.... We have enshrined this picture in our hearts and it will go with us into future battles.[7]

THE CONQUEST OF DENMARK AND NORWAY

For Hitler, the conquest of Poland was only the prelude to a German empire that would stretch from the Atlantic to the Urals in Russia. When conditions were right, he would unleash an offensive in the West. Meanwhile, the six-month period following the defeat of Poland was nicknamed the "phony war"

---

*In 1943, the Germans discovered these bodies, but the Soviets insisted that they were murdered by the Nazis. Not until 1990 did Soviet authorities finally admit that those murdered in the Katyn Forest and other Polish officers had been executed by the Soviets.

because the fighting on land consisted of only a few skirmishes on the French-German border. Then, in early April 1940, the Germans struck at Denmark and Norway. Hitler wanted to establish naval bases on the Norwegian coast from which to wage submarine warfare against Britain and to ensure delivery of Swedish iron ore to Germany through Norwegian territorial waters. Denmark surrendered within hours. Nazi sympathizers in Norway led by Vidkun Quisling, the country's former war minister, provided the Germans with useful military information. The Germans rapidly secured control of Norway's principal ports and airfields. A British-French force tried to assist the Norwegians, but the landings, badly coordinated and lacking air support, failed. However, the Norwegians and British did succeed in sinking a substantial number of German ships—ten destroyers, three cruisers, and eleven transports—and seriously damaging three cruisers and a battleship.

A defeated Norway lost its independence. According to Nazi racial ideology, both Norwegians and Danes were Nordic Aryans and hence could serve the Third Reich in a variety of ways, including fighting in special SS units. Germany was assured of getting the vital iron ore from Sweden. It also extracted from neutral but cowed Sweden several concessions: Sweden would permit German soldiers to be transported on Swedish trains and would construct warships for the German navy.

Despite the German victory, the Norwegian campaign produced two positive results for the Allies: Norwegian ships escaped to Britain to be put into service, and the German victory in Norway eroded Chamberlain's support in the House of Commons. On May 10, the day Germany invaded Holland and Belgium, Winston Churchill, who had opposed appeasement, replaced Chamberlain as prime minister. Dynamic, eloquent, and courageous, for whom defeat or surrender was foreign to his nature, Churchill had the capacity to stir and lead his people in the struggle against Hitler and the Third Reich. In his first address to Parliament as prime minister on May 13, he left no doubt about the grim realities that lay ahead:

> I have nothing to offer but blood, toil, tears, and sweat…. We have before us many, many long months of struggle and suffering. You ask, what is our policy? I will say: It is to wage war by sea, land, and air with all our might, and with all the strength that God gave us; to wage war against a monstrous lamentable catalogue of human crime. That is our policy. You ask: What is our aim? I can answer in one word: "Victory!" Victory at all costs, victory in spite of all terror, victory however long and hard the road may be; for without victory there is no survival.[8]

THE LOW COUNTRIES AND FRANCE

Prewar French Strategy

Achieving Lebensraum by conquering vast areas of Russia was central to Hitler's worldview. Before invading the Soviet Union, it was necessary to eliminate the threat of an Anglo-French offensive against Germany to the west. German plans called for quickly subduing neutral Holland, Belgium, and Luxembourg and invading France. The defeat of Poland and the pact that had been signed with the Soviet Union enabled Germany to move large numbers of troops from the east to its western borders.

Based on their World War I experience, the French relied on a defensive strategy of which the key element was the Maginot Line, which stretched for eighty-seven miles from the Swiss frontier nearly to where the French and the Belgian-Luxembourg borders converged. The French High Command believed that the Maginot Line was impregnable—that the Germans would suffer huge losses trying to break through the carefully planned fortifications, which included concrete and steel forts, numerous concrete pillboxes for machine guns, heavy artillery firing from deep underground, plenty of well-placed antitank defenses, and miles of barbed wire intended to ensnare attacking infantry. But French strategy had a fatal flaw: the Maginot Line could be bypassed because only weak fortifications stood in the area across from the Ardennes Forest on the border with Belgium. Believing that the Ardennes was impenetrable, that no large force, particularly tanks and heavy artillery, could get through the forest's wooded hills and narrow twisting roads, and that the Meuse River was an effective barrier against tanks, the French High Command gave little thought to defending this sector. Despite leading generals' reluctance to confront what was at the time considered a formidable French military machine, Hitler supported General Erich von Manstein's plan for an offensive across neutral Belgium and through the Ardennes into France near Sedan. This plan would result in far fewer casualties than if German forces attacked the Maginot Line.* Once across the Meuse River, they would race to the coast. Hitler liked von Manstein's strategy because it coincided with his view that successful military operations required surprise, boldness, and hammer-like blows that paralyzed, routed, and annihilated the enemy.

To keep the Germans off French soil for as long as possible, the French High Command, headed by General Maurice Gamelin, intended to rush troops to the Dyle River, the main Belgian defense line. Together with substantial Belgian and British forces, they would halt a German offensive at the river. But would these troops not be needed in France if the Germans chose an invasion route that circumvented the Maginot Line?

The German Offensive

On May 10, 1940, Hitler launched his western offensive with an invasion of the three Low Countries. Hitler simply dismissed concern over their neutrality: "No one will question that when we have won."[9] Immediately, France sent troops to Holland and, according to plan, to the Dyle River in Belgium where they were joined by the British Expeditionary Force (BEF).

---

*This was not the original plan, which was a replay of Germany's invasion of France in 1914. But on January 10, 1940, a German courier plane made an emergency landing in Belgium; on board was an officer carrying the original plan. The Belgian authorities seized his documents before they could be destroyed. Hitler now turned to von Manstein's Ardennes stratagem.

MAP 2.1   The German Conquest of Western Europe, 1940

From April to June 1940, the Germans overran Western Europe. Britain stood alone.

Anticipating that the British and French troops would rush into Belgium, German strategists planned to move a massive motorized force through the Ardennes Forest into France just north of where the Maginot Line ended, taking the French by surprise. After establishing bridgeheads on French soil, their panzers would rapidly sweep across the open plains of northern France to the sea, encircling and trapping the Anglo-French forces in Belgium.

While German armored forces penetrated Dutch frontier defenses, airborne units seized strategic airfields and bridges. The French army sent to aid the Netherlands was forced to retreat into Belgium. In a deliberate attempt to terrorize the population, the Luftwaffe methodically and leisurely bombed a defenseless Rotterdam, destroying the center of the city that was made up mostly of wooden buildings that caught fire easily and causing death and injury to several thousand civilians. (In one of the mishaps of war, the city had already surrendered, but the radio orders to the German bombers in the air to abort the mission failed to get through to all the German planes.) The Dutch army had not been vanquished, but fearing further destruction of its cities, the Netherlands capitulated on May 14 after only five days of fighting.

A daring attack by glider-borne troops enabled the Germans quickly to capture a supposedly impregnable concrete Belgian fortress and two key bridges over the Albert Canal. The British and French had expected the fort to stall the German advance for weeks, but its guns were not designed to ward off an attack from the sky. German troops, transported by gliders, descended on the fort's roof and mined the exits, sealing inside the Belgian defenders who quickly surrendered when German infantry surrounded the fort.

On May 14, near the Belgian village of Hannut, in what was the largest tank battle ever fought until then, the French inflicted substantial losses on the Germans. Approximately 160 German and 121 French tanks were put out of commission. However, since the battlefield remained in their hands, the Germans were able to repair or rebuild many of the disabled tanks, whereas the French had to leave their losses behind. The next day, the Allies, performing admirably, withstood a German attack at the Dyle River. But at precisely this time, the French forces in Belgium were needed to counter the German drive into France against a weakly defended sector. By rushing troops north into Belgium and Holland, the Allies had fallen for Germany's clever feint that was designed to draw attention away from the principal offensive to the south through the Ardennes Forest and into France.

Through the Ardennes

The French had sent their best forces into Holland and Belgium to prevent a German breakthrough, including mobile tank and motorized infantry reserves; other reserves were sent to strengthen the Maginot Line, which the Germans never intended to test in force at this early stage. The real danger for France lay on the Franco-Belgium frontier in the vicinity of Sedan. But the French forces arrayed there consisted mainly of recently mobilized, poorly trained and aging reservists, including officers. The forces were also woefully short of antiaircraft and antitank weapons, although they did have quality artillery. The French forces deployed to counter a German drive in this region were not only deprived of their most modernly equipped and most mobile armies but were also depleted of ready reserves. Not having a general reserve to buttress the defense of this region was a fatal miscalculation, particularly since reports from both Belgian and French intelligence indicated that an attack there was likely.

The French were out of position to repulse a German assault, particularly one directed against the least fortified stretch in the French lines. When informed of the French decision to deploy their troops north into Belgium, the Germans were ecstatic; one officer exclaimed, "It looks as though the enemy is doing exactly what we hoped he would do! He is making himself strong on the northern wing and attaching less importance to [General Karl Rudolf Gerd von] Rundstedt's attack through the Ardennes."[10] When the Germans crossed the Ardennes and reached the Meuse River, they would confront an enemy about half their strength, with no substantial mobile reserves and deplorably deficient in antitank and antiaircraft guns.

Virtually undetected and meeting only slight resistance, a huge concentration of German armored forces—134,000 soldiers, 1,600 tanks, and 41,000 other vehicles—moved through the narrow mountain passes of Luxembourg and the dense Forest of Ardennes in southern Belgium. On May 12 they reached the Meuse, much to the great astonishment of the French. Had the Allies grasped the situation early enough, their aircraft could have done considerable damage to the fifty-mile-long column of German armor moving slowly in close formation over the Ardennes Forest's steep hills, heavily wooded valleys, and narrow, twisting roads that produced bottlenecks. Unable to maneuver in these conditions, German tanks would have been easy targets. Operating further north in Belgium and Holland where the Allies thought the main German attack would come, the French and British air forces missed an opportunity.

The French in a Rout

Because much heavy artillery could not be moved over the narrow mountain roads in the Ardennes, the Germans had to rely on Stuka dive bombers to bombard French positions. On the morning of May 13, hundreds of shrieking Stukas attacking in waves blasted French command posts, communication networks, and bunkers for eight hours. Resembling diving vultures and with sirens emitting nightmarish howls, the Stukas shattered the nerves of stunned French defenders, many of whom fled before the bombs fell. As terrified French soldiers cowered in their bunkers, they could not help but notice the absence of French and British aircraft, which were now operating against the Germans in Belgium.

> A hundred and fifty German planes! It is breathtaking! The noise of their engines is already enormous and then there is this extraordinary shrieking which shreds your nerves.... And then suddenly there is the rain of bombs.... And it goes on and on and on! ... Not a French or British plane to be seen. Where the hell are they! ... My neighbour,

a young bloke, is crying.... Nerves are raw.... Few men are actually hit but their features are drawn, tiredness rings in their eyes. Morale is affected. Why are our planes not defending us? No one says it, but everyone is thinking it.[11]

Although casualties were light, the fierce aerial bombardments confused and demoralized the French troops who sought cover. While the pounding from the air softened French positions, German infantry attempted to cross the Meuse in rubber dinghies. At first, intense French gunfire took its toll of the assault crafts. But German artillery and tanks firing point blank from across the river and the incessant Stuka attacks pinned down French gunners in their bunkers, which enabled German troops to cross the Meuse in three places. German engineers quickly hooked rafts together to ferry troops and vehicles across the river and constructed pontoon bridges enabling German armor to cross. The success of the crossing was due largely to General Erwin Rommel's skillful handling of his soldiers and armor.

In several sectors, the Germans faced stiff resistance and suffered considerable casualties. However, in the center of the river bend, resistance was weak and the Germans quickly overran French positions. The Allies made a frantic attempt to destroy the German bridgehead by air, but they lacked sufficient bombers and their fighters were badly outnumbered. The Luftwaffe and superbly accurate antiaircraft guns shot 150 Allied planes out of the sky. In order to protect their own country against possible air attacks, the British had not sent to France their Spitfires, which were a match for the best German aircraft, and most of the French air force was now in Belgium.

France's failure to counterattack with armor and infantry before the pontoon bridges were completed and during and immediately after the crossing was a costly tactical mistake that enabled the Germans to establish and expand their bridgeheads. If the French had immediately and decisively attacked the exposed German bridgeheads, even with their limited reserves they might have crushed them. By the time the timorous French commanders ordered counterattacks—and the delays once they started—it was too late to stop the German thrust. The French command seemed paralyzed by the speed and daring of the German assault.

Contributing to the debacle was the flight of thousands of French soldiers, including those who manned the vital artillery batteries needed to bombard the Germans as they crossed the Meuse. At times, officers joined the fleeing soldiers. The panic had already started *before* the Meuse crossing; many soldiers, still in shock from the dive-bombing Stukas, began deserting their posts and abandoning their guns when unfounded rumors that German tanks were already behind them spread through their ranks. In actuality, no German tank had yet crossed the river.

Immediately following the successful crossing of the Meuse, and concerned about a French counterattack, the German High Command wanted to consolidate the bridgehead before advancing. But General Guderian, a key innovator in tank warfare who stressed speed, took the initiative. His panzers broke out of the bridgehead and furiously raced west across the flat countryside that was ideal for tanks to the English Channel. The rest of the German forces followed Guderian's panzers. The Luftwaffe bombed and strafed the few fortified positions in the panzers' path, disrupted the French supply chain and communication networks, and broke up the few limited and badly coordinated counterattacks on the panzers' flanks. Shocked French units were surrendering in large numbers, although in some fortified areas the Germans faced fierce resistance. At Arras, British tanks fought well and temporarily delayed the German advance. But as earlier, the Allies responded too late with too little. Guderian's panzers reached the coast on May 20; more units quickly followed. The Germans were succeeding beyond their hopes.

On the same day, General Maxime Weygand replaced Gamelin as supreme Allied commander, but his counteroffensive amounted to nothing. The situation for France was becoming more perilous as the BEF and French troops in Belgium were now cut off from the Allied forces in France. Caught in a collapsing pocket, the Anglo-French forces were left with only one option: withdraw to England immediately. Desperately, they retreated to the northern French port of Dunkirk, the last port of escape. On May 28, King Leopold of Belgium surrendered—274,000 soldiers and all their equipment—another setback for the Allies, who were relying on Belgian resistance to hold off the Germans while the evacuation was in progress.

The "Miracle of Dunkirk"

The Germans now sought to surround and annihilate the Allied forces converging on Dunkirk. Probably fearing that German tanks would lose mobility in the rivers and canals around Dunkirk, General von Rundstedt called them off just as the panzer force prepared to take the port. Von Rundstedt also thought the panzers, whose number had already been diminished in battle and by mechanical problems, were needed to guard against French counterattacks south of the Somme River and to continue with the offensive campaign that would lead to France's surrender. Von Rundstedt was also concerned that after the long advance many tanks required maintenance and armored units a rest. Hitler agreed and confirmed the order. Moreover, Field Marshal Hermann Goering, who wanted the Luftwaffe to be in on the kill, persuaded Hitler that his planes could finish off the Allied troops trapped on the beaches. Fog and rain prevented German planes from operating at full strength, though, and British pilots inflicted heavy losses on the attackers. Most German generals in the field were outraged and frustrated over the decision to hold back the panzers just before the trap was closing on the Allied troops whose backs were to the sea. But they could not change Hitler's mind. Chief of Staff Franz Halder wrote in his diary: "[T]he pocket would have been closed at the coast if only our armor had not been held back. As it is, the bad weather has grounded our air force and now we must stand by and watch how countless thousands of the enemy are getting away to England, right under our noses."[12]

Hitler quickly reversed himself, but the Allies were able to take advantage of an almost three-day breathing space to tighten their perimeter defenses and

The Art Archive/Art Resource, NY

This famous picture depicts the "Miracle of Dunkirk," during which the Allied soldiers were evacuated from the beaches and harbor of Dunkirk, France.

prepare for a massive evacuation. Although the operation proceeded, it faced continuous artillery fire and attacks by the Luftwaffe, which, weather permitting, bombed and strafed both the unprotected soldiers crowding the beaches and the rescue ships. Given that Luftwaffe bombing had made much of Dunkirk's harbor largely inoperable, small craft ferried the soldiers to the transport ships and destroyers. Waiting for the soldiers to be brought on board, these ships were often prime targets for the Luftwaffe. At times, German torpedo boats and submarines operating in the English Channel sank British ships packed with soldiers. More than two hundred British ships, mainly small craft but also six destroyers, were lost. Many more were badly damaged. The Royal Air Force (RAF) Spitfires and Hurricanes provided protection during the nine days of evacuation at a cost of 177 planes; the Luftwaffe lost about twice as many. Because they were close to their home bases, RAF pilots had the advantage of being able to stay in the air longer than Luftwaffe pilots, who needed sufficient fuel for the flight home. However, the greatly outnumbered RAF could not provide full cover for the men congregating on the shore, and the Luftwaffe waited for opportunities to attack the vulnerable beaches. And as the Germans advanced, the beaches came within their artillery range, adding to the Allied casualties.

Dead and dying men were sprawled on the shore and in the water, victims of German planes and artillery. Adding to the death toll were the not infrequent drownings caused by desperate and leaderless men struggling to get on the small craft that would carry them to the large ships farther out. Some men drowned wading and swimming to the transport ships as the water level suddenly rose, but fortunately the waters of the Channel remained essentially calm.

All during the embarkations, Allied troops, principally French, fought bravely to hold the Germans back in the towns and canals that comprised the perimeter. They were not strong enough to hold the perimeter for more than a few days, but their determined defense gave the Allies precious time to proceed with the evacuation. More than thirty thousand French defenders became prisoners of war.

Despite considerable Allied casualties, the operation was a huge success. Goering, who was given to "shooting his mouth off" as one German general remarked, could not deliver on his assurance that his Luftwaffe would annihilate the Allied forces on the beaches. Some 338,000 Allied troops, including 123,000 French, were transported across the English Channel chiefly by destroyers and troop transports, but also by merchant ships, motor boats, fishing boats, tugboats, barges, and private yachts. In an extraordinary display of patriotism, civilian volunteers manning small craft worked tirelessly moving the men from the beaches to waiting ships or taking them directly to Britain. In all, an estimated 850 vessels participated in the evacuation.

The desperate evacuation forced the British to abandon their heavy equipment on the beaches, including 400 tanks and almost 64,000 vehicles, and tons of ammunition and stores. Nevertheless, they saved their veteran soldiers and most qualified officers to fight another day. Hitler's decision to hold back the tanks—one of the worst military mistakes of the war—the efforts of the Royal Navy, the dedication of small craft owners, and the courage of RAF pilots made the "miracle of Dunkirk" possible. True, as Winston Churchill said, "wars are not won by evacuations," but had the BEF been unable to escape, Britain would have had very little left to continue the struggle. It is problematic that Churchill could have survived the growing political pressure to make peace with Hitler. For the British, Dunkirk was a memorable deliverance that boosted British morale.*

The Fall of France

Meanwhile, the battle for France was turning into an even worse disaster for the French. The German armored divisions that had swept across northern France to the Channel now moved south in a new offensive. As in the first stage of the battle, the Luftwaffe worked in close cooperation with the panzers. Roaming the skies at will, German aircraft attacked key targets, including

---

*Was it also an act of deliverance for the Soviet Union? Had the British forces been killed or captured, Britain would have posed no immediate threat to Nazi Germany. Nor was Hitler eager to invade the island nation. He preferred making peace with Britain on condition that it did not interfere with German domination of the Continent. With Britain gravely weakened, even if still unwilling to make peace, Germany was not compelled to deploy large numbers of troops to guard the Atlantic Wall and to fight the British in North Africa. Then when Germany invaded the Soviet Union in June 1941, Hitler could have concentrated all that manpower, airpower, and armor against the Soviet forces, increasing substantially German offensive strength.

Hitler and his aides rejoicing in front of the Eiffel Tower after the fall of France. Hitler (center right) saw the fall of France as proof of the invincibility of the Reich and a predestined reversal of the humiliation felt by Germans at their defeat in World War I.

© SZ Photo/Scherl/The Image Works

industrial and communication centers, and terrorized the civilian population, at times machine-gunning fleeing refugees. German armor moved relentlessly into the French heartland. Although there were instances of great courage and effective defense, French resistance was rapidly crumbling; whole divisions were cut off or in retreat. Defeatism showed on the faces of French soldiers and civilians. Millions of refugees in cars and carts and on motorcycles and bicycles fled south and west in panic to escape the advancing Germans; also in flight was the French government, depriving the people of leadership.

On June 10, Mussolini declared war on France and Britain in a move that President Franklin Roosevelt called a "stab in the back." On June 14, German troops entered Paris, which, unlike Warsaw, capitulated without a fight. French leaders had taken no steps to defend their capital or its approaches. On June 16, Marshal Henri Philippe Pétain, a World War I hero, was appointed prime minister. With authority breaking down and resistance dying, the French cabinet appealed for the armistice that was signed on June 22; in accordance with Hitler's order, it was signed in the same railway car in which Germany had agreed to the armistice ending World War I. A veteran of the Great War who had never accepted Germany's defeat, this was Hitler's way of humiliating his old enemy and redeeming German honor.

It was France's darkest hour: its vaunted military machine had been ignominiously vanquished in just six weeks, and 1.9 million French soldiers were prisoners of war.* The Germans had accomplished in just a few weeks what they had failed to do in World War I after more than four years of brutal conflict. For Hitler, it was a personal triumph that recklessly inflated his ego. He had already interpreted his rise to power as evidence of his political genius; now he also saw himself as a military genius in the tradition of Frederick the Great, one of his heroes. Had he not intuited that France and Britain would not come to Poland's aid? Had he not recognized the merit of sending his panzers through the Ardennes? Increasingly, Hitler would rely on his own intuition and imagination, which he now considered infallible, even if they conflicted with the reasoned judgment of his senior generals. For Hitler, strength of will and the nerve to take great risks were more important virtues in politics and war than professional expertise. This overweening pride, what the ancient Greeks called hubris, would contribute to his downfall.

The German people were euphoric. The shame of the Versailles Treaty had been erased and German honor restored. In one audacious stroke, the Wehrmacht had driven Holland, Belgium, and France out of the war and expelled Britain from the Continent. Western Europe, with all its economic potential, was at Germany's feet. The German people's devotion to Hitler increased immeasurably. Much of the nation shared in one German housewife's sentiments:

> The French had now had the tables turned on them, and the British too. Germany stood once again in her true place in Europe.... Naturally we were all intoxicated by our victories.... [T]the strongest feeling of all was our pride in Germany, showing the world that the Treaty of Versailles, with its bitter humiliations, had been broken. I was proud to be German. I was also proud of Hitler. Indeed, all those who formerly had had doubts about Hitler were now carried away in respect and admiration. He had put Germany back as a great nation in the world.[13]

Adding to the jubilation of ordinary Germans were the expensive French silk stockings, perfumes, toiletries, champagnes, and delicacies that veterans brought home with them. The Nazi authorities had artificially fixed the exchange rate for the French franc in order to greatly increase the value of the German Reichsmark, thus enabling German soldiers to buy luxury products that they normally could never have afforded.

And yet the greatest reason for jubilation was the overwhelming relief that there would be no repetition of the trench warfare of World War I with its massive casualties. After the fall of France, most Germans simply wanted the fighting to end.

---

*The Germans' abuse of black French West African soldiers was an early sign of how deeply Nazi racial ideology had penetrated German troops. Although senior officers did not order or sanction this mistreatment, writes Dennis Showalter, "there is nevertheless no question that German soldiers, including men from the mobile divisions, disproportionately refused quarter to black combatants, singled out black prisoners for brutal treatment including large-scale executions in non-combat situations, and justified themselves on racial grounds. Only the degenerate French would put subhumans into uniform, call them soldiers, and give them license to mutilate German wounded. It was an evil portent." *Hitler's Panzers: The Lightning Attacks That Revolutionized Warfare* (New York: Penguin Books, 2009), 132.

After the crushing defeat of France, the Ministry of Popular Enlightenment headed by Joseph Goebbels launched a propaganda barrage to promote Hitler's image. Since Hitler's rise to power, Goebbels had exalted the Führer as an inspired savior with infallible judgment; sinister and cunning, he wanted the German people to view their leader as a demigod who deserved total loyalty. Now in newsreels, posters, and newspapers, Nazi propaganda depicted the victorious German soldiers, united in their devotion to Hitler and National Socialism, as an invincible fighting machine and Hitler as history's most brilliant military strategist. Goebbels' propaganda also spewed Nazi racist doctrines. The German people were told that France was a nation contaminated by Jewish-Negro cultural influences and racial mixing, that the victory of German Aryans saved European civilization from these destructive forces.

Reasons for France's Defeat

How can the collapse of France be explained? France had somewhat fewer pilots and planes, particularly bombers, than Germany, but many French planes never left the airfields. And because French airfields lacked early warning systems and sufficient antiaircraft guns, the Luftwaffe was able to destroy numerous aircraft on the ground, and, unlike the French, German antiaircraft gunners demolished many Allied planes in the air. Nevertheless, French factory production replaced the losses. France had planes, but the High Command either did not use them—which is still a cause of astonishment—or did not deploy them properly. And because of a terrible deficiency in antiaircraft weapons, German planes often could operate freely. Another reason for the Allied aerial weakness was the British decision to keep large numbers of its best planes at home for defense of their island.

The French air force simply lacked competent command. Unlike the Germans, the French were not proponents of a tactical air force, particularly dive bombers that operated in close support of infantry and tanks. In contrast, the German air force was an integral part of an offensive operation, providing close support for advancing ground forces and bombing behind enemy lines. Operating like aerial artillery, screeching Stuka dive bombers accurately bombed French positions, terrifying French troops and disorienting their command structure. Dominating the air, the Luftwaffe disrupted Allied reconnaissance efforts and decimated tanks and infantry attempting to counterattack.

As for tanks, the French had as many as the Germans, some of them superior. The heavy damage inflicted on German panzers in Belgium showed the quality of both French tanks and the crews that operated them. But the French High Command had not learned the sobering lesson of the German blitzkrieg in Poland. For them, the function of tanks was to support infantry advances and not to achieve breakthroughs. Clinging to the doctrine of static warfare along a linear line, the French spread their tanks among the various infantry divisions in the belief that this would strengthen ground forces across the fronts. Intending to fight a war of mobility and maneuvering, the Germans concentrated their tanks in panzer divisions designed to power through enemy lines. Against such a large

French civilians of Marseilles show the shock of France's defeat in 1940. Hitler's army accomplished what the German generals of World War I had planned but not brought about: the capture of Paris and the fall of France. The might of motorized warfare had prevailed over the French army and its outmoded World War I methods.

array of attacking panzers with air support, the handful of defending tanks and antitank guns could offer only feeble resistance. In his memoirs, General Charles de Gaulle pointed out the weakness of the French approach. A newly formed motorized division, he said, "was immediately split up between the battalions of an infantry division and was engulfed fragment after fragment in an abortive counterattack. Had they been grouped together beforehand, these mechanized units, for all their deficiencies, would have been able to deal the invader some formidable blows. But isolated one from another, they were nothing but shreds."[14] Moreover, unlike the panzers, most French tanks did not have radios, which were essential for the rapid deployment of tank units. Communicating by radio, German tank crews lured French tanks into traps where they were destroyed by antitank guns.

Nor was German manpower overwhelming. Actually, French, British, Dutch, and Belgian armies combined had some four million soldiers compared to about three million in the Wehrmacht, but the British did not send sufficient troops to buttress their French ally. France met disaster largely because its military leaders, unlike the Germans, had not mastered the psychology and tactics of motorized warfare. The Germans had developed a new and modern approach to warfare: rapid breakthroughs into the enemy's rear by concentrating at one point motorized armor closely supported by aerial bombardment and strafing and mobile artillery; forcing a breakthrough in the enemy lines; penetrating with lightning speed deep into the enemy's rear before it had time to react; and encircling and destroying or capturing the surrounded enemy forces. Not drawing a lesson from the German blitzkrieg in Poland, the French were overwhelmed by the speed and power of the German offensive. "The French commanders, trained in the slow-motion methods of 1914 to 1918, were mentally unfitted to cope with Panzer pace, and it produced a spreading paralysis among them," said respected British military analyst Sir Basil H. Liddell-Hart.[15] Moreover, both French and British command systems were geared to following rigid plans that were worked out in advance to the last detail, which left little room for officers at the front to adapt to changing battlefield situations. Unlike their French counterparts, German commanders and even junior officers were encouraged to take the initiative, to deviate from a set battle plan and improvise in order to exploit an opportunity. Also unlike their French counterparts, who were commanding from dugouts miles away, German panzer commanders—Guderian and Rommel, for example—were in the front line directing and inspiring their troops, observing the battlefield, and communicating by radio with their tank crews. Put succinctly, the French were badly outgeneraled.

The Germans exploited the element of surprise by moving rapidly through the Ardennes Forest and arriving unexpectedly at the Meuse River, where they had the good fortune of facing weak French units at critical points along the Meuse crossing. King Leopold of Belgium informed the French High Command that he had evidence that Germans hoped to draw the principal French and British forces into Belgium while their main force headed south toward the area of Sedan. And French reconnaissance pilots reported the movement of large German columns through the Ardennes. However, unwilling to rethink their conviction that a major offensive through the Ardennes was impossible, the French High Command largely ignored these warnings; at best, they regarded these signs as a weak secondary offensive. Fixating on the Maginot Line, the French did not transfer divisions stationed there in order to counter the German's advance; many of these divisions remained inactive as the Germans established bridgeheads across the Meuse and raced to the sea.

The slowness of the French High Command's response to vulnerable German salients was a failure as costly as their earlier failure to decipher the route the German offensive would take. Overly cautious, overrating German strength, and not fully comprehending modern motorized warfare, the baffled French command either neglected or delayed a counterattack when the Germans were crossing the Meuse and establishing precarious bridgeheads on the other side, particularly near Sedan. Had French tanks in the vicinity moved quickly to the Meuse, which was only a few miles away, they could have been lying in wait as the panzers crossed and set up their formations. By the time French armor arrived, the Germans had expanded their bridgehead and deployed their tanks and antitank guns to rout the French thrust. And the French failed to counterattack exposed German flanks in sufficient strength as the panzers were racing westward to the sea. Throughout the campaign, the French military generally remained rigid, unable to adapt to changing battlefield conditions; the Germans, on the other hand, constantly seized the initiative and moved with speed. Exploiting slow French responses, the Germans were able to explode from their bridgeheads and race to the Channel.

Compounding these mistakes were the French High Command's fatal decision to commit the cream of their armies to Holland and Belgium, leaving only weak units to repel an invasion force driving through the Ardennes, and their failure to retain a sufficient strategic reserve to check the Germans in case of a breakthrough. When Churchill rushed to Paris during the crisis, he was "dumbfounded" to learn that the French had no such reserves to "counter-attack at the moment when the first fury of the offensive has spent its force.... I admit that this was one of the greatest surprises I have had in my life."[16] In contrast to the poor performance of French military leaders, the German High Command fought an imaginative campaign, effectively implementing Napoleon's battlefield injunctions: create a secondary front that diverts the opponent's forces, rapidly move troops to an unexpected destination that surprises and shocks the enemy, and concentrate a superior force against a weak segment of the opponent's strung-out positions.

Not only did German generals outperform the French High Command but also German soldiers in the field generally evidenced a higher level of morale and battlefield skill and daring than the French. Highly trained German noncommissioned officers (NCOs) demonstrated resourcefulness and daring in leading their squads to destroy a bunker or gun position. Although many front-line troops fought well, it was not uncommon for panicky French soldiers to abandon viable positions and their vehicles, actions that clogged the roads and impeded the movement of troops. Surrender and flight were common.

One also senses a failure of will among the French people, a defeatist attitude that afflicted civilians and many front-line soldiers. This loss of confidence was a consequence of internal political disputes dividing the nation, poor leadership, the years of appeasement and lost opportunities, and German propaganda, which depicted Nazism as irresistible and the Führer as a man of destiny. For many bourgeois and upper-class Frenchmen, Hitler's domination was preferable to a government controlled by French socialists and Communists. And the French people were still traumatized by World War I, which had been fought largely on their soil. Some 1.5 million men had been killed and 1 million wounded, many of them permanently crippled and disfigured. This painful memory shattered the martial spirit of the French people, for whom war was now hateful.

According to the terms of the armistice, Germany annexed Alsace and Lorraine and occupied northern France and the Atlantic coast, France's most industrialized regions. The French military was forced to demobilize. The French government, now located at Vichy in the south, was headed by Marshal Pétain, who favored authoritarian rule and collaboration with the German authorities in occupied France. Vichy France continued to control France's overseas empire, including Algeria, Morocco, and Tunisia. Germany seized France's arsenal, including thousands of tanks and artillery that would be used in other campaigns, and French industry and resources, along with those of Holland and Belgium, were now at the Third Reich's disposal, which significantly increased its military capacity. In a few weeks, France had been reduced to a second-rate power subservient to the Third Reich. Refusing to recognize defeat, General Charles de Gaulle escaped to London and organized the Free French forces. The Germans gloried in their revenge, the French wept in their humiliation, and the British gathered their courage, for they now stood alone.

THE BATTLE OF BRITAIN

Hitler expected that after his stunning victories in the west, Britain would make peace. The British, however, continued to reject Hitler's peace overtures, for they envisioned only a dark future if Hitler dominated the Continent. "The Battle of Britain is about to begin," Churchill told his people. "Upon this battle depends the survival of Christian civilization.... if we fail, then ... all we have known and cared for will sink into the abyss of a new Dark Age."[17] In these dire circumstances, Britain's greatest threat in its long history, Churchill's stirring oratory, inspired leadership, and unyielding will mobilized the morale of the British people. Against all odds, a defiant Britain would continue to fight Hitler and his Third Reich.

With Britain remaining defiant, Hitler proceeded with invasion plans code-named Operation Sea Lion. He anticipated that the plans would materialize in mid-September. Not eager to invade the British Isles, Hitler retained a glimmer of hope that if threatened with invasion, Britain would recognize reality and accept his peace offering—an end to hostilities if Britain would not interfere with German rule of conquered Europe.

Unlike the battles in Poland and France where motorized armor prevailed, the Battle of Britain was fought entirely in the air. It was the first such campaign of its kind in history. Starting in mid-July, the Germans concentrated a large number of barges and other transport craft in English Channel ports in occupied lands, and troops practiced amphibious landings on French beaches. But a successful crossing of the Channel and the establishment of beachheads on the English coast depended on control of the skies. A sizable invasion force could not establish a beachhead while the RAF continuously strafed and bombed. And the Royal Navy, which was far superior to the German naval fleet, had to be prevented from annihilating the invasion transports. To protect the beachheads and to make the British fleet vulnerable to German dive bombers, it was necessary to destroy the RAF. (Some analysts maintain that the Royal Navy could have repelled a German invasion even if the Luftwaffe had destroyed British air power, but this is arguable.) Given the Luftwaffe's past performance and its superiority in numbers, Goering assured Hitler that his Luftwaffe could destroy the RAF. On August 1, he arrogantly informed German generals: "The Führer has ordered me to crush Britain with my Luftwaffe. By means of hard blows I plan to have the enemy, who has already suffered a crushing moral defeat [in France], down on his knees in the nearest future, so that an occupation of the island by our troops can proceed without any risk."[18] However, Goering both overestimated the strength of his Luftwaffe, which had lost 1,284 planes in the campaign in France and the Low Countries, and underestimated the proficiency of RAF aircraft and pilots.

Fighter Command and Britain's Air Defense

In early July 1940, the Luftwaffe, from bases in Holland, Belgium, and northern France, began attacks on British ports and ships in the English Channel. In the 1930s, Hugh Dowding, commander in chief of Fighter Command, had with foresight and skill developed an effective air defense system for Britain. He promoted the development of radar and advanced fighter planes called Spitfires and Hurricanes. Providing early warning, the fifty radar stations situated on the coast provided the island with a valuable shield. Technicians studying the route of German planes phoned the details to a central office where members of the Women's Auxiliary Air Force (WAAF) plotted the course of the incoming German planes on a huge map. Even when bombs were falling around them, killing some, these women coolly and effectively did their job. To complement the radar stations, the British established the Observer Corps consisting of some thirty thousand sky watchers posted in different places who scanned the skies for hostile planes and telephoned their sightings to Fighter Command. Utilizing the data supplied by radar stations and the observer posts, Fighter Command officers then radioed instructions to the fighter squadrons. RAF fighters, Hurricanes and Spitfires, were more than a match for the Luftwaffe's Messerschmitts, and RAF pilots understood that they were fighting for the very life of their country. Fortunately, Dowding had fought against sending more planes to aid the French in what had become a lost cause. If the British lost more aircraft in France, he feared, there would be only a handful left to protect the island. As it was, after the losses suffered protecting the exodus from Dunkirk, the British had fewer than four hundred Spitfires and Hurricanes left. Working day and night, British factory workers labored tirelessly to replenish the RAF. Nevertheless, the Luftwaffe had a significant numerical superiority over the RAF.

Virtually every day during the Battle of Britain, weather permitting, hundreds of planes dueled in the sky above Britain. Watching from the ground, tens of thousands saw aircraft moving in for the kill or maneuvering to escape an attacker, exploding in the air, or desperately attempting to crash-land. Some pilots were volunteers from Commonwealth countries—Canada, New Zealand, Australia, and South Africa. A large number of highly motivated Polish (141) and Czech (86) pilots who had sought refuge in Britain distinguished themselves—Joseph František, a Czech pilot in the Battle of Britain, had the second-highest kills in the RAF. Seven idealistic American volunteers also fought with the RAF.

Dowding instructed his pilots to go after bombers rather than the fighters that accompanied them. The Germans would find it more difficult to replace the highly trained crew of four that manned the bombers than they would a fighter pilot, and it was considerably more expensive to produce a bomber than a fighter. Moreover, fighter-to-fighter combat could lead to a high death toll of

British pilots. But destroying bombers, which were protected by thick armor plating and escorted by fighters, was an immense challenge.

The air battle over Britain is usually divided into four phases. Lasting from July 10 to August 11, the first phase, the "Channel battles," consisted of German attacks on British convoys in the English Channel; because of the large number of ships lost, the British Admiralty diverted these convoys away from the Channel. In the second phase, "Eagle Attack," from August 12 to August 23, the Luftwaffe targeted British airfields and the radar stations, both extremely vital to British defense. Dowding was greatly alarmed. On August 12, the Germans managed to damage five radar stations, one of which was out of action for eleven days. But, because the bombings did not render the stations totally inoperable, on August 15, in what was a major blunder, Goering abandoned these targets; the radar stations had to deal with only two more attacks. Also on August 15, from bases in Denmark and Norway, an unprecedented number of bombers, escorted by large formations of fighters, attacked airfields, air defenses, and factories in the north of England; British fighters shot down seventy-one planes—three times as many as the RAF lost. Surviving Luftwaffe pilots referred to this painful defeat as "Black Thursday."

On August 24, German pilots dropped bombs on London. Although accounts differ, it was probably an accidental bombing by German bomber pilots who, because of a navigational error, were unaware that they were over the city. Hitler had directed that the Luftwaffe should refrain from attacking London unless he ordered it. The bombs caused little damage, but Churchill was determined to retaliate. On the next night, the RAF bombed Berlin and would continue to do so. The RAF bombing enraged Hitler, who now approved of bombing the British capital. Although the damage to Berlin was also negligible, the raid did have a psychological effect on the Berliners. William L. Shirer, an American journalist in Berlin, wrote in his diary: "The Berliners are stunned. They did not think it could happen. When this war began, Goering assured them it couldn't.* … They believed him. Their disillusionment today, therefore, is all the greater. You have to see their faces to measure it."[19] For the German people, the bombing of Berlin was an unthinkable occurrence; for Hitler, it was an abomination, and he ordered the construction of several flak towers—steel and concrete structures protected by antiaircraft guns and with a capacity to shelter as many as eighteen thousand people. In a speech on September 4, he vowed that if the British attacked German cities on a large scale, their cities would be erased. In time, British and (American) air raids would become frequent and deadly. They would bring much pain to the German people.

In the third phase, also starting on August 24, the Luftwaffe concentrated on damaging British airfields and destroying as many RAF fighters as they could on the ground and in aerial combat. The Germans also intended to eliminate the

---

*Actually, Goering had said, "You may call me Meyer [an unmistakably Jewish name] if one single enemy plane ever enters German airspace."

sector stations, the "nerve centers" of Fighter Command, which relayed to fighter squadrons intelligence from radar and ground observation posts regarding the location of German planes, information that gave British pilots an advantage in combat. Although Fighter Command lost fewer planes than did the Luftwaffe in this stepped-up fighting, it was weakened by the damage to its forward airfields—deep craters made them unserviceable for days—and the indispensable sector stations and the continuous loss of veteran pilots. By September 1, 181 pilots had died and another 145 were out of action because of injuries in only about a week of third-phase fighting.

Replacing experienced pilots was a great concern for Fighter Command. Not enough pilots were being trained, and many pilot replacements, sometimes boys in their late teens, were thrown into the maelstrom after only nine hours of flying time and no training in aerial combat. Replacement squadrons with untried pilots usually suffered more losses than the formations they had replaced. Moreover, the daily air battles were grueling; pilots sometimes landed, refueled, and then immediately flew back into combat. This, combined with the incredible danger they experienced—lethal dog fights, bailing out of burning planes, perilous forced landings, and damaged planes crashing into the waters of the Channel—stretched the nerves of surviving pilots to the limits. At times, exhausted pilots fell asleep in their planes before taking off to do battle again and again.

Dowding had only to hold off the Luftwaffe until the end of September. After that, storms and the resultant high seas would make the English Channel too treacherous for an amphibious attack. But could he keep his squadrons flying and intercepting Luftwaffe bombers if the Germans accelerated their air war of attrition?

From August 31 to September 7, Fighter Command went through its darkest period. During this time, Fighter Command lost 161 planes, which was more kills than were inflicted on the Luftwaffe. An anxious Fighter Command now feared that if this slugging match with the Luftwaffe continued much longer, it would soon suffer a severe shortage of pilots, a situation that flight training schools could not remedy, and that the losses in planes might outpace factory production. The RAF would not have the strength to stop an invasion that military intelligence thought could occur any day, based on aerial photographs and reports from agents on the Continent.

But on September 7, a decision that turned out to be fatal for the Luftwaffe gave Fighter Command a reprieve. On that day, Luftwaffe Command shifted its focus from bombing British airfields and aircraft factories to massive terror raids on London and major industrial cities. More than nine hundred German planes—up to that point the largest air attack ever undertaken—assailed London in several waves. They bombed docks, warehouses, factories, oil refineries, power stations, and other targets; 306 Londoners perished in the raid and 1,337 were seriously wounded. This marked the beginning of the fourth phase of the Battle of Britain—the "Blitz" (see "The Home Front" in Chapter 5). One reason for this tactical shift away from air fields to cities was to please Hitler, who wanted to retaliate for the RAF's bombing of Berlin.

A second reason was to break the morale of the English people. To end the terror from the skies, the Germans hoped that the British would come to terms, saving them the need to invade the island nation. The third and most important reason was the expectation that great numbers of British fighters would take to the air to defend the capital, making it possible to accelerate the annihilation of the British air force, which Germans mistakenly believed was now spent. However, like the reversal of orders to attack radar stations, this move backfired. By destroying planes on the ground, hangars, repair shops, and runways, leaving some so damaged that they were unusable for days, the daily raids on airfields had seriously weakened British air defenses. Now these raids were greatly reduced; so too were the raids on the critically important sector stations, the operation rooms that were the nerve center of Fighter Command. This shift in German targets, and the improved performance of replacement pilots, greatly eased the pressure on Britain's imperiled defense system. True, the incessant pounding of London would cause mounting civilian casualties, but the country was saved. The German High Command's failure to continue the Luftwaffe's raids on airfields and sector stations was a fortunate mistake for Britain.

Nazi Germany's First Defeat

On September 15, the decisive day in the Battle of Britain, two hundred bombers escorted by six hundred fighter planes made an all-out effort to destroy the British air force and, as Goering hoped, to bring Britain to its knees. The RAF, with virtually every available Hurricane and Spitfire seeing action, shot down sixty aircraft; only twenty-six British planes were downed. Relentless attacks by RAF fighters broke up Luftwaffe formations and prevented the bombers from hitting their targets. The mass attack on London had failed, much to Hitler's displeasure.

When added to the heavy losses of the past two months, the loss of about 175 planes since September 7 convinced Hitler that Goering could not fulfill his promise to destroy British air defenses. Hitler now had misgivings about invading Britain. Without control of the air, the Germans could not risk an invasion across the English Channel. And soon autumn's storms and high seas would make the English Channel hazardous for an amphibious assault. Moreover, unwilling to absorb more losses of planes and highly trained pilots that he would need for an attack on the Soviet Union, on September 17 the Führer postponed the invasion of Britain "until further notice."

After a succession of spectacular victories, Nazi Germany had suffered its first defeat: the Luftwaffe had not neutralized Britain's air force or its aircraft production facilities, Hitler's plan for an amphibious landing on the British coast never did take place, and Britain did not withdraw from the war. Nazi Germany's failure to achieve these goals demonstrated that it was not invincible and strengthened the English people's determination to continue the struggle against Hitler.

In addition to Germany's tactical errors, several other factors account for the British victory. First, radar developed by British scientists provided early warning of the approach and location of German planes. Second, Luftwaffe fighter pilots had to check constantly their fuel supply for the trip back, limiting their combat time to no more than twenty-five minutes; although bombers could hover over Britain longer, they depended on fighter escorts for survival. Flying back with virtually empty fuel tanks, many German pilots did not make it. British pilots, on the other hand, could land, refuel, and rejoin the fight. Third, a RAF pilot who was either shot down or forced to bail out landed on friendly territory and could soon return to battle, sometimes the same day. A German pilot who was shot down over Britain and survived became a prisoner of war. Fourth, much credit goes to British ground crews and factories. Demonstrating exceptional skill, ground crews speedily refueled, rearmed, and tested and replaced equipment of landed planes, which enabled them to reenter the battle in minutes. Factories operated around the clock to replenish losses; in the summer of 1940, these factories produced about 125 planes a week, far more than the German output. But ultimately it was the skill and courage of British pilots— over five hundred of whom made the ultimate sacrifice—fighting to protect their homeland that saved Britain. "Never in the field of human conflict was so much owed by so many to so few," said Churchill famously of these heroes. These words also apply to the foreign volunteers who wanted to strike at Hitler and the Third Reich. Perhaps the achievement of these brave young men was even greater: they rose to the challenge at a time when a new barbarism threatened to overrun Western civilization. The summer of 1940 was indeed Britain's "finest hour" as Churchill said.

During Britain's time of troubles, the United States was supplying it with massive amounts of military hardware that helped it to continue the struggle against the Axis. Consistent with his racial delusions, Hitler saw American aid as proof that President Roosevelt was being manipulated by Jews. Britain by itself had no hope of defeating the Third Reich. Two events ultimately changed the course of the war: Germany's invasion of the Soviet Union on June 22, 1941, and Japan's attack on the United States on December 7, 1941, which was followed four days later by German and Italian declarations of war. With the entry of the Soviet Union and the United States, an anti-Nazi coalition was created that had the human and material resources to reverse the tide of battle. Churchill saw the alliance with America as Britain's salvation. He described his feelings on hearing the news of Pearl Harbor:

> I knew the United States was in the war up to the neck and in to
> the death.... I thought of a remark which Edward Grey had made
> to me more than thirty years before—that the United States is like
> "a gigantic boiler. Once the fire is lighted under it there is no limit to
> the power it can generate." Being saturated and satiated with emotion
> and sensation, I went to bed and slept the sleep of the saved and the
> thankful.[20]

CHRONOLOGY

September 1, 1939	Germany invades Poland
September 3, 1939	Britain and France declare war on Germany
September 17, 1939	Soviet Union invades Poland
September 27, 1939	Poland surrenders
November 1939	Soviet Union invades Finland
April 1940	Germany attacks Denmark and Norway
May 10, 1940	Germany attacks Belgium, Holland, Luxembourg, and France
May 13, 1940	German troops cross the Meuse
May 27–June 4, 1940	Allied troops are evacuated from Dunkirk
June 22, 1940	France surrenders
August–September 1940	Battle of Britain
September 17, 1940	Hitler postpones indefinitely the invasion of Britain

NOTES

1. Peter Gay, *Freud: A Life for Our Times* (New York: Norton, 1988), 348.

2. Roland Dorgelàs, "After Fifty Years," in *Promise of Greatness*, ed. George A. Panichas (New York: John Day, 1968), 14–15.

3. Barbara Tuchman, *The Guns of August* (New York: Macmillan, 1962), 145.

4. James Joll, "The Unspoken Assumptions," in *The Origins of the First World War*, ed. H. W. Koch (New York: Taplinger, 1972), 318.

5. Alistair Horne, *To Lose A Battle: France 1940* (New York: Penguin Books, 1990), 91.

6. Heinz Guderian, *Panzer Leader*, trans. Constantine Fitzgibbon (New York: De Capo Press, 1996), 97.

7. Excerpted in *Blitzkrieg in Their Own Words: First-Hand Accounts from German Soldiers 1939–1940*, trans. Alane Bance (St. Paul, MN: Zenith Press, 2005), 27–28. This was first published in 1942 in Nazi Germany with a foreword by Heinz Guderian.

8. Winston S. Churchill, *The Second World War*, vol. 2, *Their Finest Hour* (Boston: Houghton Mifflin, 1949), 25–26.

9. Alan Bullock, *Hitler and Stalin: Parallel Lives* (New York: Alfred A. Knopf, 1992), 650.

10. William L. Shirer, *The Collapse of the Third Republic: An Inquiry into the Fall of France in 1940* (New York: Simon and Schuster, 1969), 638.

11. Julian Jackson, *The Fall of France: The Nazi Invasion of 1940* (New York: Oxford University Press, 2003), 164.

12. *The Halder War Diary, 1939–1942*, ed. Charles Burdick and Hans-Adolf Jacobsen (Nivato, CA: Presidio, 1988), 172.

13. Else Wendel, *Hausfrau at War: A German Woman's Account of Life in Hitler's Reich* (London: Odhams Press, 1957), 81–82.

14. Charles de Gaulle, *War Memoirs*, vol. 1, *The Call to Honour 1940–1942* (New York: Viking Press, 1955), 36.

15. Basil H. Liddell-Hart, *History of the Second World War* (New York: Putnam, 1970), 73–74.

16. Churchill, *The Second World War*, vol. 2, *Their Finest Hour*, 47.

17. Ibid., 225–226.

18. John Keegan, *The Second World War* (New York: Viking, 1989), 91.

19. William L. Shirer, *Berlin Diary* (New York: Galahad Books, 1995), 486.

20. Churchill, *The Second World War*, vol. 3, *The Grand Alliance*, 608–610.

Chapter 3

✳

Operation Barbarossa

The obliteration of what he called the "Jewish–Bolshevik" system and the conquest, exploitation, and colonization of the Soviet Union* were cardinal elements of Adolf Hitler's worldview. In *Mein Kampf*, he wrote:

> [W]e National Socialists must hold unflinchingly to our aim in foreign policy, namely *to secure for the German people the land and soil to which they are entitled on this earth.*... Just as our ancestors did not receive the soil on which we live today as a gift from Heaven, but had to fight for it ... no folkish grace will win soil for us and hence life for our people, but only the might of a victorious sword.... [We must] turn our gaze toward the land in the east.... If we speak of soil in Europe today, we can primarily have in mind only Russia and her *vassal* border states.[1]

Hitler saw the conquest of European Russia as the culmination of his life's work. Conquest would establish German control over the Continent's agricultural resources, raw materials, and industrial capacity from the Atlantic coast to the Ural Mountains, which would significantly increase German military power and domestic prosperity. Even with the aid of its Commonwealth countries, Britain could not hope to challenge such a powerful German empire.

Hitler also conceived a conflict with the Soviet Union as an ideological-racial war that would end not in a negotiated settlement but in annihilation.

---

*In 1941, the Soviet Union consisted of many different nationalities—Russians, Ukrainians, Belorussians, Crimean Tartars, Georgians, ethnic Germans, and many others. Of these, Russians comprised slightly more than half the population. Many non-Russians resented Communist rule, which they equated with Russian domination. During the war, the terms "Soviet Union" and "Russia" were used interchangeably: Germans saw themselves as fighting Russians; to the United States and Britain, Soviet Union and Russia were synonymous and remained so until the breakup of the Soviet Union in 1991. In this chapter, "Russia" and "Russians" are used mainly when referring to German perceptions of their enemy and Anglo-American perceptions of their ally. But for this relatively new stylistic concern, one cannot be a purist.

The Germans would destroy the Soviet system that threatened the very life of the Volk; take control of and settle the fertile Russian plains with Germans; and exploit, enslave, deport, or liquidate racial enemies. The Ural Mountains would divide Germany's European empire and Asiatic barbarism. Many Wehrmacht commanders, junior officers, and common soldiers who ardently fought for Führer, fatherland, and race shared Hitler's dream of a Europe dominated by a greater German racial state. German soldiers were filled with a sense of duty and idealism in a war against what many considered a Jewish-Bolshevik threat to German security and survival. They also shared Hitler's expectation that the Soviet Union—a "rotten structure," he called it—would quickly crumble when attacked by the world's mightiest army.

For Hitler, German expansion in the East could not wait for Britain to be subdued. Crushing the Soviet Union, he thought, would deprive Britain of a much-needed European ally. With no Soviet ally, Britain would be forced to give up the struggle and reach a settlement that would give the Third Reich unchallenged domination of the Continent. But what if the Soviet Union did not prove an easy victim? Germany would then face a prolonged two-front war, something the High Command dreaded. Attacking the Soviet Union while Britain remained a formidable foe was a major blunder.

In July 1940, Hitler instructed his generals to formulate plans for the invasion of Russia. On December 18, he set May 15, 1941, for launching Operation Barbarossa, the code name assigned for the massive blitzkrieg. (Barbarossa or "Red-beard" was the nickname of Frederick I, the twelfth-century Holy Roman Emperor, idolized as a German hero.) But problems of training and equipping the vast force, finalizing detailed plans, and events in the Balkans led Hitler to postpone the date to the latter part of June.

THE BALKANS FIRST

Seeking to establish a new Roman Empire in the Mediterranean and to win glory for himself, Benito Mussolini ordered an invasion of Greece. In late October 1940, Italian troops stationed in Albania—which Italy had occupied in 1939—crossed into Greece. The poorly planned operation was an instant failure, the first of many humiliations for the Italian dictator. Within a week, the counterattacking Greeks advanced into Albania. Hitler feared that Britain, which was encouraging and aiding the Greeks, would use Greece to interfere with the forthcoming invasion of the Soviet Union and to attack the oil fields of Romania that were vital for the German war machine.

Another problem emerged when a military coup overthrew the government of Prince Paul in Yugoslavia. Just two days earlier, the Yugoslav government had signed a pact with Germany and Italy, but Hitler feared that the new government might gravitate toward Britain. To prevent any interference with Operation Barbarossa, the Balkan flank had to be secured.

On April 6, 1941, Germany attacked Yugoslavia. Like the Poles, the Yugoslavs sought to defend virtually the entire length of the country's borders instead of concentrating their forces in a strategic area such as Belgrade, their capital. The stretched Yugoslav army made it easier for the Wehrmacht, which excelled at breakthrough and envelopment. Also working to the disadvantage of the Yugoslavs were ethnic animosities, particularly between Catholic Croats and Orthodox Serbs, who dominated the government. Many Croats were not eager to fight the Germans alongside Serbs.

The Luftwaffe demolished the small and obsolete Yugoslav air force, pulverized Belgrade in raids that killed many civilians, and destroyed Yugoslav command and control networks, severing links between the High Command and units in the field. When the Wehrmacht divisions crossed the frontier, they confronted uncoordinated Yugoslav forces that were without orders. Smashing and encircling Yugoslav defense positions, panzer corps raced to capture Belgrade and Zagreb (the capital of Croatia), both of which quickly fell. Many Croats greeted the Germans as liberators. On April 17, an armistice was signed. As in the campaign against Poland, the Germans, moving with speed and power, shocked and overwhelmed their opponent. Serb and Croat Yugoslav soldiers who escaped capture sought refuge in the mountains, where they formed partisan units that fought the Germans and each other until the end of the war.

The Nazis partitioned Yugoslavia, establishing an Italian zone of occupation and the puppet states of Croatia and Serbia. Because of its pro-Nazi sentiments, the Croatian state was given Serbian territory, and a truncated Serbia also had to surrender land to Italy, Hungary, and Bulgaria, Germany's allies. The new Croatia was dominated by the Ustashi, extreme nationalists and Fascists who wanted a religiously and ethnically pure country. With the tacit approval of local Catholic authorities, priests accompanied by armed Ustashi forcibly converted tens of thousands of Serbs to Catholicism; those who resisted conversion faced imprisonment or death. Although some Catholic leaders did protest against the Utashi's outrages, a number of Catholic clergy openly urged Croatians to rid their country of non-Catholics by force if necessary. Some priests even participated in the killings. With great cruelty, the Ustashi murdered tens of thousands of Serbs, Roma (that is, "Gypsies," which is a term no longer used), and Jews. (There is a wide discrepancy regarding the number of victims; estimates range from eighty thousand to two hundred thousand and more, but for the most part these are only guesses.) Many of the victims were killed in several death camps set up to commit genocide. Croatian killing squads, at times encouraged by Franciscan friars, carried out mass murder with sadistic brutality that rivaled SS atrocities against the Jews.*

---

*To escape the Nazis, some 4,500 Yugoslav Jews fled to the Italian zone of occupation, where they were placed in internment camps. Italian military authorities would refuse to comply with German and Croatian demands to deport these Jews to Nazi extermination camps. Nor did the Italians harm Roma who had found refuge in Italian-occupied Croatia.

On the same day that Germany invaded Yugoslavia, it also moved against Greece. Although fifty thousand British, New Zealand, and Australian troops aided Greece, they soon found themselves caught between two German pincers. In their retreat south, the Commonwealth forces were ceaselessly attacked by Luftwaffe dive bombers. Many did manage to evacuate the Greek mainland, but, as with Dunkirk, they had to abandon most of their equipment. Athens was captured on April 27, and the war there ended three days later. Greece fell under German occupation, and the British had suffered another humiliation.

After their conquest of the Greek mainland, the Germans invaded the island of Crete, one hundred miles to the south. Crete was defended by some thirty-five thousand British and Commonwealth troops and a Greek garrison, most of whom had had just fled Greece. To Britain, Crete was a valuable base for possible air attacks on the Romanian oilfields at Ploesti. A German attempt at an amphibious landing failed utterly as the Royal Navy sank fourteen small Greek ships transporting the German troops, forcing the other ships in the flotilla to return to the mainland. The Germans followed with an air attack consisting of paratroops and glider-borne troops—the first time that a multidivision military operation was carried out solely by air. (Earlier German airborne assaults in 1940 consisted of far fewer aircraft and soldiers and were subordinate to the invasion by land and sea.) Although suffering heavy casualties, the airborne troops managed to capture the island's airfields, enabling transport planes to land with additional troops and supplies. The RAF had few planes on hand to support the ground troops, who were under attack by German fighter planes and dive bombers. Once again, the Royal Navy was called upon to evacuate defeated troops to safety, this time to Egypt, a British protectorate.

The evacuation went smoothly on one part of the island, but on another part the Luftwaffe, virtually unopposed by the RAF, zeroed in on the British ships, sinking three cruisers and six destroyers and damaging an additional seventeen ships. So deadly were the German planes that the evacuation had to be called off. British and Commonwealth troop losses on Crete amounted to 3,967 killed, wounded, and missing; naval casualties were 2,000 killed and 183 wounded. In addition, 11,370 troops were captured on the island. Because of their high losses, about 7,000 casualties, for the rest of the war the Germans refrained from engaging in another major airborne attack on enemy territory.

THE OPENING PHASE

A War of Annihilation

The speedy and successful campaign in the Balkans enabled the Germans to implement Operation Barbarossa in late June as they intended in their revised timetable. Nevertheless, because the Russian winter arrived unexpectedly early, the five-week postponement would eventually hamper the German offensive. For the war against the Soviet Union, Hitler assembled what Joseph Goebbels, the minister of propaganda, called "the biggest concentration of forces in the history of the world":[2] over three million Germans; 3,300 tanks; 2,700 combat planes; and, by April 1942, almost one million troops from Hitler's allies, Romania, Hungary, Slovakia, Croatia, Italy, and Finland. Included in the German arsenal were tanks built in Czechoslovakia and antitank guns and vehicles captured in France. Ironically, in the weeks prior to Barbarossa, the Soviet Union continued to provide Germany with petroleum rubber, copper, tin, grain, and other vital resources that would aid the Nazi invaders.

Evidence of an imminent German attack abounded: The numerous German reconnaissance flights over Soviet frontier defenses were a clear warning, and an effective Soviet spy network in several cities, including Berlin, informed Joseph Stalin of German intentions. Britain also gave information to Stalin. Border guards captured hundreds of Germans attempting to cross into the Soviet Union; the mission of these men, who were carrying weapons, radio transmitters, and Soviet passports, was obviously sabotage. And in June, German diplomats were leaving Moscow and destroying their files. But the stubborn and distrustful Soviet dictator ignored these warnings. Certain of his own judgment, he simply dismissed facts that suggested a different interpretation. On the eve of the invasion, Soviet commanders received reports that three German deserters stationed on the front lines said an attack was about to happen. Stalin considered this disinformation and ordered one of the deserters, a young Communist, shot. He did not believe that Hitler would open a second front while still at war with Britain—in *Mein Kampf*, Hitler declared it folly to engage in a two-front war. He also did not believe that Hitler would invade in late June, only a few months prior to winter. And surely, reasoned Stalin, Hitler was aware that the Soviet Union, which possessed more troops, tanks, planes, and artillery pieces than did the Third Reich, would not be a pushover. Moreover, ever mistrustful, Stalin suspected Britain's warnings of an impending German invasion as a devious ploy to involve the Soviet Union in the war against Germany. Desperate to avoid a war with Nazi Germany at this time, Stalin would take no action, particularly deploying troops in appropriate defensive positions that he feared Hitler would regard as a provocation. Stalin's misjudgment left the Red Army vulnerable to the German blitzkrieg.

One hour before the start of a war in which German forces would commit crimes of plunder, enslavement, and systematic genocide that would forever dishonor their nation, Hitler's order of the day, which inverted reality, was delivered to the troops. That order was not only to fight for Germany's existence and future but also "to save the whole of European civilization and culture." In succeeding months, several Wehrmacht commanders would echo this message, commanders who shared Hitler's expansionist aims, anti-Bolshevism, and racist ideology. In November 1941, Colonel-General Hermann Hoth instructed his troops: "More than ever we are filled with the thought of a new era, in which the strength of the German people's racial superiority and achievements entrust it with the leadership of Europe. We clearly recognize our mission to save European culture from the advancing Asiatic barbarism."[3]

With Napoleon's failed Russian invasion as a reminder, Germany feared getting sucked into a protracted war of attrition with Russia, whose large population, vast land mass, and fierce winters put an invader at a disadvantage. Germany aimed for another blitzkrieg operation, a swift and decisive victory in a single campaign, as in Poland and France, that must be achieved by early autumn. The German military intended a hammer blow that would annihilate the Soviet military and topple what Hitler and Wehrmacht leaders saw as a decaying Communist regime. The Red Army had to be thoroughly demolished in the frontier zones and prevented from escaping, falling back, and regrouping in the Soviet interior, where it would require considerable time and blood to inflict a final defeat. And Hitler was supremely confident. After the victory in France, Hitler told Field Marshal Wilhelm Keitel: "Now we have shown what we are capable of.... Believe me, Keitel, a campaign against Russia would be like a child's game in a sandbox by comparison."[4]

The German plan called for massed mobile spearheads to smash through the Soviet lines, envelope the Soviet forces, and then, in an ever-tightening circle, crush and capture whole armies before they could escape. Goebbels expected that "Bolshevism will collapse like a house of cards. We face victories unequalled in human history."[5] After the war, some generals said that they did have reservations about attacking Russia, but at the time few of them cautioned Hitler of the perils of invading such a vast and heavily populated land. Nor would Hitler have heeded such warnings; conquering European Russia was at the center of his worldview and a driving force in his life.

The German High Command believed that the German army's superior training, impressive technical skills, and bold tactical deployments, brilliantly demonstrated in the campaigns in Poland and France, would demolish the Red Army, which the High Command deemed inferior to the French military. The High Command believed that German officers, selected for their competence and rigorously trained, were far superior to their Soviet counterparts and that Red Army soldiers were no match for German infantry and tank crews whose battlefield skills had been demonstrated and sharpened in Poland and France. Indeed, the speed with which the Germans had overrun France had produced what turned out to be a fatal hubris among both the Führer and the German military. Not only were German generals overconfident of the Wehrmacht's strength but many also now shared Hitler's delusion that he was a military genius. There is no doubt that the Wehrmacht was the best trained, best equipped, and best led army in the world, but it was not invincible as the German High Command now fervently believed.

Contributing to the Germans' confidence was the Soviets' poor performance in their recent war with Finland, the Winter War (November 30, 1939–March 12, 1940), in which the Soviet Union suffered two hundred thousand casualties. Its military credibility suffered even though it eventually won. German reports on the performance of the Red Army described its shoddy equipment, the poor training of front-line soldiers, and the low level of tactics employed by Soviet commanders.

National Socialist ideology also generated confidence. For a large number of Hitler's generals, junior officers, and rank-and-file soldiers indoctrinated with Nazi dogma, the Wehrmacht was composed of the cream of the Aryan race. These true believers did not doubt Nazi propaganda that described the citizens of the Soviet Union as primitive, racially degenerate Slavs and Asiatics led by criminal "Jewish Bolsheviks." Hitler himself called the Russians "brutes in a state of nature."[6] Moreover, German soldiers believed they were fighting for a worthy cause—also propagated by Nazi propaganda—that the war against Russia was necessary for the self-preservation of both Germany and European civilization. In their eyes, Germany was leading a European crusade against Bolshevism. The letters of Karl Fuchs, a young idealistic German soldier, clearly illustrate contempt for Russians, a sense of participating in a noble mission to create a better future for Germany and Europe, and reverence for Hitler. Viewing Russian POWs, Fuchs wrote to his wife on August 3, 1941: "Hardly ever do you see the face of a person who seems rational and intelligent. They all look emaciated and the wild, half-crazy look in their eyes makes them appear like imbeciles. And these scoundrels led by Jews and criminals wanted to imprint their stamp on Europe, indeed on the world. Thank God that our Führer, Adolf Hitler, is preventing this from happening." And to his parents on that same day: "This war against these sub-human beings is about over. It's almost insulting when you consider that drunken Russian criminals have been let loose against us.... They are ... the mere scum of the earth! Naturally they are not a match for us German soldiers." And to his father on the following day: "Everyone, even the last doubter, knows today that the battle against these sub-humans, who've been whipped into a frenzy by the Jews, was not only necessary but came in the nick of time. Our Führer has saved Europe from certain chaos." On October 15, in the midst of the German drive on Moscow, he reiterated his faith in Hitler and righteousness of the German cause: "Our duty has been to fight and to free the world from this Communist disease. One day, many years hence, the world will thank the Germans and our beloved Führer for our victories in Russia."[7] Fuchs died in a tank skirmish on November 21.

The Germans were told that in waging war against Bolshevism they were fighting the Jews, who were supposed to be pulling the strings in the Soviet Union. Most commanders accepted without question Hitler's equating Bolshevism with Jews and Judaism. Of course, "Jewish-Bolshevism" was another absurd anti-Semitic myth that defied the facts.* Jews as an organized body exercised no power in the Soviet Union, and by 1939 there were virtually no Jews in the

---

*In 1917, most Russian Jews identified with either the Zionist movement that sought the establishment of a Jewish state in Palestine or the Bund, a Jewish labor party that advocated democratic socialism. In February 1917, the Bund supported the revolt against the tsar and the establishment of a liberal, constitutional government and opposed the Bolshevik seizure of power in October 1917. Jewish Bolsheviks were few in number and had no interest in Jewish concerns. In the ensuing civil war, the Whites killed some one hundred thousand Jews. As a result of these pogroms, marked by sickening brutality against the Jewish victims, Jews came to view the Red Army as their protector. Once in power, the Communists, in contrast to the tsarist regime, permitted Jews to enter the universities and attain careers in the professions. Taking advantage of these new opportunities, Jews in substantial numbers served the Soviet state as administrators and professionals. For a short time, they even played a prominent role in the NKVD, the feared secret police, until they were purged in the Great Terror of 1937–1938. In 1939, Jews were 4 percent of the ranking officers in the NKVD. Most Jews who had achieved status in the Communist Party had already repudiated their Jewish heritage and identity. Certainly, they did not use their positions to promote "Jewish interests." Nor could they: the Soviet regime, hostile to both Jewish nationalism and religion, would never permit this. Many of these educated and trained Jewish functionaries were victims of Stalin's purges from 1934 to 1939; they were either executed or sent to the Gulag. See Zvi Gitelman, *A Century of Ambivalence: The Jews of Russia and the Soviet Union, 1881 to the Present* (Bloomington: Indiana University Press, 2001).

ruling circles of the Communist Party. Moreover, many Communists, Russians, and ethnic minorities harbored a traditional anti–Semitism. During the war, the Soviet Union would give no recognition to Jewish concerns or even reveal Nazi war crimes directed at Jews. But the association of Jews with Communism and the labeling of Jews as an existential threat to the nation, staples of Nazi propaganda, were deeply embedded in the Wehrmacht's psyche (see also Chapter 8, pages 298-299) as the following letter from the front illustrates: "The political doctrine of Bolshevism is … but a purely political act of world Jewry. And just as the Talmud teaches nothing except murder and destruction, so Bolshevism knows but one science: murder and destruction, cruel and barbaric murder."[8]

Few now question whether Nazi racial doctrines led the Wehrmacht, including senior generals, to condone, look away from, or participate in the atrocities inflicted on the Soviet people, including the mass murder of Jews. To be sure, the camaraderie, loyalty, and devotion to the fatherland stressed in army training and reinforced by battle experiences accounted for the Wehrmacht's motivation and superior performance. Moreover, the Wehrmacht was the best trained and best led army in the world. But many rank-and-file German soldiers and their junior officers were also driven by National Socialist ideology with which they had been indoctrinated in their schools and the Hitler Youth. The anecdotal evidence derived from soldiers' letters and diaries—and their actual behavior toward Jews and Slavs—indicate that not just the SS but also substantial numbers of the Wehrmacht were committed to Hitler's worldview and were willing to execute it. These soldiers were strong supporters of Hitler and believed that in the Soviet Union they were fighting an ideological racial war just as their Führer, Goebbels' propaganda, and their officers, particularly younger junior officers, had told them. Seeing themselves as agents of a noble mission, the Wehrmacht became an active instrument in Hitler's war of annihilation. Ideological goals fused with military needs. The burning of villages, the shooting of women and children, and the killing of prisoners were perceived as normal acts of war. Now fighting for survival, many were not morally troubled by these atrocities. And those who were troubled had little option. Vociferous protests or refusal to fight could mean a death sentence. The intervention of commanding generals may have stifled atrocities. But this rarely occurred. And given the regime's ideological commitment to a war of annihilation, protests by individual generals would have had little effect on the policy makers or their fellow senior officers, many of whom shared, in varying degrees, Hitler's antipathy to Slavs, Jews, and Bolsheviks.

German Successes

German plans called for an offensive over an 1,800-mile front. Attacking from East Prussia through the Baltic states, Army Group North, with the support of the Finnish army, would strike toward Leningrad; Army Group Center, the most powerful, would advance from Poland to Minsk, the capital of Belorussia (now Belarus) and then proceed to Smolensk and Moscow; and Army Group South, supported by Romanian, Hungarian, and Italian divisions, would drive into the

Ukraine and capture Kiev, its capital. German staff officers intended to encircle then destroy Soviet forces in a series of double envelopments. When diagrammed on an operation's map, the enemy forces would be caught in a kettle—hence the name cauldron battle—with the Wehrmacht providing the iron sides and the helpless Russians trapped in the pot. The Prussian General Staff had successfully used such tactics in the past.

In the early hours of June 22, 1941, German planes bombarded Soviet cities and airfields and German armies crossed into the Soviet Union. Taken by surprise, the Soviet forces were thrown into a state of confusion. Unprepared, disorganized, only partially mobilized, inadequately trained, and poorly led, the Red Army could not cope with the Wehrmacht's breathtaking speed and power generated by panzers, mechanized artillery, and motorized infantry. The shock of the coordinated panzer and Luftwaffe attacks caused a breakdown of the Red Army's command and control, spreading confusion at the front. Soviet commanders were not prepared to avoid and break out of encirclements. In crucial situations, they failed to withdraw their forces while there was still time to escape the encircling panzers and motorized infantry. Adding to the disorientation at the front were poor communications due to an insufficient supply of radio equipment and the Germans' deliberate targeting of command posts. Penetrating into the Soviet rear by parachute drops or infiltration, German commandos destroyed cables, depriving Red Army commanders of their communication system. Unable to receive messages from the fronts, Soviet commanders did not have a clear picture of what was happening, nor were their orders received in the front lines. Under these circumstances, infantry divisions, tank units, and airplane squadrons foundered despite their numerical superiority. There was just too much happening in too many places for the Soviet High Command to master the situation. So confused were Stalin and his High Command about the debacle their troops were facing that they ordered divisions on the border to take the offensive and move into German territory—as if this were possible.

Raiding Russian airfields, the Luftwaffe claimed to have destroyed 1,200 aircraft on the first day, most of them lined up in rows on the ground, a painful indication of Stalin's gross miscalculation. Eight hundred more were destroyed in subsequent days. With only a few hours' worth of flying experience, many Soviet pilots knew nothing of the tactics required in aerial combat. Also, they were often flying antiquated planes, which were quickly shot down by better trained and more experienced German airmen flying superior aircraft. "Our pilots feel that they are corpses already when they take off," a squadron officer would later confesss.[9] By early October, the Soviet Union had lost 5,316 aircraft, many of them due to accidents caused by poorly trained Soviet pilots. Control of the air facilitated German ground forces that rapidly encircled and destroyed the disoriented Russian troops.

Soviet tank crews, some with only a few hours' worth of operating experience, were often ineffective against the panzers, and appalling maintenance and lack of spare parts immobilized even more tanks than did German weaponry. Moreover, the Red Army's obsolete tanks were chewed up by the panzers; the Soviets' T-34 and Kv-I were superior to the German Panzer-IV, but there were insufficient numbers available at the front. Duplicating the mistake made by Poland in 1939 and France in 1940, Soviet tanks were parceled out across the front; these thinned-out armored units were no match for the massed panzers striking at key locations. Marshal Mikhail Tukhachevski had advocated concentrating large numbers of tanks that would break through the enemy lines and encircle its forces. But in 1937, this brilliant Soviet marshal became another victim of Stalin's purge of the military. His execution left the Red Army without an effective strategy for tank warfare. In many instances, the superior tactics of panzer divisions that had been honed in earlier battles overwhelmed Soviet tank forces. On the first day, attempting to counterattack Guderian's panzers, a Soviet mechanized corps lost nearly half of its 478 tanks within 48 hours. Freely roaming the skies, the Luftwaffe destroyed numerous Soviet tanks before they were able to enter the fray and inflicted huge losses on Soviet infantry. The Stuka dive bombers with their terrifying screams and the encircling panzers caused panic in the Soviet formations. The Red Army was in shambles. Whole units simply dissolved, and amidst the chaos thousands deserted and more thousands surrendered without a fight.

Other factors contributed to the rout as well. In 1937–1938, Stalin imprisoned nearly forty thousand army and navy officers, many of whom were able professionals attuned to the new doctrines of motorized warfare. Of these, fifteen thousand were executed. Many of the survivors were restored to duty in time to fight the Germans, but their imprisonment limited their military experience. Lacking training and experience, both Soviet senior and junior officers were no match for the consummately professional Wehrmacht officer corps. Moreover front-line commanders had to contend with the always suspicious commissars (political officers assigned to every staff) and the secret police (NKVD, People's Commissariat for Internal Affairs) constantly looking over their shoulders. Generals were terrified of making independent decisions lest they be reported for disobeying orders, punishable with a death sentence or the Gulag. As it was, within a month after the invasion Stalin executed several senior generals for "criminal behavior in the face of the enemy." Thus when the situation required flexibility, daring, quick reaction, and initiative, commanders were often paralyzed and rigid, unable to exploit an opportunity to punish the enemy or to fend off a catastrophe.

A militarily incompetent Stalin ordered Soviet counterattacks, usually frontal assaults by weakened and disorganized troops without air protection and against concentrated fire. The assaults showed no imagination and were miserable failures. No doubt some Soviet commanders wanted organized tactical retreats, not futile human wave attacks, but they feared challenging an order. Massive numbers of brave Soviet soldiers were simply massacred in these death charges. A German machine-gunner described such an attack in which wave after wave of Soviet infantrymen marched virtually shoulder to shoulder into what he called:

> an unbelievable sight, a machine-gunner's dream target.… At 600
> metres we opened fire and whole sections of the first wave just
> vanished, leaving here and there an odd survivor still walking stolidly

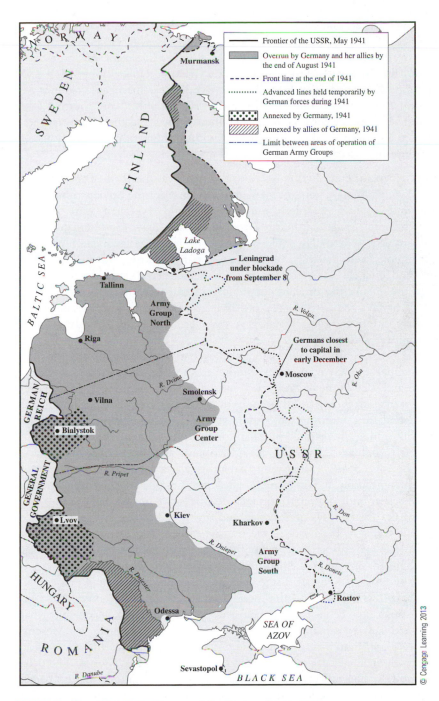

MAP 3.1 Operation Barbarossa and the Eastern Front, 1941

By the end of August 1941, the Germans had overrun large areas of the Soviet Union and by December 1941 had advanced to the outskirts of Moscow.

forward. The second wave ... marched around and across the bodies of their comrades who had fallen.... The first three waves had been destroyed by our fire.... The rush by the fourth wave came on more slowly for the men had to pick their way through a great carpet of bodies.... About an hour later a further five lines of men came on in a second attack. We smashed this and then crushed a third and fourth assault. The numbers of the enemy seemed endless and the new waves of men advanced across their own dead without hesitation.... The Ivans kept up their attacks for three days and even during the nights.[10]

Another major contributing factor to the rout was the Red Army's strategic blunder. From a military point of view, it made sense for the Soviets to surrender territory and conduct an orderly retreat that would save their army. Trading space for time to strengthen their reserves would also draw the Germans deeper into the country, where they could be fought under more favorable terms. The frontier regions were precisely where the German blitzkrieg was most likely to overrun and encircle Soviet forces. Instead, Stalin demanded that no land be ceded to the enemy and ordered counterattacks that were monumental failures. Fearful of Stalin's response if they ordered a withdrawal, Soviet commanders held their positions too long, which gave the Germans an opportunity to encircle and capture whole armies.

In the first few days, Stalin met with key party and military officials in an effort to repel the German attack whose magnitude they could not grasp. When the full scale of the disaster struck him, it appears that he sank into depression and went into hiding in his home. His confidence restored, Stalin emerged on July 3 and gave a stirring radio address, telling his countrymen of the great danger confronting the nation. He called for guerrilla resistance and for the Russian people to fight this patriotic war with courage and determination.

The opening phase of Operation Barbarossa was a catastrophe for the Soviet Union. Uncoordinated and disorganized attempts to escape encirclement produced horrific losses in both dead and captured. As the situation rapidly became more chaotic, small, broken units of leaderless and frightened soldiers were captured or killed while trying to break out of the ring where they were exposed to massive German firepower. Within a few months, some four million soldiers had been killed, wounded, or captured. The number would grow. The Germans destroyed thousands of tanks and aircraft. Large areas of the country, including rich agricultural lands of the Ukraine and the most productive industrial centers, had fallen into German hands; Leningrad was besieged; Smolensk, Minsk, Kiev, and Kharkov, key cities, were captured; and German forces were advancing on Moscow, the Donets Basin industrial area, and the Crimea. Soviet counteroffensive efforts to halt the German advance almost always failed and with heavy losses. The debacle the Soviet Union suffered, writes historian Robert M. Citino, "has no parallel in military history: the world's largest army was essentially destroyed and the richest portions of the world's largest country overrun."[11]

Both the German High Command and Western military analysts felt certain that the Red Army was in the final stages of disintegration. They believed it

United States Holocaust Memorial Museum, courtesy of Archiwum Dokumentacji Mechanicznej

Russian women make their way through the ruins of Smolensk, which was destroyed by the Germans in the summer of 1941.

impossible for the Soviet Union to continue fighting after enduring such losses. And yet huge casualties, encirclement, and mass surrender were not the full story. There were also numerous instances where the Red Army tenaciously contested every yard, causing the Germans considerable casualties, and there were times when small units fought to the death rather than surrender. On June 28, Field Marshall Fedor von Bock noted that in a row of Soviet bunkers behind the front, each bunker "has to be taken one at a time. In spite of the heaviest fire and the employment of every means the crews refuse to give up. Each fellow has to be killed one at a time."[12] This unexpected doggedness of Soviet soldiers began to alarm the Germans. And in the battle of Smolensk, which commanded the road to Moscow from the west, the Germans suffered a battlefield reversal. Despite inflicting huge casualties on five Soviet armies and conquering and nearly destroying the city, the Germans were denied a quick and painless victory. Refusing to surrender, the encircled Soviet forces continued fighting through July and August, and in early September newly mobilized Soviet armies launched powerful counterattacks that sapped the Wehrmacht's strength. The extended battle for Smolensk cost the Germans some 250,000 dead, wounded, and captured and interfered with the Wehrmacht's timetable for attacking Moscow. Moreover, some 200,000 trapped Soviet troops succeeded in breaking out of the pocket. Although the Germans were victorious and Soviet casualties were considerable, the battle of Smolensk was a foreboding sign: the Red Army was tougher than anticipated, and the Wehrmacht might be drawn into a protracted war.

With his armies suffering one staggering defeat after another, Stalin turned to saboteurs and partisans to attack the German rear. In the 1930s, Soviet military planners had trained large numbers of men in guerrilla warfare and stockpiled arms and explosives in different parts of the country. However, fearing that these trained saboteurs threatened his rule, in 1937 Stalin ordered their execution and eliminated their arsenals. To fight a guerrilla war now required a fresh start.

Describing the war as an ideological crusade to save Europe from "Jewish-Bolshevik subhumans," German propaganda claimed that victory was assured, a sentiment shared by the highest echelons of the military, who expected it to be all but over before the onset of winter. On July 31, 1941, less than seven weeks after the start of Operation Barbarossa, a euphoric Franz Halder, Chief of the General Staff, recorded in his diary that the campaign had been won in fourteen days. (In September 1942, Hitler retired Halder for challenging his military decisions.) An overconfident Hitler, anticipating victory in a matter of weeks, informed Nazi officials that Germany's new borders would stretch to the Urals, Germans would settle the conquered regions, and the Jews would be eliminated as one would "bacteria." On October 3, Hitler told a cheering audience in Berlin that Soviet military power had been broken and the outcome of the war decided.

SOVIET RESILIENCE AND GERMAN MISCALCULATIONS

Despite their triumphs, Germany had failed to bring the Soviet Union to its knees. There would be no repetition of the collapse of Poland and France, no lightening victory in less than three months, as both Hitler and the German High Command had anticipated at the start of the campaign. With immense reserves safely barracked east of Moscow, the Soviets were able quickly to reconstitute wrecked divisions, and the Soviet people were willing to make incredible sacrifices for their land. Even when Hitler claimed victory, Nazi invaders noticed disquieting signs that would become increasingly more troublesome as the war evolved into a brutal, drawn-out life-and-death struggle.

Russian Tenacity and Courage

The Soviet people had a proven capacity to endure hardships. They often fought doggedly and courageously, turning out to be a tougher opponent than the German High Command expected. On July 3, 1941, a Luftwaffe general said of the Soviets: "The will to resist and the toughness of the masses exceeded all expectations."[13] The government encouraged citizens to see themselves as defenders of the Russian motherland in what Stalin astutely called the "Great Patriotic War." (The war against Napoleon was known as the "Patriotic War.") Soviet propaganda cleverly stressed traditional Russian patriotism rather than fighting to protect the Communist state that many Soviet citizens abhorred; and, starting

Lyudmilla Pavlichenko, a student majoring in history at Kiev University, volunteered to fight the invading Germans. Holding a certificate in marksmanship, she soon became one of two thousand female snipers in the Red Army. Credited with 309 kills, Pavlichenko was proclaimed a national hero.

in July 1942, medals awarded for bravery on the battlefield were named after legendary tsarist commanders. At the same time, many believers in the socialist experiment, particularly urban youth, volunteered to serve. Hundreds of thousands of soldiers who had escaped the German blitzkrieg formed partisan groups or were absorbed into new fighting units being assembled in the rear.

More than eight hundred thousand women increased the Red Army's strength, several hundred thousand of whom saw action as artillery and antiaircraft gunners, fighter pilots, tank personnel, and snipers. All women who fought at the front were volunteers, and some became recognized heroines. Sniper Lyudmila Pavlichenko achieved legendary status for her 309 confirmed kills, including 36 enemy snipers. The women who served in a completely female aviation corps that reconnoitered and fought over German positions also achieved fame. Called "Night Witches" by the Germans, thirty-three of these pilots, bombardiers, and navigators were designated Heroes of the Soviet Union, the highest decoration awarded.

In an extraordinary feat of organization involving 1.5 million freight cars and trucks, within five months the Soviets dismantled and moved east—beyond the Ural Mountains and far beyond the reach of the Luftwaffe—1,523 industrial facilities and a huge number of workers. To keep out of German hands what they were unable to relocate, the Soviets destroyed as much as possible. The Germans had expected to utilize captured factories, industrial equipment, loco-motives and railcars, and raw materials for their war effort. Although the Germans did seize a considerable portion of Soviet industrial infrastructure, the transfer and destruction of industries left them with far less than they had anticipated—to the displeasure of their economic planners.

Employing modern methods of production acquired in large measure from American technical assistance provided before the war, by early 1942 the Soviets had more than replenished the massive amount of armor and weapons that had been lost during the first six months of the war, and full-scale armaments pro-duction would continue throughout the conflict. With complete ruthlessness, the Soviet government immediately geared all its material and human resources for total war. In contrast, because Germany delayed until 1943 to mobilize its economy for total war it consistently faced shortages in equipment. Driven by patriotic fervor and by fear of the omnipresent NKVD agents searching for mal-ingerers, factory workers toiled relentlessly, often eleven hours a day, seven days a week. By using the wives and daughters of soldiers, fourteen-year-old boys, the elderly, and invalids in the factories, Soviets freed men to serve in the armed forces.

By early 1942, the Soviets were producing three times as many guns, twice as many combat planes, and four times as many tanks as Germany. And the qual-ity of their tanks both impressed and surprised the Germans. Wider tracks on the T-34 gave it more mobility than German tanks whose narrow treads made for poor traction in snow and mud, and the armor on the T-34s and even heavier Kv-1s was impervious to the antitank weapons then used by the Germans. It would take time for the Germans to build and transport more powerful antitank weapons to the front, particularly the 88mm antiaircraft gun that could damage the heavy Soviet tanks. And, in contrast to the Germans, who manufactured complex tanks with sophisticated equipment that were immobilized when a spe-cific part failed to function or required replacement, the Soviets produced tanks that were easy to assemble and easy to maintain. Improved Soviet combat planes reduced the enormous advantage German aircraft had in the opening phase of the war. Also aiding the Soviet Union's war effort was the Lend-Lease aid, including some 337,000 trucks and jeeps, 7,056 tanks, 14,834 airplanes, and enor-mous quantities of food, sent mainly by the United States but also by Britain. Relatively modest in 1941–1942, Lend Lease aid increased substantially in 1943 and afterward.

Unforeseen Challenges

At first, many Soviet citizens greeted the Germans as liberators, hoping they would free them from the hated Stalinist regime. Peasants loathed the forced collectivization and the attack on their churches. A German officer recalled, "I was astonished to detect no hatred among them. Women often came out of their houses with an icon held before their breast crying, 'We are still Christians. Free us from Stalin who destroyed our Churches.'"[14] In particular, people in the

Baltic states recently annexed by the Soviet Union and Ukrainians, who had suffered greatly under Stalin, welcomed the Germans. Infuriated by the Ukrainians' strong nationalist sentiments and their resistance to forced collectivization, Stalin had imposed a famine on the region in which some 3.3 million Ukrainians perished in the early 1930s (it appears that the 7 million figure often given is inflated). In the Great Terror of 1937–1938, the NKVD shot 70,868 Ukrainians accused of having kulak (more prosperous peasants whose lands had been collectivized) backgrounds or of supporting Ukrainian nationalism that threatened the territorial unity of the Soviet state. A German soldier on leave told family and friends of his experiences in Ukraine: "I was one of those who marched in to be received, not as a conqueror but as a friend. The civilians were all ready to look on us as saviours. They had had years of oppression from the Soviet. They thought we had come to free them.... What did we do? Turn them into slaves under Hitler. Worse, we deported their women for labour in Germany." And he added forebodingly, "Do you think they won't revenge themselves somehow. Of course they will."[15]

Occurrences like the one witnessed by a sympathetic German officer were quite common: "The villages are burning and little is spared from the flames. Some of the women kneel before our soldiers, crying hysterically, because we are taking their last cow or chicken from them.... If only our people behaved better and showed a little human decency."[16] The protests of some officers and soldiers repelled by these atrocities had no effect. Had the Nazis taken advantage of the initial reaction among oppressed Russians and subject nationalities who hated both Stalin and the socialist state, it would have been extremely difficult for Soviet leadership to marshal the country against the invader. But brutal treatment of the indigenous Slavic population, including prisoners of war (see Chapter 4), whom Nazi ideology designated a primitive, inferior race marked for servitude, alienated potential collaborators and fueled a fierce hatred for the German invaders and a desire for vengeance. Soviet propaganda whipped up support for these feelings. In early 1942, a Soviet soldier expressed these feelings in a letter to his wife: "I've been in some of the places where the beasts have been. I've seen the burned-out towns and villages, the corpses of women and children, the unhappy, plundered residents, but also I have seen the tears of joy when these people encountered us.... The spirit of these places has affected me and it has grown in all our soldiers."[17] To be sure, various ethnic groups resented both Stalin's rule and Russian domination. Both eluding conscription and desertion by non-Slav nationalities were common. Nevertheless, most Soviet citizens were united in their determination to drive out the hated German invaders. They saw themselves fighting for their families, homes, villages, and towns.

The German High Command, with a reputation for meticulous planning, launched the war against the Soviet Union very much ignorant of its enemy's capabilities. Relying on poor intelligence evaluations, senior Wehrmacht commanders made three major miscalculations that hampered their operations. First, they underestimated both the size of the Soviet Union's army and its reserve strength. In a short time, the Soviets were able to organize new armies from shattered units and from its large population spread out over the vast country. And as fear of war with Japan diminished, they could transfer to the European theater large contingents stationed in Siberia that were highly skilled in winter warfare. To the anguish of Germans in the field, even after killing and capturing millions of soldiers, the Soviet pool of manpower seemed inexhaustible. On August 11, 1941, seven weeks after the start of Operation Barbarossa, Franz Halder wrote in his diary, "The whole situation makes it increasingly plain that we have underestimated the Russian colossus.... At the outset of the war, we reckoned with about 200 enemy divisions. Now we have already counted 360.... [And] if we smash a dozen of them, the Russians simply put up another dozen. The time factor favors them, as they are near their own resources, while we are moving farther and farther away from ours."[18] No doubt, because of their disdain for Slavs, the Germans underrated not only the fighting capability of the Soviet soldier but also the operational planning of the Soviet High Command. After an initially poor performance, Soviet commanders showed they could learn the principles of mechanized warfare both for defensive and offensive operations. And the soldiers of the Red Army would demonstrate considerable courage in their resolve to liberate their land from the hated Nazi invaders. Although many Soviet soldiers did surrender in large numbers, many also fought with a ferocity— sometimes to the very end; this is something that invading Germans did not anticipate. Contrary to the assumptions of the German High Command, the Red Army would not be quickly defeated.

Second, the Germans underestimated both the speed with which the Soviets could replenish their aircraft that had been largely demolished in the opening weeks of the war and their ability to produce quality aircraft. In 1942, the Soviets claimed to have produced 25,000 planes, 60 percent more than in the previous year. As with the Soviet tanks, which were being replaced with the formidable T-34s and Kv-1s, many of the planes that had been destroyed in the opening phase of Barbarossa were obsolete slow-flying machines. They were replaced in large numbers with new first-rate fighters and dive bombers that compared favorably with German aircraft. Even before the outbreak of war, aircraft production had been greatly increasing. By the end of 1941, the Soviets had considerably more planes than the Germans and could match the Luftwaffe in quality of aircraft, and the Luftwaffe's initial advantage diminished further as Soviet pilots gained experience in aerial combat. Moreover, as the war progressed, Germany had to divert its air force to other fronts in the Mediterranean and Western Europe, whereas the Soviet air force remained entirely on the Eastern Front.

Third, the overwhelming German victories in the opening phase of Operation Barbarossa did not cause the Communist regime to collapse as Hitler and several senior generals had anticipated. The Soviet Union was not an unstable colossus ready to fall apart, as they thought. Indeed, Soviet leadership effectively mobilized millions of soldiers, transferred and built factories that mass produced vital military equipment, and skillfully galvanized public opinion by defining the conflict as the Great Patriotic War rather than a defense of the Communist system.

Other factors diminished Germany's chances of conquering the Soviet Union. Although the Soviet Union suffered far greater losses in the opening months of the war, German casualties were also considerable: 686,000 killed, wounded, and captured by November 1, 1941. Moreover, in contrast to the

Soviets, the Germans had a difficult time finding replacements. Anticipating victory before winter, Germany did not have enough reserves to replenish the loss of manpower. After the war, describing conditions in early November, Field Marshal Wilhelm Keitel wrote that, including replacements, "the army in the field was reduced in numbers by 60,000 to 70,000 men each month. It was a piece of simple arithmetic to work out when the German front would be exhausted."[19] The need for replacements forced the military to rush poorly trained recruits to the front, where their chances of survival were considerably less than for trained soldiers. It was a vicious spiral that endured for the rest of the war.

The Germans also failed to plan adequately for the loss of armor and equipment at the front. Whereas the Red Army was close to its sources of supplies, the deeper the Wehrmacht penetrated into the Soviet Union the farther it moved away from supply lines. The overextended Wehrmacht suffered acute shortages of ammunition, replacement tanks and other vehicles, and spare parts needed to repair damaged vehicles. Most important, Germany lacked the fuel reserves needed to wage an ongoing war in a country as large as the Soviet Union. And expecting the conflict to be over by autumn, the German High Command had not prepared for a winter war. Without antifreeze, guns jammed and vehicles, including tanks and supply trains, were inoperative; without warm uniforms, frostbite immobilized tens of thousands of German soldiers.

The Russian climate and difficult terrain—wide marshes, dense forests, and broad rivers—impeded the movement of supplies and military operations, disrupting the German timetable. For example, grit carried by dust clouds choked engines causing vehicles, including tanks, to break down. Also obstructing travel were the primitive unpaved roads that turned into seas of mud when the autumn rains came. The Russians call these months the *rasputitsa*—the "time when the roads dissolve." One German general described the ordeal: "The infantryman slithers in the mud, while many teams of horses [600,000 horses, used mainly to move artillery and supplies, were part of the invasion force] are needed to drag each gun forward. All wheeled vehicles sink up to their axles in the slime. Even tractors can only move with great difficulty. A large portion of our heavy artillery was soon stuck fast.... The strain that all this caused our already exhausted troops can perhaps be imagined."[20] These conditions led to the frequent disablement of German tanks because their narrow tracks hampered movement through the mud. Many trucks and carts in supply convoys were rendered useless before attaining their destination; unable to traverse through the mud, they simply sank into the ground. Horses needed to haul supplies and heavy equipment, including artillery, sank up to their necks in the mud and many died of exhaustion struggling to extricate themselves.

German generals were not prepared for these primitive conditions, as one of them later commented: "Our maps in no way corresponded to reality. On those maps all supposed main roads were marked in red, and there seemed to be many, but they often proved to be merely sandy tracks."[21] Ironically, in this instance, not modernization but backwardness worked to the Soviet Union's advantage. If the Soviet Union had possessed a road system comparable to that of Western Europe, German mechanized units would have faced far fewer battlefield and supply problems. Compounding the supply problem was the lack of railways in the Soviet Union, their destruction by the retreating Red Army and partisans, and the removal of locomotives farther east. Moreover, German locomotives could not operate on Soviet rail tracks because they used a different gauge than that used in Europe. Converting the tracks to make them usable took time and manpower. Under these circumstances, the blitzkrieg, whose essence was movement and speed, could not maintain its momentum. Adding to the Germans' difficulty in supplying their troops were the raids behind their lines by Soviet partisans who destroyed railway tracks and bridges and attacked supply convoys.

A major reason for the Wehrmacht's ruinous supply problem was Hitler's initial failure to prepare the German nation for total war. Anticipating a short war with light casualties, Hitler and the German High Command gave little thought to the replacement of soldiers and armor. Soon, the Wehrmacht would be lacking numbers and arms. "Hitler's fundamental irresponsibility," declares Antony Beevor, "[was] to launch the most ambitious invasion in history while refusing to gear the German economy and industry for all-out war."[22] Had Hitler mobilized the home front from the start of Operation Barbarossa rather than after Stalingrad in early 1943, logistical difficulties might have been surmounted. Or maybe not, for ultimately Germany may have lacked sufficient strength in numbers; in natural resources, particularly oil; and in industrial capacity to crush the Soviet Union. Several statistics show the enormous task confronting the German invaders. Operation Barbarossa began on June 22. Between that day and December 1, 1941, the Soviet Union inducted 3,241,000 men. During that same period, German replacements on the Eastern Front numbered about 100,000. From July to December 1941, the Soviets produced 5,173 fighter planes as compared to the Germans' 1,619.

The aim of Operation Barbarossa—the destruction of the Red Army and the Soviet regime in one decisive blow—was not achieved. The Wehrmacht had been immensely successful fighting campaigns of no more than six weeks in countries with road networks that facilitated rapid movement by tanks and armored units and where the distances to be covered were short. It would be less successful fighting a protracted war where poor roads, vast distances, swamps, forests, freezing weather, and partisan attacks hampered mobility. Despite the Wehrmacht's striking victories, the vastness of the Soviet Union and the seemingly prodigious supply of replacements at the fronts of both soldiers and armor would begin to seem insuperable challenges. Increasingly German soldiers, exhausted from long marches often over difficult terrain, and constantly fighting a relentless enemy, felt that they were being sucked into a quagmire with no speedy or safe exit. Barbarossa may have been fatally flawed from the start: in the Soviet Union, the Germans would win battles but not a war.

Stalin's Continued Terror

Stalin fought the war with the same spirit and methods that he had employed in ruling the Soviet Union prior to the war. Forced collectivization of agriculture had led to the murder and deportation of millions of peasants to the Gulag.

Seeing enemies and threats to his power everywhere, the always suspicious and vengeful Stalin unleashed raw terror, decimating the Old Bolsheviks who had fought alongside Lenin, the cultural elite, and the officer staff. In the historic struggle to construct a powerful socialist state and to retain personal power, human life was of no concern to the Communist dictator, nor did it matter now in the life-and-death struggle with the Nazi invaders. Consistent with his domestic rule, Stalin employed terror to deal with armies that were disintegrating because of surrender and desertions. In July 1941, the Soviet dictator ordered the arrest and trial of four senior generals, a commander of a rifle corps, and four divisional commanders "for disgracing their rank." Three weeks later, they were stripped of their ranks and executed. On August 16, Stalin issued Order 270: "I order that anyone who ... surrenders should be treated as a malicious deserter whose family is to be arrested.... Such deserters are to be shot on the spot. Those falling into encirclement are to fight to the last and try to reach their own lines. And those who prefer to surrender are to be destroyed by any available means while their families are to be deprived of all state allowances and assistance."[23] Stalin would soon follow this with other orders that called for executing those who deserted, retreated without explicit orders, displayed a defeatist attitude, and deliberately wounded themselves. In the first few months after the German invasion, the NKVD arrested 26,000 people, 10,000 of whom were executed, more than 3,000 of them in front of their comrades. It is estimated (but not confirmed) that during the war Soviet authorities sentenced 158,000 soldiers to death for alleged cowardice or desertion; at the front commanders ordered tens of thousands more shot. And in the opening weeks of the war, the NKVD massacred political prisoners in Ukraine and other regions that the Germans were about to overrun.

Surrender was strictly forbidden; Stalin demanded that Soviet soldiers fight to the death. Soldiers who allowed themselves to be taken prisoner were considered traitors or deserters or in collusion with the enemy, and their families were subject to arrest. When Stalin's son was taken prisoner, he ordered the imprisonment of his son's wife. After the war, Russian POWs who managed to survive the war in captivity were tortured, sent to the Gulag, and frequently executed. There is no way of knowing how individual soldiers reacted to Stalin's terror tactics, but generally they feared being shot if they fled. They also feared being captured, which meant confinement in a German prisoner of war camp and possible death at the hands of the Germans or eventually their own government. These fears no doubt stiffened resistance and discouraged flight and surrender.

Hunted down by special NKVD units, "traitors"—virtually anyone accused of cowardice or disobeying orders—were often assigned to penal battalions that were forced to clear minefields or engage in suicide attacks against German emplacements; if they retreated, armed guards shot them from behind. Between 1942 and 1945, more than four hundred thousand soldiers and prisoners from the Gulag served in these units, which offered little chance for survival.

Ethnic cleansing was another component of Stalin's terror. The Soviet dictator feared that the 1.5 million ethnic Germans living in the Soviet Union would assist the German invaders. Because they had settled in Russia many generations ago and large numbers no longer spoke German, many

Russian-Germans considered themselves loyal Russians. But thousands of others volunteered to serve the Nazis in both noncombat and combat capacities. Stalin saw only the danger. He also suspected the loyalty of the various nationalities in the Caucasus and Central Asia that were still angered over being reabsorbed into the Soviet Union in the 1920s, the forced collectivization of agriculture in the next decade, and the Communist state's antireligious campaign that impinged on their Islamic faith. By the end of 1942, more than one million ethnic Germans, Crimean Tartars, Chechens, and other ethnic minorities were forcibly uprooted from their homes without notice and herded into cattle cars to journey to Central Asia or Siberia. Given little food or water and no protection from the cold, tens of thousands perished before reaching their destination. To carry out the population transfers, valuable human and transportation resources were diverted from the war effort—more than 100,000 soldiers and police and 180 railway cars. And the deportees included many skilled workers and farmers. Undoubtedly, the Soviet Union paid a price for Stalin's paranoia—his failure to distinguish between traitors and loyal Soviet citizens. And yet Stalin succeeded in forging solidarity within his heterogeneous population; many members of the ethnic minorities accepted Stalin's dictum that the nation was embroiled in a "Great Patriotic War" and fought courageously to drive out the invaders.

Stalin's policies in the 1930s—forced collectivization, liquidation of the kulaks, the Ukrainian famine, the elimination of ethnic Poles living in the Soviet Union, and the eradication of imaginary opponents of his regime during the Great Terror of 1937 and 1938—deliberately killed millions. And his wartime policies—ethnic cleansing and the murder and deportation of Poles while eastern Poland was in Soviet hands—added to his butchery. Although fighting to preserve freedom, the Western democracies were compelled to ally themselves with the Soviet dictator, a notorious mass murderer. Such were the demands of the war and the vicissitudes of history.

THE WEHRMACHT THWARTED: MOSCOW AND LENINGRAD

At the Gates of Moscow

The German General Staff considered the capture of Moscow to be a major objective. The fall of the Russian capital, they reasoned, would demoralize the Russians and deprive them of leaders who would be forced to flee east. Moreover, as an important communication center and railway junction and as a major source of arms production, Moscow was essential to the Soviet war effort. Given that Soviet leaders regarded Moscow as absolutely vital, they were certain to deploy much of their remaining forces to defend the city to prevent the Soviet Union's destruction.

Hitler planned to obliterate the city by flooding it; a giant human-constructed lake would cover the region where Moscow once stood. However, in August 1941, just as German forces were closing in on Moscow, Hitler clashed with his senior generals. The generals wanted to press the assault in full strength in order to capture the capital before winter. Hitler instead chose to divert forces southward for economic reasons: to seize the Ukraine, the bread-basket of Russia, which also had an abundance of raw materials and metal plants; and to secure the oilfields of the Caucasus. German economic planners warned of oil shortages. Obtaining these resources, Hitler reasoned, would greatly strengthen Germany and incapacitate the Soviet war machine, paving the way for further advances, including taking Moscow. The Wehrmacht inflicted another catastrophic defeat on the Soviets by encircling, trapping, and pounding with artillery a huge force in Kiev, the capital of the Ukraine. In the battle for Kiev, 665,000 Soviets were taken prisoner, the largest number of soldiers captured in any one battle in history. Rejecting the advice of Georgi Zhukov and other field commanders, Stalin stubbornly and foolishly refused to evacuate Kiev before the Germans sealed the pocket. For challenging Stalin, Zhukov was dismissed as field marshal.

Historians debate whether this diversion for economic ends cost Germany the opportunity to take Moscow. At the time, Franz Halder and several other senior generals regarded it as a great strategic blunder: by dividing its forces, they maintained, Germany wasted the opportunity to capture Russia's capital and perhaps end the war before winter. The loss of Moscow, the German High Command believed, would compel the Soviet leaders and their remaining military to retreat east of the Ural Mountains, giving the Germans total control over European Russia. And with Stalin forced to flee, the Communist state might have collapsed. Instead, the Soviets gained time to replenish their shattered divisions and to strengthen defenses around the capital, particularly antiaircraft batteries that took a huge toll of German planes. However, Robert M. Citino urges caution "in using the word *blunder* to describe ... the greatest victory in German history" and the greatest double envelopment on the Eastern Front, particularly because many of the 665,000 Soviets taken prisoner would have been used against the Germans attacking Moscow.[24]

At the beginning of October, after a delay of one month, the Germans resumed their drive on Moscow, replicating their stunning victories in the opening weeks of Operation Barbarossa: they encircled Soviet armies, killed and captured hundreds of thousands of Soviet soldiers, and overran towns and villages. Almost all the routes to Moscow were now open. Hitler's headquarters predicted that this powerful blow marked the end of the Red Army, and headlines in German newspapers trumpeted the imminent conquest of Moscow. These catastrophic losses drove Moscow into a state of panic. Government officials and bureaucrats burned documents, and some fled the city without permission. Workers looted stores and factories. The NKVD restored order through terror—on October 16, 200 people were executed. The government then instituted procedures for evacuation. By November 25, some two million Muscovites had been moved east.

Heeding Stalin's orders, Soviet officials made preparations to demolish power stations, railway stations, trolleybus yards, office buildings, manufacturing plants—most of them small factories because major industrial complexes had already been transported east—and anything else that could be of value to the Germans. But these plans were not enacted, for contrary to the Germans' expectations, the Red Army maintained a tenacious defense rather than collapsing.

Furthermore, the Germans had a serious supply and replacement problem. Panzer divisions were nowhere near full strength. When the torrential autumn rains came, unpaved Russian roads were a muddy quagmire; men and horses up to their knees in the sludge strained to extricate sunken vehicles. Tanks could barely move. Transporting equipment and fuel from supply depots in the rear to the front became a horrendous ordeal, stalling the advance. By mid-November the rains lessened and the ground was hard enough for tanks and armored vehicles to move forward. In some sectors, the Germans advanced to within twenty-five miles of the capital by the beginning of December. But the Germans were meeting stiff resistance in what had become a battle of attrition, and whereas the Soviets were able to rush new divisions to the front, the Germans were unable to replace their losses. Increasingly, German soldiers now had doubts about a speedy and decisive victory and a new respect for their Russian adversary, as one infantryman wrote at the end of November:

> They say that the campaign will end before the onset of real winter but I do not see much sign of this happening. It is best not to set one's hopes on miracles. Even if we capture Moscow, I doubt whether this will finish the war in the east. The Russians are capable of fighting to the very last man, the very last square metre of their vast country. Their stubbornness and resolve is quite astonishing.[25]

Suffering unsustainable losses in men and armaments and near the end of their strength, the Germans in early December were forced to halt the attack entirely. Early and bitter subzero weather—the most severe winter in many years—for which German soldiers were not properly outfitted, caused widespread frostbite, further debilitating the physically and emotionally exhausted troops, many of whom had been in action since the first day of Operation Barbarossa. Recalls a veteran of the battle: "Those Arctic blasts that had taken us by surprise … had scythed through our attacking troops. In a couple of days there were one hundred thousand casualties from frost-bite alone; one hundred thousand first-class, experienced soldiers fell out because the cold had surprised them."[26] Tens of thousands of these incapacitated soldiers, some of them now amputees, would never see combat again. Malnutrition and dysentery also took their toll. A considerable reduction in tank strength and other vehicles, often due to the difficulty transporting spare parts, meager fuel supplies, and deleterious effect of icy cold—engines frozen solid—weakened the Wehrmacht still more. A principal reason for the monumental supply problem was insufficient number of locomotives and the inability of trains and the railroad installations to operate effectively in the brutal winter. With reinforcements and replacements reduced to a trickle, neither panzer nor infantry divisions were operating anywhere near full combat strength.

A Soviet Counterattack

On December 6, the Red Army launched a carefully planned counterattack that took the Germans totally by surprise. The commander of the army was Georgi Zhukov, whom Stalin turned to despite having removed him as chief of staff in the summer. Not detecting the size and strength of the army the Soviets had assembled in the rear, German intelligence continued to maintain that the Red Army lacked the reserves to conduct a counteroffensive. Zhukov's divisions were reinforced by the secret arrival of large numbers of well-trained veteran troops from Siberia with a demonstrated capacity to fight in subzero weather; 1,700 tanks, whose broad tracks were better suited for maneuvering on snow and ice than the German panzers; and aircraft squadrons that gave the Soviets air superiority. Soviet aircraft flew from airfields close to Moscow with heated hangers and concrete runways, whereas German planes, parked in open airfields, had to deal with snow and ice and makeshift earthen runways.

Rested and equipped for the weather—quilted uniforms, fur hats, and felt boots—Soviet soldiers, some of them on sleighs and skis, broke through the German lines and forced a retreat. During the retreat, the Soviets inflicted heavy casualties and destroyed or captured large numbers of abandoned artillery pieces, tanks, and trucks, many of them immobilized by blizzards and cold. Soviet planes, tanks, ski patrols, and partisans relentlessly hounded the exhausted and demoralized Germans retreating in a desperate flight, and large numbers surrendered, which was unusual for the Wehrmacht at this time. Lacking winter clothing, weakened in body and mind, and suffering from frostbite that caused ears, noses, and fingers to fall off, many German soldiers collapsed in the snow, which soon covered them. Their corpses froze solid. The narrow roads were littered with dead Germans, broken-down vehicles, and the cadavers of horses. The conviction of German superiority, of which there was no doubt in the early stage of Barbarossa, now rapidly eroded. "The triumphalism with which we began our advance on Moscow has completely evaporated," Horst Lange, a German infantryman wrote in his diary. "Instead we are conscious of a growing fear of the Russians. And it is more than fear, it is verging on hysteria."[27] Goebbels' appeal to the German people just before Christmas to donate winter clothing for the troops also diminished the home front's triumphalism.

Recognizing the crisis, several German generals urged a large-scale withdrawal to a shorter and more sustainable defensive line. Screaming criminal betrayal, Hitler relieved several of these senior generals of their duties, including Field Marshal Walther von Brauchitsch, head of the German army, and Field Marshal Fedor von Bock, commander of Army Group Center. Hitler took personal command of the German army and, demanding "fanatical resistance," ordered his troops "not one step back." First, retreating from the Russians, whom he had constantly described as racial inferiors, would be a blow to his prestige that he was not willing to take. Second, with Napoleon in mind, he feared that a retreat would cause morale to plummet and precipitate a demoralizing rout. Third, the Germans would have to abandon their heavy armaments—artillery, tanks, and antitank weapons—which were not easily replaced and would fall into Russian hands. And when the retreat would come to a halt, they would be without heavy weapons to confront the advancing Russians. Finally, the essential principle of Hitler's military strategy, which he imposed over and over again with sometimes disastrous consequences, was never to surrender conquered ground. General Heinz Guderian, the brilliant panzer leader, initiated a retreat in order

The invading Germans treated the Russian people, whom they regarded as racial inferiors, in a savage manner. They deliberately starved to death Russian prisoners of war and engaged in atrocities against civilians. Here, Russians are looking for relatives and friends among seven thousand Crimean villagers slaughtered by the Germans.

to wage a flexible defense on December 26; Hitler placed him on inactive duty. (In time, he would be called back to active service.)

The German soldiers dug in where they could and tried to establish connecting strongpoints in and near towns and villages. In mid-January, Hitler did allow some withdrawal in small stages in order to set up improved defensive positions; he also ordered the withdrawing forces to burn all villages before evacuating them and not to abandon any weapons. As German troops pulled back, in accordance with Hitler's orders they destroyed bridges, vehicles, and anything else that might sustain the Soviet war effort. They confiscated the warm winter clothing of Russian civilians and set fire to whole villages, farms, and buildings, condemning many villagers to death by hunger and cold. They also killed and deported civilians to Germany. One villager described the retreat:

> They slaughtered all the cattle and chickens. They didn't let us into our cottages. We had to sleep in the open and cook on bonfires.... They burned the village as they left. They left two houses at the request of the women, so that there would be somewhere to shelter the children. But [some two miles] away the Germans were hanging and beating people.... They hanged the woman teacher and the chairman of the collective farm and they raped the girls.[28]

When Soviet soldiers moved into these devastated areas and heard survivors' harrowing tales of torture, pillage, the wailing of frozen children, enslavement, and murder, their hatred of the German occupiers intensified. At times, their determination to attain retribution was cruelly gained; they frequently killed prisoners, even wounded soldiers in a captured German field hospital.

In their counteroffensive, the Soviets pushed back the German forces, recaptured several towns that were approaches to Moscow, and inflicted punishing losses on German soldiers, whose morale was suffering. Moscow was saved and the German forces were in dire straits, but the Red Army could not sustain its offensive and inflict a knockout blow. Moving farther from its supply lines, it fell short of artillery shells needed to bombard German strongpoints, and it lacked fresh units. This was largely Stalin's fault. Instead of concentrating his armies for a massive assault on the weakened German Fourth Army, as Zhukov advised, Stalin diverted forces to other fronts, including the transfer of a key unit needed in the Moscow counteroffensive. Stalin hoped to envelop and demolish the German invaders in one great counteroffensive, a strategy that overreached the capacities of the Red Army and resulted in considerable casualties.

Also helping to rescue the Wehrmacht was the appointment of General Walther Model as commander of the Ninth Army. An ardent Nazi, he was also brave, aggressive, and devoted to his troops, whose hardships he shared by visiting them on the front line. Model believed that the way out of the crisis was to halt the retreat, boldly attack the flanks of the pursuing Red Army, close the gaps in the Wehrmacht's lines, drive a wedge between attacking Soviet armies, and encircle and entrap one of them. Model's aggressive tactics, which completely surprised the Soviets, who felt the Germans incapable of recovering from the Red Army's offensive, succeeded. The Germans now repulsed renewed Red Army attacks and stabilized the front, restoring confidence in the army ranks. The Soviets had not been able to hammer the Wehrmacht into submission, but the threat to Moscow had been lifted, and the Germans, like the Soviets, suffered massive casualties.

What saved the German army from a complete rout, Hitler insisted, was his iron will, which forbade a full-scale retreat that could have produced a general panic. It is true that in their exhausted condition, many soldiers would not have survived marching for days in frigid weather through snow and ice with the Red Army in merciless pursuit. From senior generals to common soldiers, all would be thinking of Napoleon's fateful retreat from Moscow, and morale, already fragile from the ordeal, might have totally collapsed. But an earlier tactical retreat, which senior commanders had urged, would have avoided severe losses in men and materiel. Moreover, it was Stalin's diverting of forces that weakened the Red Army offensive at a critical point. Had the Red Army remained at full strength, it might have overpowered the Wehrmacht's holding positions and overrun withdrawing units. Hitler drew a simple lesson from the winter of 1941–1942: in a crisis, never surrender territory but always stand fast. Hitler's rigid commitment to this strategy, which was successful in the Moscow ordeal, would prove disastrous for the Wehrmacht at Stalingrad and in other campaigns.

Some seven million soldiers from both sides were engaged in the battle for Moscow. Losses—killed, missing, wounded, and taken prisoner—amounted to

1,896,000 (Soviet) and 615,000 (German). No other battle before or since has reached these numbers. After achieving a string of impressive victories in Poland, France, and other lands, the Germans were hurled back before the gates of Moscow. Hitler and many of his senior commanders had been confident that Moscow would be taken. The German people were told that the Red Army was being obliterated and the fall of the Russian capital was imminent. The failure of the Moscow campaign illustrated Germany's underestimation of the Red Army's strength and the resolve of the Soviet people. And the Soviet regime, which Hitler and his generals thought would collapse, remained firmly entrenched. Although Germany still occupied large areas of the country, the key objective of Operation Barbarossa—a quick, decisive, crushing blow that would cause the collapse of the Soviet Union—had been foiled and the image of German military invincibility shattered. Contrary to the assurances the Nazi regime gave to the German people, the war against the Soviet Union would not be short, and with American entry into the conflict in December 1941, the prospects of an Allied invasion of the Continent loomed. Germany now had little chance of winning a prolonged war against the combined might of the Allies. Moreover, months of combat, including the Moscow counteroffensive, had depleted the Wehrmacht of manpower, including experienced officers, and equipment, both of which were difficult to replace. The Third Reich lacked the human and material resources to fulfill its goal of conquering European Russia.

In their memoirs written after the war, German generals stressed weather conditions as the principal reason for their defeat in Russia. An especially brutal winter certainly contributed to the Wehrmacht's woes, but it was the effectiveness of Red Army soldiers and their commanders that ultimately halted the German offensive. The performance of the Red Army in the Moscow offensive proved unsettling to German soldiers indoctrinated with the Nazi belief that their opponents were primitive, racially inferior Slavs. In accounting for the failure to capture Moscow, a German officer provided a new perspective of the Russian enemy. "[T]he truth is we totally underestimated our opponent. He showed a strength and resilience we did not believe him capable of— indeed, resilience greater than most of us imagined humanly possible."[29] The successful outcome of the battle for Moscow raised Soviet morale both on the home front and on the front lines; there was a growing confidence that the German aggressor could be defeated. And to the dismay of senior German commanders, the campaign demonstrated the growing competence of a new breed of Red Army commanders, who skillfully employed flanking attacks and encirclements.

Perhaps the most outstanding of these generals was Georgi Zhukov. Of peasant background, Zhukov was decorated for valor in World War I and served in the Red Army during the civil war that followed the Bolshevik Revolution. He excelled in the use of intelligence reports to anticipate German tactics and in planning an operation in minute detail. In preparing for battle, Zhukov relentlessly scoured the country for men and equipment in order to have a massive concentration of power; ruthless, he was willing to absorb horrendous casualties in the pursuit of his battlefield objectives, and he ordered soldiers retreating without orders to be fired on with machine guns. Zhukov was also brave; in daring to challenge Stalin's military judgment, he was fortunate to survive.*

The Epic Siege of Leningrad

Leningrad (the former tsarist capital of St. Petersburg, renamed in honor of V. I. Lenin, the leader of the 1917 Bolshevik Revolution, and today once again called St. Petersburg) was a chief objective of Operation Barbarossa. From a military standpoint, it was a principal center for arms production and the base for the Soviet Union's Baltic fleet. For Hitler, conquering Leningrad would also have great symbolic value; he believed that the loss of what he regarded as the birthplace of Bolshevism would undermine Soviet morale and accelerate the Soviet Union's collapse.

By early September 1941, the Wehrmacht had encircled the city, cutting off supply routes. Hitler did not want to risk considerable casualties fighting through the Red Army's strong defenses, including antitank ditches, minefields, barbed-wire entanglements, and pillboxes, constructed with the labor of five hundred thousand citizens of Leningrad. The Führer decided simply to starve to death Leningrad's almost three million besieged inhabitants and utterly destroy the city with artillery barrages and aerial bombardments. Then in the spring the Wehrmacht would send the survivors into captivity and with high explosives raze the city to the ground. Hitler ordered that all offers to surrender should be rejected; the Führer did not want capitulation but annihilation of the civilian population and obliteration of the city. On September 16, 1941, he told the German ambassador in occupied France: "The 'venomous nest Petersburg' out of which Asiatic poison had so long gushed ... would have to disappear from the face of the earth."[30] German soldiers besieging the city understood what their commanders intended for Leningrad, as one infantryman at the scene observed.

> We had erected an impenetrable ring around Leningrad. All its inhabitants had been sentenced to death through hunger and disease. We did not think the Russians would be able to break through to the city or provide its people with provisions. The population was inevitably going to starve to death and that was the real intent of our higher command.[31]

During the epic nine-hundred-day siege, the citizens of Leningrad endured incessant shelling and bombings that destroyed residential areas, food warehouses, schools, hospitals, and factories. Supply convoys had to cross the frozen Lake Ladoga to relieve the besieged city, which was desperate for food, water, electricity, and heat; many civilians were also evacuated to safety across the

---

*He was also fortunate that the Germans did not take Moscow. Years later, Zhukov told a Russian historian that Stalin warned him his "head will roll" if he surrendered Moscow. See Victor Anfilov, "Zhukov," in *Stalin's Generals*, ed. Harold Shukman (New Haven, CT: Phoenix, 2001), 351.

lake. Constant German bombardment made this lifeline a perilous journey as did ice that gave way. Hundreds of thousands who remained perished from cold, starvation, and exhaustion; the shelling and bombardments killed additional thousands. At the height of the famine, a doctor observed the following "horrible sight":

> A dark room covered with frost, puddles of water on the floor. Lying across some chairs was the corpse of a fourteen-year-old boy. In a baby carriage was a second corpse, that of a tiny infant. On the bed lay the owner of the room—dead. At her side, rubbing her chest with a towel, stood her eldest daughter.... In one day she lost her mother, a son and a brother who perished from hunger and cold.[32]

There is little doubt that virtually the entire population of Leningrad would have perished from slow starvation had imagination and courage not sustained the route across Lake Ladoga. Estimates for the number of civilians who died in Leningrad and its suburbs and in the evacuations vary, but a death toll of one million is generally accepted, a figure that far surpasses the combined fatalities of both the United States and Britain for the entire war.

Pushed to the limits of physical and emotional endurance, the people of Leningrad displayed an unconquerable spirit. Emaciated and exhausted Leningraders toiled long hours in arms factories and in constructing and repairing defense fortifications and buildings damaged by shelling. They also had to deal with the NKVD, which interrogated and imprisoned "enemies of the people." In a heroic struggle to maintain human values, Leningraders kept schools open, staged and attended concerts and dramatic performances, recorded their experiences in diaries, and performed acts of altruism. They also remained defiant. In September 1941, the poet Anna Akhmatova recorded these words for her fellow citizens:

> The Germans want to destroy our city—the city of Peter, the city of Pushkin, of Dostoevsky and Alexander Blok, the city of great culture and achievement. This city is part of my life. In Leningrad I became a poet—I, like all of you, live with one unconquerable belief—that Leningrad will never be fascist.[33]

But there were times when human values collapsed, a consequence of the desperate struggle to survive. Unable to endure the strain of food deprivation—at times, just a few slices of bread a day—some Leningraders resorted to stealing food even from family members and friends; and more than a few were driven to cannibalism. Police records kept secret until 2002 record that the authorities executed more than three hundred people for cannibalism and imprisoned more than fourteen hundred for the same horrifying act.

In January 1944, a Soviet offensive drove German forces from the outskirts of the city, ending the nine-hundred-day siege. The courage and tenacity demonstrated by the citizens of Leningrad, which surprised Hitler and the German High Command, made a mockery of the racial arrogance that littered the propaganda fed to German soldiers at the front.

THE TIDE TURNS: STALINGRAD

More German Conquests

To Hitler's great displeasure, his armies did not succeed in annihilating Moscow and Leningrad by the end of 1941, goals that accorded with his Social Darwinian and racist worldview. However, by the spring of 1942, the Soviet Union's losses in territory, manpower, military equipment, and industrial capacity were gargantuan: some 3.1 million soldiers had been killed and more than 3 million captured; replenishing the thousands of tanks and planes destroyed in combat was an immense challenge; the loss of the Donets (also known as Donbas) industrial sector reduced by three-quarters coal, steel, and iron ore production; and the loss of rich agricultural lands in the Ukraine greatly reduced the food supply. Nor did the military situation look promising, despite breaking the encirclement of Moscow and preventing the Germans from capturing Leningrad. Stalin's misguided attempt to retake Kharkov in May 1942, as a part of an ambitious plan to regain German-occupied territory and to divert the Wehrmacht away from Moscow, ended in a debacle as the Germans encircled and then captured whole armies. Zhukov, who had distinguished himself in the defense of Moscow, warned Stalin that the Red Army was not ready for such a large-scale operation. Whereas Stalin aspired to win the war in one all-embracing offensive, Zhukov, who had a more sophisticated understanding of the military situation, urged a sequence of carefully planned offensives. Had a stubborn Stalin heeded this advice, hundreds of thousands of lives could have been saved.

Between May and July, the Soviets suffered two other major setbacks in campaigns that added to Erich von Manstein's reputation as Germany's most able general—he had devised the plan for attacking France through the Ardennes. First, von Manstein seized the Kerch Peninsula in the Crimea. Effectively employing air power, massive concentration of artillery, and panzer assaults, German forces broke through Soviet positions and inflicted punishing losses in men and material on the defenders, who outnumbered the Germans two to one in personnel, artillery, and tanks. An elite Luftwaffe air unit of six hundred aircraft flying some two thousand sorties a day gave massive support to von Manstein's ground forces. Tightly packed Soviet units waiting to be evacuated from the port of Kerch were slaughtered by von Manstein's artillery situated on cliffs overlooking the shore. The victory at Kerch was followed by another stunning triumph, the capture of Sevastopol, the Soviet Union's principal Black Sea naval base and fortress and gateway to the Caucasus. A delighted Hitler elevated von Manstein to the rank of field marshal.

In smashing and enveloping Soviet forces on the Kerch Peninsula and at Kharkov and seizing Sevastopol, reputed to be the world's strongest fortress, the Germans had completely obliterated six Soviet armies, taking five hundred thousand prisoners. German panzer divisions were again performing at their best—opening gaps and encircling and entrapping the enemy. And commanders were leading aggressively by exploiting weaknesses and improvising creatively. It seemed like a repetition of the first weeks of Operation Barbarossa. After its terrible ordeal before the gates of Moscow, the Wehrmacht had demonstrated great resilience and resourcefulness. These victories restored both the morale of German soldiers and the confidence of senior command.

Operation Blue

The conquest of the Crimea had eliminated a threat to the Wehrmacht's southern flank, a necessary precondition for launching Operation Blue. Hitler had two goals for Operation Blue: control of Caucasus oilfields, which would provide the Reich with a vital resource at the same time denying it to the Soviet forces; and capturing Stalingrad (now Volgograd), the great industrial and supply center located on the Volga River. Control of Stalingrad would give Germany command of vital rail transportation, deprive the Soviets of a key center of war industry, and protect the Wehrmacht's operations in the Caucasus. Hitler expected that the Soviets would pour in what he believed was the last of its manpower to defend this vital area. Inflicting crippling casualties on an already exhausted Red Army in a series of encirclements and gaining Stalingrad and the Caucasus, he thought, would irreversibly weaken the Soviet military, which would assure a final German victory. Moreover, conquering this city that bore Stalin's name would be a personal triumph and a great propaganda victory for the Third Reich. Hitler had made plans for Stalingrad's future: kill all the male inhabitants, deport women and children, and destroy the city forever.

Because of the losses incurred in previous months of hard fighting, the number of soldiers available for Operation Blue was limited. Germany was forced to call on its allies, Romania, Hungary, and Italy, to provide troops. But lacking the dedication, skill, and superior armor of German soldiers, these satellite armies were not very reliable. The Wehrmacht had been stretched to its limits in its drive on Moscow in the previous winter and in the major campaigns at Kharkov and in the Crimea. So soon after these engagements, Germany lacked sufficient combat troops, armor, equipment, and air power to launch simultaneously complex offensives on two fronts covering vast stretches of territory. Moreover, the armies headed for the Caucasus and those for Stalingrad were moving in different directions, away from each other. This dispersal of forces was a departure from the tactic the Germans had so successfully employed in the past—concentrating forces in a unified front against a specific target. And the German High Command, relying on poor intelligence, badly underestimated the number of Soviet planes, tanks, and artillery they would have to face.

Operation Blue began on June 28, 1942, as a dual operation, splitting the armies between the Caucasus and Stalingrad. German forces drove south toward the Caucasus, devastating the Red Army units in their path. Rostov, at the mouth of the Don River, fell in the last week of July. That the soldiers responsible for defending Rostov had offered little resistance and were in flight dismayed Soviet authorities. However, hampered by diminishing air strength, great distances, and dreadful roads that impeded the flow of supplies, the German advance slowed in late August. In October and November, although fighting in forbidding mountain terrain in freezing cold and snowstorms, the First Panzer Army still made considerable gains.

The German invasion of the Soviet Union caused millions of Soviet children to lose one or both parents. Here, two orphaned children wander alone among the smoldering ruins of Rostov-on-Don, 1941.

But short of tanks and with significantly reduced front-line strength and no reserves, the Germans, threatened with encirclement, pulled back. The German High Command could hope for no more than a stalemate in the Caucasus. The Germans managed to capture the Maikop oil fields, but the Soviets had destroyed them. Germany never did get the oil of the Caucasus.

Meanwhile, in their advance toward Stalingrad, which they reached in late August and September, the German Sixth Army had demolished Red Army counterattacks. Hitler was convinced that the weakened Red Army could not save Stalingrad. However, although the Sixth Army inflicted huge casualties on the Soviets, it also suffered significant losses that would hamper its efforts in the struggle for Stalingrad. Moreover, Hitler and the German High Command had again underestimated the Soviets' ability to mobilize fresh armies to replace those destroyed in the approaches to Stalingrad.

On August 23, in a deliberate attempt to terrorize the citizens of Stalingrad, wave after wave of German planes dropped one thousand tons of bombs on residential areas; civilians driven from homes and hospitals were mowed down by machine guns fire. Two days later, the Germans resumed the aerial raids. Some forty thousand civilians perished in the inferno ignited by more than one thousand German planes. Orphaned children wandered about in a trance. Continuous bombardment in the months that followed transformed Stalingrad into a vast landscape of skeleton buildings and mountains of rubble. The Luftwaffe, which controlled the skies, made it difficult for supplies to reach the Soviet defenders by air or by ferry across the Volga River. German pilots also intentionally slaughtered civilians seeking to cross the Volga to safety, as one survivor of the conflict recalls.

> The pilots must have been able to see that all the people on the riverbank were civilians. But they were acting like professional assassins. They opened fire on defenseless women and children, and chose their targets so as to kill the maximum number of people. They dropped their bombs on the crowds just as the people were beginning to get on the ferries. They strafed the decks, they bombed the islands where there were hundreds of wounded.[34]

In September, Soviet authorities permitted three hundred thousand Stalingrad inhabitants to escape across the Volga, but tens of thousands more remained trapped in the city, seeking shelter in the shells of bombed buildings and in caves and sewers. Emaciated women and children foraged for berries, roots, or meat cut from dead horses lying in the street; desperate, they sometimes risked stealing food from the Germans. If spotted, German sentries would shoot them. The Sixth Army also herded civilians into camps, some sixty thousand of whom were sent to Germany as slave laborers. Thousands more died in the camps that were largely without shelter.

Urban Warfare

For the two dictators, the battle for Stalingrad became a test of wills. Hitler's obsession with conquering Stalingrad was matched by Stalin's determination to hold on whatever the cost. Vasily Chuikov, commander of the Sixty-Second Army, was given the responsibility to defend the city at a time when defeatism and defections were rampant. Tough and courageous, Chuikov was able to lift up morale when conditions looked hopeless and inspire his defenders to feats of great bravery. He shared his troops' rations, frequently could be seen where the fighting was most brutal, and demanded that battalion and regimental commanders remain in the front line and fight alongside their men. He was also ruthless, ordering counterattacks that wasted lives and the execution of men accused of cowardice and incompetence. It is estimated that some 13,500 "betrayers of the motherland" were shot at Stalingrad. And both his officers and men resented his striking them in a fit of anger.

Chuikov was flexible and inventive, capable of discarding battle blueprints and finding different ways for his undertrained soldiers to fight a disciplined professional army. Realizing that he could not match the Germans' superior firepower, Chuikov avoided engaging the panzers in the open plains outside the city. Instead he would fight the Germans in Stalingrad's streets, houses, railway stations, grain elevators, and factories. He turned key buildings, particularly three giant industrial complexes (a steelworks, a weapons plant, and a tractor factory that had switched to building tanks) into strongholds; he ordered night attacks by small storm units to unnerve the Germans and told his soldiers to get as close to the Germans as possible in order to restrict their use of artillery and aerial bombardments. Instead of moving heavy artillery across the Volga into Stalingrad, he ordered that they remain on the east bank where they could be more easily supplied with shells and were safer from aerial attack. Defenders manning the observation posts in the city would report the enemy's position to the artillery units. And he promoted the use of snipers, recognizing that they demoralized the enemy and lifted the morale of Stalingrad's defenders, who eagerly read of their exploits in the army newspaper. Chuikov made certain that all the defenders knew that there could be no retreat from the city. It was their patriotic duty to fight to the death, as Chuikov said: "We cannot surrender the city to the enemy.... The loss of it would undermine the nation's morale.... I swear I shall stand firm. We will defend the city or die in the attempt."[35]

The battle of Stalingrad was an epic struggle in which Soviet soldiers and civilians contested for virtually every building and street of the city. Launches ferrying desperately needed supplies across the Volga were horrifically bombed and strafed. As the Germans closed in on the Volga, the Red Army's prospects seemed bleak. For example, one division suffered 80 percent casualties in one week of fighting. But the tenacity of the defenders of Stalingrad astonished the Germans, who could not fathom how the Soviets continued to resist. In this urban battlefield, the combatants were separated by mere yards; sharp-shooting snipers with nerves of steel, some of them women, lurked in the maze of ruins, and tough Soviet soldiers stealthily and ceaselessly attacked at night, causing the enemy considerable anxiety. In a war of movement, German soldiers had out-performed the Red Army, but Soviet soldiers proved superior in close quarters, fighting hand-to-hand with daggers and bayonets. This is what Chuikov was counting on. Ironically, massive German bombing raids that had left almost every structure in ruins provided the Soviet fighters with perfect cover from which to harass the enemy. Vaunted German technical skills and generalship were of no value in combat in basements and sewers and in the twisted skeletons of buildings that had to be cleared floor by floor. They were also no help in combat situations where no clear front line separated the two sides. Here the blitzkrieg, whose sweeping panzer maneuvers and encirclements had brought the Germans immense success in earlier campaigns, did not apply. Tanks, unable to maneuver in narrow streets piled with rubble, were sitting ducks for Soviet antitank gunners hidden in the wreckage. Soviet ground units deliberately placed their gun emplacements as close to the enemy as possible, discouraging the Germans from employing air support and artillery bombardments in fear of killing their own men, thereby neutralizing their superior firepower. Chuikov's astute tactics reduced losses and raised the morale of his men.

The Stalingrad defenders quickly learned the most effective methods of urban warfare that unsettled German soldiers and their officers used to engaging the enemy in open plains. From upper stories of buildings, Russians hurled bottles of inflammable liquid wrapped in gasoline-soaked cloth—"Molotov cocktails"—at German tanks. They also crossed through sewers, linked cellars, and attics and ambushed German patrols, and they planted booby traps in buildings and mines in streets that killed and disabled numerous Germans. Another tactic involved moving from lair to lair so that one sniper could kill ten or more Germans in a day; the Red Army trained and deployed more than a few of these sharpshooters. Frequently, important targets—a strategic hill, factory, grain elevator, or railway station—changed hands several times in one day of battle. A German lieutenant wrote:

> We have fought during fifteen days for a single house, with mortars, grenades, machine-guns and bayonets. Already by the third day fifty-four German corpses are strewn in the cellars, on the landings, and the staircases. The front is a corridor between burnt out rooms; it is the thin ceiling between two floors. There is a ceaseless struggle from noon to night.... [W]e bombard each other with grenades.... [Everywhere] floods of blood, fragments of human beings. Ask any soldier what half an hour of hand-to-hand struggle means in such a fight.... The street is no longer measured by meters but by corpses.[36]

So brutal was the fighting that at night half-crazed dogs sought to escape the city by swimming across the Volga.

Throughout the campaign, Soviet soldiers were told there could be no retreat east across the Volga River, and NKVD agents patrolled the river crossings, summarily executing soldiers trying to flee the city. The Russian soldier in Stalingrad was expected to fight until the last bullet and die. And that is exactly what many did: more than three hundred thousand troops perished defending the city. But the deadly urban warfare, particularly assaults to clear Soviet forces from factory districts, was bleeding the German Sixth Army to death.

The Death of the Sixth Army

In November, Operation Uranus, a Soviet counterattack planned by Zhukov, caught the Germans in a trap. In part, Zhukov's plan called for keeping the Sixth Army pinned down within the city while Soviet forces broke through its overextended left flank. The left flank was defended by Romanian armies, but they were poorly led and inadequately armed—they lacked antitank guns and their obsolete tanks were no match for the formidable T-34. Soviet armor would then move through the breached Romanian lines deep into the rear of the German Sixth Army, leaving it surrounded, cut off from retreat, and extremely difficult to supply. The German command had left the Sixth Army in and around Stalingrad without adequate flank protection, a grievous error that placed the entire army in danger of envelopment.

The success of Zhukov's strategy depended on exhausted Soviet fighters within the city holding out in the brutal fighting until everything was in place, a seemingly impossible assignment given that the Germans already controlled some 90 percent of the city. And the Soviet soldiers, short of food and ammunition and at the limit of their endurance, could not be apprised of the counterattack, for secrecy was paramount. In mid-October, the Germans launched an all-out assault intended to capture the remaining sections of the city. Artillery, tanks, and planes ferociously bombarded remaining Red Army strongpoints.

The defenders' astonishing courage and sacrifices fighting in streets and ruins and Chuikov's unflagging leadership prevented the Germans from overrunning the city and reaching the Volga. Chuikov and his defenders had given Zhukov the time he needed.

The Soviets assembled a powerful force of over one million soldiers and nearly one thousand tanks. The Germans spotted the Soviet build-up and also received information from Soviet deserters and warnings from the Romanians, but they grossly underestimated its size and did not detect its purpose, a huge failure of German intelligence. Not believing that the Soviets had sufficient reserve strength—ironically, a principal reason for the German Sixth Army's defeat at Stalingrad was insufficient reserves—or the competence to launch a massive counteroffensive, German commanders were unprepared for the Red Army's drive that began on November 19. But with no reserves to transfer to its flanks and limited fuel to maneuver against Soviet tanks, how was the Sixth Army to prepare for an attack by such a superior force? And given Hitler's fixation on Stalingrad and his personal clash with Stalin, withdrawal was not an option. When senior generals advised withdrawal, Hitler flew into a rage.

Following a heavy bombardment, Soviet forces quickly tore through Romanian lines, which collapsed in panic, and raced to Stalingrad, preparing to envelop the Sixth Army. The planning of this complex operation and its deft execution demonstrated that the Soviet Supreme High Command (Stavka) was now a match for Germany's vaunted General Staff.

An army can encounter no worse disaster than encirclement in a pocket with supply lines severed and reinforcements denied while being subjected to constant aerial and artillery bombardment. Its soldiers frozen; desperately short of food, medical supplies, fuel, and ammunition; and physically and emotionally drained, the beleaguered Sixth Army faced an agonizing and fast-approaching death. Friedrich Paulus, commander of the Sixth Army, urged Hitler to order a breakout before the Red Army sealed the ring. For the Führer, such a withdrawal was unthinkable. On September 30, Hitler had told the German people, "You may rest assured that nobody will ever drive us away from Stalingrad."[37] He would not now permit the loss of personal prestige that withdrawing from Stalingrad would entail. Moreover, retreating would mean leaving behind valuable equipment and admitting that the campaign was a failure. Refusing Paulus' plea, Hitler ordered the Sixth Army to dig in and defend "Fortress Stalingrad." Paulus lacked the courage to override Hitler, even though it meant certain death for his men. (It is questionable if the weakened Sixth Army had sufficient transports and fuel for a breakout to succeed.)

Hitler was persuaded, in part, by the pompous Herman Goering's assurance that his Luftwaffe would be able to supply the beleaguered Sixth Army by air. Goering's previous promises that the Luftwaffe would annihilate the Allied forces on the beaches of Dunkirk and that no British bombers would ever reach Germany had proved empty. So too did this latest assurance. The Luftwaffe had insufficient available transport planes, and terrible winter weather limited the number of flights and hampered maintenance crews that had to work outdoors on primitive Russian airfields. Moreover, these slow-moving transports were ideal targets for Russian antiaircraft guns and high-speed fighter interceptors. Often, the dropped provisions missed the target and fell into Soviet hands or could not be reached by the besieged Germans. The airlift provided between 100 to 140 tons of supplies a day, far less than the 750 tons the Sixth Army required just to maintain its position, and on some days no supplies reached the beleaguered soldiers. The airlift failed. So too did efforts of a relief force, commanded by von Manstein, to open up a corridor through the encircling Red Army to supply and aid the besieged Sixth Army. Von Manstein's force was simply not strong enough to fulfill this mission. The German public was not informed of von Manstein's failure.

Soviet forces moved rapidly to tighten the noose around the Sixth Army trapped in the pocket. Their situation rapidly deteriorating, the Germans suffered tens of thousands of additional casualties. The temperature was often twenty, thirty, or more degrees below zero, and soon the starving, exhausted, and frozen soldiers were capable only of feeble resistance. Thousands of largely unattended and unsheltered wounded, tortured by lice and rats, simply froze to death. Misery and death lurked everywhere. One German soldier wrote in his diary at the end of December: "The horses have already been eaten.... The soldiers look like corpses or lunatics looking for something to put in their mouths. They no longer take cover from Russian shells; they haven't the strength to walk, run away and hide."[38]

Hitler's promise to rescue the army from the Russians, delivered in a New Year's message, brought hope to the beleaguered men as they indicated in their letters home.

> "We're not letting our spirits sink, instead we believe in the word of the Führer."

> "We're maintaining a firm trust in the Führer, unshakeable until final victory."

> "The Führer knows our worries and needs, he will always—and I'm certain of this—try to help us as quickly as possible."[39]

As revealed by their letters, many soldiers retained a passionate devotion to their Führer and his ideology even as their plight gravely deteriorated, so powerful was the Hitler mystique.

A desperate Paulus asked for permission to surrender, to which Hitler responded on January 23, "Surrender is out of the question. The troops will defend themselves to the last."[40] Willpower had prevented a rout a year earlier at the time of the Soviet counteroffensive at Moscow; it would also prevail at Stalingrad. On January 30, 1943, Hitler promoted Paulus to field marshal. Knowing that no German field marshal had ever been taken prisoner, Hitler expected Paulus to fight to the last man or to commit suicide. The next day, Soviet soldiers made their way into Paulus' headquarters where his staff agreed to surrender terms. Paulus, fully aware that the situation was hopeless, surrendered formally on February 2, 1943. On February 1, a fuming Hitler denounced Paulus for allowing himself to be captured by Bolsheviks rather than taking his own life.

On February 3, while Beethoven's Fifth Symphony was broadcast, the German people were informed of the Sixth Army's defeat. Nazi propaganda tried to bolster morale for a public horrified by the magnitude of this unexpected disaster—the complete destruction of an entire German army. The propaganda did not acknowledge the Sixth Army's surrender, but instead manufactured a legend of altruistic sacrifice for the nation as a communiqué from the Führer's headquarters stated, "[B]eneath the swastika flag ... officers and men fought shoulder to shoulder down to the last bullet. They died so that Germany might live."[41] German newspapers and magazines were instructed to tell their readers: "The word Stalingrad must become a holy symbol for the German people. The immortal heroism of the men of Stalingrad will unleash even more than before the spirit and strength of the German nation, which will ensure the victory it is now even more fanatically determined to win."[42] Hitler dealt with the disastrous military defeat and blow to his pride by forbidding all discussion of Stalingrad either by the public or in the press. And he, himself, never referred to Stalingrad again.

Visiting Stalingrad right after the surrender, Alexander Werth, a British correspondent reporting from the Soviet Union, saw many gruesome scenes, including a basement full of two hundred German prisoners "dying of hunger and frostbite" and suffering from dysentery. In the yard "lay more horses' skeletons ... an enormous horrible cesspool.... [and] yellow corpses of skinny Germans ... piled up—men who had died in that basement." Reflecting on the horror, Werth "wished the whole of Germany were there to see it.... [T]here seemed a rough but divine justice in those frozen cesspools with the diarrhea and those horses' bones, and those starved yellow corpses."[43]

Soviet losses for the whole Stalingrad front (not just the city) amounted to 1.1 million, of which about 480,000 were killed or missing. Casualties (killed, wounded, and captured) for the Germans and their Italian, Romanian, and Hungarian allies came to about 850,000. Some 260,000 German soldiers perished and another 91,000, including 23 generals, were taken prisoner. Many died, often shot where they collapsed, in the long march through the snow either directly to prison compounds or to trains that would transport them to camps; more died from their wounds, exhaustion, and starvation in the long journey on these packed trains. At times, the prisoners even killed each other to get at the scraps of food thrown to them every other day. Still others perished from disease and abuse in the camps. Only some 5,000 would survive captivity and return to Germany several years after the war. Also captured were more than 20,000 Soviet turncoats—deserters, volunteers, and prisoners—fighting for Germany; many of them died violently at the hands of the NKVD or were worked to death in the Gulag.

The death of the Sixth Army was a turning point in the war, and it also had symbolic meaning. Again the Russians had demonstrated their determination to defend the motherland. While Soviet morale soared, Germans were deeply shaken by the human tragedy and the enormity of military setback—the most troops ever lost in battle in all of German history. They were compelled to ponder the Nazi doctrines of the invincibility of the German army, the certainty of German victory, and the providential leadership of the Führer, whom Nazi propaganda continually depicted as an infallible military genius. Was the Stalingrad catastrophe an ominous sign of what awaited their nation? Was the invasion of Russia a dreadful mistake, an act of hubris that would not go unrequited? In 1962, Joachim Wieder, an officer who had survived Stalingrad and Soviet captivity, described his feelings as the ring closed on the trapped Sixth Army. Other Germans no doubt shared his feelings.

> A foreboding I had long held grew into a terrible certainty.... Misery and death had been initiated by us and now they were inexorably coming home to roost.... In the sad events on the Volga I saw not only the military turning-point of the war. In the experiences behind me I felt and apprehended something else as well; the anticipation of the final catastrophe towards which the whole nation was reeling. In my mind's eye I suddenly saw a second Stalingrad, a repetition of the tragedy just lived through, but of much greater, more terrible proportions. It was a vast pocket battle on German soil with the whole German nation fighting for life or death inside.[44]

In the months after Stalingrad, the Security Service of the SS reported that civilians, many of whom had been apprehensive about embroiling the nation in a war with Russia and distressed by the failure to achieve a rapid victory, were now expressing pessimism about an eventual German victory and were criticizing Nazi Party officials, even the Führer himself. Civilians expressed all criticisms cautiously. Nevertheless, although the defeat at Stalingrad produced a deep gloom among some Germans, for a great number of soldiers and civilians faith in the Führer's person and leadership remained steadfast. And Goebbels' propaganda machinery worked assiduously to keep it that way.

After the crushing defeat at Stalingrad, the momentum on the Eastern Front was slipping away from the Germans. The Wehrmacht could not duplicate the series of victories employing the blitzkrieg that had characterized the opening phase of the war. For many military historians, an even more decisive turning point was Germany's failure in the summer of 1943 to eliminate the Kursk salient. The battle of Kursk was Germany's last offensive in the Soviet Union. Unable to reverse the tide of battle that had turned against it, the Wehrmacht entered a period of virtually unbroken retreats.

KURSK: GERMANY'S LAST OFFENSIVE
ON SOVIET SOIL

After the disaster at Stalingrad, Hitler resolved to regain immediately the initiative on the Eastern Front. Russia had to be subdued before Britain and the United States opened a second front in the West. Exploiting their victory at Stalingrad, in February 1943, the Soviets launched an offensive to recapture Kharkov, which Hitler ordered defended as a fortress. Encircled and also facing an uprising within the occupied city, the SS panzer divisions, disobeying orders to defend Kharkov to the last man, broke out to join another panzer force. Then reversing themselves, the panzer divisions in a successful counterattack enveloped the Soviets in several areas and retook Kharkov in three days of hard fighting, destroying or capturing some six hundred tanks. This was Germany's last victory on Soviet territory.

In May 1943, a group of generals seeking to seize the strategic initiative that would ensure victory presented Hitler with an ambitious plan that called for encircling and destroying the Red Army defending the Kursk salient, the bulge that protruded for more than seventy-five miles into German-held Soviet territory. The German High Command felt certain that within a short time the Red Army would use the salient as a springboard for a large-scale breakthrough with the objective of driving the Germans out of the occupied Ukraine and Crimea. Some generals, including Guderian, opposed a preemptive offensive that would drain Germany of men and armaments; it would be preferable, they argued, to inflict huge losses on the Red Army when it attempted a direct assault against German positions that were supported by powerful mobile reserves. These generals were overruled.

Code-named Citadel, the German operation called for a pincer attack intended to encircle and destroy the Soviet armies in the Kursk bulge. Hitler had doubts about such an ambitious operation, but wanting to continue the momentum following the successful counteroffensive at Kharkov, he decided to take the gamble. Moreover, he was concerned, correctly so, that there was little time left to crush the Soviet military before an Allied invasion of the Continent. A decisive victory would also have a salutary effect on morale both at the front and at home after the Stalingrad disaster.

Soviet Preparations

The Soviet High Command, which had performed poorly in the early days of the German offensive, had distinguished itself in the defense of Moscow and at Stalingrad. At the battle of Kursk in July 1943, Stavka again demonstrated an increasing ability to master the techniques of modern mechanized warfare. Analyzing correctly German intentions—and warned by a Soviet spy ring in Switzerland—Zhukov turned the area into a fortress and waited for the Germans to make the first move. Von Manstein wanted to attack before the Soviets could organize a formidable defense, but Hitler postponed the offensive for more than two months in order to assemble the new Panther and Tiger tanks that were designed to outperform the Soviet T-34s. The postponement caused von Manstein to have misgivings about the operation and he urged, without success, abandoning it. The delay, as von Manstein feared, enabled the Soviets to strengthen their strategic reserves and their defensive fortifications, to produce more tanks, and to learn more about German plans through aerial reconnaissance, deciphering German radio communications, reports from partisans, and the interrogation of captured soldiers.

The Soviets had assembled more than 1,300,000 combat troops and set in place eight defensive belts containing 20,000 artillery pieces; 503,993 antitank mines; 439,348 antipersonnel mines; 3,400 tanks and assault guns; and over 2,100 planes, including almost 1,000 dive bombers capable of destroying tanks. The defenders operated from a vast network of trenches protected by barbed wire.

The minefields and antitank gun placements were masterfully camouflaged. A huge reserve force that included mobile armor and antitank units was positioned to repair breaches opened by panzer attacks and to exploit weaknesses where German progress had been blocked. The in-depth fortified defensive belts were designed to ensnare and destroy the panzers and bleed the infantry; then, with fresh reserves, the Red Army would switch to an all-out counteroffensive. In one defensive line, the Soviets had buried hundreds of tanks with only their turrets showing. Difficult to spot, these hidden guns were expected to tie down the advancing Germans. Stopping the panzers with artillery, antitank guns, and tanks was Zhukov's major objective. And, extremely important, Soviet commanders had calculated correctly about where and when the Germans intended to strike.

In the past, the German blitzkrieg had succeeded because the enemy, taken by surprise, could not prevent a breakthrough and encirclement by fast-moving panzers and mobile infantry. This time, however, the Soviets did not have to guess where the attack would take place; a formidable force supported by powerful and well-positioned tank and infantry reserves awaited the German assault. Attacking panzers would be confronted by a large and well-armored tank force led by battle-tested commanders. Benefiting from the government's policy of maximizing tank production, Soviet tanks outnumbered the German panzers. Hurling panzer divisions, whose proven skill was mobile war on open plains, against what one German general later called "the strongest fortress in the world" proved to be a tactical mistake.[45]

A Stalled German Offensive

Information garnered from a captured German soldier and a deserter along with the observed movement of German troops to battle stations convinced the Soviet High Command that the attack was imminent. Very early on the morning of July 5, about two hours before the German offensive was scheduled to start, the Soviets opened one of the heaviest bombardments of the war. Although the bombardment unnerved the Germans burrowing themselves in their shelters, the Germans were able to begin their offensive as planned. German troops, among the best Germany had, did gain substantial ground in several places, but heavily fortified defense positions, including extensive minefields, camouflaged antitank emplacements, effective bombardments by Soviet artillery and fighter bombers, and fierce counterattacks on exposed flanks, repelled and bled white the German attackers. When after bitter fighting they broke through one defensive position, they were confronted with another one. In much of the front, the offensive's forward progress slowed from day to day. Bogged down in Zhukov's deep defense system, the German panzers lost the advantage they had held in mobile warfare. Nevertheless, although there were no stunning breakthroughs, the Germans were slowly and painfully gaining ground as relentless aerial bombardment by Stukas and the long-barrel 88mm guns of the new Tigers, which had a much greater range than the Soviet T-34s, took a heavy toll of Soviet tanks and infantry. But unlike in previous encounters, Soviet troops, neither overwhelmed nor overrun, were able to retreat in orderly fashion. In one area, crack panzer divisions advanced considerably, threatening to penetrate to the rear of Soviet defenses and to reach Kursk. But strengthened by the timely arrival of reserves and an elastic defense that called for withdrawing troops and tanks to fortify another defensive line, the Soviets, in furious fighting, halted the panzer drive.

In another attempt to surround and annihilate Soviet forces and open the road to Kursk, the same panzer armies then drove to the small town of Prokhorovka. The Germans did make considerable headway, capturing twenty-four thousand Soviet soldiers and a large number of tanks. To counter this sudden development, the Soviets called on their reserves, which reached the front on July 10 after an arduous four-day trek. On July 12, the two armies clashed on the rolling plains in the area of Prokhorovka. For years, based largely on embellished Soviet figures, it was said that some 1,200 to 1,500 German and Soviet tanks and armored vehicles fought in what was called the "greatest tank battle of all time." Recent analysis of operational documents has led military historians to modify the earlier estimates. According to David M. Glantz, whose works on the war on the Eastern Front are considered authoritative, "830 Soviet and 420 German [combat vehicles] fought along the long eastern flank of the Kursk Bulge and about 572 met on the field of Prokhorovka itself. Moreover, Prokhorovka was not a single titanic struggle of legend. In reality, it was a confused and confusing series of meeting engagements and hasty attacks, with each side committing its forces piecemeal."[46]

Prior to and during the tank battle, hundreds of German planes sent to attack Soviet lines were intercepted by an equivalent number of Soviet fighters; numerous aircraft on both sides were downed. From morning to night, at times in pouring rain, tanks clashed in a war of metal, and infantry engaged in hand to hand combat. Since the T-34s' cannons could not penetrate the Tigers' or Panthers' massive armor at more than 1,500 feet, Soviet tankers were instructed to get as close as possible and aim at the German tanks' vulnerable sides. The Tigers were fearful monsters. In a previous engagement, one Tiger fought some fifty T-34s, destroying twenty-two and forcing the others to retreat. Hovering above, German and Soviet planes waited for an opportunity to attack the tanks below, but poor weather conditions and the thick smoke from burning tanks that covered the sky blocked the pilots' vision, reducing the effectiveness of air support. While the battle raged, Soviet forces prevented German reinforcements from entering the fray and outflanking their tanks. At the battle's end, the plains were a graveyard of smoking tank hulks and thousands of burned, blackened bodies. The Prokhorovka engagement, of which the tank battle comprised the most important part, is seen as the "culminating moment" in the battle of Kursk. Despite far greater losses, the Red Army had successfully countered the blitzkrieg, preventing a German breakthrough at Prokhorovka and advancing to Kursk. Meanwhile, the Allies landed in Sicily, which was a second front that the Führer and his High Command had feared. Not wanting to lose more men and hard-to-replace tanks in a costly battle of attrition, the next day Hitler called off the offensive, which was the largest armored campaign of the war, and transferred divisions to Italy and the Balkans.

On the basis of recently opened Russian archives, Soviet casualties—killed, wounded, and missing—in the Battle of Kursk are given at 177,847; German casualties amounted to 49,822. Although suffering significantly more losses in soldiers and tanks, in less than two weeks the Red Army had beaten back the best combat units of the Wehrmacht, inflicting costly human and materiel losses in the process. Nor did German panzers achieve a breakthrough that enabled them to penetrate to the rear of the Red Army as they had done so effectively in the past. To be sure, the Tigers dominated the Soviets' T-34s, and the German offensive did manage to make some inroads against a superbly planned defensive network and a larger enemy force. Nevertheless, Operation Citadel failed to achieve its principal objectives: eliminating a Russian base around Kursk from which offensive operations could be launched and destroying enough Soviet forces to discourage the Soviet High Command from undertaking such an offensive. Instead, the ferocious battles had cost the Germans heavily, both in armor and men, particularly highly trained panzer crews. The losses weakened elite divisions. The operation had depleted the German military of almost all its reserves on the Eastern Front. The Red Army had learned how to cope with the blitzkrieg—in-depth fortifications and mobile reserves—that had brought the Germans so much success in the glory days of the past.

NO PROSPECT OF A GERMAN VICTORY

Hitler and His Generals

After Kursk, Hitler, who was always suspicious if not contemptuous of Germany's traditional aristocratic senior officers, railed at what he called the generals' incompetence. Growing more mistrustful of his generals and with continued unwavering confidence in his own military judgment, he increasingly took direct control over military operations. He was certain that the same iron will that had propelled him to lead Germany would prevail over Germany's enemies.

A number of generals had come to view Hitler as a gifted military strategist. They gave him credit for his inspired leadership in the Wehrmacht's early victories and were awed by his diplomatic daring, strategic military boldness, granite willpower, and astonishing memory that enabled him to reel off rapidly and accurately a mass of technical details regarding artillery, tanks, planes, and other weapons. Hans Ulrich Rudel, an ace Stuka pilot and Germany's most decorated soldier in World War II, wrote in his memoirs that Hitler "discusses the minutest details in the field of ballistics, physics, and chemistry with an ease which impresses me who am a critical observer in this department."[47] Another fighter ace, Günther Rall, recalled many years later that "Hitler had every facet of the war at his fingertips. He was well informed with details and facts and figures that astounded me. He recited statistics, logistics, the order of battle, and had knowledge of every military operation and its problems. He knew production numbers, exactly how many aircraft, guns, antiaircraft, submarines and battleships were built and where they were to be deployed."[48] Generals were also impressed with his ability to almost instinctively gauge and exploit an adversary's weakness as he had done at Munich in 1938 and when he gambled that France would not interfere with the remilitarization of the Rhineland in 1936, the annexation of Austria in 1938, and the German invasion of Poland in 1939.

After the war, it was common for German generals to blame Hitler exclusively for starting the war and for the nation's defeat. But contrary to their postwar protestations, German generals were not simply apolitical soldiers doing their duty, and Hitler was not solely responsible for costly military mistakes. Virtually all senior generals supported Hitler's policy of German territorial expansion, an objective the general staff had sought since prior to World War I. Although there were reservations, most generals agreed with his decision to invade Poland, France, and the Soviet Union. The generals shared Hitler's mistaken convictions that the blitzkrieg would cause the Soviet government to collapse and that the Red Army, comprised of Slavs and Asiatics, was no match for German soldiers. And, like Hitler, they woefully underestimated Soviet reserve strength. They also share Hitler's guilt for permitting their men to wage a war of annihilation.

Also contrary to their postwar memoirs, generals were not simply innocent soldiers compelled to carry out the orders of a ruthless dictator. Senior generals very often went along with, if not endorsed, Hitler's military strategy. And increasingly German generals and junior officers, either to promote their careers or for ideological reasons, embraced National Socialist principles and strove to show their loyalty to Hitler. Many were ardent admirers of Hitler and willingly supported his leadership, even when it was certain that the war was lost and Germany faced destruction. That so few senior officers were involved in the July 20 plot to assassinate Hitler (see Chapter 4, page 149) is a clear indication of the support given to him by the officer corps. Generals rarely had the courage to challenge him, for those who angered Hitler risked losing their command, and they shrank back from facing the Führer's rage. Nor would they disobey Hitler's orders, for as both head of state and commander of the armed forces Hitler was their superior, and the German High Command traditionally interpreted refusal to carry out a superior's commands as treason. In making Hitler solely accountable for both starting and losing the war—that is, in sidestepping their own complicity, the generals manufactured a myth, one that paralleled their avowed innocence regarding the war crimes committed in areas of occupied Soviet Union that were under their control.

But it is also true that as the war progressed and Germany's successes were fewer, several members of the German High Command came to view Hitler as "that corporal"—his rank in World War I—an untrained, meddling amateur, who had never commanded troops in the field and often relied more on intuition and impulse than sound military judgment. With his inflated sense of self-esteem, Hitler let his generals know that his combat experience in World War I made him more qualified to command than all their training in military schools. In addition to being impulsive, Hitler was also inflexible: he refused to change his mind once he had made a battlefield decision. If presented with evidence that contradicted his assumptions, he generally dismissed it. When reliable sources informed Hitler of the increasing number of Soviet tanks and soldiers, he flew into a furious rage and forbade his officers to present him with such "idiotic nonsense" that conflicted with his conviction that the Soviet Union was near collapse. He was particularly stubborn and furious when generals appealed for an orderly tactical retreat in order to save their troops from total destruction. Unwilling to abandon conquered territory for ideological reasons and the need to maintain his image, often Hitler's highest battlefield wisdom was to fight to the death, the "Stand or Die" order that prevented troops from escaping a certain trap and wasted tens of thousands of lives unnecessarily. German generals had the operational skill to lead a strategic withdrawal that could throw the enemy off balance and then to launch a surprise counterattack that could regain the initiative. But Hitler saw such retreats as cowardly. In order to comply with the Führer's rigid orders to stand fast, generals had to abandon flexibility and mobility, tactics at which they excelled. He denounced as cowards and defeatists those generals who questioned him, and he frequently removed them, including veteran commanders who had demonstrated their skills in several campaigns. Hitler also would never concede to having made an error of judgment. Always he attributed a military setback to his generals, whom he accused of incompetence, disloyalty, disobeying orders, and weakness in the face of the enemy.

Accounting for German success in the opening phases of World War II and in previous wars was the tradition of "flexible command" that granted senior commanders and junior officers considerable independence on the battlefield. After being told an operation's goal, they were given the responsibility of figuring out how to achieve this goal on the battlefield. Consequently, in World War II and previous wars, both generals and junior officers had excelled at improvisation and ingenuity. By scrapping this practice and insisting on personal loyalty and total obedience to all his orders, by constantly dismissing generals and often replacing them with commanders whose principal virtues were commitment to National Socialist ideology and an unwillingness to challenge his orders, and by making arbitrary and rash decisions that went against the advice of his senior generals, Hitler contributed significantly to Germany's eventual defeat.

The Momentum Changes

In the early stages of the war, Stalin was guilty of poor judgment for which the Red Army paid a heavy price. But, in contrast to Hitler, while still exercising hands-on leadership, Stalin did learn to rely more and more on the expertise of his professional commanders. This was a valuable lesson because these senior officers were becoming more adept at planning and carrying out complex large-scale operations that required a mastery of mechanized warfare. In the course of his dictatorial rule, Stalin had never hesitated to order the execution of people for daring to challenge him, but as the war progressed he did, at times, accept the judgment of his top military commanders even when he held a dissenting view. To strengthen the Red Army's professionalism, he relegated to a secondary role commanders who had been promoted largely for political reasons, and he kept commissars who were responsible for assuring ideological commitment to Communism and loyalty to Stalin from interfering with commanders. Less fearful of Stalin's purges, generals were willing to take the initiative.

After Kursk, the Wehrmacht lost the strategic initiative on the Eastern Front; it would never again launch a major offensive on Soviet territory. The days of the blitzkrieg, of rapid and decisive operations that enveloped and destroyed huge Soviet forces, were over. The Wehrmacht and its panzer armies were now on the defensive. The strategic initiative had passed to the Red Army, which possessed overwhelming superiority in men and weapons. Transitioning from defense to offense, the Red Army relentlessly hammered away at the German forces, which were greatly limited in both soldiers and arms. Any prospect of a German victory over the Soviet Union was gone. And with tens of thousands of deaths every month on the Eastern Front, the Wehrmacht faced an overwhelming replacement crisis that it tried to meet by conscripting teenagers and middle-aged men, including those badly needed in armaments plants, and then sending these inadequately trained recruits to the front.

As they retreated from Soviet soil, the Germans wreaked havoc, systematically burning villages, carrying off or killing livestock and horses, removing cartloads of food, and taking with them civilian hostages and forced laborers. In March 1944, a panzer corps of the German Ninth Army arranged for the deportation of able-bodied Belorussians to Germany. The elderly, the frail, mothers, and children were forced-marched to camps. As one prisoner reported after her liberation that same month, stragglers were "immediately finished off. One of the women had three small children. The youngest slipped in the mud, and a German soldier immediately shot him. When the other two turned round, frozen in terror, the soldier shot them as well. The mother let out a heart-rending cry—but this was cut short by the final bullet."[49] Soviet intelligence reported: "The camps were in the open fields—surrounded by barbed wire. Their approaches had been mined. There was no shelter at all, not even of the flimsiest kind. Those imprisoned inside it were forced to lie on the ground. Many of them—already weak—lost the ability to move, and lay unconscious in the mud. The prisoners were forbidden to collect brushwood to make fires—for the slightest breach of this rule the Germans would shoot people."[50]

Soviet soldiers were determined to make the Germans pay the price for the murder and mayhem they had inflicted on their country. Hardened by combat and much better led and armed, the Red Army was far superior to the forces that the German blitzkrieg had chewed up in 1941. Also, Nazi brutality in their homeland had infused Russian soldiers with an ardent patriotism, an all-consuming hatred for Germans, and a determination to win—attitudes that made for a more determined combat soldier. Moreover, with its great reservoir of manpower, the Red Army could withstand frequently appalling losses—Soviet generals were generally willing to accept high casualty rates—in attempts at a breakthrough. Effectively replacing losses in armaments, Soviet factories continued to supply the Red Army with what seemed to the Germans to be unlimited quantities of first-rate weapons and ammunition. In contrast, the Germans could only replace a limited proportion of their losses on the Eastern Front. For the rest of the war, the Wehrmacht was forced to defend an overextended Eastern Front with reduced armor and hurriedly trained replacements who had to face seasoned and hardened Red Army soldiers. Less than four months after the failure of the Kursk offensive, Goebbels wrote in his diary that "our eastern campaign has cost us 3,000,000 casualties—men killed, missing, or wounded.... At some point or other we simply must try to get out of this desperate bloodletting. Otherwise we are in danger of slowly bleeding to death in the East."[51]

Now the Germans were also forced to deploy large numbers of troops and equipment in Italy and Western Europe to check the Americans and British, who had just defeated them in North Africa. Trying desperately but unable to stave off a powerful and vengeful Red Army's inexorable drive to Berlin, the Wehrmacht would bleed to death, as Goebbels feared.

CHRONOLOGY

April 6, 1941	Germany attacks Yugoslavia and Greece
April 17, 1941	Yugoslavia signs armistice with Germany
April 30, 1941	Greece surrenders
June 1, 1941	Germany completes conquest of Crete
June 22, 1941	Germany invades the Soviet Union
July 3, 1941	Stalin delivers a stirring radio address to rally the Russian people
April 16, 1941	Stalin issues Order 270 that condemns as traitors those who surrender
September 4, 1941	Start of nine-hundred-day siege of Leningrad
September 19, 1941	Germany conquers Kiev
November 15, 1941	Germany renews its attack on Moscow
December 5, 1941	Red Army launches a counterattack on Moscow front, halting the German offensive against the capital
December 19, 1941	Hitler takes personal command of the Wehrmacht
June 28, 1942	Start of Operation Blue: Germans move toward the Caucasus and Stalingrad
April 23, 1942	Start of terror attacks on Stalingrad by the Luftwaffe
November 19, 1942	Start of Soviet counteroffensive at Stalingrad
January 23, 1943	Hitler rejects Paulus' appeal to surrender his trapped army
February 2, 1943	Sixth Army surrenders
July 5, 1943	Battle of Kursk begins
July 12, 1943	Tank battle at Prokhorovka
January 26, 1944	Red Army lifts German siege of Leningrad

NOTES

1. Adolf Hitler, *Mein Kampf*, trans. Ralph Manheim (Boston: Houghton Mifflin, 1943), 652–654.

2. *The Goebbels Diaries 1939–1941*, trans. and ed. Fred Taylor (New York: G. P. Putnam's Sons, 1983), 423.

3. Omer Bartov, *Hitler's Army: Soldiers, Nazis, and War in the Third Reich* (New York: Oxford, 1992), 131.

4. Albert Speer, *Inside the Third Reich*, trans. Richard and Clara Winstom (New York: Macmillan, 1970), 173.

5. *The Goebbels Diaries*, 414.

6. *Hitler's Table Talk, 1941–1944*, with preface and essay by H. R. Trevor-Roper, trans. Norman Cameron and R. H. Stevens (New York: Enigma Books, 2008), 33.

7. *Your Loyal and Loving Son: The Letters of Tank Gunner Karl Fuchs, 1937–1941*, trans. and ed. Horst Fuchs Richardson (Washington, DC: Brassey's, 2003), 118–120, 139.

8. Stephen G. Fritz, *Frontsoldaten: The German Soldier in World War II* (Lexington: The University Press of Kentucky, 1995), 197.

9. Antony Beevor, *Stalingrad: The Fateful Siege: 1942–1943* (New York: Penguin Books, 1998), 22.

10. James Lucas, *World War II through German Eyes* (London: Arms and Armour Press, 1987), 172.

11. Robert M. Citino, *Death of the Wehrmacht: The German Campaigns of 1942* (Lawrence: University of Kansas Press, 2007), 35.

12. Fedor von Bock, *The War Diary 1939–1945*, ed. Klaus Gilbert, trans. David Johnston (Atglen, PA: Schiffer Military History, 1996), 231.

13. Chris Bellamy, *Absolute War: Soviet Russia in the Second World War* (New York: Alfred A. Knopf, 2007), 152.

14. Hans von Luck, *Panzer Commander: The Memoirs of Colonel Hans von Luck* (New York: Dell Publishing, 1989), 70.

15. Else Wendel, *Hausfrau at War: A German Woman's Account of Life in Hitler's Reich* (Long Acre London: Odham's Press, 1957), 143.

16. Michael Jones, *The Retreat: Hitler's First Defeat* (London: John Murray Publishers, 2010), 17.

17. Catherine Merridale, *Ivan's War: Life and Death in the Red Army, 1939–1945* (New York: Henry Holt, 2006), 127.

18. *The Halder War Diary 1939–1942*, eds. Charles Burdick and Hans-Adolf Jacobsen (Novato, CA: Presidio, 1988), 506.

19. John Ellis, *Brutal Force: Allied Strategy and Tactics in the Second World War* (New York: Viking, 1990), 66.

20. Günther Blumentritt, "Moscow," in *The Fatal Decisions*, ed. Seymour Freidin and William Richardson, trans. Constantine Fitzgibbon (New York: Berkley, 1958), 68.

21. H. Liddell-Hart, *The German Generals Talk*, (New York: William Morrow, 1979), 179.

22. Beevor, *Stalingrad*, 33.

23. Andrew Nagorski, *The Greatest Battle: Stalin, Hitler, and the Desperate Struggle for Moscow That Changed the Course of World War II* (New York: Simon and Schuster, 2007), 71.

24. Citino, *Death of the Wehrmacht*, 43.

25. Jones, *The Retreat*, 98.

26. Excerpted in Desmond Flower and James Reeves, eds., *The War 1939–1945: A Documentary History* (New York: Da Capo Press, 1997), 222.

27. Jones, *The Retreat*, 144.

28. Rodric Braitwaite, *Moscow 1941: A City and Its People at War* (New York: Vintage Books, 2007), 291.

29. Jones, *The Retreat*, 195–196.

30. Gerd R. Ueberschär, "The Military Campaign," in *Hitler's War in the East A Critical Assessment*, ed. Rolf-Dieter Müller and G. R. Ueberschär, trans. Bruce D. Little (New York: Berghahn Books, 2002), 107.

31. Michael Jones, *Leningrad: State of Siege* (New York: Basic Books, 2008), 41.

32. Richard Overy, *Russia's War* (New York: Penguin Books, 1998), 107.

33. Jones, *Leningrad*, 7.

34. John Bastable, *Voices from Stalingrad* (Cincinnati, OH: David & Charles, 2006), 44.

35. Michael Jones, *Stalingrad: How the Red Army Survived the German Onslaught* (Philadelphia: Casemate, 2007), 68.

36. Fritz, *Frontsoldaten*, 44–45.

37. Aristotle A. Kallis, *Nazi Propaganda and the Second World War* (New York: Palgrave Macmillan, 2008), 126.

38. Richard Overy, *Why the Allies Won* (New York: W. W. Norton, 1995), 82.

39. Beevor, *Stalingrad*, 318.

40. Earle F. Ziemke, *Stalingrad to Berlin: The German Defeat in the East* (New York: Barnes & Noble Books, 1996), 78.

41. Excerpted in Max Domarus, ed., *The Essential Hitler: Speeches and Commentary* (Wauconda, IL: Bolchazy-Carducci Publishers, 2007), 768.

42. Kallis, *Nazi Propaganda and the Second World War*, 129.

43. Alexander Werth, *Russia at War 1941–1945* (New York: E. P. Dutton, 1964), 562–563.

44. Joachim Wieder, *Stalingrad: Memories and Reassessments*, trans. Helmut Bogler (London: Arms and Armour, 1993), 131.

45. F. W. von Mellenthin, *Panzer Battles*, trans. H. Betzler (Old Saybrook, CT: Konecky & Konecky / University of Oklahoma Press, 1956), 217.

46. David M. Glantz and Jonathan M. House, *The Battle of Kursk* (Lawrence: University Press of Kansas, 1999), 152.

47. Ronald Smelser and Edward J. Davies II, *The Myth of the Eastern Front: The Nazi-Soviet War in American Popular Culture* (New York: Cambridge University Press, 2008), 113.

48. French L. Maclean, *2000 Quotes from Hitler's 1000-Year Reich* (Atglen, PA: Schiffer Publishing, 2007), 270.

49. Michael Jones, *Total War: From Stalingrad to Berlin* (London: John Murray, 2011), 142.

50. Ibid., 142–143.

51. *The Goebbels Diaries, 1942*, trans. and ed. Louis P. Lochner (Garden City, NY: Doubleday, 1948), 493.

Chapter 4

✳

The Racial Empire: Exploitation, Enslavement, Extermination

B y 1942, Germany ruled virtually all of Europe from the Atlantic to deep into the Soviet Union. Some conquered territory was annexed outright; German officials administered other lands; in still other countries, the Germans ruled through local officials sympathetic to Nazism or willing to collaborate with the German occupiers. Over this vast empire, Adolf Hitler and his henchmen imposed a New Order designed to serve the interests of the "master race." In particular, they intended to exploit the natural resources, industries, agriculture, and labor supply of these countries and to establish military bases in key areas. A crucial objective of the New Order was a radical racial reordering of Europe—the subjugation, enslavement, and liquidation of people deemed to be racial inferiors. Eastern European Slavs, for example, were low on Hitler's racial hierarchy, as he informed intimates on August 6, 1942: "As for the ridiculous hundred million Slavs, we will mould the best of them to the shape that suits us, and we will isolate the rest of them in their own pigsties; and anyone who talks about cherishing the local inhabitant and civilizing him, goes straight off into a concentration camp!"[1] Unlike the Roman Empire, which conferred citizenship on many different nationalities, or the British Empire, which introduced many of the benefits of modern civilization to Asian and African lands—of course, there was a dark side to both Roman and British rule—the Nazi Empire brought, in varying degrees, repression, exploitation, enslavement, terror, and genocide to occupied lands.

In particular, the Slavic lands of the East would serve the German master race. Hitler regarded "our Eastern conquests ... as the foundations of our very existence." In these conquered territories, he said on April 11, 1942, "Our guiding principle must be that these people have but one justification for existence—to be of use to us economically. We must concentrate on extracting from these territories everything that it is possible to extract."[2] Other leading Nazis echoed this principle. Heinrich Himmler, head of the SS,* declared on October 23, 1943: "I do not care what happens to the Russians or the Czechs. I am interested in other people's prosperity or death from hunger only to the extent that these people can be used as slaves to our culture."[3] In March 1943, Erich Koch, *Reichskommissar* for the Ukraine, replicated Hitler's sentiments in a speech to party members: "We are a master race, which must remember that the lowliest German worker is racially and biologically a thousand times more valuable than the population here."[4] And for these ideologues, the Nazi master race had a historic mission to rid the world of Jews, a task that they pursued with dedication, efficiency, and a sycophantic desire to please their Führer.

Nazi indoctrination that Poles, Russians, and Jews were *Untermenschen*, a lower form of humanity, propelled the Germans to commit atrocities more than did the circumstances of a brutal war. SS-*Obergruppenführer* Erich von dem Bach-Zelewski, who was a witness for the prosecution at the Nuremberg trials after the war (a deal that saved him from being tried for war crimes), maintained that mass murder was the result of Nazi ideology and earlier racist thinking: "I am of the opinion, when for years, for decades, the doctrine is preached that the Slavic race is an inferior race, and the Jews are not even human, then such an explosion was inevitable."[5]

EXPLOITATION AND TERROR

The Germans systematically looted the countries they conquered, taking gold, art treasures, machinery, and food supplies back to Germany and exploiting the industrial and agricultural potential of these lands to aid the German war economy. Some foreign businesses and factories were confiscated by the German Reich, and others produced what the Germans demanded. In every country occupied by the Nazis, Jewish property and assets were "Aryanized"—that is, stolen in what one German historian calls "the most single-mindedly pursued campaign of murderous larceny in modern history."[6] German civilians acquired confiscated Jewish businesses; they lived in apartments, decorated their homes with the furniture, and wore the clothing taken from Jews deported to concentration camps.

---

*Formed in 1925 to guard Hitler, the SS grew into a powerful organization under Himmler's leadership. Regarded as an elite unit that best represented the master race, recruits were selected on the basis of loyalty to Hitler and National Socialist ideology and racial purity; that is, looking like the Aryan ideal and proving they had no Jewish ancestry. A principle duty of the SS was enforcing Nazi racial and anti-Semitic policies, including staffing the concentration camps. After the war, some SS murderers were put on trial for war crimes; many, however, escaped justice, some by fleeing to South America.

German war production depended heavily on the resources of occupied Europe. German soldiers fought with weapons produced in Czech factories. German tanks ran on oil delivered by Romania, Germany's ally. German factories and farms relied on labor forcibly deported from the new German empire. And Germany requisitioned food from the conquered regions, significantly reducing the quantity available for local civilian consumption.

Forced Labor

Forced laborers played an important part in Germany's war economy. With so many men in the service, Germany was desperately short of labor. The Nazis compelled conquered peoples to work on farms and factories in Germany. Replacing German factory workers with slave laborers enabled Germany to draft more men into the armed services as replacements for the large number of casualties suffered on the Eastern Front. As more men were drafted and the war economy moved into high gear, Albert Speer, Minister of Armaments and Munitions, kept demanding more workers, and he didn't seem to care how they were obtained and did precious little to ease their treatment, despite the image he presented after the war. By the autumn of 1944, more than seven million people from occupied lands, including prisoners of war compelled to work, toiled in Germany. They made up more than 20 percent of the workforce. The largest contingents came from Poland, the Soviet Union, and France.

About two hundred thousand foreigners had volunteered to work in Germany, lured by the promise of good wages and working conditions, but when news of their arduous toil spread, the number of volunteers declined considerably. Consequently, in some occupied lands the Germans rounded up people for transport to the Third Reich. It was not uncommon for Germans to shoot Poles, Russians, Ukrainians, and others who refused to report for deportation. Sometimes the Nazis seized their victims from churches, marketplaces, festivals, and villages in organized manhunts—"catching humans like dog catchers used to catch dogs," declared one Nazi official. Most conscripted labor came from the East, where officials ruthlessly imposed Nazi racial ideology. Because Slavs were low in the Nazis' racial hierarchy, they were generally treated far worse than Western Europeans. In Western Europe, public protests, including work stoppages and strikes, and thousands of men going into hiding or joining the resistance, forced the Nazis to modify the conscription levies; it was decided that in Western Europe people working in their native countries for firms producing for the German war economy would not be subject to conscription.

Jews penned in ghettos toiled relentlessly for the German war economy before they were sent to the death camps. So too did Jewish concentration camp inmates. At times, Jews deemed fit to work were not immediately sent to the gas chambers; their fate was "extermination through labor," as the Nazis called it.

By the end of 1944, some seven hundred thousand concentration camp inmates, both Jews and non-Jews, labored for their German masters in factories and on construction sites in German-occupied Europe. The SS Business Administration Main Office (WVHA) provided them. Those with the least chance of

survival toiled for large–scale industrial projects owned by the SS or in construct–
ing the underground sites where the V missiles were produced. Prisoners from
Dora–Mittelbau labor camp dug these tunnels. Because of the breakneck pace of
work deep underground and insufficient rations, and because of the abuse sadistic
guards inflicted on them, the life expectancy of the sixty thousand slave laborers
who dug these tunnels in the mountains was generally only a few months (pris–
oners who possessed certain needed skills were kept alive). Supervisors hanged
underperforming workers as an example, and the tunnel had to be constantly
cleared of the bodies of workers who had died of exhaustion and starvation.
Some thirty thousand laborers perished. Those too weak to work were sent to
the gas chambers at death camps. A French survivor describes the conditions
endured by these "missile slaves":

> In the beginning, they drilled, expanded and fitted out this tunnel
> almost without tools, with their bare hands. The weight of the machines
> was so great that the men, walking skeletons at the end of their strength,
> were often crushed to death beneath their burden. Ammonia dust burnt
> their lungs. The food was even insufficient for lesser forms of life…. The
> deportees only saw daylight once a week at the Sunday roll call…. There
> was no drinkable water. You lapped up liquid and mud as soon as the
> SS had their backs turned, for it was forbidden to drink "undrinkable"
> water…. No heat, no ventilation, not the smallest pail to wash in. As for
> latrines, they were barrels cut in half with planks laid across. Often, when
> the SS spotted a deportee sitting on the plank, they would … laugh, go
> up to him and roughly push him in the barrel. Irresistible! Never had
> these gentlemen laughed so much.[7]

In many German towns and cities, civilians could observe emaciated and
despondent forced laborers marching, at times at an indecent speed, from their
fenced compounds to toil for their German masters. The bureaucrats who
transported slave laborers to places where their labor was needed and those
who worked them beyond endurance were concerned only with efficiency.
When the brutalized "human material," as these slave laborers were called,
were no longer fit for work, they were often liquidated and replaced by other
concentration camp inmates or captives. If these Nazi bureaucrats ever
questioned the morality of their actions, they were certain that their efforts on
behalf of Hitler, National Socialism, and the German nation were necessary and
commendable; they believed in what they were doing and took pains to do their
job well.

Prisoners of war were included among the slave laborers, but mistreatment
deprived the Germans of this large labor pool. When the order was given to send
Soviet POWs to Germany, a camp commander wrote in his diary: "Now all the
POWs capable of work are to be sent to Germany to free up armaments workers
there for the front. Of the millions of prisoners only a few thousand are capable
of working. So unbelievably many have starved to death, many are ill with
typhus and the rest are so weak and pitiful that they can't work in this state."[8]
And the mistreatment continued when Soviet POWs were sent to labor in

Germany. It is estimated that about half of the Soviet POWs working in Germany did not survive toiling for their German masters.

Those forcibly moved to Germany from the East, particularly Soviet citizens and Poles, whom Nazi ideology classified as biological inferiors, were confined in one of thousands of special camps set up across the country; they slept on straw mattresses in wretched, unheated barracks, cellars, and barns, were poorly fed, and overworked. Many died of disease, hunger, and exhaustion. A German factory foreman observed: "The Russians' food consisted of a dirty, watery soup containing a few foul potatoes and a bit of cabbage. When the food containers were opened, the whole works stank. Our people often held their noses. The Russians were so hungry that they ... would let themselves be beaten half to death for a piece of bread and never murmur."[9] A German doctor recalled that the mattresses on which the people slept were full of lice and bugs. "Every day at least ten people were brought to me whose bodies were covered with bruises on account of the continual beatings with rubber tubes, steel switches, or sticks. Dead people often lay for two or three days until their bodies stank so badly that fellow prisoners ... buried them somewhere. The dishes out of which they ate were also used as toilets because they were too tired or too weak from hunger to get up and go outside."[10] Those no longer able to work—"useless mouths" they were labeled—were simply killed.

No doubt the wretched physical appearance of these millions of Poles and Russians, and their low status in the labor force, led many Germans to accept Nazi propaganda that depicted these people as racial inferiors—"human animals," Himmler called them. On the other hand, the SS Security Service (SD) reported that those who worked alongside Russians found them intelligent and quick to understand complex mechanical processes, an observation, said the report, which undermined the Nazi image of Russians. The authorities insisted that Germans refrain from having any social contact with Slavic "subhumans." To assure their identification, the letter "P" was sewn on the clothing of Polish workers; Russian workers wore a distinctive badge identifying them as Eastern laborers. Local police were always on the alert for what was considered racial defilement—Germans fraternizing with Slavs from the East—and ordinary citizens were encouraged to denounce to the police and the Gestapo (secret police) any of their neighbors having social contact with or showing sympathy for the forced laborers. Such people would be publicly humiliated, and the foreign workers could be sent to a concentration camp or hanged in public, particularly for a sexual encounter with a German. (There were, of course, cases where Poles and Russians working for German farm families or family-owned businesses were treated decently.) As Germany neared defeat, the SS and the Gestapo death squads, either fearing that forced laborers might turn on Germans or to fulfill their blood lust and racial fantasies, killed the laborers in large numbers throughout Germany.

Many of Germany's most prominent firms involved in the manufacturing of munitions and arms—Daimler-Benz, BMW, Volkswagen, I. G. Farben, Krupp—collaborated in the enslavement of foreign workers. They welcomed this gift of cheap labor. Any misgivings they might have had at the outset were overridden by the desperate need for labor for the war effort and the opportunity for profit. The exploitation of foreign laborers, the plundering of occupied lands, and the expropriation of Jewish property throughout Europe contributed to the home front's general well-being until the last year of the war.

Occupied Poland

The German administration in Norway, Denmark, Belgium, Holland, and France was less harsh than in occupied Poland and the Soviet Union, although in these Western countries the Nazis were capable of executing hostages in reprisal for partisan actions and of torturing suspected members of the resistance. And, of course, Jews were despoiled of their property and deported to death camps. From September to December 1939, before and immediately after Poland's surrender, the Wehrmacht, SS units, German police, and ethnic German militias engaged in a merciless campaign of destruction and mass shootings of civilians; they burned 531 Polish towns and villages and executed sixty-five thousand Poles and Jews in compliance with Hitler's order to treat "without pity or mercy, all men, women, and children of Polish descent or language."[11] An English woman observed one example of indiscriminate murder:

> The first victims of the campaign were a number of Boy Scouts, from twelve to sixteen years of age, who were set up in the market place against a wall and shot. No reason was given. A devoted priest who rushed to administer the last Sacrament was shot too…. A Pole said afterwards that the sight of those children lying dead was the most piteous of all the horrors he saw. That week the murders continued.[12]

This was the beginning of Hitler's racial war in which those designated as biologically inferior would serve the German master race.

Poland was partitioned between Germany and the Soviet Union. The Germans annexed western Poland and some other regions directly into the Third Reich. They intended to remove all Jews and the majority of Poles from this territory and settle it with ethnic Germans who were not living inside the Third Reich. To make way for these Aryan colonists, Nazis forcibly expelled hundreds of thousands from their homes and farms and transported them to the General Government, the region of Poland not annexed but occupied by Germany and administered as a colony under the brutal rule of Dr. Hans Frank.

The expellees were transported in the winter in unheated freight cars or open wagons to the General Government, where they were simply dumped. At times, the trains stood idle on the tracks for days causing thousands of deportees to freeze to death. The Germans confiscated the property and possessions of the expelled Poles, permitting them to take only a suitcase, some food, and a little money. The German police who evicted Mrs. J. K. told her "that not only must I be ready [in a few hours], but that the flat must be swept, the plates and dishes washed and the keys left in the cupboards so that the Germans who were to live in my house should have no trouble."[13] As a rule, the Germans allowed those Poles to stay who, upon a racial examination, appeared to have German blood; these people would undergo Germanization under the supervision of the SS and the German police. Those Poles who refused Germanization were often executed and their children sent to Germany to be raised as Germans.

After deporting many Poles and Jews, ethnic Germans from the Baltic States, eastern Poland under Soviet control, and the Tyrol region in northern Italy settled the annexed Polish territory. The Nazis also moved ethnic Germans living in the Soviet Union to the annexed Polish lands after the invasion of the Soviet Union. In all, 650,000 or more ethnic Germans were resettled in the incorporated Polish territory.

Poles were ranked just above Jews and Roma (Gypsies) in the Nazi racial hierarchy. Hitler set the tone. On October 10, 1939, Joseph Goebbels recorded in his diary:

> The Führer's verdict on the Poles is damning. More like animals than human beings, completely primitive, stupid, and amorphous. And a ruling class that is an unsatisfactory result of a mingling between the lower orders and an Aryan-master race. The Poles' dirtiness is unimaginable. Their capacity for intelligent judgment is absolutely nil…. The Führer has no intention of assimilating the Poles.[14]

Goebbels expressed similar sentiments. "The Poles understand only force. Moreover, they are so stupid that no rational argument has any effect on them. The fact is quite simply that Asia starts in Poland. The nation's civilization is not worth consideration."[15] Many German soldiers, indoctrinated in Nazi racial ideology, shared this contempt for Poles.

The Nazis imposed a ruthless racial policy on the Poles. In the territory incorporated into the Reich, they sent to concentration camps or executed potential organizers of a resistance movement—priests, aristocrats, the intellectual and political elite, and army officers. To eliminate Polish influence and eradicate all traces of Polish culture in the incorporated territory, the Nazis closed all Polish schools, libraries, theaters, and most churches; forbade Poles from holding professional positions and writers and journalists from practicing their craft; barred the Polish language from use in public; and destroyed Polish monuments. Germans who fraternized with Poles could face severe punishment; a pamphlet distributed to Germans instructed: "There are no decent Poles, just as there are no decent Jews."

In remarks to leading Nazis, on October 2, 1940, Hitler set guidelines for the Nazi administration of the General Government, the un-annexed but occupied regions of Poland:

> Under no circumstance should the Government General become a self-contained and uniform economic area producing all or some of the industrial articles needed by it; it must be a reservoir of manpower for us to perform the most menial jobs…. It is therefore completely in order for a large surplus of manpower to exist in the Government General so that every year there would be a supply of labour for the Reich….

> The Poles can only have one master, and that is the German; ...
> therefore all representatives of the Polish intelligentsia should be elimi-
> nated. This sounds harsh, but such are the laws of life. The Government
> General is a reservation for Poles, a huge Polish work camp.[16]

Hans Frank and his officials followed these guidelines. Polish factories produced what the Germans wanted, Polish businesses were expropriated, and Polish
resources, including farm animals and agricultural products, were requisitioned.
Poles were required to salute German officials and police and were beaten if they
did not salute. Food rations for Poles were set at a starvation level, because as
Robert Ley, head of the German Labor Front declared, "a lower race needs less
food."[17] Without the food smuggled in from the countryside, starvation in the
cities would have been rampant. Tens of thousands of Polish Catholics were sent
to concentration camps, and Poland's three million Jews were forced into ghettos
and then systematically exterminated. Seeking to eliminate Poland's "leadership
elements," Frank imprisoned thousands of members of the Polish elite. Thousands
more were shot. Poles who tried to help Jews and hostages in reprisal for
attacks on Germans were also executed, as were their families. Most schools
above the fourth grade, including universities and technical colleges, were shut
down. Heinrich Himmler insisted that it was sufficient for Polish children to
learn "simple arithmetic up to five hundred at the most; writing of one's name; a
doctrine that it is a divine law to obey the Germans and to be honest, industrious,
and good."[18] The occupiers seized Poland's cultural institutions—museums, art
galleries, libraries, theaters—and used them for their own purposes.

In November 1942, the Nazis began to categorize by racial characteristics
Poles in the Lublin area of the General Government. Those Poles who seemed
to possess desirable racial traits were removed to another Polish city where "racial
experts" evaluated them for possible Germanization. Polish sources estimate that
two hundred thousand Polish children who passed a selection test for what the
Germans defined as Aryan qualities—blue eyes, blond hair, a well-proportioned
head, good behavior, and superior intelligence—were taken from their parents,
guardians, and orphanages and deported to the Reich, where they were sent to
Nazi-led schools and institutions. Every effort was made to strip these youngsters
of their Polish identity and to transform them into Germans. The Nazi authorities forbade them to speak Polish, gave them German names, drafted them in
Nazi youth organizations, and placed them in German homes.

The Nazis conscripted some two million Poles to toil in industry and agriculture in Germany or to serve as domestics: most of them were seized in round
ups, sometimes as Poles were leaving church or the cinema; some of them
were prisoners of war. Polish farm workers forcibly brought to Germany were
barred from riding bicycles, going to church, participating in cultural events, or
using public transportation. Domestics were permitted to leave the house three
hours a week but could not attend church, dine in restaurants, or enter cinemas.
As with farm workers, engaging in sexual intercourse with a German could
mean death or transfer to a concentration camp. The Gestapo hung Polish farm
workers for infractions and required Poles in the area to witness the spectacle.

As war casualties mounted, the Germans in manhunts dragooned tens of thousands of Poles into the army as auxiliaries to do whatever was needed. Had the war been prolonged, it is possible that Poles, like the Jews, would have been subject to planned campaigns of systematic killings. Even without implementing a genocidal policy, the Nazis killed more than two million non-Jews in occupied Poland.

Occupied Soviet Union

The Germans were also ruthless toward the people of the Soviet Union. Three months before the invasion, Hitler told his commanders-in-chief, "This is a war of extermination.... Commanders must make the sacrifice of overcoming their personal scruples."[19] Hitler ordered that Soviet commissars, political officials attached to the Red Army, were not to be treated as prisoners of war but were to be immediately liquidated. A propaganda tract distributed to German soldiers said of the commissars: "We would insult the animals if we described these mostly Jewish men [of course, most were not Jews] as beasts. They are the embodiment of Satanic and insane hatred against the whole of noble Humanity."[20] German propaganda literature and broadcasts circulated among the troops and were promoted by junior officers. The propaganda portrayed the Russians as a lower and brutal form of humanity, a description that senior commanders sometimes endorsed. In an order to his men, Colonel-General Hermann Hoth declared, "Here in the east spiritually unbridgeable conceptions are fighting each other: German sense of honor and race; and a soldierly tradition of many centuries, against an Asiatic mode of thinking and primitive instincts, whipped up by a small group of Jewish intellectuals."[21] Five weeks after Operation Barbarossa began, Hitler told confidants his plans for the Soviet Union: "We'll take the southern part of the Ukraine, especially the Crimea, and make it an exclusively German colony. There'll be no harm in pushing out the population that's there now. The German colonist will be the soldier-peasant."[22] Three weeks later, he continued with this theme.

> This Russian desert, we shall populate it.... We'll take away its character of an Asiatic steppe, we'll Europeanize it.... We shan't settle in the Russian towns and we'll let them go to pieces without intervening. And above all no remorse on the subject! We're absolutely without obligation as far as these people are concerned.... [L]et them know enough to understand our highway signs, so that they won't get themselves run over by our vehicles. For them the word "liberty" means the right to wash on feast days.... There's only one duty: to Germanize this country by the immigration of Germans and to look upon the natives as Redskins.... In this business I shall go ahead, cold-bloodedly.[23]

Erich Koch, in charge of the Ukraine, told his subordinates: "Gentlemen: I am known as a brutal dog. Because of this reason I was appointed *Reichskommissar* of the Ukraine. Our task is to suck from the Ukraine all the goods we can get hold of, without consideration of the feeling or property of the Ukrainians. Gentlemen: I am expecting from you the utmost severity toward the native population."[24]

The treatment of prisoners of war accorded with Nazi ideology. Impacted by Nazi indoctrination that dehumanized the Russians, German soldiers frequently and indiscriminately shot prisoners. As columns of POWs were marched away from the front over great distances, guards barred civilians from giving the half-starved and wounded men food, and they routinely whipped and shot those who fell behind. POWs were herded into unsheltered holding pens where they lay under the open sky during rain and snow. Within a few weeks, many died of exposure, dysentery, typhus, and starvation. Political personnel and Jews were identified and immediately killed. Guards routinely brutalized prisoners on work details and flogged and shot civilians who tried to pass food through the camp fence. It was not uncommon for the wounded to beg guards to shoot them. The guards often complied. In all, the Germans took prisoner some 5.5 million Soviets, of whom more than 3.5 million perished, principally from starvation. Desperate POWs were driven to cannibalism. The prisoners of war were supervised not by the notorious SS who ran the extermination camps but by the regular army, the Wehrmacht, whose commanders made deliberate decisions to starve the prisoners. This was a notorious criminal act committed by a professional army. Some Wehrmacht officers and soldiers protested this inhumane treatment, but their protests had no effect. (In the opening stage of the war, it was not uncommon for Soviet soldiers to kill and mutilate prisoners. The Soviet government did not authorize these actions, though, and when Stalin realized that such cruelty spurred Germans to fight to the death, he instructed his troops to refrain from such atrocities. But as the war grew more brutal, Soviet soldiers and partisans often took savage revenge against German captives, particularly members of the SS.)

German armies were ordered to live off the land—that is, to plunder food from occupied Soviet territory and to send back to Germany a minimum of seven million tons of grain a year, taken principally from the Ukraine. Deprived of food reserves, thousands of Soviet civilians were condemned to starvation, as a German report produced seven weeks before the invasion predicted: "Thereby tens of millions of men will undoubtedly starve to death if we take away all we need from the country."[25] A significant reduction in the Soviet Union's population was desired by the Nazis, who intended to repopulate fertile agricultural regions with German colonists.

German soldiers, not just the SS, routinely abused innocent Soviet civilians: they stripped peasants of their winter clothing and boots before driving them into the freezing outdoors to die of cold and starvation, tore up cottages looking for hidden food, deported massive numbers of people for slave labor, burned tens of thousands of villages to the ground, and slaughtered large numbers of hostages in reprisal for partisan attacks. For every German killed, fifty to one hundred Soviet citizens were generally executed. Nazi ideology and the strains of battle turned German soldiers into heartless moral nihilists.

Recent studies, largely by German historians, dispel the myth that the Wehrmacht had "clean hands," that the Nazi leadership and the SS were solely responsible for war crimes. These studies reveal how committed many Wehrmacht officers were to Nazi ideological aims, how willing they were to propagate Nazi ideology among the troops, how ideologically devoted common soldiers were to Nazism, and how complicit both officers and rank-and-file soldiers were in war crimes, including the extermination of the Jews (see also Chapter 8, pages 307–310). Some commanders withheld from their troops the orders to kill immediately all Soviet political officials and issued injunctions to their troops warning against excesses. Some officers protested the behavior of Nazi special units that massacred Jews. Realizing that the brutal treatment of the population only fostered hostility and resistance and was detrimental to the German economy, some officers and administrators sought to modify Nazi policy in the occupied territory. In November 1941, a German official in the Ukraine described the consequences of German behavior: "In the last analysis only the Ukrainians can produce objects of economic value through their work. If we shoot the Jews, let the prisoners of war starve to death, allow much of the big city population to starve to death, we cannot answer the question: *Who will then produce economic assets here?*"[26]

THE HOLOCAUST: THE EXTERMINATION
OF EUROPEAN JEWRY

The Nazis carried out a program of extermination against the Sinti and Roma, commonly called Gypsies (which is now seen as a pejorative term). Originally from northern India, the Roma and Sinti migrated into Asia Minor and Europe in the Middle Ages. Although many became Christians, for centuries they were victims of prejudice and persecution by Europeans who disliked their itinerant ways and customs. Because they dressed differently and spoke a strange language, wherever they roamed these people were viewed as social outcasts, as thieves and beggars, a perception that persisted for centuries. Deeming Sinti and Roma living in Germany as asocial criminals, the Nazis placed many in concentration camps or, like German Jews, deported them to Poland. With the invasion of the Soviet Union, the Nazis moved from persecution to extermination. The same SS and police units that slaughtered Jews also rounded up and killed the Sinti and Roma. Those sent to the Auschwitz death camp or other concentration camps died of disease, hunger, and abuse or perished in the gas chambers alongside the Jews. And as with the Jews, German physicians used Roma as guinea pigs in medical experiments. And Croatians, Romanians, and other Eastern Europeans slaughtered Roma on their own initiative, just as they did the Jews. Some 220,000 Sinti and Roma were murdered in what survivors call the *Porajmos* (the Devouring).

As terrible as it was, the Nazis' liquidation of European Roma and Sinti was not as planned, systematic, or thorough as was the Holocaust, the destruction (*Shoah* in Hebrew) of European Jewry. Nor were the Roma an overriding concern for Nazis, whereas anti-Semitism was central to the Nazi worldview and the driving force of Hitler's life. Had the killing machinery specifically designed to annihilate Jews not already been in operation, the Roma would not have been targeted. The Germans waged a war of biological extermination against the Jews of Europe that required considerable organization and utilization of the nation's personnel and resources; for Nazi planners, administrators, and perpetrators, the "Final Solution of the Jewish Problem" required considerable ideological fanaticism and justification and personal dedication. Not to diminish the suffering of others, the Holocaust was a unique evil.

The SS Mentality

The task of implementing the Final Solution was given to Heinrich Himmler's SS, whose thinking about Jews was dominated by crude myths. The following tract issued by SS headquarters reveals SS sentiment.

> Just as night rises up against the day, just as light and darkness are eternal enemies, so the greatest enemy of world-dominating man is man himself. The sub-man—that creature which looks as though biologically it were of absolutely the same kind, endowed by Nature with hands, feet and a sort of brain, with eyes and mouth— is nevertheless a totally different, a fearful creature, is only an attempt at a human being, with a quasi-human face, yet in mind and spirit lower than any animal. Inside this being a cruel chaos of wild, unchecked passions: a nameless will to destruction, the most primitive lusts, the most undisguised vileness. A sub-man—nothing else! ... Never has the sub-man granted peace, never has he permitted rest.... To preserve himself he needed mud, he needed hell, but not the sun. And this underworld of sub-men found its leader: the eternal Jew.[27]

The SS adopted Hitler's visceral hatred of Jews, the irrational ideology on which this hatred rested, and the propaganda that propagated it. Nazi ideology held that Jews were not only the scum of humanity and biologically worthless but also they were evil and dangerous, a threat to Germany. Nazi propaganda repeatedly stressed that a Jewish conspiracy had instigated the war in order to destroy the German people; therefore, liquidating them was seen as an act of self-defense, a logical and appropriate preventive measure that was often expressed in biological terms. Himmler and his SS believed with Hitler that they were doing Germany and Europe a service by cleansing the Continent of a dangerous disease—Jews were often referred to as vermin and parasites. Hitler told the head of the SS that "the discovery of the Jewish virus is one of the greatest revolutions that has taken place in the world. The battle in which we are engaged today is of the same sort of battle waged during the last century by Pasteur and Koch. How many diseases have their origin in the Jewish virus! ... We shall regain our health only by eliminating the Jew."[28] British psychiatrist Henry V. Dicks, who interviewed members of the SS murder squads and concentration camp personnel after the war, concluded that "the grandiose delusional basis of the SS's mission," was to see themselves as "the chosen instrument of the saviours and cleansers of the world."[29] The SS saw themselves as high-minded idealists who were writing a glorious chapter in the history of Germany and for which posterity would one day be grateful. Few were faced with a moral dilemma, for they believed that killing the Jewish archenemy—every Jew, including infants and young children—was necessary to achieve a better future for Germany.

The liquidation of the Jews, a core element in Hitler's plan for the racial reordering of Europe, became an ideological priority as important as the acquisition of territory for German exploitation and colonization. (When it was that Hitler decided on the Jews' physical extermination rather than expulsion from Germany and the rest of Europe is a subject of historical debate.) Liquidation was pursued even when it interfered with needs of the military. The timetable of the extermination camps had to be met even if it deprived the Eastern Front of urgently needed skilled armaments workers and rolling stock to transport supplies. And, "as the fortunes of war turned against Germany," observes German historian Eberhard Jäckel, for Hitler and the SS, "the destruction of the Jews became National Socialism's gift to the world."[30]

As soon as the SS entered Poland, SS members began to abuse, humiliate, and murder Jews indiscriminately. In a sign of what was to come, a Wehrmacht officer noted: "[A] number of Jews were herded into a synagogue and forced to crawl among the pews, singing, while being beaten constantly by the SS with whips. They then were forced to drop their trousers in order to be beaten on their naked backsides. One Jew who soiled himself out of fear was forced to smear excrement in the faces of other Jews."[31] The Germans turned many synagogues into stables and latrines and burned others, destroyed sacred scrolls, and tore out the beards of pious Jews.

Mobile Death Squads

Special mobile killing squads of SS (the *Einsatzgruppen*) and police battalions followed the German army into Soviet territory, including Soviet-occupied Poland. Entering captured villages, towns, and cities, the killing squads rounded up Jewish men, women, and children and herded them to execution grounds, where they forced them to undress and then slaughtered them with machine guns, rifles, and pistols. The bodies fell into open pits that sometimes were piled high with thousands of victims, including some wounded, who would suffocate when the pit was filled with soil and sand. After the massacre, some movement from within the pit would cause the ground to heave for many hours; Ukrainian villagers today tell researchers that the ground would move for up to three days.* Miraculously, there are a handful of instances where a victim managed to claw past the corpses

---

*Sixty years later, Father Patrick Desbois journeyed to Ukrainian execution sites and interviewed elderly Ukrainian eyewitnesses to the massacres, including some who were requisitioned to dig pits and stamp on the bodies and cover them with sand in order to make room for the next batch of victims. Because of flowing blood and the smell of death, the Germans forced these villagers to cover the pits with sand and chlorine. Desbois's moving narrative personalizes and humanizes both the Jewish victims and the Ukrainian villagers who witnessed the mass killings, sometimes of neighbors and friends. See his account in *The Holocaust By Bullets* (New York: Palgrave MacMillan, 2008).

and through the earth to escape the death pit. But survival was rare; most perished. In September 1941, the SS murder squads slaughtered 33,761 Jews in two days of continuous shooting at Babi Yar, a ravine on the outskirts of Kiev.

Aided by Ukrainian, ethnic German, Lithuanian, and Latvian auxiliaries—who at times simply bludgeoned or axed their victims to death—along with contingents from the Romanian army, the Einsatzgruppen in these *Aktions* massacred some 1.3 million Jews in what was euphemistically described as "cleansing operations." The commanders kept meticulous records of each *Aktion*, boasted to Berlin of their success and, as instructed, kept Hitler informed of their activities. In February 1942, Karl Jäger, commander of Einsatzgruppen 3 reported that his unit had executed 138,272 people, all Jews except for 1,851 non-Jews (most likely many of them Communists). He broke the figures down this way: 48,252 men; 55,556 women; and 34,464 children. By the end of 1942, the Jewish population in German-occupied Soviet Union was largely liquidated.

Many Einsatzgruppen leaders were university graduates, several with doctorate degrees, but despite their education they believed that they were doing their endangered country a great service by annihilating an evil race of subhumans. They had been indoctrinated for years with Nazi biological racism. As such, they did not doubt Nazi propaganda, which linked Bolshevism with Jews and blamed the Jews for starting the war in order to destroy Germany and later for organizing a British, Soviet, and American alliance against Germany. Interrogated after the war, Robert Ley, head of the German Labor Front, expressed this irrational fear that governed the SS mentality: "We National Socialists … saw in the struggles, which now lie behind us, a war solely against the Jews—not against the French, English, Americans, or Russians. We believed that they were only the tools of the Jew…. We were on the defensive."[32] The SS agreed with the thoughts Goebbels expressed in his diary on March 27, 1942:

> A judgment is being visited upon the Jews that, while barbaric, is fully deserved by them. The prophecy which the Führer made about them for having brought on a new world war is beginning to come true in a most terrible manner. [On January 30, 1939, Hitler prophesized that if Jewish financiers succeed in starting a world war, "the result will be … the annihilation of the Jewish race in Europe."] One must not be sentimental in these matters. If we did not fight the Jews they would destroy us. It's a life-and-death struggle between the Aryan race and the Jewish bacillus.[33]

In the Nazi worldview, Germans were always victims defending themselves against enemies led by demonic Jews. In October 1941, a Nazi assassin in the Soviet city of Mahileu demonstrated this bizarre logic in a letter to his wife:

> During the first try, my hand trembled a bit as I shot…. By the tenth try I aimed calmly and shot surely at the many women, children, and infants. I kept in mind that I have two infants at home, whom these hordes would treat just the same, if not ten times worse. The death that we gave them was a beautiful quick death compared to the hellish torments of thousands and thousands in [Soviet] jails…. Infants flew great

United States Holocaust Memorial Museum, courtesy of Instytut Pamieci Narodowej

United States Holocaust Memorial Museum, courtesy of Instytut Pamieci Narodowej

German death squads methodically murder Soviet Jews; most of the victims in this *Aktion* were women and children.

arcs through the air, and we shot them to pieces in flight before their bodies fell into the pit and into the water.[34]

And still another justification for the killings quickly emerged: the Jews were all partisans who threatened German forces in conquered lands. This was only a myth; nevertheless, the executioners widely accepted it because they wanted to believe that their actions fulfilled a military need. In actuality, the liquidation of Jews served no military purpose, as Lieutenant Colonel Dr. Otto Bradfisch, who commanded an Einsatzgruppen unit, confessed at his trial in 1958. "The shooting of the Jews was not a matter of destroying elements that represented a threat to the fighting troops or to the pacification of the field of operations behind the lines; it was simply a matter of destroying Jews for the sake of destroying Jews."[35]

The SS murder units prided themselves on their ability to suppress all human feelings that might interfere with carrying out their orders, which virtually no one ever refused to obey. Helping them to do what they considered their duty was the conviction that the order to kill unarmed Jewish civilians, including women and children, made good sense because Germany was engaged in total war against the Jewish-Bolshevik enemy. The Jews' very existence, they were convinced, imperiled the realization of Hitler's goal of a new and better Europe based on a racial restructuring. The Einsatzgruppen proceeded with the slaughter routinely, expeditiously, and with a sense of accomplishment. On September 26, 1941, a German member of an antitank battalion recorded in his journal a conversation he had with a nineteen-year-old SS "killer commando." For two days, said the Einsatzkommando, Jews had to dig a series of trenches that could accommodate 250 people each. When the trenches were ready,

> everybody from baby to oldest senior had to strip naked. The first 250 have to step to the edge of the ditch, the throaty barking of 2 machine guns—the next ones are herded forward, they have to climb into the ditch and position the dead bodies nicely next to each other, no room must be wasted—the larger spaces are nicely fitted with the dead children—forward, forward, more than 1500 must fit! Then the machine guns rip the air again, here and there somebody moans, a short reshooting of the machine guns: next! And this continues through the evening. We have so little time, too many Jews inhabit this country!

Taken to an execution site by the young SS executioner, the soldier then observes that when "the one-thousand quota is filled, the heap of dead bodies is detonated and closed up. 'Well isn't that a great idea, the detonation?' asks the blond with the smiling boy-face."[36] At the end of an *Aktion*, the murder squads often celebrated with festive banquets, a tribute to a job well done.

Unlike the SS members, who were chosen for their ideological fervor, those who served in the liquidation squad Reserve Police Battalion 101, maintains Christopher Browning in *Ordinary Men* (1992), were simply ordinary middle-aged citizens of Hamburg; they had not evidenced any special National Socialist dedication or violence-prone character traits that would make them suitable for hunting and killing Jews. Rather, continues Browning, they engaged in mass murder in order not to appear weak in the eyes of their comrades and to be praised by their superiors for a job well done, attitudes fostered by an organizational culture. And although no member of the battalion was ever executed or severely punished for refusing to kill Jews—nor were any SS members—between 80 and 90 percent of the battalion became heartless and proficient murderers, even of children and infants. It would seem that Jew-hatred and anti-Bolshevism had at some point permeated their consciousness, that they were motivated by more than peer pressure, that the Nazis racial denigration of Jews and their identification with Communism along with the thrill of killing had psychologically transformed these police from ordinary men into willing executioners who felt malice or at least indifference toward their dehumanized Jewish victims. The photographs they took of battalion members playfully abusing and humiliating Jews while others in the unit laughed and smirked tell us how much they relished the limitless power they had over these helpless innocents and the pleasure they derived from killing them. Or they felt, as one wrote, that the slaughtered Jews "were not human beings but ape people."[37] They never saw their genocidal acts as criminal but as military duty, which is why they performed them exceptionally well.

For decades after the war, Germans insisted that the Final Solution was the work of a small group of criminals that stood apart from the army, which retained its honor. But several recent studies have shown that a substantial number of German soldiers were aware of the massacres; they heard about mass executions, witnessed them, or took part in them.

Wehrmacht commanders knew of the extermination of Jews, and several even sanctioned the extermination. They cooperated with grateful Einsatzgruppen commanders, providing them with transport, equipment, and lodging, and ordered Wehrmacht units to participate in what was called "Jew hunts" and "ghetto actions" that involved mass executions. General Eberhard Wildermuth gave the following statement, which the British secretly recorded during the war:*

> In carrying out the mass executions the SS did things which were unworthy of an officer and which every German officer should have refused to do, but I know of cases where officers did not refuse and *did* do them, those mass executions.... It would have been a very good thing politically if the German officers' corps were to say: "We dissociate ourselves in that way from these people," but the [SS] could immediately confront us and say: "But if you please, in this instance the German Hauptmann [Captain] So–and–so, or the German Oberst [Colonel] So-and-so did exactly the same thing as the SS."[38]

Some field commanders protested that these shootings were a stain on the German military's honor, but the High Command, submissive to Hitler, did nothing. Most commanders in occupied territory probably adopted the outlook of Colonel-General Ernst Busch, commander of the Sixteenth Army in Army Group North. In the autumn of 1941, from his hotel room in the Lithuanian city of Kovno, he could hear the gunfire that was massacring Lithuanian Jews but was not disturbed; he merely said, "Well I can't do anything about it; these

---

*Unknown to captured German senior staff officers, British intelligence installed listening devices in their meeting rooms. The recorded words of General Wildermuth and other generals implicate the Wehrmacht in the crimes committed in the East. These conversations provide remarkable insights into how some Wehrmacht generals felt about Jews, the SS, the conduct of the war, Hitler's leadership, and the July 20 conspiracy to assassinate Hitler.

are political matters which don't interest us, or rather they interest us but we shouldn't do anything. These things don't concern us."[39] But many commanders were more than just passive and indifferent. Politically indoctrinated with Nazi ideology, they worked together with the Einsatzgruppen. After the war, staff officers denied any knowledge of the extermination policy. However, evidence from their own files reveals that they knew that extermination was state policy, and they also knew that the Wehrmacht was helping the SS to implement this policy. On October 10, 1941, Field Marshal Walter von Reichenau told the Sixth Army:

> The main aim of the campaign against the Jewish-Bolshevist system is the complete destruction of its forces and the extermination of the Asiatic influence in the sphere of European culture.... In the eastern sphere the soldier is not simply a fighter according to the rules of war, but the supporter of a ruthless racial ideology and the avenger of all the bestialities which have been inflicted on the German nation.... For this reason, the soldiers must show full understanding of the need for the severe but just atonement being required of the Jewish subhumans.[40]

Von Reichenau gave the order for Ukrainian militiamen to kill ninety hungry, thirsty, terrified, and wailing Jewish children, some just toddlers, who had been locked in a house after their parents had been murdered a day earlier. And in the same month, General Hermann Hoth told his troops:

> Every sign of active or passive resistance or any sort of machinations on the part of Jewish-Bolshevik agitators are to be immediately and pitilessly exterminated.... These circles are the intellectual supports of Bolshevism, the bearers of its murderous organisation, the helpmates of the partisans. It is the same Jewish class of beings who have done so much damage to our own Fatherland by virtue of their activities against the nation and civilisation, and who promote anti-German tendencies throughout the world, and who will be the harbingers of revenge. Their extermination is a dictate of our own survival.[41]

In early October 1943, Himmler proudly told a meeting of high-ranking SS officers, "I also want to talk to you, quite frankly, on a very grave matter ... and we will never speak of it publicly. I mean ... the extermination of the Jewish race.... This is a page of glory in our history."[42] On January 26, 1944, he addressed several hundred generals, admirals, and general staff officers in which he declared that his SS had successfully completed Hitler's assignment: the Jewish problem no longer exists. An eyewitness tells us that upon hearing this, the assembled "generals and admirals sprang to their feet and broke into thunderous applause."[43]

Extermination Camps

In Poland, where some 3.3 million Jews lived, the Germans established ghettos in the larger cities. Jews from all over the country were crammed into these ghettos, which were sealed off from the rest of the population. There, the Jews worked as slave laborers for the German war machine. The German administration deliberately curtailed the food supply—369 calories per day in 1941—and tens of thousands of Jews died of malnutrition, disease, shootings, and beatings. In the ghettos, the Polish Jews struggled to maintain community life and to preserve their spirit. They established schools (forbidden by the German authorities), prayed together (also forbidden), organized social services, and kept hidden archives so that future ages would have a historical record of their ordeal.

The largest of the ghettos was in Warsaw, the Polish capital, where 450,000 Jews were confined in an area of about two square miles; a ten foot wall sealed them off from the rest of the Polish population, which the Germans considered the "Aryan side." Guards with attack dogs stood at the gates and killed anyone who tried to escape from the ghetto, including starving children desperately trying to smuggle food in from beyond the wall. As many as two hundred Jews died from starvation each day. For sport, the Germans beat and humiliated the ghetto inhabitants; some roamed the ghetto looking for random targets, including children, to improve their marksmanship.

In their resolve to liquidate all of Poland's Jews, the SS would not rely on the mobile death squads because mass killings posed problems. First, they were too public. Nazi leaders wanted to keep the Final Solution as secret as possible because they knew that the German people would not approve such mass murder. Second, the face-to-face killing of civilians, including women and children, could be hard on the psyche of the murder squad charged with carrying out such orders even when plied with liquor. Third, because of the amount of ammunition required to kill thousands of people, mass shootings were costly; they were also time-consuming. To overcome these problems, the Germans tried gas vans, which were not entirely satisfactory: they still involved close contact with the victims and, when fresh air came in through the door seals, it took too much time for the victims to die. They then built death camps with gas chambers that could kill hundreds of people impersonally, inexpensively, and in minutes.

Some 2.5 million to 3 million Jews were gassed in Nazi death factories built in Poland—Chelmno, Treblinka, Sobibor, Belzec, Majdanek, and Auschwitz-Birkenau, the largest and most notorious. Often, thousands of people a day were gassed in each camp. Jews from all over Europe were rounded up for "resettlement," they were told. Adolf Eichmann headed the Race and Resettlement Office that administered the deportation of Jews from Germany and the occupied countries. Eichmann conscientiously, obsessively, and efficiently performed his duty to send European Jews to the gas chambers. The victims dismissed rumors that the Germans were engaged in genocide. They simply could not believe that the Germans, with a reputation of being a highly civilized people, could sink to such evil. "Why did we not fight back?" a survivor asked, and answered: "I know why. Because we had faith in humanity. Because we did not really think that human beings were capable of committing such crimes."[44] (See Jewish resistance on pages 146–147.)

Jammed into sealed cattle cars, eighty or ninety to a car, Jews from all over Europe traveled sometimes for days without food or water, choking from the stench of vomit and excrement and shattered by the crying of children. Many died before the cattle cars reached their destination. Disgorged at the concentration camps, the Jews entered another planet, more grotesque than Dante's *Inferno*.

MAP 4.1 Main Deportation Centers

From all over Europe, Jews were rounded up, packed into trains—usually boxcars used for cattle—and deported to Auschwitz and its gas chambers.

Corpses were strewn all over the road; bodies were hanging from the barbed-wire fence; the sound of shots rang in the air continuously. Blazing flames shot into the sky; a giant smoke cloud ascended about them. Starving, emaciated human skeletons stumbled forward toward us, uttering incoherent sounds. They fell down right in front of our eyes gasping out their last breath. Here and there a hand tried to reach up, but when this happened an SS man came right away and stepped on it. Those who were merely exhausted were simply thrown on the dead pile…. Every night a truck came by, and all of them, dead or not, were thrown on it and taken to the crematory.[45]

Guards brandishing whips and with dogs at their side, often assisted by Nazi-trained Ukrainians, made sure the Jews unloaded from the cattle cars followed orders. SS doctors quickly inspected the new arrivals, "the freight," as they referred to them. Rudolf Höss, the commandant of Auschwitz described the procedure:

The "final solution" of the Jewish question meant the complete extermination of all Jews in Europe. I was ordered to establish extermination facilities at Auschwitz in June, 1941…. It took from three to fifteen minutes to kill people in the death chamber, depending upon climatic conditions. We knew when the people were dead because their screaming stopped. We usually waited about one-half hour before we opened the doors and removed the bodies. After the bodies were removed our special commandos took off the rings and extracted the gold from the teeth of the corpses…. The way we selected our victims was as follows…. Those who were fit to work were sent into the camp. Others were sent immediately to the extermination plants. Children of tender years were invariably exterminated since by reason of their youth they were unable to work…. We endeavored to fool the victims into thinking that they were to go through a delousing process. Of course, frequently they realized our true intentions, and we sometimes had riots and difficulties due to that fact. Very frequently women would hide their children under clothes, but of course when we found them we would send the children in to be exterminated.[46]

The naked bodies, covered with blood and excrement and intertwined with one another, were piled high to the ceiling. To make way for the next group, a squad of Jewish prisoners emptied the gas chambers of the corpses and removed gold teeth, which were carefully collected and shipped back to Germany for the war effort, along with the victims' hair (used for mattresses), eyeglasses, clothing, and jewelry.* Christian Wirth, the SS commandant of the Belzec death camp, bragged to an SS colonel while holding a can of gold teeth: "See for yourself the weight of that gold! You can't imagine what we find every day—currency, diamonds, gold."[47] Later, the bodies were burned in crematoriums specially constructed by J. A. Topf and Sons of Erfurt. The chimneys vomited black smoke, and the stench of burning flesh permeated the entire region. The killing process went on relentlessly. Between 1.1 million and 1.5 million people died in Auschwitz—90 percent of them Jews. Non-Jewish victims included Roma, political prisoners, and Soviet prisoners of war.

Auschwitz was more than a murder factory. It provided the German industrial giant I. G. Farben, which operated a synthetic rubber factory three miles from the extermination facilities, with slave laborers, principally Jews and Poles. In 1942, a member of the managing board of I. G. Farben wrote to another leading executive: "Our new friendship with the SS is proving very profitable."[48] The working pace at the factories and the ill treatment by guards were so brutal, reported a physician and inmate, that "while working many prisoners suddenly stretched out flat, turned blue, gasped for breath, and died like beasts."[49] Some twenty-five thousand Jews perished laboring for this corporate giant. And, of course, all I. G. Farben officials at the rubber factory knew of the gas chambers.

---

*Not infrequently, SS officers accumulated wealth by taking for themselves a proportion of Jewish possessions and the money received from business firms for providing slave laborers. After the war, they used these funds to escape to South America and to start a new life.

Auschwitz also allowed the SS, the elite of the master race, to shape and harden themselves according to the National Socialist creed. The SS relished their absolute power over the Jews, which they exercised with sadistic pleasure. A survivor recalls seeing SS men and women amuse themselves with pregnant inmates. The unfortunate women were "beaten with clubs and whips, torn by dogs, dragged by the hair, and kicked in the stomach with heavy German boots. Then, when they collapsed, they were thrown into the crematory—alive."[50] The SS devised numerous gruesome tortures that they took pleasure in inflicting on Jewish (and other) victims—placing inmates in boxes too small for them to stand, burning their genitals, having them torn to pieces by dogs, practicing knock-out blows on an inmate who was kept from falling, and so forth. Replacing their names with an identification number tattooed on their arms; systematically overworking, starving, beating, terrorizing, humiliating, and dehumanizing Jewish inmates; making them sleep sprawled all over one another in tiny cubicles: these were methods the SS deliberately employed to strip prisoners of all human dignity, to make them appear and behave as subhumans, and even to make them believe that they were subhuman, as National Socialist ideology asserted.

Many inmates went mad or committed suicide; some struggled desperately, defiantly, heroically to maintain their humanity. When prisoners became unfit for work, which generally happened within a few months because of exhaustion, starvation, disease, and beatings, they were sent to the gas chambers. This daily brutalization and humiliation of Jewish inmates produced a psychological distance between the SS and their victims. SS members could feel no sympathy for people who were frequently depicted as a lower form of humanity, repulsive lice and vermin who poisoned humanity. Tormenting and murdering Jews also reinforced the SS members' own sense of superiority and gratified their urge for power.

SS officers were ideologues committed to racist doctrines that they believed were supported by the laws of biology. A Jewish physician-inmate at Auschwitz asked one of the Nazi doctors who selected Jews for the gas chamber how he could reconcile extermination with the Hippocratic Oath he took to preserve life. The Nazi replied, "Of course I am a doctor and I want to preserve life. And out of respect for human life I would remove a gangrenous appendix from a diseased body. The Jew is the gangrenous appendix in the body of mankind."[51*] Most members of the SS were true believers, driven by a utopian vision of a new world order founded on a Social Darwinist fantasy of racial hierarchy. To realize this mythic vision of ultimate good, the Jews had to be destroyed because they were biological trash yet immensely evil, powerful, and dangerous enemies of the fatherland. Ridding the world of Jews was for the SS a sensible and justifiable policy.

---

*A remark uttered by a badly wounded SS sergeant in the last weeks of the war also reveals the SS mentality. When an American medic started to give him plasma, the sergeant asked in perfect English if the plasma contained any Jewish blood. When informed that Americans made no such distinction, he responded calmly, "I would rather die than have any Jewish blood in me." He had his wish. Stephen E. Ambrose, *The Victors: Eisenhower and His Boys—The Men of World War II* (New York: Simon and Schuster, 1998), 332.

The extermination process required assembly-line efficiency on the part of the SS who ran the death camps and the army of bureaucrats, transportation employees, town officials, local police, and others involved in rounding up and deporting the Jews. Many of these Germans and collaborators in occupied lands were ordinary people doing their duty as they had been trained, following orders the best way they knew how. Thus, as Konnilyn G. Feig observes, thousands of German railway workers "treated the Jewish cattle-car transports as a special business problem that they took pride in solving so well."[52] The German physicians who selected Jews for the gas chambers were concerned only with the technical problems and orderliness, observes Robert Jay Lifton. "Nazi doctors in Auschwitz … reduced everything to technique. As one of them said to me. 'Ethics was a word we never used in Auschwitz; we only focused on what worked.' The Nazi doctors were involved in a kind of absolute, almost diabolical pragmatism."[53] And those doctors and scientists who performed unspeakable medical experiments on Jews, including children, viewed their subjects as laboratory animals ("rabbits," they were called), as the following correspondence between an I. G. Farben plant and the commandant of Auschwitz testifies.

> In contemplation of experiments of a new soporific drug we would appreciate your procuring for us a number of women…. We propose to pay not more than 170 marks a head. If agreeable, we will take possession of the women. We need approximately 150…. Received the order of 150 women. Despite their emaciated condition, they were found satisfactory…. The tests were made. All subjects died. We shall contact you on the subject of a new load.[54]

The German industrialists whose foremen worked Jewish slave laborers to death considered only profits and cost-effectiveness in their operations. So too did the firms that built the gas chambers and the furnaces whose durability and performance they guaranteed. An eyewitness reported that engineers from Topf and Sons experimented with different combinations of corpses that would be burned in pits, deciding that "the most economical and fuel-saving procedure would be to burn the bodies of a well-nourished man and an emaciated woman or vice versa together with that of a child, because as the experiments had established, the dead would continue to burn without any further coke required."[55] It is likely that many executives who headed the German railways that deported Jews to the death camps, and the heads of German firms involved in the Holocaust, were motivated less by ideology and more by careerism and demonstrating their professional competence.

Höss, the commandant of Auschwitz who exemplified the bureaucratic mentality, noted that his gas chambers were more efficient than those at Treblinka because they could accommodate far more people. In mid-1944, killing more than three hundred thousand Hungarian Jews in less than two months created an assembly-line problem for Höss. He had to prod the manufacturers of Zyklon-B gas to speed up production and delivery. Because even the high-quality crematoriums that he had insisted on could not handle so many corpses, Höss resorted to burning pits, a technique that he had considered primitive and inefficient when he inspected the early death camps. The Germans' concern with efficiency and cost was extreme. For example, toddlers were taken from their mothers and thrown live into burning pits or mass graves in an effort to conserve ammunition or gas and to prevent slowing the pace from the time victims were ordered to undress until they were hurried into the chambers.

The Uniqueness of the Holocaust

Perhaps the vilest assault on human dignity ever conceived, Nazi extermination camps were the true legacy of National Socialism, and the SS were the true end product of National Socialist indoctrination and perverted idealism. When the war ended, the SS murderers and their German and non-German accomplices—many of whom never paid for their crimes—returned to families and jobs and resumed a normal life, free from remorse and untroubled by guilt. "The human ability to normalize the abnormal is frightening indeed," observed sociologist Rainer C. Baum.[56] Mass murderers need not be psychopaths. It is a "disturbing psychological truth," noted Robert Jay Lifton, that "ordinary people can commit demonic acts."[57]

There have been many massacres during the course of world history. And the Nazis murdered many non-Jews—particularly Roma, Poles, Russians, and Ukrainians in prisoner of war camps, concentration camps, and in reprisal for acts of resistance. What makes the Holocaust an unprecedented crime was the Nazis' determination to murder without exception every single Jew who came within their grasp, and the fanaticism, obsessiveness, ingenuity, cruelty, and systematic way—industrialized mass murder—with which they pursued this goal. The SS murdered Jews whose labor was needed for the war effort, and when Germany's military position had greatly deteriorated, the SS still diverted military personnel and railway cars to deport Jews to the death camps. As Germany's situation became progressively worse, notes Saul Friedländer, "no effort would be spared, no roundup deemed too insignificant in the final drive toward the complete extermination of European Jews."[58] Thus from May 15 to July 8, 1944, the Germans devoted considerable energies deporting to Auschwitz the last sizable European Jewish community within their reach. Despite military reversals, the Germans were still gripped by their genocidal mania, and in this last deportation they received help from the overly enthusiastic Hungarian police. Of the 437,000 Jewish deportees, 327,000 were gassed and 110,000 were selected for labor. Adolf Eichmann, always the dedicated bureaucrat, oversaw the operation to make sure it proceeded quickly and smoothly, an accomplishment that brought him great satisfaction.

Driven by National Socialist racist ideology, Nazi executioners performed their evil work with dedication, assembly-line precision, and moral indifference, if not moral fervor. It was a gruesome testament to human irrationality and wickedness. Using the technology and bureaucracy of a modern state, the Germans killed approximately 6 million Jews: two thirds of the Jewish population of Europe. Some 1.5 million of the murdered were children; almost 90 percent of Jewish children in German-occupied lands perished. Tens of thousands of entire families were wiped out without a trace. Centuries-old Jewish community life vanished, never to be restored. Burned into the soul of the Jewish people was a wound that could never entirely heal. For generations to come, Germans would be compelled to reflect on this most shameful period in their history. Written into the history of Western civilization was an episode that would forever cast doubt on the Enlightenment conception of human goodness, rationality, and the progress of civilization.

THE GERMAN PEOPLE AND THE HOLOCAUST

Germany

The response of Germans to the persecution of the Jews requires a nuanced assessment. For hard-core Nazis and rabid anti-Semites, the destruction of the Jewish racial enemy was a burning issue, particularly as the war on the Eastern Front descended deeper into barbarism. For the general German public, however, the Jewish question was not an overriding concern, although before and during the war it is more than likely that some Germans—or perhaps many, we will never know—supported the Nazis' exclusion of Jews from the life of the nation and favored their expulsion from Germany. However, knowing that the great majority of Germans would not support the mass murder of Jews, the Nazi leadership tried to keep the extermination process secret; nevertheless, a significant number of Germans were aware, for soldiers returning home from the Eastern Front told of Jews being rounded up and massacred by the thousands. Some carried photographs of the grisly executions. "Take care otherwise you'll go up the chimney" was a familiar expression that circulated widely throughout the country. One myth that German scholars have shattered is that Nazi crimes were committed by a small number of killers and very few people were involved or knew of them. German historian Ulrich Herbert responded forcefully to this distortion.

> [T]he number of those involved directly or indirectly in the National Socialist policy of murder reaches far—*very far*—beyond those who held the rifles or locked the gas chamber doors…. [T]he mass murder of Jews in the East was by no means secret. Too many officials of the German occupation administration, representatives of the party and government offices, members of police and Wehrmacht units, employees on economic staffs and in industrial ventures, from organizations such as the railroad and the labor department, were devoting their time and energy to … deporting, classifying, forcing into ghettos, recruiting for forced labor, and ultimately carrying out the murders themselves. From these groups knowledge, or suspicion, of mass murder spread rapidly. Anyone who has read how various German authorities and representatives of industries … haggled over 1,000 Jews here, 200 there, another 3,000 somewhere else—all in the implicit knowledge that those who could not work would be killed immediately, and those who could probably not much later—will surely view the notion of a secret plan for murder with some cynicism.[59]

Denying knowledge that Jews were suffering a terrible fate became a national lie both during and after the war. And yet it is true that many Germans who heard about the mass shootings of whole families, thousands of them, and thousands more being herded into gas chambers found it impossible to believe that it was actually happening. That their country was engaged in systematic killing on a vast scale seemed beyond the imagination, as it was for many Jewish victims. Moreover, if the rumors were indeed true, it was safer to block them out lest they arouse the suspicion of the authorities.

When the deportations—the program was called "resettlement"—of German Jews to Polish and Russian ghettos and then to concentration camps and to Baltic regions for immediate execution in death pits first started in 1941, there was not a ripple of protest; most Germans simply ignored them.* The plight of Jews, they reasoned, was not their concern. Others welcomed the chance to "liberate" Jewish apartments and acquire Jewish possessions, which were either given to them by the state to compensate for their losses due to bombings or were sold at auctions for low prices. (Often, Nazi officials just took what they wanted for themselves.) Or, swallowing Goebbels' relentless propaganda that Jews were responsible for the war and the British air raids (which in 1941 were still on a small scale), they convinced themselves that the deportees deserved this fate. As the Jews were assembling under guard for transport, some Germans watched with shame; others gathered to torment the deportees. There were also many Germans, their baser impulses and perverted idealism mobilized by the Nazis, who assisted with the deportation process, as Christopher R. Browning relates: "At the highest level the Finance Ministry, Foreign Office, and Transportation Ministry had all been eager participants. At the local level small-town mayors ensured that their handfuls of Jews were included, cleaning ladies collected overtime pay to conduct strip searches of female deportees, and the German Red Cross expressed profuse gratitude for the perishable foods of deported Jews turned over to its care for charitable distribution."[60] And Peter Fritzsche reminds us that "Germans were not merely spectators." After the first one thousand Jews were deported from Nuremberg on November 29, 1941, Fritzsche writes, "The Gestapo, their secretaries, and the cleaning ladies gathered together for a party. While a local tavern keeper served drinks, the group snacked on food pilfered from the evacuated Jews, raffled off items found in their stolen bags, and danced the polka to accordion music. Eleven Jews from this transport survived the Holocaust."[61] And more than a few Jews in hiding were reported to the authorities by people believing that they were dutifully serving the fatherland. The indictment of Eric A. Johnson seems inescapable:

[T]ens of thousands of ordinary Germans participated in the mass
murder of the Jews, many actively, many more passively. While some

---

*Even Jewish World War I heroes could not escape deportation. Helmuth James von Moltke, scion of a prominent German family, wrote to his wife about the suicide of a Jewish war hero: "Yesterday I said goodbye to a once famous lawyer who has the Iron Cross First Class and Second Class, the Order of the House of Hohenzollern, the Golden Badge for the Wounded, and who will kill himself with his wife today, because he is to be picked up tonight." Thousands of German Jews chose the same fate. Roger Moorhouse, *Berlin at War* (New York: Basic Books, 2010), 179.

rounded up Jews, guarded Jews, interrogated Jews, sentenced Jews, or placed Jews on trains, others clamored for their removal, denounced them to the authorities, liquidated their assets, pronounced them medically fit for transport, and arranged for their deportation in myriad ways. Much of this was done in the open in full view of a German population that came to be well informed about the ultimate fate of European Jewry well before the end of the war.[62]

And more than a few Germans benefited from the seizure of Jewish property. Martin Dean, who has done extensive research in the despoiling of the Jews in Germany and other countries, concluded:

> The deportations left a very large economic footprint. Many contractors and private individuals became involved; among those were property assessors, auction houses, trustees, estate agents, notaries, and transport companies. Hundreds of thousands of individuals benefited from the sale of cheap household items or the availability of apartments. The Nazis attempted to maintain a hierarchy of beneficiaries ranked according to the Party's racial and social priorities. However, rampant corruption ensured that Nazi potentates and hangers on, as well as police and finance personnel, secured the best items for themselves. The processing of property became a pivotal act in the destruction process, involving hundreds of thousands of ordinary Germans who thereby became complicit in the destruction of their Jewish neighbors.[63]

Before the war, most Germans looked away when the Nazis deprived Jews of citizenship, banned them from the civil service and professions, confiscated their property, and humiliated and degraded them with anti-Semitic legislation, insults, and physical abuse. Jews who managed to emigrate from Germany in the 1930s were devastated knowing that they were abandoned by their friends who had become Nazi sympathizers or did not consider it in their self-interest to fraternize with Jews. (Ironically, Christians who remained loyal to their Jewish friends and colleagues did them a "disservice" because such good behavior gave Jews hope about the future and discouraged them from emigrating while there was still a chance. As it turned out, most Jews who remained in Germany ultimately perished.) Germans continued to look away when Jews were rounded up and deported. Even when they knew that something dreadful was happening to the Jews, most Germans, including the clergy, remained indifferent to their fate. Only a small minority suffered moral torment for the victims and shame for the nation. As the war progressed, Germans had too many immediate worries to be concerned about Jews, and many were influenced by years of Nazi propaganda that consistently depicted Jews as Communists and fifth columnists, blamed them for causing the war in order to destroy Germany, and demonized them as an evil race, an alien *other* beyond the pale of caring. Moreover, showing compassion for Jews or aiding them was perceived as a traitorous act that could result in severe punishment.

This is not to say that the German people were afflicted with a genocidal mania to exterminate the Jews and were therefore collectively guilty for the

Holocaust. Or that a particularly malevolent form of Jew-hatred characterized historic German culture and society that led straight to Auschwitz, although, to be sure, deeply rooted anti-Jewish sentiments contributed to the behavior of both perpetrators and bystanders. Rather, the moral failing of ordinary Germans was their lack of concern and passive response first to the Nazis' abusing and denigrating fellow citizens who were Jewish and then to their deportation. This massive indifference and insensibility meant that the Nazis would face no public outcry of disapproval, no committed opposition that might have constrained them in their persecution of Jews. Because of protests by the public and clergy, the Nazis did stop their euthanasia policy of killing physically and mentally handicapped Germans. (But they later resumed the practice, although more surreptitiously.) When large numbers of German Catholics in Bavaria vigorously protested the Nazis' removal of crucifixes from school classrooms, Hitler acquiesced and ordered their reinstatement.

There was an incident where a large public protest did deter the Nazis from deporting Jews to the gas chambers. In February 1943, the Nazis moved to rid Berlin of all remaining Jews. The SS and the Gestapo swept some ten thousand Jews from factories, the streets, and their apartments to which they were confined in the Jewish quarter and prepared to deport them to Auschwitz. Included in the roundup were eighteen hundred Jewish men married to Christians; up to now, these men had been spared. In a spontaneous display of courage, wives, Christian relatives, and sympathizers crowded around the building where the men were held. For about a week, hundreds of leaderless people at different times—the total number of protesters may have been as many as six thousand—gathered each day at different times and loudly demanded the release of the men. Most of the protesters were the wives, and they were sometimes accompanied by children. The Gestapo set up machine guns and ordered the women to disperse. Displaying great courage, the women refused and shouted "murderer, murderer, murderer" at their husbands' jailers. Goebbels realized that he could not order the massacre or arrest of such a large throng of German women, and he wanted to stifle a display of public dissent that might provoke anti-Nazi demonstrations or encourage Germans to ask uncomfortable questions regarding the destination of the deportees. Thus in the end, he permitted the prisoners to return home. If more Germans, perhaps led by the clergy, had demonstrated such moral courage when the deportations started, it is possible that the hands of the SS and Gestapo would have been tied. But such courageous displays were extremely rare. As Wehrmacht commanding officers and soldiers turned a blind eye to the genocide in the East or cooperated with the SS, so too did German civilians when it came to the persecution and deportation of their fellow townspeople, neighbors, and even friends.

This is not to dismiss the efforts of small networks of brave and compassionate Germans who hid Jews from the Gestapo and those individuals who extended a kind gesture to a Jew. For example, when as a symbol of their degradation Jews were required to wear on their clothing a yellow Star of David with the word "Jude" centered, Goebbels complained: "People everywhere are showing sympathy for them. This nation is … full of all kinds of idiotic sentimentality."[64]

He also complained when the final roundup of Berlin's Jews scheduled for just one day was thwarted "owing to the shortsighted behavior of industrialists who warned the Jews in advance. In all, we failed to seize four thousand Jews."[65]

Not all Germans were insensitive to the plight of Jews. However, the German response to the Nazi evil illustrates how easily individual moral feeling can be deadened and how quickly civilized standards can collapse if people do not rally to defend them.

Austria

The behavior of Austrian Germans toward Jews was uniformly dreadful. For decades after the war, Austrians preserved the historical fiction that the *Anschluss* in 1938 made them Hitler's first victims. Manufactured by the Western Allies, Austrians eagerly adopted the myth of their nation's victimization. By insisting that the Germans annexed their country against their will, Austrians consciously overlooked the great joy with which they greeted the Nazis and their brutalizing and humiliating of Jewish citizens. The brutality was so intense that it shocked foreign observers and even Nazi officials, as Evan B. Bukey recently reminded us:

> On Friday 11 March 1938, tens of thousands of Viennese took to the streets bellowing "Down with the Jews! Heil Hitler! … For weeks gangs of Nazis roamed the streets of the city, desecrating synagogues, cleaning out department stores, and raiding apartments…. Surrounded by jeering mobs they dragged Jewish families from their homes "put scrubbing-brushes in their hands, splashed them with acid, and made them go down on their knees to scrub away for hours." … [T]he rebellious masses … stole cash, jewelry, furs, clothing and furniture; they tore Torah rolls from the synagogues; they forced Jewish patriarchs to scrub toilet bowls with prayer bands; they sheared the beards of rabbis with scissors and rusty knives…. Eyewitness accounts by diplomats, foreign correspondents, and Jewish survivors make it unmistakably clear … that ordinary Austrians were anything but indifferent to the fate of the Jews…. [E]normous crowds welcomed the Anschluss by joining Nazi gangs to attack, rob, and humiliate Jews…. Most Jews recalled … that nearly all Gentiles were hostile even those long regarded as friends.[66]

Anti-Semitic outrages continued in succeeding months, and on Kristallnacht in November the Viennese burned 42 synagogues, looted 4,038 Jewish shops, murdered 27 people, and severely injured 88. Traumatized by this orgy of violence and hatred, several hundred Jews committed suicide.

During the war, more than one million Austrians served in the German armed forces. Of those, a disproportionate number of them volunteered to join the SS and held key positions in the concentration camps. Austrian soldiers participated in numerous massacres of civilians in the Balkans, and Austrian authorities rounded up and deported Jews to the concentration camps. At Mauthausen concentration camp in Austria, 119,000 inmates perished from the brutal treatment. They were mainly political prisoners, Soviet POWs, and Jews.

For many years after the war, Austrians would not talk about what happened at the camp.

EUROPE, AMERICA, AND THE HOLOCAUST

Complicity

The Holocaust raises several questions that concern historians and both dismay and give hope to moralists. To what extent did people and governments in occupied Europe aid the Nazis in carrying out the Final Solution, as the Nazis called it? To what extent did they try to help the persecuted Jews? What was the position of the United States, Britain, and the Vatican? In discussing the behavior of a particular nation during the Holocaust, no simple generalization suffices. In every country where the native population committed dreadful outrages against Jews, there were also "righteous gentiles" who protected Jews, a topic discussed in the next section.

German historian Michael Wald raises a distressing issue. "[T]he Germans on their own," he says, "wouldn't have been able to carry out the murder of millions of European Jews."[67] In occupied lands they relied on the help of state authorities, local organizations (including police forces and transportation networks), and Jew haters and lackeys who sought material gain by betraying Jews to the German authorities. So involved were non-Germans in the Final Solution, says Berlin historian Götz Aly, that the Holocaust can be viewed as a "European project." Further, those who assisted the Nazis knew that a terrible fate awaited the deported Jews; knowledge of the mass murder of Jews was widespread throughout the Continent. Martin Dean, who studied the confiscation of Jewish property in the Nazi era, states: "One important consequence of recent research on Holocaust-era assets has been to dispel the myth that few people in Europe were aware of the disappearance of the Jews and their likely fate. The vast number of institutions, organizations, companies, and individuals mentioned in this book makes this point abundantly clear."[68] But it required Hitler's mania and Nazi presence and policy to initiate and sustain this murderous violence against Jews. Without the war, anti-Semitism would have been confined largely to social and professional discrimination and sporadic assaults and desecrations perpetrated by extreme nationalists and anti-Semites.

The motive of many of these participants in Jewish persecution was simply greed. Numerous public officials, business leaders, police, and others profited from the confiscation of Jewish businesses, homes, art objects, and other valuables. But there was also hatred and an ill-considered sense of duty. In Eastern European lands under Nazi control, there were instances where the local population massacred Jews with little or no urging from the Nazis. In virtually every country occupied by or allied to Nazi Germany, local officials and the police willingly participated in the confiscation of Jewish property and the rounding up, hunting down, and deportation of Jews to the camps, many of them also staffed with non-Germans. Throughout Europe, informers denounced Jews in hiding or trying to pass as Christians to the German authorities who paid the informers for their services. At times, they were turning in neighbors. Ridding their country of Jews was appealing to many people, including even some members of the clergy.

In Holland, Belgium, and France, railway bureaucracies and railway workers had the responsibility for getting the deportees to the German border, a task that they fulfilled efficiently. In the Netherlands, bureaucrats provided the German occupiers with a precise list of Jews. Between March and June 1943, a Dutch agency paid informers for tracking down more than 6,800 Jews. In 1944, a Dutch informer betrayed the teenage Anne Frank to the Nazis. Frank's sensitive record of her ordeal in hiding gained her international fame after the war, but she was only one of thousands of such Jews Dutch informers betrayed. Like most of the other betrayed Jews, Frank perished in a concentration camp (Bergen-Belsen). Dutch policemen, complying with Nazi orders, arrested Jews; Dutch security officers guarded them in the Westerbork transit camp; and Dutch railway personnel transported them to their death. Heinrich Himmler was pleased with the performance of Dutch police: "The new ... Dutch police do an excellent job in the Jewish question and arrest the Jews by the hundreds day and night. In doing so the only risk that occurs is the fact that in places some policemen step out of line and enrich themselves out of Jewish property."[69]

Welcoming the opportunity to rid their lands of Jews, many nationalists and anti-Semites in the Baltic countries and Ukraine eagerly helped the Nazis. In the summer of 1941, Ukrainian nationalists organized massacres in numerous cities, towns, and villages immediately after the German invasion. They saw themselves as avengers for the wrongs done to Ukrainians by Soviet Communists, whom they equated with Jews. To be sure, Ukrainians suffered greatly during the Nazi occupation: the Germans starved them, shot them, worked them to death, and burned their villages. Ukrainians served in large numbers in the Red Army and fought as partisans. Some even sheltered Jews, which would result in a death sentence if they were caught (about one hundred were). At the same time, with a long history of violent anti-Semitism—Ukrainian folk songs and legends glorified centuries-old massacres of Jews—Ukrainians murdered Jews independently of German orders or assistance. Killing Jews became a policy of some Ukrainian nationalists who wanted to break away from the Soviet Union as one leader indicated:

> Moscow and Jewry are Ukraine's greatest enemies and bearers of corruptive Bolshevik international ideas. Although I consider Moscow ... and not *Jewry*, to be the *main* and *decisive* enemy, I nonetheless fully appreciate the undeniably harmful and hostile role of the Jews, who are helping Moscow to enslave Ukraine. I therefore support the destruction of the Jews and the expedience of bringing German methods of exterminating Jewry to Ukraine, barring their assimilation and the like.[70]

In Ukrainian villages and cities, the Germans organized local police units to round up Jews, search for those in hiding, and assist the Einsatzgruppen in the killing fields. Informers were plenty, say survivors. The SS also recruited and trained Ukrainians to serve as guards in the extermination camps.[*]

In the Baltic states of Latvia, Lithuania, and Estonia, nationalists also viewed Jews as Communists who had welcomed the Soviet Union's invasion of their country. Latvian gangs initiated murderous pogroms against Jews without any German orders. "The greatest tragedy," stated a survivor, "was that these crimes were committed not by strange, invading forces, but by local Latvians, who knew their victims by their first names."[71]

In Lithuania, it was more of the same. A German officer reported seeing in the Lithuanian city of Kaunas a crowd cheering and clapping and mothers raising their children to get a better view of a blond man clubbing to death one Jew at a time as each, in silent submission, was sent by armed guards into the death courtyard. After some forty were bludgeoned to death, the assassin climbed on the heap of corpses and played his accordion while the crowd joined in singing the Lithuanian national anthem. In a particularly vicious pogrom in Kovno, Lithuanian thugs clubbed to death some fifteen hundred helpless Jews before the Germans occupied the city. Among the thousands of Lithuanians who participated in the murder of Jews were clergy and intelligentsia, not just common criminals.

Right-wing nationalist gangs proved so competent at murdering Jews, often with clubs and pickaxes, that the Germans organized them into police battalions that massacred in a more systematic way. Lithuanian police battalions, nationalist militias, and local individuals were responsible for murdering more than half of the country's 140,000 Jewish victims. In all, 96 percent of Lithuania's Jewish population ultimately perished. The SS recruited Latvians, Estonians, and Lithuanians to aid the Einsatzgruppen murder squads in the Soviet Union, and Balts also served as guards in the death camps.

In Slovakia, Croatia, Romania, and Hungary, countries allied to Nazi Germany, radical right-wing nationalists killed Jews on their own initiative— often taking delight in torturing their helpless victims—and the authorities helped the Nazis arrest and deport their Jewish citizens to the death camps. Croats killed the majority of Croatia's Jews. Germany's ally Romania murdered perhaps as many as three hundred thousand Jews, many of them in the Soviet Union. Only Germany killed more Jews. Marshal Ion Antonescu, leader of Romania, told his soldiers, "There has never been a more suitable time in our history to get rid of the Jews, and if necessary, you are to make use of machine

---

[*]After Ukraine gained its independence from the Soviet Union in 1991, it continued the Soviet practice of not revealing the Jewish identity of the victims of Nazi massacres. Yaroslav Hrytsak, a Ukrainian historian, notes that for the Ukrainians, "the Holocaust was and to a large extent remains one of the most silenced subjects in historical memories of Ukrainians." Omer Bartov, *Erased: Vanishing Traces of Jewish Galicia in Present-Day Ukraine* (Princeton, NJ: Princeton University Press, 2007), 90. One reason for this neglect of the Holocaust in contemporary Ukraine is the uncomfortable truth that some of the same Ukrainian nationalists who are regarded as heroic precursors of an independent Ukraine sided with the Nazis and participated in the massacre of Jews. One gets a different impression from Father Patrick Desbois's experience (see footnote, page 114). The Ukrainians he interviewed wanted to talk about their painful wartime memories of the murder of Jews, some of them neighbors and friends, and they expressed genuine sorrow and sympathy for the victims. Recently, with the end of the Soviet taboo on discussing the Holocaust, considerable knowledge has been gained regarding the valiant efforts of some Ukrainians to rescue Jews.

guns against them."[72] In a pogrom staged in Bucharest in January 1941, the Fascist Iron Guard killed at least 120 Jews, many of them taken to a slaughterhouse and butchered like animals.* In some eight weeks in 1944, Hungarian police, railway officials, and workers ably assisted the Nazis in deporting 438,000 Hungarian Jewish citizens to Auschwitz.[†]

In parts of Poland, particularly in the region where the Soviet occupiers were driven out by the Germans in 1941, Polish civilians abused and killed Jews. To Catholic Poles, many of them reared in a rabid anti-Semitic environment nurtured by clergy, Jews were traitors because they had welcomed the Soviet invasion of Poland in the hope that the Germans, who were already murdering Jews in western Poland, would not come in. For much of the war, right-wing Polish nationalists, anti-Semites, and criminals hunted down Jews in hiding and either killed them, blackmailed them, or denounced them to the German authorities.

The publication of Jan T. Gross's *Neighbors: The Destruction of the Jewish Community in Jedwabne* (2002) was a cause for much soul searching in Poland. On July 10, 1941, responding to a German order that all the Jews in the town of Jedwabne should be destroyed, Poles first mercilessly clubbed their Jewish neighbors, colleagues, and friends, including newborn babies, and then herded them into a barn that was doused with kerosene and lit. The Poles then searched Jewish homes for sick people and children, who were thrown into the smoldering coals. The Polish mayor and the town council coordinated the pogrom, which succeeded in burning alive the town's sixteen hundred Jews. Had the Germans not occupied the town, no massacre would have occurred, but on July 10, German participation was largely limited to taking pictures, says Gross. Compounding the tragedy of Polish-Jewish relations were the pogroms that occurred immediately after the war; it is estimated that Poles murdered some fifteen hundred to two thousand surviving Jews who tried to return to their former homes and rebuild their lives.[‡]

Vichy France actively assisted the Germans in deporting Jews to death camps. Without pressure from the Germans, the Vichy government, prodded by a powerful group of anti-Semites, enacted racial laws that legalized the seizure

---

*No doubt Antonescu, a viscous and violent anti-Semite, was a war criminal who ordered the plundering, massacre, and deportation of hundreds of thousands of Jews. But as the war turned against the Axis powers and he was pressured by the Romanian royal family, the diplomatic corps, and a Romanian archbishop, Antonescu resisted German demands to deport Romania's remaining Jews to Polish death camps. Because of his resistance, some 290,000 Jews survived the war.
[†]Miklos Horthy, leader of Hungary, had introduced anti-Semitic legislation before and during the war. However he resisted Hitler's demands to construct ghettos, require Jews to wear a yellow star, and deport them to the death camps. When German victory seemed unlikely, Horthy sought to break his alliance with the Third Reich, leading Hitler in March 1944 to threaten Horthy with a German invasion. Horthy immediately accepted the installation of a pro-Nazi government that agreed to deport Hungary's Jews to the death camps. But in July, responding to the pressure of Allied governments, the International Red Cross, and the Vatican, Horthy put a stop to the deportations. Although their ordeal was not over, several hundred thousand Hungarian Jews did survive.
[‡]Although only a few thousand Jews dwell in Poland today, there have been some anti-Semitic incidents. On the positive side, in recent years, there has been a reawakening of Jewish life in Poland, including exhibitions, festivals, and musical and theatrical performances. Poles are expressing considerable interest in the history and culture of Polish Jewry, including anti-Semitism, and increasingly the government, the church, intellectuals, and students are extending a hand of reconciliation and friendship to the Jewish people.

of Jewish property, prohibited the sale of books by Jewish authors, and dismissed Jews from the civil service, teaching, law, medicine, the arts, and the media. On July 16 and 17, 1942, in collaboration with the Gestapo, French police went house to house and rounded up thousands of foreign refugee Jews in Paris; in August, they seized thousands more in Vichy. The Jews were interned in concentration camps under French control in preparation for deportation in cattle cars mainly to Auschwitz. Drancy, the central internment camp, was guarded by French police, who along with French government officials, indigenous Fascist militias, and French railway executives and workers, assisted the Germans in deporting seventy-five thousand Jews—including eight thousand children under the age of thirteen—to Auschwitz; only twenty-five hundred survived. French railway men never interfered with the smooth flow of the special trains used to deport Jews, and without the assistance of the French police and the national railway the Germans could not have deported as many Jews as they did. Although willing to cooperate with the Nazis in sending refugee Jews to concentration camps, at first the Vichy authorities did resist Nazi efforts to deport Jews who were long-standing French citizens. However, when the Germans occupied Vichy in late 1942, no differentiation was made between foreign- and native-born Jews. Auschwitz was the destination for all Jews.

After the war, there was little inclination for the various occupied countries and neutral Switzerland, which had turned away many Jewish refugees seeking asylum, to examine their behavior toward Jews during the Nazi years. Thus for decades, France simply buried its collaboration with the Nazis in the Holocaust; its role in the extermination of Jews was a taboo subject. Some fifty years later, several countries began to look at the past more honestly. For example, French and Austrian officials acknowledged that their citizens had committed criminal acts against Jews in their lands, and French and Austrian Catholic bishops apologized for their moral failures. In 1995, the French government officially recognized Vichy's responsibility in the deportation process, and in 2010 the director of France's national railway, the SNCF, expressed the company's "profound sorrow and regret for the consequences of its act" in deporting Jews. The apology, the first ever and some sixty-five years after the war, came after lawmakers in Florida and California moved to block SNCF from obtaining contracts to build high-speed trains in their states until it admitted its part in the Holocaust.

Righteous Gentiles

Undoubtedly, the Germans had considerable assistance carrying out the Final Solution from people in the lands under their control. But in every country there were also people of conscience—a small minority to be sure—who, at the risk of their own lives, tried to help Jews by providing false documents and by hiding them in their own homes, in safe houses, and in convents and monasteries. In Israel, Yad Vashem, The Holocaust Martyrs' and Heroes' Remembrance Authority, lists 22,211 Righteous Gentiles who saved Jews during the war, and the list continues to grow. Most of them are Christians from German-occupied lands, including 6,066 from Poland, 4,863 from Holland, 2,833 from

France, and 2,213 from Ukraine. Some of these saviors of Jews were captured and executed by the Nazis. Following is a small sample of the actions taken by courageous people who resisted Nazi efforts to exterminate Europe's Jews.

In February 1941, several hundred thousand people participated in a general strike in Amsterdam, Holland, partly to protest Nazi measures against Jews. The Nazis supressed the strike and executed some of the participants. Networks of Dutch citizens hid as many as forty thousand Jews, many of them children, although between one-quarter and one-half, including Anne Frank, were eventually found and deported. Belgian resistance fighters stopped a train transporting Jews to a death camp, enabling some of the victims to escape. The Danish resistance smuggled into neutral Sweden almost all of Denmark's eight thousand Jews just before they were to be deported to the death camps. Pressured by Hitler, Mussolini's Fascist government imposed harsh legislation on Jews, but Italian authorities were often lax in enforcing it. In parts of Yugoslavia, Greece, Albania, and Italian-occupied France, Italian army commanders resisted German demands to deport Jews. When the Germans occupied Italy in September 1943, they immediately began transporting Italy's small and ancient Jewish community to the death camps. Although Italian police serving the German puppet government hunted Jews down, some police informers warned them. Many Jews fled and were hidden by compassionate fellow Italians, including the clergy; much to the anger of their German ally and later occupier, most Italians were not receptive to Nazi racist policies and were uncooperative in carrying them out. Largely because of the aid fellow Italians provided, 80 percent of Italian Jews survived.*

Risking death, French citizens, including Catholic clergy, hid Jews and arranged for escape routes to Spain and Switzerland. The Huguenot (Protestant) village Le Chambon-sur-Lignon sheltered five thousand Jews fleeing the Nazis, and French Resistance groups also helped. Revolted by the inhumanity of the roundups and deportations, particularly of young children whose parents had already been deported, French people, including some police and their office staff, warned Jews of an impending roundup, giving them an opportunity to flee. Their help enabled some 250,000 Jews to survive.

In Hungary, Swedish official Raoul Wallenberg set up safe houses in Budapest and provided Swedish passports for more than thirty thousand Jews destined for deportation to Auschwitz. In 1943 in Bulgaria, strong resistance from parliamentarians and the Holy Synod, the leadership of the Bulgarian Orthodox church, forced the government to cancel the deportation of Bulgarian Jews to Polish death camps. At the risk of their own lives, some Ukrainians hid Jews from the Nazis. Monasteries and convents also provided Jews with sanctuary and forged documents. The Nazis executed more than one hundred Ukrainians for aiding Jews.

The Polish underground radio informed the Polish government in exile in London of the massacres carried out by the Germans, and the information was

---

*Dating back to the Roman Empire, the small Jewish community was well integrated into Italian society. It was virtually indistinguishable from other Italian communities. Numerous Jewish generals and junior officers had served in the Italian army during World War I and more than a few Jews had been members of Mussolini's early Fascist movement. For the most part, Italians were not afflicted with anti-Semitism.

relayed to the Allied governments and to the press. Officials of the Polish government in exile pressed both London and Washington to institute bombing reprisals against Germany and to drop leaflets telling the German people that the bombing raids were punishment for the crimes committed in their name against the Jews. In the Warsaw Ghetto Uprising (see page 147), the Polish Home Army provided Jewish resisters with some arms—a mere token, lamented the desperate Jewish fighters—and when the end was near helped smuggle survivors to safety. In its underground press, The Council for Aid to the Jews (Zegota), admittedly a small group in a vast sea of indifference and even hostility, condemned Poles who blackmailed Jews on the run or informed on them to the Germans and warned of retribution; indeed, several hundred were executed by the Polish resistance. These actions did deter blackmailers and informers. Zegota forged documents that enabled thousands of Jews to hide their identity; smuggled Jews, particularly children, out of the walled ghettos where the Nazis confined them; and tried to get food to the starving Jews behind the walls. Rescuing Jews took great courage because the Nazi authorities executed Poles and their families, and sometimes their neighbors, for aiding Jews. Martin Gilbert recalls the events of December 6, 1942:

> at Stary Ciepielow the SS locked thirteen Poles—men, women and children—into a cottage and ten more into a barn and then burned them alive on suspicion of harbouring Jews.... In the village of Bialka, ... Jews found refuge with the villagers. But on ... December 7, the Germans entered the village and shot ninety-six Poles for helping Jews. Three days later, in the village of Wola Przybyslawska, seven Poles were executed by the Germans for hiding Jews.[73]*

Rescue efforts also took planning and the cooperation of dedicated people, for it often required an entire network to hide a single Jew.

A legendary heroine was Irena Sendler, who worked for Zegota. Assisted by some thirty volunteers, she secreted some twenty-five hundred Jewish children out of the Warsaw Ghetto. Sometimes they were sedated and placed in coffins or potato sacks. They would be taken to a church, given forged papers indicating that they were Catholic, and then placed in a Catholic home, convent, or orphanage. Sendler kept a record of each child so his or her Jewish identity could be restored after the war.

---

*Captured Poles engaged in resistance activity had a better chance of surviving than did a Pole caught sheltering a Jew. Polish resisters would be sent to a concentration camp, no doubt after being tortured; their spouses were often arrested and interrogated but then released, and their children were generally not harmed. Poles caught hiding Jews, however, were almost always executed along with their spouses and children. Rescuers had to be wary not only of the German police but also of fellow Poles, including their neighbors, many of whom had a pathological hatred of Jews. It was not uncommon for ordinary Poles, not just criminal extortionists, to report hidden Jews and their protectors to the authorities. In February 1946, about a year after the Nazis had been driven from Poland, a U.S. embassy official in Krakow commented on the plight of saved Jewish children: "Until this very day those children are kept in the garret of the house hidden away from the neighbors for fear that the neighbors discover that the Christian family saved the Jewish children and vent their vengeance on the whole family, and this one year after liberation." Michael C. Steinlauf, "Poland and the Memory of the Holocaust," in *Humanity at the Limit: The Impact of the Holocaust Experience on Jews and Christians,* ed. Michael A. Signer (Bloomington: Indiana University Press, 2000), 309.

Germans are included among the Righteous Gentiles as well. In several cities, sympathetic Germans helped Jews hide from the Gestapo, a risky undertaking because informers were everywhere. Before the war when Jewish emigration was possible, Ernst Leitz II, who manufactured the famous Leica camera, deliberately hired Jews from the town of Wetzlar, where his optics factory was located, so that he could place them in show rooms and sales offices in France, Britain, Hong Kong, and the United States, where they were housed and trained at company expense. It is estimated that several hundred Jews, counting employees and their families, were saved by the "Leica Freedom Train." Oskar Schindler was a German businessman who employed more than one thousand Jews in his factory in Poland and shielded them from extermination throughout the war. Through bribes and charm, he managed to convince the SS that he needed his Jewish laborers to produce items vital for the war effort.

Bombing of Auschwitz Controversy

Both the United States and Britain, which knew very early about Nazi genocide against the Jews, have been criticized for doing so little to help the victims. Critics argue that if Britain and the United States had not virtually closed their doors to persecuted Jews in the 1930s—a policy largely motivated by anti-Semitism—tens of thousands of Jews would have been saved. However, at that time Jews were facing persecution, not genocide.

Certainly, say the critics, from bases in Italy the United States could have bombed the railways leading to Auschwitz and its gas chambers in which more than three hundred thousand Hungarian Jews were gassed in the late spring and early summer of 1944. The United States had bombed I. G. Farben's synthetic oil facilities less than five miles away; that no attempt was made to destroy the gas chambers is attributed to the Allies' indifference to the fate of Europe's Jews.

Those who reject this view argue that German air defenses in the area would have shot down numerous American planes with their crews. These were resources that could not be spared immediately before and after D-Day when the American air force was raiding German fuel installations, the French transportation system, and German V-1 missile sites. They argue further that because there was little chance of hitting just the gas chambers, which were a small target, the bombs would have killed many inmates in the camp—heads of major Jewish organizations took the same position. Moreover, if the gas chambers had been destroyed, the Germans would have reverted to older methods to kill their victims. No doubt, slave laborers would have quickly repaired the bombed railway lines from Budapest to Auschwitz. In the interim, the Germans would have simply machine-gunned the Hungarian Jews as they had done in the Soviet Union or kept the victims in the cattle cars or in the departure centers where they would have perished from lack of food and water. For those holding this view, the bombing of Auschwitz would have been no more than a symbolic act. Moreover, Britain and the United States, which were locked in a total war against a brutal and determined enemy, had their own pressing concerns that precluded diverting precious resources for aiding Jews. Bombing Auschwitz, which served no military purpose, was seen as a diversion. If the Jews were given any thought, it was maintained that a speedy end to the conflict was the best way to help them. Furthermore, neither the United States nor Britain wanted to give the impression to their citizens, a considerable number of whom harbored anti-Semitic feelings, that they were fighting a costly war to save Jews.

The Vatican's Policy of Silence

The Vatican has been criticized for not speaking out forcefully while Jews were being rounded up, deported, and gassed. Throughout the war, the Vatican, in line with its policy of strict neutrality, deliberately remained silent even after receiving reports from its nuncios in several lands and Allied diplomats that Jews were being systematically murdered. Pope Pius XII told the French ambassador to the Vatican that he had no objection to the anti-Semitic legislation introduced by the Vichy government as long as it was implemented humanely. And because he promoted Catholicism, the pope refused to cut diplomatic ties with or denounce Croatian dictator Ante Pavelić's regime, which tortured and massacred Orthodox Serbs, Roma, and Jews. Despite knowing of these mass murders, the Vatican failed to intervene or take action against the priests and monks who had participated in the slaughter. Nor did Pius XII threaten with excommunication Hitler, Goebbels, and other leading Nazis who were Catholic. Indeed, no Catholic was excommunicated during or after the war for their involvement in the mass murder of European Jewry. In several countries individual Catholics and Catholic institutions rescued Jews. But they were acting largely on their own; there is no evidence that Pius XII was active in organizing rescue missions either in Italy or beyond.

In refraining from publicly condemning Nazi genocide, it is argued, Pius XII failed to exercise his moral obligation. Had the Vatican's disclosure of the death camps with their gas chambers been broadcast over the Vatican radio and widely circulated in the Catholic press, and had Pope Pius XII designated the murder of Jews a grave sin, more Catholics might have stopped collaborating with the Nazis or assisted their Jewish countrymen. And Jews, who then would have had no doubt about German intentions, might have reacted less passively to Nazi roundups and deportations. When the Germans planned to round up the Jews of Rome for deportation to Auschwitz and the gas chambers, Pius XII sent the victims no warning message. And on the day of the roundup, virtually in front of the pope's window, he resisted pleas from Catholic officials to demonstrate the church's revulsion. The relieved German ambassador to the Holy See wrote Berlin that the pope, although pressured to voice a "demonstrative censure of the deportation of the Jews of Rome ... has nonetheless done everything possible even in this delicate matter in order not to strain relations with the German government and the German authorities in Rome."[74] What would the Nazis have done had Pope Pius XII, in full regalia and accompanied by church officials, appeared at the railroad station as more than one thousand Roman Jews were being herded into boxcars? What repercussions would this have had throughout Europe?

It has been suggested that the reason for the pope's silence is that he was a cautious diplomat who wanted to preserve the Vatican's neutrality lest the Nazis punish the church and Catholics in Germany and other countries. It has been suggested that regarding Communism as a greater threat to Christian Europe than Nazism, the pope did not want to create a problem for German Catholic soldiers who were fighting to destroy the godless Soviet regime.

Defenders of the Vatican point out that papal officials and Catholic bishops did try to help. They argue that working behind the scenes was more effective than public outcries because such outcries would have brought the wrath of the Nazis down on the church and would have intensified persecution of converts and Jews married to Catholics. For example, in 1942, Dutch bishops issued a pastoral letter denouncing the Germans for their mistreatment of Jews. The Germans responded by hunting down converted Jews in monasteries and convents and shipping them to Auschwitz.

There are numerous examples of the church extending aid to Jews. In 1942, papal nuncios protested Slovakia's plan to deport eighty thousand Jews to their death. Although a priest, Jozef Tiso, headed the government, the Vatican's intercession had little effect. In France, when children whose parents had already been deported were shoved into freight cars headed for Auschwitz, the papal nuncio voiced a strong protest. In Hungary, the papal nuncio set up safe houses for Jews, and Pius XII was the first head of state to urge regent Miklós Horthy not to give in to the Nazis who demanded that he repeal his earlier decision to discontinue deportation of Jews, a contributing factor in the survival of 40 percent of the Hungarian Jewish population. The Vatican issued false documents enabling Jews to pass as Christians, and almost everywhere in occupied Europe, thousands of Jews found refuge in Catholic monasteries, convents, and parish houses, many of them in Rome. The Vatican itself provided sanctuary for hundreds of Jews, as did the pope's summer residence at Castel Gandolfo. And throughout Europe, monks, nuns, and priests were executed or imprisoned for harboring Jews.

The question of Pius XII's policy during the Holocaust will not be resolved until the Vatican unseals its wartime records. So far, only select documents have been released.

COLLABORATION WITH THE NAZIS IN

OCCUPIED EUROPE

Each occupied country had its collaborators who welcomed the demise of democracy, saw Hitler as Europe's best defense against Communism, approved of Nazi measures against Jews, and profited from the sale of war supplies and the confiscation of Jewish property. These collaborators included government officials, business elites, police, right-wing intellectuals, and Nazi sympathizers. Particularly enthusiastic about serving the Third Reich was the German minority living in Nazi-occupied countries. No doubt, for many collaborators the profit motive, not ideology, was the driving force. Dutch and French industrialists profited handsomely through economic collaboration that aided the German war effort. And they certainly welcomed the banning of strikes by their workers. In their defense, they feared that the occupying power would seize their businesses and perhaps deport their employees to Germany if they did not comply.

Some collaborators were idealists who wanted to be a part of Hitler's New Europe. To them, this meant the death of Communism and liberalism and putting Jews in their place. In their eyes, Hitler represented the dawning of a new and better Europe. Under the occupation, many members of right-wing and Fascist parties and Nazi sympathizers welcomed an opportunity to serve the Third Reich, which, as one French Nazi sympathizer stated, "is leading a veritable crusade for European salvation against all the communist and Judeo-masonic international forces…. We hope for the victory of those who will deliver Europe from Bolshevism and will at the same time liberate it from Judeo-capitalist power, for only then will Europe be able to live!"[75] And several weeks after the Nazi invasion of the Soviet Union, the Cardinal-Archbishop of Paris said in a sermon that "Hitler's war is a noble undertaking in defence of European culture."[76] No doubt, many of these extreme Right ideologues also expected that they would share power with the Nazis. However, Nazi administrators saw them as little more than useful tools for exploiting the country's resources needed for the war.

Not all collaborators were right-wing extremists. The great majority were just realists and pragmatists who thought it was simply expedient to make an accomodation with the Nazis who held all the power. These people had their dealings with the Nazis as police, government officials, merchants, manufacturers, café proprietors, performers, mistresses, and so forth. They saw collaboration as a means for advancing their careers, improving incomes, or just finding work. Parisian nightclubs and theaters did booming business entertaining German soldiers, and French musicians and artists toured Germany. In addition to prisoners of war, concentration camp inmates, and conscripted labor, the German labor force was augmented by volunteers from occupied lands who went to Germany to find work that was often not available in their homeland. And many people who stayed home found employment in German-controlled enterprises serving the war economy.

In a desperate but often futile attempt to survive, Jews even collaborated with the Nazis. In Berlin, the Gestapo used Jewish informers to detect Jews in hiding or attempting to pass as gentiles. In Polish ghettos, Jewish communal authorities who hoped to save a remnant of their bretheren and Jewish police who hoped to save themselves and their families assisted their masters in rounding up fellow Jews for deportatation to the death camps. The collaboration of the communal authorities and Jewish police with the Nazis did not save Jewish lives, not even their own—they too perished in the gas chambers. In the Warsaw Ghetto Uprising (see next section), Jewish fighters executed Jewish spies who revealed to the Nazis the location of the bunkers set up by the resistance.

France is often used as a case study in collaboration. France's collapse in the face of the German blitzkrieg in 1940 discredited the liberal parliamentary system and stengthened the radical Right. The heads of Vichy and their supporters, many of them prominent intellectuals and anti-Dreyfusards* in their youth, shared in the antidemocratic, anti-Marxist, and anti-Semitic tradition of the radical Right that had arrayed itself against the Third French Republic since the late nineteenth century. Under the leadership of Marshal Philippe Pétain, the revered World War I hero who had asked Germany for an armistice in 1940, the government of Vichy selected hostages, principally Communists, to be executed by the Nazis in retaliation for the killing of a German soldier by the French Resistance. The government also arrested members of the Resistance, coordinated the recruitment of French men and women to work in armaments factories in Germany, and actively participated in the deportation of Jews to the death camps. It was not uncommon for French collaborators to denounce Jews and Resistance fighters to the authorities. The Nazis paid several thousand French men and women to spy on fellow citizens.

Hundreds of thousands of non-Germans from several countries volunteered for the Wehrmacht and SS battalions and served at the front and as guards in concentration camps. Himmler especially sought Danish, Norwegian, and Flemish Belgian recruits for his SS, believing that they were close to German racial stock; often they had German ancestry. Sixty thousand recruits came from the Netherlands, more than from any other Western country. Together, neutral Switzerland and Sweden provided some nine hundred volunteers. Germany's war against the Soviet Union persuaded many people in occupied Europe to fight for Germany in an anti-Communist crusade. Croats, Hungarians, Slovaks, and Bosnian and Albanian Muslims also were accepted into Himmler's SS, which by the end of the war had more non-Germans than Germans in its ranks. The 125,000 men from occupied Western European lands and Scandinavia that had joined the Waffen-SS (battlefield SS) were often held in contempt by their families and countrymen, and many were punished after the war.

French volunteers fought with the Wehrmacht in Russia, and in 1943, facing a manpower shortage, Hitler authorized the formation of the Charlemagne regiment, French volunteers who served with the Waffen-SS. The Vichy government gave its approval to this all-French regiment that fought in the Soviet Union and in eastern Germany and Berlin in the closing months of the war. Marshal Pétain sent a message of approval to these French soldiers fighting for Nazi Germany: "By taking part in this crusade, command of which has been assumed by Germany, you are earning justified claims to the world's gratitude and are helping deflect the bolshevik threat from us. It is your land that you are defending, while at the same time saving the hope of a reconciled Europe."[77]

Ironically, the largest number of foreign volunteers came from the Soviet Union, the country that suffered the most from Hitler's war and whose Slavic and Central Asian populations Nazi propaganda degraded as racial misfits. Soon

---

*In 1894, Captain Alfred Dreyfus, a Jew, was falsely accused of having sold secrets to the Germans. After a court martial, in which he was framed by the army, Dreyfus was condemned to life imprisonment on Devil's Island. The French Right—monarchists, army leaders, nationalists, clerics, and anti-Semites—blocked attempts to clear the innocent Dreyfus. The affair bitterly divided the nation. After many humiliations, Dreyfus was finally cleared in 1906 to the anger of the Right, an anger that lasted into World War II.

after Operation Barbarossa, large numbers of Soviet prisoners of war and deserters volunteered to serve the Germans; it was one way of escaping death by starvation in a prisoner-of-war camp. Often, volunteers were non-Russian ethnic minorities and Cossacks who had suffered greatly under Stalin and now welcomed the Germans as liberators. Also viewing the Germans as liberators were the people of the Baltic states that the Soviet Union had invaded and annexed in 1940: Latvia, Lithuania, and Estonia. When Germany invaded these states, it recruited the local population for service in both the Wehrmacht and the SS, with whom they fought on the Eastern Front and participated in numerous atrocities. For the Baltic peoples, Communist Russia not Nazi Germany was the enemy. It is estimated that one million or more Soviets were serving the Germans in various capacities: in noncombat positions such as drivers, orderlies, laborers; in police battalions and as concentration camp guards under the supervision of the SS; in armed units fighting partisans and guarding German installations; and at the front fighting alongside the Wehrmacht. By the end of the war, the Russian Army of Liberation consisting mainly of Soviet prisoners of war and headed by Lieutenant General of the Soviet Army A. A. Vlasov mustered some fifty thousand men. Returned to the Soviet Union after the war by the Americans, Vlasov was executed in 1946 along with many of his men.

RESISTANCE MOVEMENTS

Each occupied country also produced a resistance movement that grew stronger as Nazi barbarism became more visible and prospects of a German defeat more likely. Members of the resistance were enormously courageous men and women who abhorred both Nazi ideology and the German occupation of their country. Aided by the Allies, the various resistance movements did not set Europe ablaze with rebellion against the Nazis as Churchill had hoped, but acts of resistance, including the publication of underground newspapers, gave hope to people under Nazi rule. Nevertheless, fearful of brutal German retaliation, the local population often did not want resisters in their area and at times betrayed them to the Nazis. Members of the resistance lived in constant fear that collaborators and paid informers would report them to the German authorities. In France, there was an ongoing armed battle between resisters and collaborators, particularly members of the Milice, the paramilitary force created by Vichy that assisted the Nazis in hunting for resisters and Jews.

When resistance fighters did attempt to confront the German army in Italy and Warsaw in the summer of 1944, they were devastated by superior force. In July 1944, the Germans also killed a large number of French Resistance (La Résistance) fighters in southern France who had risen up in support of the Allied landings on D-Day. In these instances, courageous but untrained patriots could not hope to defeat professional soldiers capable of crushing insurrections with the utmost brutality. The Nazis retaliated against the French Resistance by torturing and executing captured fighters and killing hostages—generally fifty for every German killed. On June 10, 1944, four days after the Allied invasion of France,

© Cody Images

The Milice, an organization of Nazi sympathizers, hunted down both Jews and resistance fighters in Vichy, France.

an SS unit took punitive actions against the village Oradour-sur-Glane, slaughtering 642 villagers, including 207 children.

In Western Europe, the resistance circulated anti-Nazi newspapers, rescued downed Allied airmen, radioed military intelligence to Britain, and sabotaged German installations. Many French, Dutch, and Belgians joined the resistance to escape forced labor in Germany. After the Allied invasion, the Belgian resistance helped capture the vital port of Antwerp, and the Dutch resistance seized some important strongpoints. Norwegians blew up the German stock of heavy water needed for atomic research. The Greek resistance destroyed a vital viaduct, interrupting the movement of supplies to German troops in North Africa.

Just prior to D-Day, some two hundred thousand French men and women served in the French Resistance, and with the Allied invasion the numbers rapidly expanded. More than thirty thousand were executed and sixty thousand deported to Germany, many of them betrayed to the Germans by paid French informers. Before and after the Allies landed on the coast of France in June 1944, the French Resistance provided valuable intelligence, sabotaged German installations, delayed the movement of German reinforcements, and liberated sections of the country as the Germans retreated.

The Polish resistance, numbering some three hundred thousand at its height, reported on German troop movements, interfered with supplies destined for the Eastern Front, and occasionaly assassinated Nazi officials, for which the Germans took savage revenge. For example, on February 3, 1944, the Germans executed

300 Poles in Warsaw in reprisal for the shooting of an SS general, and a week later at Lesno, a Warsaw suburb, 140 more were executed. On February 9, the occupiers killed 60 Polish women railway workers in reprisal for an act of sabotage.

On August 1, 1944, with Soviet troops approaching Warsaw, the Poles staged a full-scale revolt against the German occupiers. The Poles appealed to the Soviets camped ten miles away for help. But Stalin, who was sheltering Polish Communists whom he intended to install in a new Soviet-dominated Poland, did not want non-Communist Poles to assume positions of leadership. He would not permit the Red Army to intervene; nor did Stalin permit Britain and the United States—at least until it was too late to matter—to use Soviet-controlled airstrips near Warsaw to drop supplies to the Polish Home Army. Eliminating potential anti-Communist resistance in Poland was a prime concern of Stalin even while the war still raged. (The Soviet High Command also had legitimate military reasons to pause at the Vistula—overstretched supply lines, exhausted troops' need to rest and reorganize, and fears of huge casualties engaging reinforced German units in urban warfare.) Anglo-American planes based in southern Italy tried to supply the Polish insurgents. However, German antiaircraft fire downed a number of Allied planes, and most of the supplies never did reach the embattled Poles.

In the opening days of the battle, the Home Army, which numbered about forty-five thousand combatants—and tens of thousands of others who in numerous ways assisted the insurgents—attacked Germans and took some prisoners. The people of Warsaw expressed their jubilation by unfurling the Polish national flag, singing patriotic songs, and wearing red-and-white armbands. Reinforced German forces launched a reign of terror ordered by Himmler, and between August 1 and 5, special murder squads went house to house massacring some forty thousand civilians, including women and children, in the Wola district alone. German soldiers used civilians, including women and children, as human shields for tanks and killed captured insurgents and hospital patients. Despite these German atrocities, the Poles continued to fight. But the shortage of food, water, weapons, and ammunition and the great loss of life—some two thousand deaths per day—forced the capitulation of the Home Army on October 2, 1944.

A furious Hitler ordered the total destruction of the city, particularly its historic religious and cultural centers; the task was given to Himmler's SS. The Nazis evacuated the remainder of Warsaw's population and then street by street, building by building, special detonation squads reduced the once beautiful Polish capital to rubble and ruins. It is estimated that more than two hundred thousand Poles died in the uprising, and many survivors were sent to slave labor camps. Some twenty-five thousand Germans were also killed.

When Soviet forces did move closer to Warsaw, the NKVD hunted down the surviving Home Army fighters, whom Stalin called "a gang of criminals," and imprisoned, deported, and executed them. These acts were a continuation of Stalin's earlier policy toward the Poles. In 1939, when both Germany and the Soviet Union invaded Poland, Stalin had ordered the execution of Polish officers who might lead an anti-Communist resistance movement.

In general, the population of occupied Western Europe did not resort to armed resistance until after the Allied invasion of France in June 1944. In the Soviet Union and Yugoslavia, partisan warfare began shortly after the invasion and occupation. The first Soviet partisans were soldiers and officers cut off from their units in the opening weeks of the war. Some of these soldiers were Communist Party officials ordered to stay behind and organize resistance behind German lines. As the war progressed, additional party and NKVD personnel were transported by air to the partisan units. Stalin wanted to make sure that the partisan forces did not become independent of party control. Soviet partisans grew to more than five hundred thousand men and women by 1943. As in other countries, Soviet civilians threatened with deportation to Germany as forced laborers fled their homes and joined the partisans.

Operating from swamps and forests behind the German lines, Soviet partisans sabotaged railways lines and attacked truck convoys, which interrupted the movement of supplies to the front; destroyed telegraph poles and railroad tracks; gathered intelligence; assassinated German officials; killed perhaps thirty-five thousand German soldiers in hit-and-run attacks; and compelled the Germans to divert forces away from the front in order to combat their guerilla operations. Partisans also tortured and killed village elders, town mayors, and police who collaborated with the German occupiers. Nor, at times, did they spare collaborators' families.

In reprisal for partisan attacks, the Germans burned whole villages and massacred civilians, often hundreds at a time, or sent them to labor camps. It is estimated that in these antipartisan sweeps, the Germans murdered some 345,000 civilians and burned down thousands of villages. Such cruel counterinsurgency methods had a dual effect: they drove more people to join the partisans, but they also led villagers not to welcome partisans in their area. Despite their accomplishments, most analysts believe that the Soviet partisans' impact on the war was limited. Nevertheless, their actions tied down German troops and forced the German occupiers, who were unable to eliminate the partisan threat, to be ever worried and ever vigilant.

The mountains and forests of Yugoslavia provided excellent terrain for guerrilla warfare. The leading Yugoslav resistance army was headed by Josip Broz, better known as Tito. Moscow-trained, intelligent, and courageous, Tito organized the partisans into a disciplined fighting force, which numbered some 150,000 by the beginning of 1943. Yugoslav partisans tied down a huge German army and, together with the Red Army, liberated the country from German rule.

Jews participated in the resistance movements in all countries. Seeking to escape the fate of their brethren, Jews joined up with Soviet partisans and were particularly prominent in the French Resistance, comprising some 15 to 20 percent of its members. Specifically Jewish resistance organizations emerged in East Europe, but they suffered from shattering hardships. They had virtually no access to weapons, and the peoples of Eastern Europe, with a long history of anti-Semitism, gave little or no support to Jewish resisters—at times, they even denounced them to the Nazis or killed them on their own. For centuries, European Jews had dealt with persecution by complying with their oppressors

AP Photo

Here, the surviving Jews of the Warsaw Ghetto Uprising in April and May 1943 are rounded up. Most would either be killed immediately or deported to the Treblinka death camp to be gassed.

so as not to make things worse, and they had unlearned the habit of armed resistance that their ancestors had demonstrated against the Romans. In the ghettos, the Germans responded to acts of resistance with savage reprisals against other Jews, creating a moral dilemma for any Jew who considered taking up arms. Nevertheless, revolts did take place in the ghettos and concentration camps, and Jewish partisans also fought from bases in forests.

In the spring of 1943, the surviving Jews of the Warsaw Ghetto resisted the Nazis' efforts to transport them to the Treblinka death camp. Armed with a few pistols, automatic weapons, and a few hundred homemade bottled explosives, the insurgents battled the German troops from April 19 to May 16. From their hiding places in buildings, the Jews rained grenades and bullets on Nazi patrols. Unable to dislodge the Jews from their positions, the Nazis systematically set fire to and blew up the buildings in the ghetto, block by block. In this ghastly inferno, the Jewish partisans continued their desperate struggle until resistance was no longer possible, some of them escaping the ghetto through the sewers.

The Axis powers also had resistance movements. After the Allies landed in Italy in 1943, bands of Italian partisans helped liberate Italy from Fascism and the German occupation. (See Chapter 5.) Communists were instrumental in organizing the resistance in cities. Including the victims of reprisals by the Germans, some forty thousand Italians perished resisting the Nazis.

German resistance to the Nazi regime consisted mainly of Communists, Social Democrats, army officers, and committed Christians, but their numbers were small. Given that the great majority of Germans remained loyal to Hitler and the Nazi regime and because the eyes of the Gestapo and their informers were everywhere, a resistance movement within the country could not hope to achieve a mass following. Indeed, it was quite common for Germans to denounce to the Gestapo someone who expressed anti-Nazi sentiments. Communist resistance groups distributed anti-Nazi leaflets and urged workers to engage in sabotage. Many members of these groups were arrested and executed. Also executed were members of the Red Orchestra, a number of whom worked in the air force and economic ministries and passed military secrets to the Soviet Union. At the University of Munich, a small group of idealistic students belonged to the White Rose, a group that circulated leaflets denouncing the Nazis for their crimes against humanity. In February 1943, Nazis executed two members of the White Rose, Hans Scholl and his sister, Sophie Scholl. Hans's last words, "Long live freedom," echoed through the prison. Students at the university loudly proclaimed their approval when the Nazi rector of the university told them of the executions.

For much of the war, German generals remained a pillar of the Third Reich. Before the war, a substantial number had been ardent supporters of the Nazi regime, including its anti-Semitic policies. Like Hitler, many were nationalists who wanted to expand German power and territory and saw the war against Russia as, what one wrote, "the old battle of the Germanic against the Slav peoples, of the defence of European culture against Moscovite-Asiatic inundation, and the repulse of Jewish-Bolshevism."[78] They agreed with the Nazis' goal to remove Jews from the German economy and state but wanted this accomplished without intolerable excesses. When it was clear that the war was lost, a small group of senior German officers plotted to assassinate Hitler, whom they held responsible for Germany's worsening military position. Hoping to make peace with Britain and the United States before the Soviet Union invaded the homeland, the officers, most of them aristocrats, wanted to show American and British leaders that a reformed Germany inspired by Christian morality would emerge after Hitler's death. Several of the conspirators were driven by moral outrage, an abhorrence of the mass murder of Jews. But for others, fighting a criminal war for a criminal cause was not the principal motivation. What dismayed them most were the military reversals, the increasing suffering of the German people, for which they blamed Hitler, and the threat of a Russian invasion. Nor were they democrats; most of these aristocratic officers had contempt for parliamentary democracy represented by the Weimar Republic. They intended to establish a semiauthoritarian government led by traditional conservatives. Staunch nationalists, they aimed to retain some annexed territories, including the Sudetenland, Austria, and the Polish Corridor, and to maintain a strong army on Germany's eastern frontier. Some were directly involved in war crimes such as persecuting and deporting Jews, forced labor conscription, and antipartisan reprisals against civilians. Under the command of Arthur Nebe, Einsatzgruppen B slaughtered 45,467 Soviet Jews; another participant enthusiastically supported the policy of starving the citizens of Leningrad.

The conspirators displayed moral courage, for which many paid with their lives: this much is without doubt. But the extent to which they redeemed themselves for their past support of Hitler and the Third Reich is open to question. Also open to question is the extent to which they redeemed the honor of the officer corps, particularly given that most military leaders would have nothing to do with the conspiracy.

On July 20, 1944, Colonel Claus von Stauffenberg planted a bomb at a staff conference Hitler attended, but the Führer escaped serious injury. Hitler demanded vengeance: "I want them to be hanged, strung up like butchered cattle."[79] Some five thousand suspects were arrested, many of them tortured. After show trials in which the accused were vilified and degraded, two hundred were executed in exceptionally barbarous fashion. Suspended from meat hooks, the condemned were slowly strangled in front of cameras; SS leaders observed the footage of these excruciating death scenes, but it is doubtful that Hitler ever saw it. Not all the arrested and executed were directly tied to the plot. The Gestapo also rounded up relatives of the conspirators and people thought to harbor anti-Nazi sentiments. In the following months, and particularly when defeat was certain, the Nazis murdered several thousand of these political prisoners.

At the time of the bomb plot, the overwhelming number of German civilians and the upper echelons of the military condemned the conspirators, whose actions during wartime they regarded as high treason. Also, having sworn a personal oath of loyalty to their Führer, which they considered dishonorable to break, most officers remained loyal to Hitler.*

The assassination attempt tightened the bond between Hitler and the German people, most of whom denounced the conspirators and expressed relief that their Führer had survived according to security reports (although the reports of the Security Service [SD] also indicated that some Germans, a minority to be sure, hoped that Hitler's death would mean a quick end to the war). Huge throngs of Germans and Austrians participated in demonstrations to show their confidence in Hitler's leadership. German generals also condemned the attempted assassination and continued to maintain their allegiance to Hitler. Even General Heinz Guderian, who had contempt for bootlicking generals trying to gain Hitler's favor, denounced the conspirators and expressed loyalty to Hitler and National Socialism. Appointed Chief of the German General Staff on July 21, he released the following order to all General Staff officers:

> The 20th of July is the darkest day in the history of the German General Staff. Through the treason of several individual General Staff officers, the German army, the entire Wehrmacht, yes the whole greater Reich has been led to the edge of ruin…. Do not let anyone surpass you in your loyalty to the Führer…. Be an example to others in your unconditional obedience. There is no future for the Reich without National Socialism.[80]

*All officers and soldiers took the following personal oath: "I swear by God this sacred oath. I will render unconditional obedience to Adolf Hitler, the Führer of the German Reich and people, supreme commander of the armed forces, and will be ready as a brave soldier to risk my life at any time for this oath."

Similar sentiments were shared by many soldiers and junior officers, one of whom wrote: "I and all members of the company were struck dumb by the announcement of this revolting infamy. Praise to God that providence has preserved our Führer for the salvation of Europe, and it is now our holiest duty to bind ourselves to him even more strongly."[81]

Hitler saw his survival as further proof that it was his destiny to lead Germany. He also saw the assassination attempt as proof that many of his senior commanders were "swine who have been sabotaging my work for years."[82] He had always felt disdain for his senior commanders, but now he was even less inclined to accept their advice; instead, he trusted his own intuition. Even more than in the past he blamed German battlefield setbacks on his senior generals, the July 20 conspirators and their colleagues who either approved the plot or had remained silent. Hitler raged against these officers, whom he denounced as betrayers and wreckers, particularly after the German failure to repulse the Allied landing in France.

The clergy were well represented among the Germans who resisted Nazism. Arrested in 1943 for conspiring to assassinate Hitler, Dietrich Bonhoeffer, a Lutheran minister and prominent theologian, was executed by hanging shortly before the end of the war. Martin Niemöller, also a Lutheran minister and prominent theologian, spent eight years in concentration camps for opposing the Third Reich's attempts to control the churches. Hundreds of Catholic priests were sent to concentration camps, and some were executed. Catholic bishops attacked the Nazis' euthanasia measures designed to put to death the mentally and physically handicapped; the bishops felt this was contrary to Christian principles.

In general, however, when the churches resisted the regime, their principal concern was protecting their institutions from Nazi domination, not challenging Hitler's core ideology. And the courageous clergy who were sent to concentration camps were not representative of the German churches that, as organized institutions, capitulated to, cooperated with, and often endorsed both Hitler and the Nazi regime, at times with great enthusiasm. Before Hitler came to power, more than 25 percent of the Protestant clergy were members of the Nazi Party. Both the German Evangelical (Lutheran) and Catholic churches found much to praise in the Third Reich, condemned resistance to the Nazi regime, urged their faithful to fight for the Führer and the fatherland, pressured conscientious objectors to serve, celebrated Nazi victories, and turned their backs on the persecuted Jews.

The German churches, which preached Christ's message of humanity, failed to take a stand against Nazi inhumanity for a variety of reasons. Many German church leaders feared that resistance would lead the Nazis to take even more severe measures against their churches. The Nazi regime had already curtailed religious instruction in public schools, censored church newspapers, and dismissed clergy thought to oppose the Third Reich. Traditionally, the German churches bowed to state authority and detested revolution. Church leaders also found several Nazi ideas appealing. Intensely antiliberal, antirepublican, anti-Communist, and anti-Semitic, many members of the clergy were filled with hope when the Nazis took power. They anticipated that Hitler would restore respect for traditional Christian morality, which they believed had been undermined by the secularism, materialism, and vice rampant in the Weimar Republic. They also believed he would declaw the Communists, who had declared war on Christianity. The prominent Lutheran theologian who "welcomed that change that came to Germany in 1933 as a divine gift and miracle"[83] voiced the sentiments of many members of the clergy. Such dedication to Hitler, which lasted throughout the war, encouraged prolonged moral nearsightedness, not a revolt of Christian conscience.

After the war, to assuage their conscience and to erase a tarnished historical record, the German churches manufactured the myth of resistance to the Nazi regime. In truth, with some notable exceptions, most German clergy either supported the Nazis or remained on the sidelines. Three months after the end of the war, Niemöller called for church leaders to show contrition: "[W]e, the church, must beat our chests and confess, we are guilty, we are guilty, we are most guilty! This is what we must say today to our people and to Christianity, that we did not stand before them as pious and righteous people."[84]

NOTES

1. *Hitler's Table Talk, 1941–1944*, edited with preface and essay by H. R. Trevor-Roper, trans. Norman Cameron and R. H. Stevens (New York: Enigma Books, 2000), 466.

2. Ibid., 319, 527.

3. Georgily A. Kumanev, "The German Occupation Regime on Occupied Territory in the USSR (1941–1944)," in *A Mosaic of Victims: Non-Jews Persecuted and Murdered by the Nazis*, ed. Michael Berenbaum (New York: New York University Press, 1990), 135.

4. Gitta Sereny, *Albert Speer: His Battle with Truth* (New York: Vintage, 1996), 311.

5. G. M. Gilbert, *Nuremberg Diary* (New York: Signet Books, 1961), 109.

6. Götz Aly, *Hitler's Beneficiaries*, trans. Jefferson Chase (New York: Henry Holt, 2005), 285.

7. Jean Michel, *Dora*, trans. Jennifer Kidd (New York: Holt, Rinehart and Winston, 1980), 62–63.

8. Mark Mazower, *Hitler's Empire: How the Nazis Ruled Europe* (New York: Penguin, 2008), 166.

9. Robert E. Conot, *Justice at Nuremberg* (New York: Harper & Row, 1983), 246–247.

10. Ibid, 247–248.

11. Richard C. Lukas, *Forgotten Holocaust: The Poles Under German Occupation 1939–1944*, rev. ed. (New York: Hippocrene Books, 2001), 3.

12. Ibid., 3.

13. Mazower, *Hitler's Empire*, 82.

14. *The Goebbels Diaries 1939–1941*, trans. and ed. Fred Taylor (New York: G. P. Putnam's Sons, 1983), 16.

15. Ibid., 20.

16. Janusz Gumkowski and Kazimierz Leszczynski, *Poland Under Nazi Occupation* (Warsaw: Polonia Publishing House, 1961), 32–33.

17. Mazower, *Hitler's Empire*, 92.

18. Gordon Wright, *The Ordeal of Total War* (New York: Harper Torchbooks, 1967), 124.

19. Chris Bellamy, *Absolute War: Soviet Russia in the Second World War* (New York: Alfred A. Knopf, 2007), 27.

20. Andrew Nagorski, *The Greatest Battle: Stalin, Hitler, and the Desperate Struggle for Moscow That Changed the Course of World War II* (New York: Simon and Schuster, 2007), 91.

21. Max Hastings, *Armageddon: The Battle for Germany, 1944–1945* (New York: Alfred A. Knopf, 2004), 109.

22. *Hitler's Table Talk, 1941–1944*, 15.

23. Ibid., 54–55.

24. Samuel W. Mitcham, Jr., *The Men of Barbarossa: Commanders of the German Invasion of Russia, 1941* (Philadelphia: Casement Publishers, 2009), 115.

25. Nagorski, *The Greatest Battle*, 91.

26. Mazower, *Hitler's Empire*, 164.

27. Norman Cohn, *Warrant for Genocide* (New York: Harper Torchbooks. 1967), 188.

28. Michael Burleigh and Wolfgang Wippermann, *The Racial State: Germany 1933–1945* (New York: Cambridge University Press, 1991), 107.

29. Henry V. Dicks, *Licensed Mass Murder: A Socio-Psychological Study of Some S.S. Killers* (New York: Basic Books, 1972), 62.

30. Eberhard Jäckel, *Hitler's Weltanschauung: A Blueprint for Power*, trans. Herbert Arnold (Middletown, CT: Wesleyan University Press, 1972), 44.

31. Richard Bessel, *Nazism and War* (New York: Modern Library, 2006), 102.

32. Excerpted in Richard Overy, *Interrogations: The Nazi Elite in Allied Hands, 1945* (New York: Penguin Books, 2001), 494.

33. *The Goebbels Diaries*, 148.

34. Timothy Snyder, *Bloodlands: Europe Between Hitler and Stalin* (New York: Basic Books, 2010), 205–206.

35. Gerald Flemming, *Hitler and the Final Solution* (Berkeley: University of California Press, 1984), 50.

36. Christine Alexander and Mason Kunze, eds., *Eastern Inferno: The Journals of a German Panzerjägeron on the Eastern Front, 1942–43* (Philadelphia: Casemate, 2010), 111–112.

37. Ernst Klee, Willi Dressen, and Volker Ries, eds., *"The Good Old Days," The Holocaust as Seen by Its Perpetrators and Bystanders*, trans. Deborah Burnstone (New York: The Free Press, 1991), 159.

38. Sönke Neitzel, ed., *Tapping Hitler's Generals: Transcripts of Secret Conversations, 1942–45*, trans. Geoffrey Brooks (St. Paul, MN: Frontline Books, MBI Publishing, 2007), 198.

39. Peter Hoffmann, *The History of the German Resistance 1933–1945*, trans. Richard Barry (Cambridge, MA: MIT Press, 1977), 269.

40. Michael Burleigh, *The Third Reich: A New History* (New York: Hill and Wang), 522.

41. Ibid., 522.

42. Excerpted in Michael Berenbaum, ed., *Witness to the Holocaust* (New York: HarperCollins, 1997), 178.

43. Gerd R. Ueberschär, "The Ideologically Motivated War of Annihilation in the East," in *Hitler's War in the East: A Critical Assessment*, ed. Rolf-Dieter Müller and Gerd R. Ueberschär (New York: Berghahn Books, 2002), 245.

44. Gerda Weissman Klein, *All But My Life* (New York: Hill and Wang, 1957), 89.

45. Judith Steinberg Newman, *In the Hell of Auschwitz* (New York: Exposition, 1964), 18.

46. *Nazi Conspiracy and Aggression* (Washington, D.C.: U.S. Government Printing Office, 1946), 6:787–789.

47. Kevin Madigan, "What the Vatican Knew About the Holocaust, and When," *Commentary* 112, no. 2 (October 2001): 47.

48. Joseph Borkin, *The Crime and Punishment of I. G. Farben* (New York: Free Press, 1978), 118.

49. Ibid., 143.

50. Gisella Perl, *I Was a Doctor in Auschwitz* (New York: International Universities Press, 1948), 80.

51. Robert Jay Lifton, *The Nazi Doctors* (New York: Basic Books, 1986), 16.

52. Konnilyn G. Feig, *Hitler's Death Camps* (New York: Holmes and Meier, 1979), 37.

53. Robert Jay Lifton, "Doubling: The Acts of the Second Self," in *A Mosaic of Victims: Non-Jews Persecuted and Murdered by the Nazis*, ed. Michael Berenbaum (New York: New York University Press, 1990), 219.

54. Erich Kahler, *The Tower and the Abyss* (New York: George Braziller, 1957), 74–75.

55. Steven T. Katz, "Technology and Genocide: Technology as a 'Form of Life,'" in *Echoes from the Holocaust*, ed. Alan Rosenberg and Gerald E. Meyers (Philadelphia: Temple University Press, 1988), 281.

56. Rainer C. Baum, "Holocaust: Moral Indifference as the Form of Modern Evil," in *Echoes from the Holocaust*, ed. Alan Rosenberg and Gerald E. Meyers (Philadelphia: Temple University Press, 1988), 83.

57. Lifton, *The Nazi Doctors*, 5.

58. Saul Friedländer, *Nazi Germany and the Jews: The Years of Extermination* (New York: Harper Perennial, 2007), 601–602.

59. Ulrich Herbert, "New Answers and Questions" in *National Socialist Extermination Policies: Contemporary German Perspectives and Controversies*, ed. Ulrich Herbert, (New York: Berghahn Books, 2000), 36–37.

60. Christopher R. Browning, *The Origins of the Final Solution: The Evolution of Nazi Jewish Policy, September 1939–March 1942* (Lincoln: University of Nebraska Press, 2004), 387.

61. Peter Fritzsche, *Life and Death in the Third Reich*, (Cambridge, MA: Harvard University Press. 2009), 257.

62. Eric A. Johnson, *Nazi Terror: The Gestapo, Jews, and Ordinary Germans* (New York: Basic Books, 1999), 381.

63. Martin Dean, *Robbing the Jews: The Confiscation of Jewish in the Holocaust, 1933–1945* (New York: Cambridge University Press, 2008), 385–386.

64. Browning, *The Origins of the Final Solution*, 390.

65. Marlis G. Steinert, *Hitler's War and the Germans* (Athens: Ohio University Press, 1977), 142.

66. Evan Burr Bukey, *Hitler's Austria: Popular Sentiment in the Nazi Era 1938–1945* (Chapel Hill: University of North Carolina Press, 2000), 133–134, 136.

67. "The Dark Continent Hitler's European Holocaust Helpers," *Spiegel* Online, www.spiegel.de/international/europe/0,1518,625824,00.html, 2–3.

68. Dean, *Robbing the Jews* (2008), 391.

69. Jan Herman Brinks, "The Dutch, The Germans, The Jews," *History Today,* June 1, 1999, 21.

70. Omer Bartov, *Erased: Vanishing Traces of Jewish Galicia in Present-Day Ukraine* (Princeton, NJ: Princeton University Press, 2007), 39.

71. Niall Ferguson, *The War of the World: Twentieth-Century Conflict and the Descent of the West* (New York: Penguin, 2006), 453.

72. Antony Polonsky and Joanna B. Michlic, eds., *The Neighbors Respond: The Controversy Over the Jedwabne Massacre in Poland* (Princeton, NJ: Princeton University Press, 2004), 28.

73. Martin Gilbert, *The Second World War*, rev. ed. (New York: Henry Holt, 1991), 384.

74. Robert Katz, *The Battle for Rome: The Germans, The Allies, The Partisans, and the Pope September 1943–June 1944* (New York: Simon and Schuster, 2003), 116.

75. Philippe Burrin, *France Under the Germans: Collaboration and Compromise,* trans. Janet Lloyd (New York: The New Press, 1996), 416.

76. Andrew Roberts, *The Storm of War: A New History of the Second World War* (London: Penguin Books, 2009), 150.

77. Fedor von Bock, *The War Diary 1939–1945*, ed. Klaus Gerbert, trans. David Johnston (Atglen, PA: Schiffer Military History, 1996), 350–351.

78. Jürgen Förster, "The German Army and the Ideological War against the Soviet Union," in *The Policies of Genocide: Jews and Soviet Prisoners of War in Nazi Germany* (The German Historical Institute, Allen & Unwin, 1986), 18.

79. French L. MacLean, *2000 Quotes from Hitler's 1000-Year Reich* (Atglen, PA: Schiffer Publishing, 2007), 153.

80. Geoffrey P. Megargee, *Inside Hitler's High Command* (Lawrence: University of Kansas Press, 2000), 214.

81. Omer Bartov, *Hitler's Army: Soldiers, Nazis, and War in the Third Reich* (New York: Oxford University Press, 1992), 172.

82. John Mosier, *The Blitzkrieg Myth: How Hitler and the Allies Misread the Strategic Realities of World War II* (New York: HarperCollins, 2003), 231.

83. Hermann Graml et al., *The German Resistance to Hitler* (Berkeley: University of California Press, 1970), 206.

84. Gilad Margalit, *Guilt, Suffering and Memory: Germany Remembers Its Dead of World War II,* trans. Haim Watzman (Bloomington: Indiana University Press, 2010), 25.

Chapter 5

✳

War on Other Fronts

At the same time that Germany was being bled dry in Russia, it had to deal with other fronts on land, on sea, and in the air that put further pressure on its manpower and resources. What greatly added to Germany's difficulties was the entry of the United States in the war. On December 11, 1941, four days after Japan's attack on Pearl Harbor, Nazi Germany and Fascist Italy declared war on the United States. With all the aid the United States was supplying Britain, including armaments shipped across the U-boat infested waters of the Atlantic, Hitler already saw America as a belligerent enemy. For Hitler, Jews engineered the alliance between Britain and the United States as part of their conspiracy to dominate Germany and the world, and he saw both Franklin Roosevelt and Winston Churchill as pawns of the international Jewish conspiracy.* Moreover, he had a low opinion of the American soldier. Because he expected the United States to be involved in a protracted war with Japan, Hitler did not think American entry would interfere with the war against the Soviet Union. After Germany defeated Russia and obtained its resources, he would then deal with the Anglo-Americans. This was a major miscalculation. In the past, Hitler had misjudged Britain's resolve not to come to terms with the Third Reich and underestimated the strength of the Soviet Union. Now he declared war on the United States at the same time

---

*According to the myth of the "world Jewish conspiracy," which was at the core of Hitler's worldview and the staple of Nazi propaganda, Jewish Bolsheviks controlled the Soviet Union (see footnote on page 57 in Chapter 3 and pages 298-299 in Chapter 8). The other half of the Jewish conspiracy myth held that Jewish plutocrats manipulated policy in the United States and Britain. And in both the Communist and capitalist countries Jews were conspiring to destroy the German people. In his diary entry for May 8, 1943, Goebbels echoed Hitler's delusions: "Our constant, untiring effort must center upon taking the necessary measures for our security…. [T]he Bolshevism of the East is mainly under Jewish leadership and … the Jews are also the dominant influence in the Western plutocracies." Such bizarre thinking illustrated again how pathologically obsessed Hitler and Goebbels were with Jews and how irrational was this obsession. In reality, Jewish influence over military decisions in the United States, Britain, and the Soviet Union was simply nonexistent.

that Britain remained unsubdued and Germany was fighting a much tougher war with the Soviet Union than it had anticipated. Germany simply lacked the industrial and human resources to defeat the combined might and numbers of three of the world's greatest powers.

The United States immediately put its enormous industrial potential into high gear and with awesome speed produced massive amounts of armaments that were employed in the war against submarines in the Atlantic, the fighting in North Africa and Italy, the air war over Europe, and eventually in the invasion of France and the march on Germany. The conflict in all these fronts demonstrated the increasing Anglo-American industrial and technological superiority over the Third Reich. For example, in 1943, the United States produced 85,898 aircraft; the United Kingdom, 26,263; and Germany, 25,024. In that same year, 42,497 tanks and self-propelled guns came off American assembly lines compared to 19,800 produced by Germany. And in 1944, Americans produced some 600,000 army trucks compared to 88,000 for Germany. Soviet armaments production also significantly outpaced Germany's. For example, the Germans managed to produce only 7,330 advanced Tiger and Panther tanks during the entire war, whereas Soviet industry manufactured more than 1,200 T–34s a month. And the war on the Eastern Front was greatly taxing the Nazi regime's forces and material resources. Nazi Germany had little chance of winning a war against such overwhelming odds.

BATTLE OF THE ATLANTIC, 1939–1943

An island nation with limited agricultural and natural resources, Britain is dependent on food and raw materials from abroad, particularly oil and rubber. From the outset of the war, in what became known as the Battle of the Atlantic, Germany attacked merchant shipping in order to deprive Britain of supplies vital for the war effort and of food to shatter the morale of the civilian population. Mines were planted outside British ports, and high-speed heavily armed warships called "pocket battleships" searched the sea lanes looking for targets. In September and October 1939, the Germans sank ninety-nine Allied and neutral ships, including a carrier and a battleship. On December 13, 1939, the *Graf Spee*, a sea raider with nine kills to its credit, engaged three British cruisers in the south Atlantic, disabling one that was forced to withdraw and damaging the other two. The *Graf Spee* also suffered damage, so it limped into the port of Montevideo in Uruguay. Forced by the Uruguayan government to leave after seventy-two hours and erroneously believing that British naval reinforcements were outside the port, the captain released his crew and scuttled the ship. The destruction of the *Graf Spee* led German naval commanders to order their warships to concentrate on merchant cargoes and to avoid risky engagements with the Royal Navy. German sea raiders troubled the British, but they accounted for only 6.1 percent of Allied shipping losses during the war compared to some 70 percent by U-boats (submarines), which was Germany's most effective weapon in the Battle of the Atlantic.

The U-Boats' "Happy Time"

Operating from ports in occupied Norway and France, marauding U-boats sank more than 500 ships in 1940. From September to December, a period they called the "Happy Time," German submariners sank 274 ships with a loss of only two U-boats. The morale of submarine crews soared. A lone merchant ship slowly crossing the Atlantic was vulnerable to attack from both U-boats and surface raiders. To counter this threat, merchant and transport ships traveled in convoys of 50 to 60 ships, escorted by cruisers and destroyers, continuing a practice that had originated in World War I.

Because of rough seas, freezing cold gales that swept tons of water across decks, and hunter U-boats, the crews that crossed the North Atlantic to supply Britain had one of the most dangerous and terrifying assignments of the war. If a ship were hit, the men struggling in the sea could not always rely on an escort rescuing them because a ship stopping to pick up survivors became too vulnerable to a U-boat attack. An escort's first duty was to continue protecting the moving convoy, not rescue sailors. To remedy this dreadful situation, special rescue ships were added to the convoys, but even then the freezing cold and powerful waves could kill the sailors in minutes, often before they could be reached. The courage of merchant seamen in the face of these dangers was exemplary. About thirty-two thousand British merchant seamen perished in the Battle of the Atlantic, 25 percent of all merchant seamen. This was a much higher fatality rate than that suffered by the infantry. The death rate for German submariners over the course of the war was even greater, more than 75 percent—thirty thousand of forty thousand submariners perished.

A particularly dangerous run was across the Arctic waters to the Russian ports of Murmansk and Archangel to provide the Soviets with Lend-Lease aid. The British and American crews had to contend with some of the world's worst seas and weather: ice, storms, fog, heaving waves, and freezing wind. In addition, convoys often had to run a gauntlet of German warships, prowling U-boats, and bombers based in Norway. Merchant seamen were the war's unsung heroes.

A catastrophe occurred on July 4, 1942, to Convoy PQ 17, which had sailed from Iceland on June 27 bound for Archangel. Believing that powerful German warships were heading to cut off the convoy, the British Admiralty made a hasty and costly decision: it ordered the cruiser escorts to turn back and the merchant ships to disperse and try to make port on their own. The German heavy ships never showed, but immediately German U-boats and dive bombers went into action against the now defenseless Allied freighters. Of the thirty-five cargo vessels that had sailed from Iceland, only eleven found their way to the Russian port; the loss of twenty-four ships and one hundred thousand tons of cargo, including 430 tanks, was the worst suffered

Photo courtesy of the U.S. Navy

Tankers were prime targets for U-boats. On July 15, 1942, a U-boat torpedoed the U.S. oiler SS *Pennsylvania Sun* some 125 miles off the coast of Florida.

by a convoy during the war. The British Admiralty learned a painful lesson: escort vessels must never desert freighters.

Heading the U-boat arm of the German navy was Admiral Karl Dönitz, a U-boat commander in World War I and a dedicated Nazi to the very end. Dönitz saw the Battle of the Atlantic as the war's most decisive campaign. Sinking freight ships with their valuable cargo at a faster rate than they could be replaced, he maintained, would achieve victory for the Third Reich. Dönitz made the U-boats more lethal by concentrating them in "wolf packs." Starting with three or four in a pack, eventually groups of twenty or more prowled the North Atlantic. He also developed an effective procedure for organizing a wolf pack. When a U-boat spotted a convoy, it would radio the location, speed, size, and other vital information to U-boat headquarters in France; headquarters then instructed other U-boats in the vicinity to converge in preparation for a concentrated assault. No attack was initiated until the U-boats were assembled in a pack. Surfacing only when it was dark in order to avoid detection, the U-boats tried to slip within the convoy, fire their torpedoes or their powerful 88 mm deck guns, and then escape, leaving behind death and destruction.

U-boat crews displayed high morale and, like Dönitz, were usually dedicated Nazis. A British interrogator of a U-boat crew captured in October 1940 reported: "The prisoners were all fanatical Nazis and hated the British intensely.... German successes during 1940 appear to have established Hitler in their minds not merely as a God but as their only God."[1] Fortunately for Britain, Germany possessed only a small number of U-boats in 1940 because Hitler did not regard submarine construction as a major priority.

Compounding the Royal Navy's difficulties in defending against the wolf packs during 1940 to 1941 was the support given to the U-boats by long-range, four-engine bombers, the Focke-Wulf Condors. Flying from bases in France and Norway, these aircraft engaged in reconnaissance missions looking for convoys. When they spotted one, they radioed its location to U-boat headquarters, which then relayed the information to nearby submarines. The aircraft also carried a sufficient load of bombs to damage and sink merchant vessels and cruiser escorts.

In early 1941, German pocket battleships, or heavy cruisers, were taking a ruinous toll of merchant shipping. In April, the newly constructed *Bismarck*, Germany's most powerful battleship yet, entered the battle against the convoys headed for Britain. Two British ships, the battle cruiser *Hood* and the *Prince of Wales*, a new battleship, intercepted the *Bismarck* and a companion cruiser, *Prinz Eugen*. The gun duel that ensued ended tragically for the Royal Navy. A shell struck the *Hood*'s ammunition storerooms, and the ensuing explosion split the ship in half. Out of a crew of more than fourteen hundred, only three survived. The damaged *Bismarck* set out for a French port while *Prinz Eugen* slipped away and prowled the Atlantic for merchant ships to destroy. Determined to avenge the loss of the *Hood*, which was one of the worst disasters in the navy's history, the Royal Navy hunted for the *Bismarck* in full force, including aircraft carriers and battleships. Spotting the German battleship from the air, the Royal Navy moved in for the kill. Blasted by torpedo planes and the warships' big guns, the *Bismarck* went under; only one hundred of its crew of more than twenty-two hundred survived.

Dönitz constantly pleaded with Hitler to build more U-boats; at times, the Führer would consent, but as Germany became bogged down in the Soviet Union, priority was given to tanks and aircraft for the Wehrmacht and Luftwaffe. In his *Memoirs*, Dönitz maintained bitterly, "[We] had failed to expand the U-boat arm, because our political leaders and their Army and Air Force advisers believed, at least until 1942, that they could win *on land* a war in which our main opponents were the two greatest *sea* powers in the world."[2]

In the first half of 1941, Dönitz's U-boats, now deployed in somewhat greater number, sank more ships than British shipyards could produce. Britain, dependent on the import of food and vital raw materials needed by the military, was slowly being strangled. Many food items were already rationed. In his history of the war, Winston Churchill said that he found the U-boat peril more frightening than the Battle of Britain: "The Battle of the Atlantic was the dominating factor all through the war. Never for one moment could we forget that everything happening elsewhere, on land, at sea, or in the air, depended ultimately on its outcome."[3] Had Hitler seen the merits of submarines earlier and before the war built a large fleet of U-boats, Churchill's fears would have been magnified.

Coping with the Threat

With its survival at stake, Britain was forced to devise effective ways of countering the U-boat threat. The British were up to the challenge. The first concern was locating a submarine before it was in a position to launch its torpedoes. This was accomplished by the development of sonar, a transmitter-receiver that could detect and locate underwater objects through sound waves that reverberated after striking the object. Not being able to detect surfaced submarines was a major limitation of this listening device. Dönitz ordered his submarines to surface and attack at night when they were less visible. To sight U-boats that surfaced and could not be seen in the dark, the British installed radar in escorts, making it much more difficult for U-boats to surprise their prey. Another achievement of British scientists was the development of a high frequency direction finder (Huff-Duff) that allowed an escort ship to track German radio transmissions and zero in on a U-boat's position.

Ultra's* success in intercepting and decrypting messages between U-boat headquarters and the wolf packs enabled the Royal Navy to learn the enemy's intentions and to plot the U-boats' current and likely future positions. With this information, they could reroute convoys to place them out of reach of the deadly marauders. Dönitz became concerned that his U-boats were finding fewer targets and the enemy was resisting more effectively, but he never suspected that the British had broken German ciphers. Instead, thinking that there was a security risk at his headquarters, he drastically reduced the staff.

The British also developed ways of providing air support for convoys. They converted merchant vessels into mini-aircraft carriers that carried six or more torpedo bombers, which provided air cover for convoys. From bases in Britain, Canada, and Iceland, giant flying boats searched for U-boats and provided convoys with an aerial umbrella. A surfaced U-boat would immediately submerge when it sighted an enemy aircraft and seek to flee the area. Finally, the escort vessels became adept at dropping high-explosive depth charges capable of destroying a U-boat. The depth charges, weighing about three hundred pounds, exploded when hydrostatic fuses were activated by water pressure at depth. These efforts proved successful. In the first half of 1941, U-boats sank 363 ships; in the second half of the year, the number dropped to 169 ships.

Immediately after Germany declared war on the United States, Admiral Dönitz, regarding the United States as the hub of enemy shipbuilding and armaments production, made an all-out effort to destroy American shipping. In particular, he targeted oil tankers going to and leaving American ports. Seeking easy targets, he ordered a full-scale U-boat offensive along America's vulnerable

---

*Ultra was the code name given to the British intelligence code breakers gathered at Bletchley Park. These cryptologists systematically decoded German operational codes transmitted by their cipher machine, code-named Enigma, which the Germans considered unbreakable. In the 1930s, a French officer obtained some pages from Enigma's instruction manual and shared his knowledge with three young and exceptionally bright Polish mathematicians who figured out how Enigma worked. Just prior to the war, Britain was apprised of the Poles' breakthrough. British intelligence took great care never to divulge this coup, which greatly aided military planning. The code breakers received a godsend when British sailors boarded a U-boat that depth charges had forced to the surface and the crew had abandoned and found an Enigma machine.

east coast. However, since many U-boats were being repaired and others, under Hitler's orders, were preying on Allied ships in the Mediterranean, Dönitz had only a few submarines available. However, the damage these submarines inflicted on American shipping was immense. The attacks threatened the entire war effort, wrote Chief of Staff General George C. Marshall to Naval Chief of Staff Ernest J. King. Unprepared for Dönitz's U-boat offensive, 216 American and neutral merchant ships were lost from January to March 1942; by the end of June, the number had risen to 500.

The failure of Americans to institute a convoy system made it easier for the prowling U-boats. In addition to a scarcity of both escort vessels and airplanes, at this early stage naval commanders thought that hunting down U-boats, rather than organizing convoys, was the better way of dealing with the threat. Also making it easier for the U-boats was the unwillingness of coastal communities, particularly the major tourist centers of Miami and Atlantic City, to dim their lights because it would hurt business. Ships outlined by shore lights became easy victims for lurking U-boats. Years after the war, a German submariner commented on this double failure.

> [T]he next few months were a period of great triumph for the German U-boats ... before the Americans got organised into a proper convoy system.... Dönitz had ordered several of our submarines to take advantage of American laxness, and he was right inasmuch as terrific slaughter took place. It became quite commonplace to see the night sky lit up by the flames from burning tankers which were en route to New York or returning to the Gulf to load up with more oil. We often saw the silhouettes of ships against the shore lights and thought the Americans were crazy to be so careless.[4]

Regarding the shore lights, Admiral Samuel Eliot Morison noted sarcastically, "Ships were sunk and seamen drowned in order that that the citizenry might enjoy business and pleasure as usual."[5] There were times when thousands of tourists could observe the destruction of oil tankers and freighters. Finally, in April and May, orders to douse waterfront lights were imposed and strictly enforced.

Based on their painful experience, the British Admiralty had warned American naval commanders to form convoys and provide escorts rather than focus on hunting U-boats in a vast ocean. The U.S. Navy has been criticized for failing to heed the British Admiralty's advice until after American shipping was badly mauled. After a short time, the naval High Command did wholeheartedly support escorted convoys. In June 1942, Admiral King wrote that, "if all shipping can be brought under escort and air cover, our losses will be reduced to an acceptable figure.... [E]scort is not just *one* way of handling the submarine menace; it is the *only* way that gives any promise of success. The so-called patrol and hunting operations have time and again proved futile."[6] Seventeen American shipyards, operating at great speed, produced small destroyers specifically designed to combat submarines. In general, five of these destroyers escorted a convoy of forty to fifty ships.

Seeking to avoid the protective convoys, the U-boats searched for easier pickings in the Caribbean, where ships departing from Cuba, Central America, and Venezuela traveled alone. Since many of the ships targeted were tankers carrying aviation fuel for the Royal Air Force (RAF), the Allies were greatly concerned. Also vulnerable were ships sailing in the Gulf of Mexico, where forty-one were sunk in May 1942. America immediately extended its defensive measures into these waters and considerably reduced shipping losses by July. Nevertheless, by August, eight and a half months after the United States had entered the war, the figures were not encouraging: U-boats had sunk 360 merchant ships in and near American waters with only eight losses. Yet, American shipyards were producing an astounding number of ships each month, far more than either Britain or Germany anticipated.

By the end of 1942, it did not appear that the Allies would win the Battle of the Atlantic. Stalking the Atlantic waters, a considerably enlarged U-boat fleet had meted out heavy losses for the year: In the first six months, Britain and the United States lost more than 140 tankers with their precious oil cargo; in October and November alone, U-boats sank 235 ships. And 1943 got off to a bad start.* In January, U-boats attacked a weakly protected convoy of nine oil tankers, destroying all but two. Between January and April, British bombers had no luck trying to attack U-boat pens in southern France; reinforced with thick concrete, the pens were impervious to bombs. After the war, Dönitz maintained that the British had erred by not bombing these pens while they were under construction and vulnerable.

March 1943 was a particularly cruel month for the Allies as U-boats sank 120 Allied and neutral merchant ships, most of them in the North Atlantic; in one battle, U-boats destroyed 22 cargo ships with only one loss. For Dönitz, these March victories meant that "[a]fter three and a half years we had brought British maritime power to the brink of defeat in the Battle of the Atlantic—and that with only half the number of U-boats which we had always demanded."[7] Given that most of the lost ships were escorted, a despondent British Admiralty began to question the effectiveness of the convoy that was the foundation of their maritime strategy. No one would admit it, but some naval commanders suspected that the U-boat menace to Britain's lifeline could not be overcome and that without the vital supplies, the country would not be able to feed its people or produce the armaments needed for the battlefield. Most important, the sinking of oil tankers would force British bombers to curtail their raids over Germany and even interfere with the movement of American troops sailing across the Atlantic.

But the British Admiralty's gloom was excessive. As Dönitz wrote fifteen years later, "The success achieved in this month, however, was destined to be the last decisive victory won by the Germans in the battle of convoys."[8] America's extraordinary industrial production was more than replacing the shipping losses,

---

*On February 3, 1943, a U-boat torpedoed an American transport ship. Of the 902 men on board, 672 perished, most of them drowning in the icy waters near Greenland. The four U.S. chaplains on board, three Christian and one Jewish, preached courage to the struggling men and gave their life preservers to those without. As the ship went down, the chaplains linked arms and prayed. A survivor later described the scene as "the finest thing I had ever seen or hope to see this side of heaven." Margaret E. Wagner, *World War II: 365 Days* (New York: Abrams, 2009), on page listed as August 5.

and many of the new ships were improved convoy escorts—faster destroyers and larger carriers able to hold as many as thirty planes—fulfilling Churchill's hope: "Until the end of 1942, the U-boats sank ships faster than the Allies could build them. The foundation of all our hopes and schemes was the immense shipbuilding programme of the United States."[9]

In February 1942, U-boat headquarters changed their communication code system, which handicapped British tracking operations. But by December, Ultra's brilliant cryptologists solved the problem, facilitating convoys in taking evasive routes and Allied escorts and long-range planes in spotting targets. Improved radar technology also enabled Allied ships and planes to locate U-boats with greater accuracy. Better training increased the proficiency of the escort crews, particularly the teams dropping the depth charges. The Hedgehog, a recently developed weapon that fired a barrage of twenty-four bombs at a time in the U-boat's vicinity, increased escorts' firing power.

RAF commanders, reluctant to divert aircraft from their goal of bombing Germany into submission, had resisted pleas to protect convoys with long-range planes, but increasing governmental pressure forced them to relent. U-boats had been extremely successful in an area of the North Atlantic known as the "air gap" because it was too far from airfields for most planes to patrol. Taking off from airfields in Greenland, Newfoundland, Iceland, and Britain, long-range bombers could now patrol the gap, which turned the U-boats' former sanctuary into killing waters. Periodically, U-boats had to surface so that they could run their diesel engines to recharge their huge batteries and the crew could breathe fresh air. Utilizing a radar system, Allied planes were able to detect, surprise, and attack surfaced U-boats. If the U-boats were able to submerge, the planes dropped depth charges. These improved countermeasures for combating enemy submarines were showing good results: the percentage of ships crossing the Atlantic in escorted convoys that reached their destination unscathed rose steadily to 90 percent, and U-boat losses started to mount substantially in the last six months of 1942, exceeding their replacement rate.

A considerable increase in both aircraft and fast escort vessels; greater coordination among British, Canadian, and American antisubmarine forces; and Ultra's decrypted messages led to the sinking of forty-one U-boats in May 1943, compared to fifteen in April. (On one of the U-boats, Dönitz's son was killed.) After the war, a U-boat commander described the abrupt turnaround; the hunter had now become the hunted.

> [T]he U-boat war was fast becoming one long funeral procession for us. The Allied counteroffensive at sea had struck with unexpected and unprecedented force. The British and Americans had quietly, steadily massed their forces. They had increased their fleet of fast corvettes, built a number of medium-sized aircraft carriers and converted a number of freighters into pocket-sized carriers, assembled squadrons of small planes for carrier duty as well as huge armadas of long-range land-based bombers. Then they hit with sudden power.... [A]ll our proud new U-boats would be turned into a terrible surplus of iron coffins.[10]

Unwilling to suffer such losses of submarines and crews, a disheartened Dönitz ordered his U-boats to temporarily withdraw from the North Atlantic and to focus on the less protected South Atlantic and the coasts of Africa and Brazil. He expected to return to the North Atlantic when German scientists had devised better ways of avoiding detection by Allied devices that could pinpoint a U-boat's location and when armaments manufacturers had designed better weapons to counter Allied aircraft. The U-boat campaign was not abandoned, but the submarines never returned to the North Atlantic in sufficient force to become a serious threat. In the last year and a half of the war, U-boats sank 630,000 tons of merchant shipping, but the Allies were not hurt given that their shipyards produced 20,000,000 tons in that period. Two related conclusions can be drawn from these figures. First, Germany lacked the industrial capacity to produce simultaneously both sufficient numbers of tanks, planes, artillery, and other weapons needed for land warfare and enough U-boats to destroy Allied merchant shipping. Second, because of their combined industrial capacity, the United States and Britain could quickly produce far more vessels than the Germans could sink.

In all, the Germans sank 2,282 ships and damaged hundreds of others. Nevertheless, the Allies won the Battle of the Atlantic. Had the U-boat threat not been contained, it is likely that the war would have been prolonged. Certainly Britain would have been denied vital war supplies and food and the United States might have hesitated to transport across dangerous waters the more than one million personnel needed for the liberation of Europe. On September 21, 1943, Churchill told cheering members of the House of Commons that convoys carrying huge amounts of essential goods, particularly fuel oil, had been docking at British ports. Britain and the United States had broken the U-boats' stranglehold on the island nation.

THE NORTH AFRICAN CAMPAIGN

Benito Mussolini had visions of turning the Mediterranean into an Italian lake and displacing Britain as the dominant power in the Middle East. Dependant on the Suez Canal to get supplies from Asia and oil from the Middle East, Britain feared that Italy's naval force in the Mediterranean and its colony, Cyrenaica (in Libya), threatened Britain's approach to the Suez Canal. From encampments in an inhospitable region of Libya known as the Western Desert, the Italians had crossed into Egypt, which was then a British protectorate, and halted at Sidi Barrani on the Mediterranean coast. In December 1940, British troops, including Commonwealth units from Australia and New Zealand, moved to drive the Italians out of Egypt. The British outflanked the Italian troops in Sidi Barrani and blocked their escape route, taking almost forty thousand prisoners. Crossing into the Western Desert, British forces captured fortresses, took more prisoners, and then moved on the Libyan port of Tobruk; its fall in January 1941 produced tens of thousands of additional prisoners.

Discovering that the Italians were withdrawing from Benghazi, another Libyan port on the Mediterranean, the British drove quickly to cut off their retreat and engaged them in battle in early February 1941. Although greatly outnumbered, British forces prevented the Italians from breaking out, and Australian forces captured Benghazi. With their forces surrounded and disorganized, and having already suffered considerable casualties, the Italians surrendered. In this brief campaign, the British took 130,000 prisoners and seized huge quantities of heavy equipment, including four hundred tanks.

Rommel and the *Afrika Korps*

Almost immediately after the rout of the Italian army, the British initiative was lost. Fearful that the British would take the port of Tripoli and drive Italy out of Libya, which would jeopardize Mussolini's rule in Italy, Hitler dispatched to Libya two German divisions, the *Afrika Korps*, and Mussolini sent fresh troops. The Afrika Korps was led by General Erwin Rommel, who had earned a reputation for daring as a tank commander in the battle for France when he employed Heinz Guderian's guidelines of massed and rapid tank attacks. Most military historians continue to praise Rommel for his willingness to take the audacious gamble; for his brilliant, swift, slashing, and outflanking deployments that brought panzer forces to the enemy's rear; for his astute maneuvers that enabled his panzers to escape when greatly outnumbered; and for his ability to get the best out of his troops. A major reason for Rommel's ability to win his soldiers' confidence was his frequent appearances on the battlefield. Although his enemies usually had an advantage in numbers and weapons and commanded the air, Rommel still won key battles. And, unlike other German armies, Rommel's Afrika Korps was not involved in war crimes. Rommel ignored Hitler's orders to execute commandos and Jewish POWs.

But Rommel also has his detractors. The sensible course to have pursued in North Africa, said his critics, was to shore up the Italians and hold the British at bay; that is, to settle for a stalemate in North Africa. Instead, consumed by ambition, he pursued an aggressive military policy whose goal was the Suez Canal and beyond, thereby involving Germany in a long and drawn-out struggle with Britain and eventually the United States. However, it is also true that when he recognized that Germany had lost the battle in North Africa, he urged withdrawal, which Hitler rejected.*

At virtually the same time that Rommel arrived in North Africa, Churchill transferred some of the most experienced British forces in Libya to Greece to help defend the country against the Axis powers. A significantly weakened

---

*After the war, Rommel was respected both in Germany and in other Western countries as a chivalrous officer who was not a Nazi racial fanatic. This image has been somewhat tarnished in recent years by German historians, who claim that Rommel had admired Hitler until even after the tide began to change. Concerned only with winning glory and furthering his ambition, he intended to invade Palestine, knowing that he would be followed by the SS, which was determined to carry out its genocidal policies against the hundreds of thousands of Jews living there. The bridgehead Rommel established in Tunisia enabled the SS to herd Jews into slave labor camps, where twenty-five hundred perished before the Germans were forced to withdraw.

British army was left to deal with Rommel, who first defeated the British at El Agheila, Libya, in March 1941, and then in April launched an offensive that overwhelmed the stretched-out British forces, capturing huge supplies and even generals.

For the British High Command and Churchill, it was essential that Rommel not seize Tobruk, a Mediterranean port from which his nearby panzer force could be supplied. As long as the British controlled Tobruk, Rommel had a major logistical problem: his supplies had to be shipped to Tripoli and then transported a considerable distance by truck or aircraft to his fighting units. In April 1941, Rommel did not succeed in capturing the port that was tenaciously defended by the Ninth Australian Division whose commander, General Sir Leslie J. Morshead, was a superb practitioner of defensive warfare. The Germans could not overcome Australian strongpoints, each held by about twelve defenders, and well-placed mines disabled the attacking panzers. After suffering twelve hundred casualties and with his ammunition depleted, Rommel was forced to halt the operation.

British attempts in May and June to throw back the Afrika Korps' forward positions and perhaps relieve the garrison at Tobruk failed completely. In the June offensive, known as Operation Battleaxe, the Afrika Korps' antitank weapons stalled the British thrust; then counterattacking German panzers tore through the British tanks. In two days of fighting, the British lost ninety-one tanks. On November 18, the British renewed their offensive, Operation Crusader, and broke through to Tobruk, forcing Rommel to retreat back to El Agheila from where he had started his first offensive.

The German-Italian army in North Africa was dependant on supplies shipped across the Mediterranean. From bases on the island of Malta, the RAF and Royal Navy, tipped off by Ultra, were devastating Italian ports, shipyards, and supply convoys destined for Axis armies. Italian sailors called these dangerous waters "the death route." Throughout the entire North African campaign, Rommel was plagued by supply problems.

To protect Rommel's supply lines, the Luftwaffe, taking off from airfields in Sicily, relentlessly raided Malta, which became the most bombed place in the war. U-boats preyed on the convoys supplying the British military and the civilians on the island. Malta was under siege and desperately short of food and fuel. The need to divert the Luftwaffe to the Soviet Union eased the pressure on Malta as did a supply convoy sent by Churchill that endured massive sea and air attacks before arriving on August 13, 1942. But not until the capitulation of the Axis forces in North Africa in May 1943 did the siege of Malta end.

In January 1942, Rommel went on a second offensive that took the British completely by surprise. By concentrating his forces against dispersed British units and using massive firepower, Rommel destroyed British heavy armor, captured supply depots, and chased the British from Cyrenaica. The fleeing British abandoned more than four thousand vehicles, many of them tanks. In addition to many dead and wounded, twelve thousand were marched into captivity.

After a brief respite, at the end of May Rommel moved again with the intention of retaking Tobruk. But first he had to overcome the British Eighth

Army that was positioned at Gazala west of Tobruk. The Eighth Army had constructed a defensive line that included miles of mines and dispersed strongpoints; the British also had a considerable number of tanks, some 290 more than Rommel. The coastal region, where it was thought Rommel would attack, was better defended than inland regions to the south. Rommel sent a diversionary force north along the coast while the bulk of his armored columns moved rapidly south during the night intending to surprise, outflank, and overrun British strongpoints. The attack met with considerable initial success as panzers maneuvered into the rear of British positions and caused havoc among the defenders. But in some sections, the flanking maneuver did not go smoothly, and German units found themselves confronting strong British defense positions. Fierce resistance by British tanks forced the German panzers to withdraw and reorganize.

Rommel was in a precarious position. His forces were trapped between a minefield and British armor in an area called "the cauldron," and his supply line was severed, leaving the Afrika Korps in great need of food, water, and fuel. If the British had counterattacked the surrounded Germans immediately, critics argue, they could have decisively defeated Rommel, who later stated that he was considering surrender. However, supply convoys did get through the minefields to the endangered panzer force, which enabled Rommel to build up his strength in the cauldron. When the British finally did attack, they were devastated by the Afrika Korps, skillfully combining powerful antitank guns and tank maneuvers; the British Eighth Army lost 260 tanks and was forced to retreat.

Then in mid-June 1942, after a massive bombardment, the Germans broke into Tobruk, which was now defended principally by a South African division. Without offering significant resistance, the British surrendered to a considerably smaller force, and thirty-three thousand troops were taken prisoner, along with huge quantities of fuel, two thousand military vehicles, and additional tons of supplies. A major reason for the disaster at Tobruk was the British military's failure to provide the quality of leadership demonstrated by General Morshead when Rommel had unsuccessfully tried to take Tobruk earlier. The ignominious loss of the fortress port, a symbol of British resolve, cast a somber mood in London. Churchill, who was at the White House conferring with Roosevelt at the time, took the news hard: "This was one of the heaviest blows I can recall during the war…. [A] garrison … [of] seasoned soldiers had laid down their arms to perhaps one-half of their number…. It was a bitter moment. Defeat is one thing; disgrace is another."[11]

Containing the Desert Fox

Newly promoted to field marshal by a delighted Hitler, Rommel now intended to drive on Egypt, threatening the oil fields of the Middle East that were vital for the Allied war machine. In July, the British Eighth Army, which had retreated back to Egypt after its defeat at Gazala, halted the Afrika Korps at the First Battle of El Alamein (also known as the battle of Alam Haifa), sixty miles west of Alexandria. Pinned down by intense artillery fire, the Germans could not advance.

Nor could Rommel outflank British defense positions as he had done in the past. The Mediterranean Sea was to the north and to the south was a vast inland depression impassable for tanks. Further, Italian units proved unreliable, at times fleeing in panic or surrendering in droves, behavior that repulsed Rommel. The Eighth Army had stopped Rommel's advance into Egypt but had lost thirteen thousand men in comparison to seven thousand for Rommel, six thousand of them Italian. Rommel's second attempt to break through Britain's Egyptian defenses in August–September was also stopped by the Eighth Army, which was now commanded by General Bernard Law Montgomery ("Monty"). Montgomery fought an effective defensive battle. The RAF, working in tandem with ground forces and in-depth minefields, enabled the British to repel Rommel's panzers.

Montgomery, who had served in the British army since 1908 and had been wounded in World War I, devoted his life to the study of war. In planning a battle, his mastery of detail was equivalent to that of the best German commanders. His overriding concern was achieving victory on the battlefield with as few casualties as possible. Eschewing improvisation and the daring gamble, Montgomery mastered the set-piece battle: careful attention to detail prior to the battle; attacking only when everything was absolutely ready and in place; and employing maximum artillery and air support for ground troops. Cautious—some said to the point of timidity—Montgomery would not move until he was absolutely certain he had the advantage. He also demanded that his troops train constantly regardless of the weather and that they stay physically fit. He possessed enormous self-confidence and energy, valuable traits that he imparted to his troops, considerably boosting their morale.

Montgomery's major flaw was an overbearing conceit and an uncontrollable urge for self-promotion. "His love of publicity is a disease, like alcoholism or taking drugs," said Lieutenant General Hastings Ismay, Churchill's chief of staff.[12] This generally did not get in the way of his relations with subordinates, who admired his devotion to his troops. However, it often interfered with good relations with American generals who resented his arrogance and attempts to steal center stage and diminish the importance of the American contribution.

In preparation for an October offensive designed to drive the Axis forces from Egypt, Montgomery systematically amassed a huge arsenal of planes, artillery, and tanks, which gave him much greater firepower than Rommel's Afrika Korps and the Italian divisions he commanded. He had 967 tanks, including 300 American-made Shermans that were superior to Rommel's Panzer IVs. Rommel had 230 panzers and 320 inadequate Italian tanks. Montgomery's Eighth Army, comprising troops from Britain, Australia, New Zealand, India, and South Africa, greatly outnumbered the Axis force 195,400 to 104,000. And short of fuel, Rommel could not sustain the mass tank battles in which he excelled.

Rather than engage the "Desert Fox," as the British called Rommel, in a battle of mobility and tactical maneuver, in which Rommel was the acclaimed master, Montgomery intended a controlled set-piece battle. He wanted to draw Rommel's forces into a slugfest in which the British had the advantage of overwhelming firepower and manpower. Since the Eighth Army had almost twice as many tanks, artillery (908 to 475), and antitank guns (1,403 to 744) as the combined German–Italian army, Montgomery reasoned that brute power would prevail in a grinding battle of attrition even against the Afrika Korps' superior training and tactical strengths, especially Rommel's deployment of deadly 88mm mounted antitank guns. Montgomery also counted on his air force to pound German tanks and infantry, preventing Rommel from employing the classic blitzkrieg envelopment maneuver. Moreover, because of Ultra intercepts, Montgomery had access to Rommel's reports to Hitler and the Führer's responses, intelligence that proved invaluable. With this information, Montgomery could pinpoint the positions of Rommel's forces and locate and sink German supply ships.

On October 23, 1942, Montgomery unleashed the Eighth Army in the Second Battle of El Alamein. The assault began with five hours of fearsome artillery barrages and aerial bombardments directed against German–Italian gun emplacements, command centers, observation posts, and any other target whose destruction would weaken the defenders. In between artillery barrages, Commonwealth infantry and engineers charged with clearing minefields moved against Axis positions. It was good fortune for the engineers that shells from the artillery barrage had already detonated thousands of the more than half a million antitank and antipersonnel mines in Rommel's "Devil's Gardens."

The first line of defense just behind the minefields was manned mainly by poorly equipped Italian troops who had little desire to risk their lives for Mussolini or Nazi Germany. Aware of this, Rommel interlaced this line with German infantry. Many Italians fled during the artillery barrage and infantry attack, but the battered German infantrymen held their ground, making it difficult for the British to break through, particularly because the engineers had not been able to fully clear lanes through the minefields. Panzer divisions stood behind the infantry, ready to throw the British who did manage to get through back into the minefields.

German artillery and antitank guns pinned down Montgomery's armor and inflicted considerable losses. But in the two days of fighting, German losses were also high—88 out of 119 tanks—and, because the British Eighth Army had considerably more men and tanks, the Germans could not hope to win a battle of attrition. Unlike the Eighth Army, the Afrika Korps could not replace lost tanks, artillery, and ammunition, nor could it quickly replenish its diminishing fuel supply. Rommel, who was in Austria recovering from illness, flew back to Africa immediately to rally and lead his troops. Montgomery was denied a quick victory, but unremitting pressure from aerial and artillery bombardments and tank battles produced heavy Axis losses, and the British were succeeding in grinding down Rommel's reserves.

There was still no breakthrough after a week of brutal combat, much to Churchill's dismay. But the Afrika Korps was hurting; it was losing a large number of tanks, many of them to British infantry skillfully wielding antitank guns. Although suffering greater losses than the Germans, Montgomery still had hundreds of tanks in reserve poised for a breakout through an open gap. Also, the RAF was carpet-bombing German positions along the route of the breakout.

The Germans, who had limited reserves, could not afford to lose more tanks. Moreover, the RAF had sunk two tankers carrying precious fuel for Rommel's panzers.

Realizing that his diminished forces, short of fuel, munitions, and food, could not hope to check the British steamroller, Rommel asked Hitler for permission to retreat. Hitler replied, "In this situation in which you find yourself there can be no other thought but to stand fast, yield not a yard of ground, and throw every gun and every man into battle…. As to your troops you can show them no other road than that to victory or death."[13] An exasperated Rommel interpreted this to mean that the Führer's headquarters intended "to subordinate military interests to those of propaganda. They were simply unable to bring themselves to say to the German people and the world at large that Alamein had been lost."[14] The remnants of the Afrika Korps, including Italian motorized units, fought with exemplary skill and courage but had no possibility of overcoming the Eighth Army's advantage in men and armor. After enduring more losses and with only a few tanks left, Rommel ordered a retreat even before he received notification that Hitler had rescinded his fight-to-the-death order.

In the Second Battle of El Alamein, the British lost more than five hundred tanks. Although Rommel lost about one-third as many, at the battle's end he was left with only ten serviceable panzers and some twenty other lightly damaged that needed repair. Rommel's shattered army retreated across Egypt west to Tripoli, pursued by Montgomery's forces and attacked by RAF fighter-bombers. Montgomery has been faulted for being overly cautious in his pursuit of Rommel. If he had been more daring, the Eighth Army likely could have dealt a crushing blow to the weakened Afrika Korps, which was desperate for fuel and was reduced to no more than thirty tanks, some of them still not operational. In Montgomery's defense, heavy rains impeded the Eighth Army's pursuit.

Rommel's masterful retreat saved most of his remaining army and added to his reputation as a brilliant tactician. Although Montgomery did not trap and destroy the Afrika Korps, his victory at El Alamein was a turning point in the war and a personal triumph. The Germans had fought effectively but were overwhelmed by superior Allied manpower and weaponry, a formula that would be repeated over and over again as the war progressed.

American Entry

Immediately after Pearl Harbor, Churchill rushed to Washington to persuade Roosevelt to focus American efforts on defeating Hitler. Japan had attacked the United States, so the public regarded Japan, not Germany, as the primary enemy. Despite this, American military planners opted for a "Germany First" strategy, with which Roosevelt agreed. Once that was decided, the American High Command, led by Chief of Staff George C. Marshall, wanted a massive buildup of forces in Britain in preparation for an early cross-Channel invasion of Nazi-dominated Europe and then a drive straight through the enemy's heart to Berlin. Remembering the horrendous slaughter in France in World War I, the British High Command and Churchill opposed opening a second front against Hitler's fortified Atlantic Wall until the odds were overwhelmingly in the Allies' favor; instead, they proposed first driving the Axis out of North Africa and then invading southern Europe, what Churchill called the "soft underbelly" of Hitler's Europe.

American military leaders, particularly Marshall, opposed diverting military resources to North Africa. They felt that with the Nazis right across the English Channel, North Africa was little more than a sideshow. Nevertheless, President Roosevelt thought a second front in North Africa would provide some immediate relief for the Soviets, who were doing most of the fighting. General Dwight D. Eisenhower was given command of the operation, code-named Torch. Although Eisenhower had no battlefield experience, he had demonstrated ability as an organizer and conciliator. He could win people's trust, get the job done, and unlike Montgomery (and Patton and Clark, discussed later in this chapter) did not seek the limelight; these were valuable assets when strong-willed and egocentric commanders in the United States and Britain were given to bickering with each other. He would allow nothing to sunder the coalition. Eisenhower scheduled the American invasion for November 1942.

Marshal Pétain ordered French troops to resist the Anglo-American invasion of Vichy-controlled Morocco and Algeria. At Casablanca in Morocco and Oran in Algeria, the Allies faced strong resistance. In Algiers, the Americans had worked out a deal with Admiral Jean François Darlan, commander of Vichy's armed forces. In return for being appointed high commissioner of French North Africa, Darlan ordered all French troops in North Africa to halt fighting and join with the Allies; he also promised to keep the French fleet, anchored in Toulon in southern France, from falling into German hands. From a military perspective the arrangement made sense because it meant fewer American casualties and secured the Allied rear when their forces moved east into French Tunisia. Nevertheless, given that Darlan was a leading French Fascist and Nazi collaborator, Eisenhower faced a storm of criticism. Hitler reacted by immediately moving troops into Vichy France and preparing to seize the warships at Toulon. Rather than allow the Germans to take control of the fleet, French admirals ordered its destruction. About 177 ships, including three battleships, were scuttled. In late December, Darlan was assassinated. Because the young Frenchman who killed Darlan was tried and executed within two days and all the court records destroyed, his motives are not certain, but he likely assassinated Darlan for having collaborated with the Nazis.

While the Allies were securing Morocco and Algeria, the Germans and Italians, crossing from Sicily with fresh divisions and heavy armor, occupied the Tunisian ports of Bizerte and Tunis. Under orders from Pétain, French commanders stationed in French-controlled Tunisia did not interfere. The Axis powers also transferred fighter planes and dive bombers to Tunisian airfields. Meanwhile, retreating from El Alamein, Rommel arrived in Tunisia at the end of January 1943, where he took up position at the Mareth Line, a series of fortifications the French built before the war to guard against an Italian attack from Libya.

It made little sense for the Axis to occupy Tunisia. With their army in Stalingrad facing destruction and their resources on the Eastern Front stretched to the limit, the Germans could not afford to divert forces to North Africa, which now had little strategic value. By 1943, it was clear that the Axis were not going to capture the Suez Canal and the oil fields of the Middle East. The force sent to Tunisia could also have substantially strengthened Axis defenses in southern Italy, which the Allies were soon to invade. Italian generals urged Mussolini to extricate his army from Tunisia before it was too late, but he refused to listen.

In late November, the Allies crossed into Tunisia with the intention of capturing Tunis and surrounding Bizerte. Supported by aircraft operating from bases close to the battlefields, the Axis inflicted a string of defeats on the Allied forces, culminating in late February 1943 with Rommel's trouncing of the green and ineptly led U.S. II Corps at Kasserine Pass in western Tunisia. Rommel's battle-experienced and hardened panzer force destroyed 112 of 120 American tanks and inflicted six thousand casualties. Distressed by the Americans' inauspicious combat debut, British officers questioned if the United States would prove to be a reliable ally. General Harold Alexander characterized the American soldier as "soft and fat ... they simply do not know their job as soldiers ... unless we can do something about it, the American Army ... will be quite useless and play no useful part whatsoever."[15]

Stung by the poor performance of American troops, Eisenhower appointed Major General George S. P. Patton, Jr., to command the II Corps. A no-nonsense commander, fearless and daring, Patton deliberately cultivated a tough image— strapped to his waist were ivory-handled revolvers, and he constantly resorted to profanity. He was convinced that projecting the image of an aggressive leader would toughen his men for the battles ahead. Patton quickly disciplined, spurred, cajoled, and molded the II Corps into a tough fighting force that could stand up to Rommel's panzer divisions.

Driving the Axis from North Africa

Now Rommel's main concern was defending the Mareth Line against Montgomery's Eighth Army that had been consolidating in front of the line since arriving from Libya. In early March 1943, Rommel's attack against a British strongpoint was beaten back by intense artillery fire. Immediately after the battle, Rommel flew to Hitler's headquarters and told the Führer that only by withdrawing from Africa could his troops be saved; but when it came to retreats, Hitler adamantly refused as usual and replaced Rommel as commander of the Axis forces in Africa.

In mid-March, the Allies went on the offensive: Montgomery struck at the southern flank of the Mareth Line and a reinforced U.S. II Corps attacked from the west. By mid-April, the Axis troops had been forced to retreat from the Mareth Line and were squeezed into a corner of northeastern Tunisia. Allied air and naval attacks on their supply lines had greatly diminished Axis strength. Their fuel supply was so limited that planes could not fly and tanks could not move from repair shops to the front. In early May, after a successful envelopment, American divisions pushed into Bizerte and the British took Tunis. The collapsing Axis armies surrendered in large numbers. The Allies took some 250,000 prisoners and enormous quantities of equipment.

Failure to heed Rommel's plea to evacuate the Axis forces to Europe was another glaring example of Hitler's limitations as a military commander. Had these troops been evacuated across the Mediterranean, the Allied invasion of Sicily and the Italian mainland would have been far more costly. Italy's expulsion from North Africa terminated Mussolini's egomaniacal dream of an Italian Mediterranean empire. Il Duce's fantasy of being honored at a victory parade while riding a white horse in Cairo in the shadow of the pyramids would never be realized. Indeed, the pompous dictator's life would soon take a decidedly different and ignominious turn.

Military historians continue to debate the effectiveness of Operation Torch. Some argue that by devoting so many troops, ships, tanks, and other equipment to the Mediterranean and North Africa, which was essentially a sideshow, the Allies delayed their cross-Channel invasion of France and gave Germany more time to strengthen its Atlantic defenses. Others argue that the North African "diversion" saved the Allies from a premature landing on the Continent that would have been a disastrous failure; the Americans, in particular, needed more time to build up their arsenal and to acquire command, logistical, and combat experience, which they gained in North Africa. Moreover, some of Germany's best soldiers were either killed or captured in the campaign, and the Third Reich lost many planes and tanks, losses that it could ill afford with the war in the Soviet Union turning against it and the Allies planning to invade the Continent.

THE ITALIAN CAMPAIGN

A major reason why Hitler had poured troops into North Africa in 1943 was to prevent an invasion of the Continent by keeping the Allies bogged down in the desert. With the termination of the North African campaign, the Allies were poised to invade Sicily—Operation Husky. At the Casablanca Conference in January 1943, attended by Prime Minister Churchill and President Roosevelt and their chiefs of staff, the Americans, who wanted to concentrate on a cross-Channel invasion of France, reluctantly acceded to British wishes for an invasion of Sicily. It was hoped that eliminating Axis air and naval bases in Sicily would reduce the danger to Allied shipping in the Mediterranean and that carrying the war to Italy would spur Mussolini's opponents to topple Il Duce and pull Italy out of the war. The island was defended by two hundred thousand Italian and thirty thousand German troops. It was a seemingly formidable force, but the Italian weapons were obsolete, the Italian air force was of little value after losing more than two thousand planes in the last eight months, and demoralized Italian troops had no stomach for fighting a war they did not support. They also did not want to fight for Mussolini, whom many now reviled. Rommel, who had experience with Italian troops in North Africa, warned that Italian units were unlikely to stand firm under fire, which was often the case.

Invasion of Sicily

The Sicilian operation that began on July 9 was not without snares. Hundreds of British airborne troops perished when gliders released in the wrong place by their tow planes plunged into the sea or crashed when the tow lines snapped. Because of an uncoded message, both American and British ships mistakenly fired on troop-carrier planes as they passed overhead, destroying or damaging fifty planes and killing or wounding more than four hundred Americans. Paratroopers who jumped too soon landed in the water and drowned, pulled under by their heavy equipment, or did not land where they were supposed to. In the amphibious landing, some infantrymen drowned in the rough waters, and mines destroyed trucks and bulldozers and killed and maimed soldiers on the beaches. Despite these ordeals, the assault succeeded. Aided by naval guns that shattered enemy positions, the amphibious troops established bridgeheads and, overcoming enemy counterattacks, pressed inland taking many Italian prisoners.

Montgomery wanted the U.S. Seventh Army, commanded by Patton, to play a secondary role, drawing enemy attacks away from his Eighth Army as it advanced to the Strait of Messina, which separates Sicily from the Italian peninsula. Unwilling to simply serve as a support for Montgomery, Patton drove rapidly inland and captured the deep-water port of Palermo, meeting little opposition. At the same time, Montgomery's Eighth Army captured the port of Syracuse and nearby airfields. Overjoyed citizens greeted the Allies as liberators, and Italian soldiers were continuing to surrender, "so fast that you have to take them by appointment," quipped an American soldier.

A principal objective of the operation was seizing the port of Messina. Control of the city would deny the Germans an exit route from Sicily; the Allies would either capture or destroy the cut-off and outnumbered German forces. However, Montgomery delayed moving north and divided his forces, sending one corps east. This gave the Germans time to strengthen their defenses that stalled both Montgomery and Patton as they drove toward Messina. The two generals, both with strong egos, were racing to reach Messina first. Although Patton won the race, it made little difference. Field Marshal Albert Kesselring, the Axis commander for southern Italy and Sicily, had successfully evacuated about forty thousand battle-hardened German troops along with most of their vehicles and weapons from Sicily to the mainland, where the Allies would have to face them again in one grueling campaign after another. (Some seventy thousand Italians also escaped.)

Patton's career was jeopardized by an incident in a field hospital. Visiting the wounded, Patton encountered a soldier who could not take the strain of battle. The volatile Patton cursed him, slapped him twice, and called him a coward and a disgrace to the army. Patton had to be restrained by the medical staff. The incident was kept under wraps, but when reports eventually reached America, there were demands for his dismissal. Eisenhower ordered Patton to make a public apology and kept him from participating in the forthcoming invasion of the Italian mainland. But Eisenhower, knowing Patton's value, was also saving him for a future command. Patton's most important contributions were yet to come.

The Allied invasion of Sicily precipitated the fall of Mussolini. Even before the invasion, dissatisfaction with the Italian dictator was apparent within his Fascist Party and among Italian generals and King Victor Emmanuel III. It was also apparent that the great mass of Italian people wanted an end to Mussolini's rule and the war he inflicted on them. They saw no justification for the death and capture of tens of thousands of Italian soldiers ordered to fight for Germany in Russia or for the sacrifice of hundreds of thousands more in North Africa to realize Mussolini's fantasy of an Italian empire in the Mediterranean. At the end of July, after the Fascist Grand Council called for Mussolini's removal, the king dismissed the dictator as premier, ordered his arrest, and appointed Marshal Pietro Badoglio as Mussolini's replacement. In Rome, ecstatic citizens, sang, danced, and embraced. The new premier dissolved the Fascist Party and, eager to pull Italy out of the war, entered into secret negotiations with the Allies. The agreement signed on September 3, 1943, called for Italy to turn its navy and air force over to the Allies and to join them in the war against Germany.

The Germans took swift vengeance against their former ally for what they deemed an act of betrayal. Italian troops throughout the Balkans, the Aegean, and Italy were disarmed, and hundreds of thousands became POWs; by February 1944, over six hundred thousand of these former Italian soldiers had been deported to Germany, many to work in armaments plants where they were treated not much differently than Soviet and Polish slave laborers, and some fifty thousand perished. Tens of thousands of other Italians were compelled to build German fortifications within Italy. The Germans seized huge amounts of military equipment from the defunct Italian army, took over Italian factories, and confiscated badly needed food and routed it to Germany. Not about to let Italy fall to the Allies, the Germans moved to occupy strategic areas, including Rome, where they met resistance by Italian troops. Some Italian units continued to fight under German command, a small number of Italian soldiers joined the Allies, and some linked up with the partisans.

Nor was it the end of Mussolini. Infuriated over the arrest of his old ally and determined not to allow Anglo-American forces to capture him—what if Mussolini decided to tell all!—Hitler ordered his commandos to free the Italian dictator. On September 12, in a daring airborne operation, German commandos led by dedicated Nazi Colonel Otto Skorzeny rescued the fallen dictator from the lightly guarded ski lodge where he was confined and installed him as ruler of a puppet Fascist state in northern Italy.

To punish the Italians further for their treachery, two German scientists arranged for formerly cleared marshlands to be flooded with seawater in order to reintroduce malaria-carrying mosquitoes into the region. To make certain that Italians would suffer, they confiscated all the quinine in the area. As expected, the number of cases of malaria soared.

Rome under Nazi Occupation

The Nazi occupation of Rome immediately after the armistice stirred anti-German feelings among the Romans, particularly after the Germans conscripted men for labor details both in Italy and in Germany. Hatred of the occupier and the expectation of the impending arrival of the Allies fostered armed resistance; the Germans responded with antipartisan roundups and imprisonments and a memorable massacre. On March 23, 1944, a small band of partisans, principally young students, attacked a column of SS police with a homemade bomb hidden in a trash can, killing thirty-three of them. Hearing of the partisan action, a furious Hitler ordered that ten Italians be shot for every German killed; on the following day, the Germans clandestinely massacred 335 men and teenage boys, including 72 Jews, in the Ardeatine Caves, the ancient Christian catacombs. Afterward, German engineers blew up the entrances in an effort to prevent the caves from becoming a shrine. As news of the slaughter leaked out, Romans were in a state of shock and grief. The massacre in the Ardeatine Caves marked the start of brutal countermeasures taken against the partisans. Field Marshal Kesselring, who approved the massacre in the Ardeatine Caves, also ordered the execution of other hostages to discourage attacks by partisans.

The war had created a problem for Pope Pius XII. Although no admirer of Hitler, he regarded godless Communist Russia as a greater threat to Christianity than Nazi Germany. Throughout the war, and particularly after the German occupation of Rome, the pope sought to preserve the Vatican's neutrality in the belief that this was the best way to discourage the Third Reich from bringing down its wrath on the Vatican and its churches. This was essentially the reason why Pius XII pursued a policy of silence when it came to German atrocities, including the annihilation of Europe's Jews (see Chapter 4, page 139). Pius XII opposed partisan attacks on the Germans in fear that they would trigger a popular uprising in the streets of Rome, which would provoke savage reprisals. At the same time, he appealed to the German authorities to act with restraint and not cause suffering for Roman citizens. Consistent with the papal policy of silence, Pope Pius XII did not intervene either publicly or privately on behalf of the men and boys about to be slaughtered in the Ardeatine Caves, despite receiving information about the impending massacre.

The German occupation of Rome created a harrowing life-and-death situation for Rome's small but ancient and thoroughly integrated Jewish community—Jews had been living in Rome for more than two thousand years. German officials in the city were ordered by the SS to round up Rome's Jews for deportation to Auschwitz, and the deportations in Mussolini's Fascist state in north Italy would soon follow. Some Nazi officials in Rome, fearful that Pope Pius XII might publicly protest transporting Rome's Jews to a death camp, urged instead conscripting the Jews for labor service, but Berlin insisted on their liquidation. Jewish men, women, and children were rounded up within sight of the Vatican, crammed into freight cars, and sent to Auschwitz, where most of them were immediately gassed. Escaping the German dragnet, some Roman Jews were hidden by Catholic friends or found sanctuary in the numerous churches and other religious institutions within Rome, while Germans searched the city looking for Jews in hiding.

Invasion of the Mainland: Salerno

After the conquest of Sicily, the Allies planned to invade the Italian peninsula in accordance with Churchill's wishes. Fearful of invading the heavily fortified French coast, Churchill urged striking against Germany's "soft underbelly"— Italy and the Balkans. Although the United States wanted no diversions from a cross-Channel invasion, it agreed to a restricted campaign in Italy for several reasons: it was still premature for the cross-Channel invasion, Allied troops were available in North Africa and Sicily, and military planners did not think that a limited engagement in Italy would imperil the build-up of forces in preparation for the assault on France. Moreover, an Italian campaign could have strategic value. Tying down German troops in Italy, some perhaps withdrawn from the Eastern Front, would both ease pressure on the Soviet Union and keep them out of northern France, the target of the cross-Channel invasion. And the capture of Italian airfields near Foggia would enable long-range RAF and U.S. bombers to strike targets in Romania, Austria, and southern and eastern Germany.

The war in Italy would be fought with limited manpower, for in preparation for the cross-Channel invasion, code-named Operation Overlord, veteran divisions were being transferred from the Mediterranean to Britain. Campaigns would be slow going and painful, for the Allies had to advance mile by mile over steep, narrow roads, through rugged mountains, and across rivers with forbidding currents and then attack skillfully and tenaciously defended German strongpoints.

The invading force, Fifteenth Army Group, comprised Montgomery's Eighth Army and Lieutenant General Mark Clark's U.S. Fifth Army; the operation was commanded by General Sir Harold Alexander. Although not noted for brilliance, Alexander was courageous, calm in a crisis, and had a good relationship with subordinates. Montgomery's Eighth Army made an uncontested landing in Calabria on September 3, the same day that the armistice was signed with the new Italian government. Supported by intense fire from the Royal Navy that silenced German coastal batteries, the British established a beachhead but had difficulty moving inland.

On September 9, the U.S. Fifth Army, with some British contingents, landed at Salerno, south of the port of Naples. The Fifth Army was commanded by Lieutenant General Mark Clark. Clark had very little battlefield experience, although he was wounded in World War I, but he was still considered a brave soldier and excellent planner with a specialty in amphibious assaults—he had planned Operation Torch in North Africa. However, at times, Clark's excessive concern with his reputation, his eagerness to promote and publicize himself, interfered with sound military judgment. His subordinates also regarded him as overbearing and close-minded, unwilling to alter a tactic to which he was committed, even if it meant taking heavy casualties. The equally vain Montgomery was angered that Clark's U.S. Fifth Army rather than his own Eighth Army was given the lead role in the campaign.

In the American sector, murderous artillery and machine-gun fire from the hills around Salerno and the bombing and strafing by the Luftwaffe destroyed landing craft as they approached shore and inflicted heavy casualties on the soldiers struggling to find cover on the beaches. The Americans were unaware that not only were they outnumbered but also they were facing a crack panzer division that had set up effective defenses, particularly artillery on the high ground. Anticipating a soft landing and not wanting to tip off the Germans that an assault was coming, the Americans had dispensed with a preliminary naval bombardment of German positions. There was also insufficient air support for the landing because planes had been withdrawn from the Mediterranean to Britain to supplement the U.S. Eighth Air Force in its bombing campaign on German cities and industrial centers. Moreover, the Allied air force, misjudging the threat from German aircraft, reduced its fighter sorties just as the Germans were mounting an air offensive. Taking off from numerous air bases in Italy, German fighters and bombers sank several transports and landing craft and a heavy cruiser, and they harassed the beachhead. Adding to the tenuousness of the beachhead was Montgomery's failure to race to Salerno to support the American landing.

Four days after the landing, the Germans launched a carefully planned assault intending to overcome the Salerno beachhead before Montgomery's Eighth Army could reach it. Dazed by the ferocity of the German counterattack, some American troops fled in disarray or surrendered. The Allied High Command in Algeria was apprehensive that the U.S. Fifth Army would not be able to hold its bridgehead. However, soon reinforced by paratroopers, seaborne landings, and the belated arrival of Montgomery's Eighth Army and bolstered by massive naval gunfire, carpet-bombing by the air force, and courageous artillerymen who fired repeatedly while being bombarded by German tanks, the Allies checked the German counterattack. After a near disaster that included 4,870 Americans killed, wounded, or missing, the Allied beachhead was secure. General Clark demonstrated personal courage and leadership by taking charge of antitank gunners who were firing at point-blank range.

The Germans made an orderly retreat, which enabled them to establish defensive positions that impeded the Allied advance on Naples. Field Marshal Kesselring skillfully employed an elastic defense—inflicting maximum casualties on the enemy while slowly withdrawing to another position where rivers and mountains gave the advantage to the defenders.

When the Allies finally took Naples on October 1, they were more than two weeks behind schedule. During that interval, German engineers totally destroyed the harbor, set fire to a university library, and planted booby traps and time bombs in museums, post offices, hotels, and other structures, adding to the destruction Allied air raids caused. At the same time, the Wehrmacht had to deal with Neapolitan insurgents who staged a spontaneous insurrection when the Germans ordered thousands of men to report for forced labor and threatened to execute those who did not show up. As the Germans were retreating north, they depleted the countryside of livestock. Naples now faced a monumental food crisis that taxed the Allied liberators to the limit. In addition to capturing Naples, the Allies secured airfields from which they could attack southern Germany and the Romanian oil fields on which Germany was dependent for fuel. The Allies' next objective was Rome, which Churchill saw as a great prize.

The war brought suffering to countless children. In this picture taken in October 1943, an Italian girl comforts her baby brother in front of their bombed-out house.

The Americans learned from the Salerno operation that contrary to their expectations combat in Italy would be exceedingly difficult and that they could not rely on assistance from the now-defunct Italian army. The Germans had augmented their forces in Italy with battle-hardened divisions led by commanders who, like many of their men, were disciplined veterans of the Eastern Front. The Allies possessed superior air and naval power and artillery but enjoyed no numerical advantage, which is an essential prerequisite for assaulting fortified defensive positions. Italy's terrain—the rugged Apennine mountain range that bisects the peninsula from north to south and numerous rivers that are difficult to cross when flooded—provided superb defensive barriers, which the Germans creatively exploited by constructing several lines with well-situated mines, pillboxes, and bunkers. Allied advances would be slow and costly.

In contrast to Churchill, U.S. commanders did not consider the capture of Rome of prime importance. Fixating on the forthcoming Operation Overlord, they continued to transfer men, bombers, troop transports, and landing craft from the Mediterranean theater to Britain. And by early 1944, many leading British and American commanders, including Eisenhower and Montgomery, had also transferred to Britain. Because of the impending Operation Overlord, the Allied High Command was reluctant to send more troops to Italy, but it was too late to withdraw. These developments did not bode well for the ground troops slogging their way up the Italian peninsula over inhospitable terrain and in dreadful weather.

Anzio: Bloody Stalemate

Along the Garigliano and Rapido rivers and with Monte Cassino as its linchpin, the Germans constructed their principal defense bulwark, the Gustav Line, a series of interlocking bunkers, rock formations, and minefields that spread across the Italian peninsula. Cassino guarded the entry to the Liri Valley and the road to Rome. Unable to batter their way through the Gustav Line, the Allies decided to outflank it with an amphibious landing at Anzio, thirty-five miles south of Rome and far behind the Gustav Line. They hoped that a surprise assault from the rear combined with a strong attack against the main front would lead to the line's collapse after which the two forces would unite and march on Rome.

The landing on January 22, 1944, completely surprised the Germans and, to the Allies' delight, met virtually no opposition. But then things went awry. The original plan called for an invasion force of forty thousand men, with more soon to arrive, to advance rapidly across good roads while the enemy was off balance and seize the Alban Hills, twenty miles inland, that controlled the two major highways leading to Rome, only fifteen miles away. The Allies hoped that the landing would force the Germans to shift their forces away from the Gustav Line in order to defend Rome, enabling Clark's U.S. Fifth Army to breach the weakened line and link up with the invasion force. However, instead of adhering to the plan, Clark warned Major General John P. Lucas, commander of the U.S. VI Corps, not "to stick your neck out." He wanted Lucas to delay the dash to the Alban Hills until the beachhead was strengthened enough to forestall a German counterattack. An overly cautious Lucas complied. He would not advance until tanks and heavy artillery had come ashore. But while Lucas awaited reinforcements, the Germans rushed troops to the bridgehead.

Clark expected his Fifth Army to crack the German line at Cassino and then move north through the Liri Valley to the Alban Hills. But cracking the Cassino line depended on a bold move by Lucas toward the Alban Hills that would compel the Germans to withdraw troops from Cassino, weakening its defenses. Failure to exploit the unopposed landing by immediately breaking out from the beachhead has been called a grievous mistake, for German troops could not have been moved fast enough to counter a strong Allied drive on the Alban Hills, which was the gateway to Rome. Moreover, German and Italian Fascist forces within Rome were numerically weak, and it is likely that the partisan-led Romans would have turned on the German occupiers. The Allies, wrote Kesselring's chief of staff after the war, had wasted an opportunity: "On January 22 and even the following day, an audacious and enterprising formation of enemy troops could have penetrated into the city of Rome itself without having to overcome any serious opposition, but the landed enemy forces lost time and hesitated."[16] On the second day of the invasion, Kesselring expressed relief that there was no imminent danger of a large-scale expansion of the beachhead.

In Lucas's defense, if he threw away a great opportunity, it was because he did not feel strong enough. He worried that an advance would mean having to defend more territory with limited manpower; he feared that the inevitable German counterattack would then ravage his thinned-out corps. Lucas wanted to wait for more troops and supplies to arrive before expanding the two- to three-mile perimeter. That the Americans now controlled the port that enabled the bridgehead to be reinforced, he considered a significant achievement of the operation. For Lucas, the real failure was launching an amphibious attack with a force too small to seize the Alban Hills while simultaneously maintaining a defensible beachhead. Yet, the question still remains: Would a general with Patton's dynamism and boldness have succeeded in taking the Alban Hills, thereby relieving the pressure at Cassino and enabling a link-up of Clark's U.S. Fifth Army and Lucas's VI Corps for a concerted march on Rome against weakened German resistance?

By the time Lucas decided to advance—he did manage to press fourteen miles inland—it was too late. With troops rapidly transferred from the Gustav Line and from beyond Italy, Kesselring had surrounded the Allied perimeter, threatening to drive the landing force into the sea. Once again, the German command demonstrated an ability to launch an immediate and effective counterattack. Hitler ordered the annihilation of the beachhead to show the Allies that an amphibious landing in France would endure a similar fate. By the end of January, the Germans greatly outnumbered the Allies about 71,500 to 41,000; by the middle of February, it was about 125,000 to 100,000.

The German buildup compelled the Allies to forgo plans to expand the beachhead and to concentrate entirely on strengthening their defenses. In February, General Lucian K. Truscott, Jr., replaced General Lucas as commander of the VI Corps. In contrast to a seemingly old, fatigued, and pessimistic Lucas, the new commander radiated aggressiveness and confidence that uplifted the troops.

For four months, German artillery and the Luftwaffe pounded the American and British troops concealed in dugouts and foxholes, and the Luftwaffe sank Allied supply ships. The VI Corps courageously held their bridgehead against a numerically superior enemy in what one historian called "the bloodiest stalemate on the western front of World War II."[17] In defending the bridgehead, Allied command made good use of Ultra intercepts that revealed German plans. Massive air and artillery support and troop reinforcements also helped protect the VI Corps, but ultimately it was the courage of the American and British infantry that prevented the Germans from driving the Allies into the sea.

Kesselring had contained but failed to destroy the Allied bridgehead. Ironically, one reason for this failure was the achievement of the discredited General Lucas securing the port from which the Allies unloaded an average of four thousand tons a day and landed reinforcements, making an eventual breakout possible. By the time of the breakout in late May, the Allies' casualties at Anzio were considerable, some 7,000 killed and 36,000 wounded and captured. Total German losses amounted to between 28,000 and 30,000. They would find it difficult to replace the loss of 10,000 dead and captured veterans, and, no doubt, many of the 17,500 wounded would never again see action.

Cassino: Costly Breakout

Two days prior to the landing at Anzio, Mark Clark's U.S. Fifth Army attacked the Gustav Line in order to keep Germans away from Anzio. The crossing of the Rapido River was a disaster. German artillery zeroed in on the infantry exposed at the crossing sites and on the rubber boats carrying them to the German side. The swift current caused a number of boats to capsize, and soldiers drowned in water that was nine feet deep. Those who reached the other side were pinned down by heavy fire coming from well-constructed German emplacements protected in front by barbed wire and mines. As their situation turned hopeless, some Americans swam back, but most were killed or captured. The two-day operation, soon called "Bloody Rapido," cost the Americans some seventeen hundred dead and wounded.

Clark planned for his Fifth Army to break through the Gustav Line into the Liri Valley and join up with the force moving north from Anzio. Together they would march on Rome. To do this, he had to overcome German defenses at the town of Cassino, which was the Gustav Line's central strongpoint some seventy miles south of Anzio. Situated on steep mountainous terrain and defended by panzer units and hard-fighting paratroops, Cassino blocked the Fifth Army's advance. German defenses at Cassino were formidable—minefields, well-protected machine-gun and mortar nests, well-situated artillery, and fortified dugouts that could withstand major assaults. The roof in a dugout, recorded famous war correspondent Bill Mauldin, "consisted of a four-foot layer of stones, a layer of crisscrossed steel rails, and beneath that a ceiling of more thick wooden ties. [The] roof indicated that many of our shells and bombs registered direct hits on it. Yet I doubt if the explosions even disturbed the sleep of the occupants."[18]

Particularly strong defenses were set around the hill on which stood the historical landmark of Monte Cassino, the historic sixth-century Benedictine monastery. The attack that started on January 24, 1944, was an instant failure, but Clark persisted in pressing the assault on the line's strongest section. This only increased American casualties. There would be no immediate link up with the Anzio force that was struggling to survive under immense German pressure.

Prior to a second attempt to take Cassino in February, Lieutenant-General Sir Bernard Freyberg, commander of the New Zealand Corps, wanted the monastery's tower closed because he feared that the Germans were using it as an observation post. Clark argued that the rubble created by the abbey's destruction would provide the Germans with superb defensive positions. But Freyberg obtained the reluctant approval of Sir Harold Alexander, Commander in Chief of Allied forces in Italy. Allied bombers and artillery barrages leveled the monastery, killing some 250 of the 800 Italian civilians who were seeking refuge within its walls. They had not heeded the leaflets dropped on the monastery urging them to leave. In retrospect, the bombing of the monastery was a senseless act because unknown to Allied commanders, no Germans were in the monastery. Publicized worldwide, the destruction of Monte Cassino earned the Allies considerable ill will. German propaganda relentlessly exploited the incident, portraying the German soldier as fighting to preserve European civilization. After the monastery's destruction, the Germans moved in and, as Clark predicted, used the ruins to good advantage to throw back the assault by New Zealanders and Indians. In March, the New Zealanders and Indians were again repulsed in the Third Battle of Cassino.

On May 11, British, Commonwealth, and American forces launched a major offensive against the Gustav Line. It was a well-planned operation. Unknown to the Germans, the Allies assembled a large force that gave them significant numerical advantage around Cassino. The Allies also had total mastery of the skies, outnumbering German aircraft by a ratio of thirteen to one. Fooled by the clever deception, Kesselring kept his reserves north of Rome and around the Anzio beachhead; he was under the misapprehension that the Allies were intending another amphibious attack in one of these sectors.

A decisive reason for the offensive's success was the French Expeditionary Corps (CEF), made up primarily of skilled North African mountain fighters under the command of General Alphonse Juin, himself a veteran of mountain combat. Juin located a weakly fortified area in the Gustav Line; the Germans did not think the Allies would attempt to move through this forbidding mountainous terrain. Working their way through the mountains, mainly on mules, the CEF opened a gap in the German lines, forcing a German pullback that the Allies then exploited.* Meanwhile, the Germans repulsed two valiant attempts by Polish troops to take Mount Cassino.† Unable to cope with Allied pressure all along the Gustav Line, Kesserling ordered a withdrawal from Monastery Hill, and the Polish troops moved in, raising their national flag over the monastery's ruins. The Gustav Line was outflanked and broken; the Germans were in retreat.

Trying to contain the Allies who were smashing through the Gustav Line at Cassino, Kesselring transferred units there from Anzio, but this weakened his beachhead defenses. In late May, the VI Corps broke out of the encirclement at Anzio and joined with other units of the U.S. Fifth Army. Now the British Eighth Army and the U.S. Fifth Army had a possibility of enveloping the German Tenth Army retreating from the Gustav Line. However, General Clark, defying orders from Alexander, did not try to block the Tenth Army's retreat; instead, he commanded the bulk of the VI Corps to proceed directly to Rome. On several occasions, Clark had feuded with the British, believing that they were assigning the Americans a secondary role in the conflict. Now he wanted to make certain that the Americans would take the prize, not the British. Clark relished the glory and publicity that American troops marching into Rome would bring him and his country. His decision permitted the German Tenth Army to escape annihilation or capture. The Americans were by no means through with Kesselring's forces. Withdrawing to northern Italy where they

---

*Entering Italian villages, Juin's Moroccan troops went on a rampage of rape and pillage.

†Defeated in 1939, a substantial number of Polish military men escaped and continued to fight the Nazis. Polish airmen fought with the RAF in the Battle of Britain, and Polish units fought alongside the British in North Africa and Italy and in the liberation of France. After first deporting and imprisoning Poles, the Soviets permitted them to fight alongside the Red Army, which they did all the way to Berlin.

built another formidable defense network called the Gothic Line, Germans fought tenaciously for the remainder of the war.

True to his word to Pope Pius XII, Kesselring retreated from the Eternal City without destroying it. The Americans entered Rome on June 4; Clark arrived on the following day. The Romans, who had been under German occupation since Italy's withdrawal from the war in early September 1943, were ecstatic at their liberation. On June 6, the cross-Channel invasion called Operation Overlord began. Clark was irritated by the timing: "Sons of bitches! They didn't even let us have the newspaper headlines for the fall of Rome for one day."[19] Until the last days of the war, the Allies continued their slow and costly drive up the Italian peninsula against fierce German resistance. But with the invasion of France happening two days after the capture of Rome, the Italian campaign had lost much of its importance to Allied planners.

The Italian Campaign: A Wasteful Diversion?

Some military analysts regard the Allied invasion of Italy as a dreadful error. Italy was not the soft underbelly that Churchill had called it. Allied forces were tied down in an unnecessary campaign where the enemy could take advantage of the rugged Italian terrain to inflict severe casualties on them virtually to the end of the war. Italy was a wasteful diversion that served no important military purpose, continue these critics. The outcome of the war depended not on conquering Italy but on a successful invasion of France, for which the Allies had to direct all their energies and resources. And because of the demands of the forthcoming Operation Overlord, the Allies would not provide the amount of troops needed in Italy for a rapid victory against an entrenched enemy. The result was a brutal and exceedingly costly conflict that was ultimately unnecessary.

Defenders of the Italian campaign raise a key point: after the successful North African campaign and with Operation Overlord still not operable, what were Allied troops stationed in North Africa to do? Joseph Stalin had already expressed outrage at the postponement of the cross-Channel operation from 1943 to 1944. How would the always suspicious Soviet dictator react if these troops stood by idly while the Red Army continued to bear the full brunt of the Nazi war machine? Would he think that Anglo-American inactivity was intended to bleed Russia before American and British leaders tried to cut a deal with Hitler? By forcing Hitler to transfer divisions from the Eastern Front, the invasion of Italy somewhat relieved the pressure on the Red Army and calmed Stalin. And keeping some of Germany's best divisions tied down in Italy—and in Greece and the Balkans, because Hitler feared expansion of the Mediterranean Front—ultimately drained German strength and worked to the advantage of Overlord. (But, respond the critics, the Allies eventually had up to as many as three times the number of troops in Italy as the Germans, troops that the Allies needed for the invasion of France and the march on Germany.) After the landing in Normandy on June 6, 1944, Hitler was compelled to fight on three fronts: the Soviet Union, France, and Italy. And from airfields in Italy, the Allies bombed many targets in Germany in addition to the vital Ploesti oil facilities in Romania, on which the Third Reich depended. The conquest of Sicily also secured Allied shipping in the Mediterranean, enabling resources from Asia and the Middle East to reach Britain faster. Finally, the Allies acquired some valuable lessons in amphibious landings that were put to good use on D–Day.

THE AIR WAR: 1941 TO D-DAY

The war had begun in September 1939, but not until the final months of the war were Britain's ground forces able to bring the fight to the German home-land. For more than four years, bombing was the only way to reach German soil, as Churchill stated: "We have no Continental Army which can defeat the German military power. But there is one thing that will bring him down, and that is an absolutely devastating exterminating attack by heavy bombers."[20]

In 1941, the RAF engaged in nighttime attacks on German industrial and port facilities. Because of poor navigational instruments and difficult weather conditions, the bombers often missed their targets. An analysis of postbombing photographs indicated that only a small percentage of the bombs fell in the vicin-ity of the targeted area. The following year, Bomber Command, headed by Arthur Harris, initiated a strategic bombing offensive directed at German oil facilities, transportation systems, and armament factories, particularly those pro-ducing airplanes and ball bearings vital for the manufacture of weapons such as aircraft. The offensive also entailed area bombing, or massive raids on population centers. Harris maintained that the increasing death toll of industrial workers, the destruction of civilian homes, the wrecking of public utilities, and the creation of an immense refugee problem would so disrupt daily life that the German people would lose the will to fight. Bomber Command believed that its strategic bombing campaign would win the war without an invasion of the Continent, particularly since advances in technology and flying patterns were enabling the bombers to hit specified targets with greater precision. At the end of May 1942, some one thousand planes in three waves bombed the venerable city of Cologne, Germany's third largest. More than 250 factories were destroyed or severely damaged, 45,000 people were made homeless, and 474 people died. The raid was instrumental in convincing the government to support massive bombing raids on German cities.

Precision and Area Bombing

Starting in January 1943, British air commanders decided to increase the pressure on Germany by pulverizing major cities in night attacks that usually consisted of an armada of five hundred heavy bombers. They chose the night because bomber losses during the day were too high. When the air raid sirens signaled, citizens huddled in the cellars of their buildings or went to public air raid shelters (which were barred to foreign forced laborers and Jews who had for the time being escaped deportation). At times the heat and flames were so intense that people died of asphyxiation; other times the shelters collapsed, burying their inhabitants in wood and concrete. When the raid was over and people emerged from the shelters, they were dazed by the fires, the blackened piles of rubble, and block after block of shells of buildings. They then faced the gruesome chore of removing the dead. Nazi propaganda repeatedly claimed that the destruction and death rained on German cities was the work of Jews who had incited Britain to launch these terror attacks.

Between March and July 1943, Bomber Command repeatedly attacked industrial cities in the Ruhr valley, the major producers of coal and steel. On March 28, the RAF hit the lightly defended port of Lübeck on the Baltic Sea. Founded in the Middle Ages, this historic city, with its wood construction, quickly went up in flames; about half the city was totally destroyed. In April, for four consecutive nights the RAF bombed another Baltic port, Rostock; in addition to setting ablaze an airplane plant, the RAF dropped their bombs on the town center. Densely populated areas were deliberately targeted in the hope of breaking the German people's spirit

Starting on July 24, the RAF and U.S. Army Airforce engaged in coordinated raids on Hamburg, Germany's second largest city. Additional raids followed. On July 29, British bombers dropped an additional 2,326 tons of high explosive and incendiary bombs. It was a lethal combination that produced a massive firestorm by coalescing numerous fires into one gargantuan inferno that generated winds of three hundred miles per hour and temperatures of more than one thousand degrees. Some forty thousand civilians perished in this sea of fire, many of them incinerated in shelters that could not protect them; others died from lack of oxygen caused by the intense heat or were sucked into the fire by the tornado force winds, including children torn from the hands of their parents. Half the city was in ruins; thousands of residential buildings were destroyed.

Between November 1943 and March 31, 1944, British Bomber Command punished Berliners in sixteen major attacks. But unlike Hamburg, Berlin's brick and stone buildings did not easily go up in flame. And an improved defense system inflicted heavy losses on RAF bombers.

In raids deep into Germany, bombers had to fly into hostile skies without fighter escorts because fighter planes could not carry sufficient fuel for the return trip. Flying slowly at low altitudes, the bombers were vulnerable to formidible German air defenses: hundreds of antiaircraft batteries and lurking Luftwaffe night-fighters that had all the advantages of speed, manuverability, long-range cannons, and surprise. The interceptors were guided by powerful searchlights from the ground that zeroed in on the bombers and, by late 1941, by an effective radar system that spotted the incoming aircraft. Between the antiaircraft guns and the enemy fighters, the loss rate for the unescorted bombers was becoming too costly—10 percent or more not returning from a mission. Bomber crews were expected to fly thirty missions before being relieved; crew members had only one chance in four of surviving a tour of duty. In the raids over Berlin alone, the British lost 492 bombers in five months, leading some British analysts at the time to regard the Battle of Berlin as a failure, if not a defeat. New technologies, including a way of jamming German radar, aided the RAF in succeeding months. So too did a new tactic introduced by Bomber Command: increasing the number of bombers while shortening the time spent over a target. This still caused considerable devastation while reducing the planes' chances of being hit by flak or brought down by Luftwaffe fighters.

Eschewing indiscriminate area bombing of urban centers, the United States Army Air Forces (USAAF) stationed in Britain opted for precision bombing of key military and industrial sites. Also unlike the RAF, which flew at night, the American Eighth Air Force commanders maintained that daylight raids would improve accuracy, particularly with the new Norden bombsight. And they thought that their well-armed bombers, B-17 Flying Fortresses and B-24 Liberators, could defend themselves against the Luftwaffe fighters. But bombers were also more vulnerable in the daylight. On August 17, 1943, a full 367 Flying Fortresses set out to bomb two targets vital for Germany's military machine: a factory complex in Regensburg that manufactured about 30 percent of the Luftwaffe's single-engined fighters and plants in Schweinfurt that produced ball bearings needed for many types of armaments. Because these targets were located deep into Germany, the bombers could have fighter escorts, whose fuel capacity was limited, for only part of the journey. As soon as the fighter escorts departed, the bombers on both missions were ceaselessly attacked by Luftwaffe interceptors. Although the American bombers scored direct hits on both targets and caused considerable damage, 107 planes were either shot down or rendered useless for future missions. Two months later, the Americans tried again; this time, the Eighth Air Force lost sixty bombers. Dismayed by these severe losses, the Americans temporarily halted their daylight raids deep into Germany.

Flying into the teeth of German air defenses without fighter escorts led to high losses in aircraft and crews that were becoming prohibitive. The development of P-51 Mustangs, fighter planes specially equipped with auxiliary fuel tanks, revolutionized air combat. The Mustangs, faster and better performers than Luftwaffe interceptors, were engineered to provide fighter escort for the bombers from take off to target. Now, weather permitting, Germany was being bombarded day and night, and Mustangs were demolishing the Luftwaffe fighters.

To curtail the threat Luftwaffe fighter planes posed, the Americans made every effort to destroy German aircraft plants, oil installations, and planes on the ground and to engage the Luftwaffe in the air. Destroying the Luftwaffe presented a great challenge because under Albert Speer's management German factories produced forty-four thousand planes in 1944, many of them of high quality. But the Allies did gain air superiority and the Mustangs made the difference, as Walter J. Boyne writes:

> The Mustang revolutionized the air battle over the year [1944]; it was the realization of the impossible dream—a fighter with enough range to escort the bombers and enough speed and manuverability to defeat the defending fighters. Air superiority had been won not by bombing the enemy's factories into oblivion; instead it was won by the long-range fighter, using the bomber formations as bait to entice the Luftwaffe to fight.[21]

In May and early June 1944, Bomber Command and USAAF bombed German installations in France in preparation for D-Day and continued to provide tactical support for ground troops after the invasion. In the autumn, they resumed their raids on the German heartland with ever greater intensity, demolishing German towns and cities.

Was It Worth It?

Analysts continue to debate both the effectiveness and morality of the Allies' bombing campaign. (For a related discussion, see Chapter 7, "Saturation Bombing," page 251.) Critics argue that bombing German cities did not force Germany to capitulate, nor did it significantly shorten the war's duration as its advocates had expected. Ultimately, the war was won not in the air but on the ground, mile by mile.

Germans used a plentiful supply of foreign recruits and slave laborers to quickly repair the damage and dispersed production to areas safe from air attack, including caves, tunnels, and forests, which meant that German production of tanks and planes did not diminish until the autumn of 1944. The cost in Allied planes and crews, say the critics, was not worth turning into rubble German cities, several of them great historic sites famous for their architectual and cultural treasures. It is also questionable whether the raids broke the morale of the German people. If German air raids did not break British morale, ask the critics, why should we have expected the Germans to respond differently? In Albert Speer's judgment, the bombing raids "spurred us to do our utmost. Neither did the bombings and the hardships that resulted from them weaken the morale of the populace. On the contrary, from my visits to armaments plants and my contacts with the man in the street I carried away the impression of growing toughness."[22]

Moreover, argue the critics, deliberately targeting densely populated urban areas was fundamentally immoral. Killing five hundred thousand to six hundred thousand German civilians, including some seventy-five thousand children, and seriously injuring hundreds of thousands more in these indiscriminate attacks on noncombatants was a war crime that tarnished the Allied cause. And, continue the critics, there was something sadistic about razing to the ground defenseless cities in the last weeks of war, cities that posed no military threat. For example, on February 23, 1945, Pforzheim was reduced to ashes. It was of no military value, but its population was reduced by nearly one-third; 20,277 of 65,000 people perished. Likewise, the beautiful medieval city of Dresden had been set ablaze ten days earlier, causing immense suffering to its civilian population and leading Churchill to question terror bombings (see Chapter 7, "Saturation Bombing," page 253).

The bombing campaign has to be analyzed on two levels. The first level is area or strategic bombing, which targeted urban centers and the civilian population. The second level is precision bombing, which aimed to destroy industrial and transportation centers and fuel depots vital to the German war effort. Precision bombing raids, carried out principally by the Americans, did produce several military benefits. By wrecking the German transportation system, these raids impeded the movement of armaments and troops to the fronts and interrupted the flow of vital resources to industrial plants, which contributed substantially to the virtual collapse of the German war economy in the closing months of the war. True, Speer's abilities (see Chapter 6, "German Recovery," page 225) meant that German arms production expanded in 1943 and for much of 1944, but the increase would have been even greater had factories not been bombed, assembled airplanes destroyed, and critical machine tools damaged. (The increase seemed so impressive because production was so limited in 1942.) Allied air raids prevented Speer from meeting the goals he set for tanks, army trucks, and aircraft. If Allied bombing had not diminished the rate of increase of German armaments production, the war could have been prolonged. The destruction of oil refineries and other fuel facilities greatly limited operations by the Luftwaffe as did the damage done to certain machine tools indispensible for the manufacturing of warplanes. From March to December 1944, for example, German oil production declined by more than 80 percent. And tanks could not operate without fuel. It is unquestionable that these attacks, particularly on oil installations in the late stages of the war, gravely weakened the Nazi military machine.

Critics of area bombing argue that had the Allies concentrated their resources on persistently bombing these critical targets—as the Americans had favored—and dispensed with terror raids on cities, the war most likely would have been shortened and numerous civilian casualties avoided. Although it cannot be said with any certainty that the massive raids on German cities shortened the war, as an integral part of the bombing campaign they did provide a military benefit, as Williamson Murray explains: "Obviously, the presence of somewhere around 10,000 antiaircraft guns [to defend against air raids], all of which were also highly capable antitank weapons, and the half-million men to operate them would have had a significant impact on any of the battles in 1943 and 1944, whether one talks about Kursk, Salerno, or Normandy."[23] The large number of fighter planes that Germany was forced to deploy in defense of its cities also deprived the Wehrmacht of air support against the Red Army and Anglo-American forces after D-Day. Consequently, these offensives were less costly than they might have been. Also hurting the German military was the considerable loss of aircraft and air staff defending against the raids; it was much easier for Britain and the United States to replenish their losses than it was for Germany. Consequently, replacement pilots in the Luftwaffe had far less training time than did their opponents, a weakness that showed in aerial combat. With the German aircraft industry virtually shut down in the last months of the war, Allied forces on all fronts could attack German ground forces with impunity. Further, there is evidence that round-the-clock bombing did cause German morale to break, particularly near the war's end, as Goebbels recorded in his diaries (see Chapter 7, "Saturation Bombing," page 252).

Moreover, strategic bombing must be understood within the context of the war. At the time, Bomber Command believed that these air campaigns would shorten the war, thereby saving the lives of hundreds of thousands of Allied soldiers. Furthermore, it was felt that the bombing of German cities was the price Germany paid for initiating the policy of deliberately targeting populated areas in order to terrorize the enemy: Guernica (1937) during the Spanish Civil War, Warsaw (1939), Rotterdam (1940), London (1940–1941), Coventry (1940), Belgrade (1941), and Stalingrad (1942). German aerial bombardment of Warsaw in 1939 left as many dead as did the horrific Allied bombing of Dresden in 1945. In four days in August 1942, systematic bombing of Stalingrad by the Luftwaffe killed some forty thousand Russians, many of them women and children. Around five hundred thousand Soviet citizens perished as a result of German bombings, virtually the same number of Germans who perished in Allied air raids. And the newly developed V-1 flying bombs and V-2 rockets, launched by Germany starting in June 1944, were designed to pulverize British cities and kill as many civilians as possible; both the German High Command and German civilians cheered these weapons in the hopes that they would lead to victory for the Third Reich.

No doubt it is improper to view the suffering of German civilians, many of them children, in the air war as legitimate retribution for their support of an evil regime that started the war and deliberately killed millions of innocents. But it certainly was a consequence, however unfortunate, of the German people embracing this regime and its leader, celebrating its military triumphs, and doing their best to achieve victory. How would slave laborers and concentration camp inmates who were dying every day by the thousands—many of them massacred by the SS—respond to the query often raised by critics of strategic bombing: Was it necessary to intensify the bombing of civilian areas when it was clear that the war was nearing its end? For these victims of Nazi savagery, shortening the war by a day or even an hour could have been the difference between life and death (as it was for thousands of brutalized inmates in Japanese prisoner of war camps just prior to the dropping of the atomic bomb.)

Finally, the destruction by air of many German cities and the death of hundreds of thousands of civilians brought home to the German people the reality of their total defeat, a goal that the Allies sought even if it required brutal means. In 1945, in contrast to 1918, no German could doubt that the nation had lost, and none wanted a repetition of the catastrophe. Unlike the years after World War I, for an overwhelming number of Germans, aggressive nationalism, militarism, and a war of revenge had lost their appeal. Also in contrast to the earlier period, most Germans would now accept a new democratic government. Ironically, the suffering the bombing campaign brought the German people helped launch a new and better Germany. This is not justification, but it is a fact of history.

THE HOME FRONT

Sustaining Morale and Coping with Hardship

The home front was an intricate part of the war. In the Soviet Union and Germany, civilian casualties resulting from invasion and aerial bombardment were far greater than in Britain, although bombing raids and later rockets and missiles launched from France and Belgium rained death and destruction on British cities, particularly London. Escaping air attacks, the United States suffered few civilian casualties. The belligerent powers sought to sustain morale at a time when domestic life was disrupted by bombing raids (and for the Soviet Union a brutal occupation) intended to crush the enemy's will to fight. All the belligerent powers used the cinema, the press, posters, and the rostrum to persuade civilians that they too were in the front line, that their cause was just, and that victory would produce a better future. The awareness of the consequences of defeat did much to promote sacrifices from their citizens for the good of the nation. Europe dominated by National Socialist Germany was intolerable to both the British and the Americans. (And for Americans there was the added factor of making Japan pay for Pearl Harbor.) Soviet citizens had firsthand experience of what the Germans were capable of doing if they won the war, and the prospect of vengeful Russians invading the fatherland terrified German civilians.

The warring powers sought to maximize armaments production, ensure that civilians had sufficient food and other basic necessities, and raise money to fight the war—bond drives in the United States featuring Broadway and Hollywood stars were common occurrences. The achievement of these goals required an enormous expansion of governmental power. To deal with shortages of food, clothing, shoes, soap, and fuel, governments instituted a strict rationing system. For example, Britain limited the purchase of meat, fish, eggs, butter, cheese, sugar, jam, and other foods and encouraged its citizens to plant vegetable gardens. (Ironically, by forcing Britons to eat more vegetables and less fat and sugar, wartime rationing fostered a healthier diet.) Shortages of food, fuel, shoes, and clothing might have dampened morale, but did not cause it to break. Governments urged citizens to collect rubber, iron, aluminum, nickel, tin, and other items that could be recycled for the production of armaments and munitions. In a complete turnaround from the Great Depression, Britain and the United States now faced labor shortages, a problem that was significantly remedied by the employment of women. Germany dealt with labor shortages by recruiting foreign laborers and conscripting slave labor.

Some aspects of the home front are treated to some extent in other chapters, such as armaments production and the effect of aerial bombardment and of the war turning against Germany on civilian morale. Here, we focus on the "Blitz," the bombing of British cities, and the impact of the war on women.

The "Blitz"

With the invasion of Britain called off in September 1940, the Luftwaffe concentrated on bombing English cities, industrial centers, and ports in the hopes of eroding Britain's military potential and undermining civilian morale. The devastation of Coventry in mid-November 1940 became a rallying symbol for the British people. In order to curtail losses, in mid-November the Luftwaffe switched from daytime to night bombings, and British planes rose time after time to make the Luftwaffe pay the price. Whole sections of London were destroyed and fires consistently burned during the "Blitz."

To escape the terror from the sky, virtually every night for months the inhabitants of London took refuge, often for the entire night, in public shelters, the

© Mary Evans Picture Library / Alamy

During the Blitz, Londoners sought shelter in the Underground stations.

tubes (underground railway stations), cellars, and specially constructed iron devices partially buried in the garden of a private home. Although generally safe, the underground stations did experience disasters. In one incident, a direct hit blew people into the path of an oncoming train, killing 111 of them. In another, a burst water main poured waves of sludge into the station, suffocating many of the 680 people sheltered there.

In May 1941, with its air force needed for the planned assault on the Soviet Union, Germany significantly reduced its bombing of British cities. More than fifty thousand Britons perished during the Blitz, but contrary to German hopes, British morale never collapsed. *The New York Times* correspondent James Reston described the exemplary courage and determination of Londoners: "One simply cannot praise the average man here too highly. Out of the history and environment of these past 1,000 years he has inherited a quality of courage which is a true inspiration…. One simply cannot convey the spirit of these people. Adversity only angers and strengthens them…. The British people can hold out to the end."[24] Churchill's speeches and visits to bombed areas helped to sustain morale.

Aerial attacks were resumed in the summer of 1944 with greater intensity, this time with flying bombs and rockets adding to the death toll. One week after D-Day, German V-1 flying bombs hit London from launching sites on the French coast. (The "V" stood for vengeance, *Vergeltung*.) Carrying high explosives, these jet–propelled bombs caused considerable damage. Fighter planes and antiaircraft fire managed to knock out more than half of the V-1s before landing but still the damage to life and property by the 2,400 bombs that got through was considerable, 6,184 killed and 12,981 seriously injured. The V-2s were more deadly because there was no defense against these guided missiles that had larger warheads. Traveling fast and noiselessly, they could not be intercepted. Five hundred hit London and caused 2,724 deaths and 6,523 injuries. Observing the death and destruction caused by these rockets, few Londoners felt any remorse for the German victims of saturation bombing. Advancing Allied armies destroyed the V-1 and V-2 launching sites in France, Belgium, and Holland, thus reducing the effectiveness of Hitler's "miracle weapons."

On the whole, the British people displayed fierce patriotism, stoic resoluteness, and good behavior as bombs rained down on their homes and neighborhoods. But not always. It was not uncommon for scavengers and even civil defense volunteers to loot bombed buildings, stealing money and jewelry from victims of air raids. In 1941, Home Intelligence reported on the bombing of Portsmouth.

> On all sides we heard that looting and wanton destruction had reached alarming proportions. The police seem unable to exercise control and we heard many tales of the wreckage of shelters and the stealing from damaged houses, and were told that some people were afraid to take shelter in an attack for fear of being robbed of their remaining possessions. This seems another illustration of the lack of community spirit. The effect on morale is bad and there is a general feeling of desperation.... [T]he worst offenders appear to be youths of 18 or 19.[25]

But these incidents do not diminish the generally sterling performance of the British public, which surprised the Germans and elated the government.

The War and Women

Women in the belligerent countries served in the armed forces in various capacities. Women were active in the resistance movements in occupied Europe, and some were captured, tortured, and killed by the Nazis. Britain also planted female spies in France, some of whom fell victim to the Nazis. In 1943, 230 women in the French Resistance were interned at Birkenau, the main women's camp at Auschwitz. Only forty-nine survived.

Soviet women were actively involved in combat. Of the 800,000 women in military service by 1945, there were 246,000 deployed in combat units. Soviet women flew fighter planes, drove tanks, and operated artillery; about 2,000 fought as snipers, some with great effectiveness. Thousands more fought with the partisans. Tens of thousands of women died in combat. More than 40 percent of doctors at the front were women. Almost 90 women were awarded Hero of the Soviet Union, their nation's supreme military honor.

In America, over 270,000 women enlisted in the armed service: Women's Air Force Service Pilots (WASPs), the Women's Army Corps (WACs), and the Women Accepted for Volunteer Emergency Service (WAVES), affiliated with the U.S. Navy. The WASPs performed such noncombat duties as flight testing, ferrying planes to different bases, and flying transport planes. WACs and WAVES drove ambulances, served as telegraphers and mechanics, cared for the wounded in hospitals, and performed administrative tasks. In addition, thousands of nurses served in the different branches of service, and more than two hundred army nurses were killed in the battle zones.

In Britain, women joined the various branches of the military but were kept out of combat. Their role in tracking incoming German planes proved invaluable in the Battle of Britain. Female pilots flew planes from the factory to an RAF base but were barred from becoming fighter pilots. Female volunteers served as air raid wardens digging for survivors in bombed-out buildings. Nurses staffed emergency shelters set up for those injured in air raids. Although not part of the military, the one million members of Women's Voluntary Service (WVS), most of them elderly, served their country well. After a bombing raid, they distributed tea and refreshments to the firefighters and to people seeking shelter in train stations, and they tended to the needs of families who had lost their homes in the aerial bombardment.

With so many men in uniform, including comparatively well paid Americans (Yanks) stationed in Britain, sexual inhibitions weakened, and prostitution, venereal disease, and unwanted pregnancies increased substantially. For example, the number of children born out of wedlock more than doubled. Wartime romances between British women and American servicemen were common, leading to over eighty thousand marriages. Because many British men were serving overseas, the presence of large numbers of American soldiers fraternizing with young British women was, at times, a source of friction.

During World War I, women in Britain, the United States, and Germany had replaced men in virtually all branches of civilian life. By performing effectively in jobs formerly held by men, women demonstrated they had an essential role to play in the economic life of their countries. By the end of the war, little opposition remained to granting women political rights, including suffrage. World War II continued this trend.

With men going off to war in both the United States and Britain, large numbers of women, many of them housewives, worked in factories producing planes, tanks, battleships, parachutes, bombs, guns, and anything else needed for the war effort. They operated forklifts, presses, hand drills, and welding machines; repaired equipment; did what was needed on the production lines; drove trucks; and performed numerous other tasks. More opportunities became available for women in management and administration, although these positions were often granted grudgingly. While 70 to 75 percent of American women chose to remain at home, that same percentage of British women was employed. When the war ended, many American women were forced to give up their jobs to provide

AP Photo

Large numbers of British women worked in armaments factories.

work for the returning soldiers, so they resumed being housewives; this was a role that many of them—and their husbands—often preferred. Nevertheless, the new possibilities created by the war gave women more confidence in their abilities, which in the 1960s helped spark a women's movement that pressed for equal opportunity in employment and education.

In the Soviet Union, the millions of men called to active duty and the demands of total war created an acute labor shortage that could only be remedied by utilizing female labor to the maximum. Soviet women comprised about 80 percent of the collective farmers, and more than half of those engaged in armaments production. They helped build defense fortifications and clear the rubble after artillery and aerial bombardments and tended the wounded in hospitals. Many women drove trucks over the hazardous ice road across Lake Ladoga to evacuate the besieged Leningraders.

Many German women aided the war effort in small family businesses and by working the land, including city women conscripted by the National Labor Service. But compared with the Soviet Union, Britain, and the United States, not until the last stage of the war were significant numbers of German women mobilized for work in the armaments sector. The reliance on foreign workers was one reason for this failure to recruit more women for the armaments industry. A second was Hitler's concern that front-line soldiers would react negatively to their wives, daughters, and mothers toiling in factories. Moreover, the Führer believed that a woman caring for home and family would do more for German morale than she would by doing factory work, and the state exhorted German women to have babies to increase the Aryan population, even if it meant having babies outside of marriage. Eventually, though, women did participate in the war effort. As the air campaign over Germany worsened, tens of thousands of women assisted antiaircraft gunners by operating searchlights and communications equipment.

CHRONOLOGY

Battle of the Atlantic

September–December 1940	"Happy Time" for U-boats, which sink five hundred ships
May 24, 1941	Cruiser HMS *Hood* destroyed in naval battle; only three of its fourteen hundred crew members survive
May 27, 1941	Royal Navy sinks the huge battleship *Bismarck*; some twenty-one hundred German sailors perish
December 7, 1941	Japan attacks Pearl Harbor
December 11, 1941	Nazi Germany and Fascist Italy declare war on the United States
July 4, 1942	Twenty-four of thirty-five British merchant ships sailing for the Russian port of Murmansk are destroyed by German U-boats and dive bombers
March 1943	U-boats sink 120 Allied and neutral merchant ships
May 1942	Allied counteroffensive at sea costs Germany forty-one U-boats; it is a turning point in the Battle of the Atlantic

North African Campaign

January 22, 1941	British capture Libyan port of Tobruk
April 1941	Rommel unable to capture Tobruk due to the capable defense of the Ninth Australian Division
January 1942	Rommel chases British from Cyrenaica
June 21, 1942	Tobruk falls to Rommel
October 23, 1942	Montgomery unleashes the British Eighth Army at El Alamein, which turns into a major defeat for Rommel

November 8, 1942	American troops land in North Africa
February 19, 1943	Africa Korps trounces green American forces at Kasserine Pass
May 7, 1943	Tunis and Bizerte fall to Allies
May 11, 1943	Collapsing Axis armies surrender in large numbers, ending the North African campaign

Italian Campaign

January 1943	At Casablanca Conference, President Roosevelt reluctantly accedes to Churchill's wish for an invasion of Sicily
July 9, 1943	Start of Operation Husky, Allied invasion of Sicily
August 17, 1943	American troops enter Messina, Sicily
July 25, 1943	Mussolini ousted as Italian premier and arrested
September 3, 1943	Italy signs armistice agreement with Allies
September 9, 1943	Allies land at Salerno, south of Naples
September 10, 1943	Germans occupy Rome
October 1, 1943	Allies take Naples
January 22, 1944	Allies land at Anzio
May 11, 1944	Start of Allied offensive against Gustav Line
May 17, 1944	Allies capture Cassino
June 4, 1944	American forces liberate Rome

NOTES

1. John Tremaine, *Business in Great Waters* (Hertfordshire, UK: Wordsworth Editions, 1999), 272.

2. Karl Doenitz, *Memoirs: Ten Years and Twenty Days*, trans. R. H. Stevens (New York: Da Capo Press, 1997), 333.

3. Winston S. Churchill, *The Second World War*, vol. 5, *Closing the Ring* (Boston: Houghton Mifflin, 1951), 6.

4. Excerpted in Edmund Blanford, *Under Hitler's Banner: Serving the Third Reich* (Shrewsbury, UK: Airlife, 1996), 79.

5. Samuel Eliot Morison, *History of United States Naval Operations in World War II*, vol. 1, *The Battle of the Atlantic 1939–1943* (Edison, NJ: Castle Books, 1947), 130.

6. Tremaine, *Business in Great Waters*, 423.

7. Doenitz, *Memoirs*, 333.

8. Ibid., 330.

9. Winston S. Churchill, *The Second World War*, vol. 5, *Closing the Ring*, 4.

10. Herbert J. Werner, *Iron Coffins: A Personal Account of the German U-Boat Battles of World War II* (New York: Bantam Books, 1978), 175.

11. Winston S. Churchill, *The Second World War*, vol. 4, *The Hinge of Fate* (Boston: 1950), 383.

12. Rick Atkinson, *The Day of Battle: The War in Sicily and Italy 1943–1944* (New York: Henry Holt, 2007), 126.

13. B. H. Liddell-Hart, ed., *The Rommel Papers*, trans. Paul Findlay (New York: De Capo Press, 1982) 320.

14. Ibid., 324.

15. Douglas Porch, *The Path to Victory: The Mediterranean Theater in World War II* (Old Saybrook, CT: Konecky & Konecky, 2004), 392.

16. Edwin P. Hoyt, *Backwater War: The Allied Campaign in Italy, 1943–45* (Mechanicsburg, PA: Stackpole Books, 2002), 145.

17. Robert Katz, *The Battle for Rome: The Germans, The Allies, The Partisans, and The Pope September 1943–June 1944* (New York: Simon and Schuster, 2003), 179.

18. Bill Maudlin, *Up Front* (New York: Henry Holt, 1944), 160.

19. Porch, *The Path to Victory*, 561.

20. Donald L. Miller, *Masters of the Air: American Bomber Boys Who Fought the Air War Against Nazi Germany* (New York: Simon and Schuster, 2006), 5.

21. Walter J. Boyne, *Clash of Wings: World War II in the Air* (New York: Simon Schuster, 1994), 337–338.

22. Albert Speer, *Inside the Third Reich* (New York: Macmillan, 1970), 278.

23. Williamson Murray "Did Strategic Bombing Work?" in *No End Save Victory*, ed. Robert Cowley (New York: G. P. Putnam's Sons, 2001), 504.

24. Michael Korda, *With Wings Like Eagles: A History of the Battle of Britain* (New York: HarperCollins, 2009), 263.

25. Stuart Hylton, *Their Darkest Hour: The Hidden History of the Home Front 1939–1945* (Gloucestershire, UK: Sutton Publishing, 2003), 138.

Chapter 6

*

Invasion: From the Atlantic Wall to the Siegfried Line

By the middle of 1944, Nazi Germany was reeling. Soviet success at Stalingrad and Kursk had turned the tide on the Eastern Front, and in 1944 the Soviets launched a series of offensives that liberated Soviet territory occupied by Germany and brought the Red Army beyond its borders. The Anglo-American forces had expelled the Axis from North Africa and forced the Germans out of southern and central Italy. By opening another front in France, the United States and Britain further drained Germany's resources and were threatening to invade the Third Reich.

Serving to reaffirm the German people's faith in the Führer, despite the success of the Allied invasion in France and the Soviet Union's relentless march west, was the dispatching over Britain of the V-1 flying bombs and V-2 supersonic rockets. (Adolf Hitler called them vengeance weapons.) Launched from several sites in France, Belgium, and Holland, these rocket attacks boosted German morale. Germans believed their leader's promise that these "miracle weapons," and others to follow, such as jet-propelled fighters more lethal than American Mustangs and deadly snorkel submarines, would lead to a quick German triumph. The myths that Hitler was an instrument of Providence, whose will coincided with what was best for Germany; that Hitler and Germany were one; and that the Führer was wise and infallible did not die easily either for Hitler himself or for the German people.

THE LANDING AT NORMANDY

Preparation

The United States and Britain disagreed over the location of a second front in Europe, for which the Soviet Union had been pressing since 1942. Winston Churchill, we have seen, favored a Mediterranean operation in which Allied troops would move through Adriatic Italy and Austria and then into Germany. This operation could be supplemented by landings either in Greece or the coast of Yugoslavia. Sometime in the future, when Germany had been bled dry, the Mediterranean operation would be followed by an invasion of northwest France. Churchill remembered the staggering losses Britain had suffered in frontal attacks against well-fortified positions during World War I. At the Battle of the Somme alone, British casualties for the first day were 57,470, including 19,240 dead; and fierce Turkish resistance on the Gallipoli Peninsula crushed a British amphibious landing at a cost of 252,000 casualties. Churchill also had vivid memory of the disastrous Anglo-Canadian raid on the French port of Dieppe in August 1942. The purpose of the raid was to see if a port in Europe could be seized, if even for a limited time. More than half of the 6,000 troops, most of them Canadian, were killed or captured; the British lost 106 aircraft and all 28 tanks that had come ashore. Churchill maintained that fighting the Italians would be less of a problem than a cross-Channel frontal assault into the teeth of Hitler's Fortress Europe. Moreover, thinking of a postwar Europe, Churchill wanted Anglo-American forces in Central and East Europe to keep these regions from falling into Soviet hands.

The United States rejected this idea, insisting that a cross-Channel invasion of France was the best approach. First, it would be supported by a massive buildup of arms and men in Britain; second, it represented the shortest path to Germany's industrial regions. American military planners objected to Britain's indirect approach. Rather than waste resources with diversionary operations on the periphery of Hitler's empire, the Americans wanted an assault with massive power on German-occupied France; from there, the Allied forces would take the war directly to German soil. After much debate, the British finally conceded, and the cross-Channel attack, code-named Operation Overlord, went into effect. Some analysts have criticized the United States for failing to recognize the geopolitical consequences of this decision—the virtual turning over of East Europe to the Red Army. Other analysts maintain that the difficult terrain of Italy and the Balkans gave the German defense a distinct advantage. Allied troops would have been tied down and the course of the war lengthened. The Americans regarded the invasions of Sicily and the Italian mainland in 1943 as secondary considerations and went along with them as long as they did not imperil the buildup for the cross-Channel operation. They also saw the Mediterranean operation as a way of pinning down a large number of German troops that would otherwise be sent to France to counter Operation Overlord, the main Allied thrust.

An invasion of France presented logistical problems. An important consideration was choosing a landing site within operating range of Allied fighter planes needed for air support. Allied commanders narrowed the choice to Pas de Calais or Normandy. Given that Pas de Calais beaches were closer to England than the coast of Normandy, the Germans would have fewer opportunities to attack the invasion fleet; and Pas de Calais was only a few days' march to the German frontier and the Ruhr, Germany's industrial heartland. But as British Lieutenant General Frederick Morgan, who in March 1943 was appointed head of planning for a future invasion of northwest Europe, warned, "The Pas de Calais is the most strongly defended area on the whole French coast."[1] Moreover, from Normandy Allied forces could move on the deep water port of Cherbourg and several other ports to the west from which needed supplies could be landed, and they could advance deeper into France and closer to Germany after securing their bridgehead.

Dwight D. Eisenhower was selected to command the Supreme Headquarters of Allied Expeditionary Force (SHAEF). His performance in the North African campaign, where he demonstrated both excellent logistical skills in coordinating the movement, equipping, and supplying of troops and an ability to work well with others, made him an ideal choice. Bernard Montgomery, who had proved himself in North Africa, was given command of the ground forces.

Allied commanders were not at all certain that the invasion would succeed, because an amphibious landing against a well-defended sector is probably the most difficult and precarious of military operations. The Germans had totally crushed the trial landing operation at Dieppe in August 1942, and they almost drove the Allied invasion force back into the sea at Salerno and Anzio. Until a massive number of troops and equipment were put on shore, the Germans would have superiority in manpower, tanks, and artillery. And they were dug in on the coastal cliffs, looking down at the Allied troops wading ashore. For the Allied forces to get ashore safely and establish a beachhead, they had to keep the Germans from knowing the precise site of the invasion and impede the flow of German reinforcements to the front. They accomplished both objectives.

Hitler was certain that an amphibious attack on the French coast was imminent, but he remained confident that German fortifications, armor, and military skill would repulse the invaders. And if the Allies were thrown back with heavy casualties, Hitler reasoned, they would not be able to attempt a second invasion in the near future. Germany then could safely transfer divisions, including elite panzer units, from the Atlantic Wall to the Eastern Front. Reinforced by these divisions, the Wehrmacht would halt a Soviet invasion of the homeland. Bolstering Hitler's confidence was a low estimation of the Americans' fighting ability, a carryover from their dreadful performance at the Kasserine Pass in North Africa. He did not realize that the Germans in France would soon face much better trained and better led American troops.

Included in Allied plans for the invasion was a clever operation designed to mislead Germany into thinking that the landing would take place at Pas de Calais. Fortunately, the British had captured and turned into British agents virtually all German spies in the country. Instructed by British intelligence, these double agents frequently reported back to Germany that a major U.S. force under the command of General George S. Patton had assembled in southeastern England for an attack on Pas de Calais. In reality, the force was nonexistent; it was disinformation that figured into German planning. At the same time, the Allies maintained tight security in the areas where British and American troops were massing in preparation for boarding transports.

To deceive German reconnaissance planes, the Allies made brilliant use of camouflage, planting dummy tanks, landing craft, and army barracks in ports opposite Pas de Calais. That this phantom force, referred to as FUSAG (First United States Army Group) was commanded by Patton, whom the Germans expected to lead the invasion force, added to the deception. And in the months preceding the assault, Allied ships and planes deliberately bombarded Pas de Calais rather than the Normandy coast. These and several other ploys convinced the German High Command that the long-awaited invasion would take place at Pas de Calais, which they heavily fortified and defended with their best troops. Armed with knowledge that Ultra successfully gathered from breaking the German code used in radio traffic at the highest levels, the British knew that Hitler and the German High Command were convinced that the Allies had chosen Pas de Calais, not Normandy, as the invasion site. And the Allies knew that Normandy was not as well fortified as it could have been. When the landings at Normandy did take place, the Germans viewed them as only a diversion and, fortunately for the Allies, held back their reserves. Ironically, on several occasions, Hitler, intuited that Normandy was the Allies' target, but he did not act on this premonition.

Just prior to the invasion, the Allied air forces made a systematic effort to neutralize the Luftwaffe in order to protect the transport ships and landings, to hit hard the beach fortifications, and to disable rail traffic in France—railroad yards, tracks, bridges, and tunnels—to prevent the Germans from rushing reinforcements to Normandy. By crippling critical rail lines and blowing up road bridges, the French Resistance compounded the Germans' reinforcement problem.

D-Day

Weather conditions ruled out June 5, the date Eisenhower had chosen for the invasion. Landing craft would be swamped by strong winds and rough seas, and low clouds impeding visibility would deprive the invasion force of vital air cover. When Eisenhower was informed that the weather, although still poor, should improve slightly the following day, he made the agonizing decision, which some members of his staff opposed, to go ahead with the operation. Eisenhower feared that further postponements would weaken the morale of the troops, who were growing impatient on shipboard and in encampments. He also feared it would enable the Germans to perceive Allied plans.

Anticipating that poor weather would persist for several days more, Field Marshal Erwin Rommel, who commanded the German defense of the Atlantic coast, left for Germany to be with his wife on her birthday and then to meet with Hitler on June 6. Senior commanders were also away from their headquarters attending a conference, leaving the German forces without leadership at a critical moment.

On June 6, 1944, D-Day, the Allies set out for five beaches in Normandy along a coastline extending for more than 50 miles. Such a large-scale operation along a broad front reduced the possibility of the Germans rushing troops everywhere to plug holes in their lines. The invasion force that crossed from England that day consisted of 156,000 soldiers, including 23,000 alighting by parachute and glider, and more than 5,000 vessels, including warships, minesweepers, cargo ships, and landing craft. It was the greatest armada in history. Such a massive display of naval power was a frightening scene to the Germans defending the beach, as one recalled: "I had a good view from the top of the cliffs and looked out at the ocean. What I saw scared the devil out of me. Even though the weather was so bad, we could see a huge number of ships. Ships as far as the eye could see, an entire fleet, and I thought, 'Oh God, we're finished! We're done for now!'"[2] Some 3,700 fighter planes guarded the ships and covered the invasion beaches; another 1,400 transport planes carried parachute battalions or towed gliders filled with infantry and equipment.

Rommel and the Atlantic Wall

In January 1944, Rommel had been given command of defending the Channel coast against an Allied invasion. He aimed to convert the coastlines of France, Belgium, and Holland into Fortress Europe. Rommel maintained that the invasion forces must be annihilated before the landing craft reached the beaches and at the water's edge as soldiers disembarked from the craft. With soldiers struggling ashore and artillery and tanks still in transport or not positioned, the Allies would be at their most vulnerable. Mobile German reserves situated close enough to the anticipated landing site would then launch an immediate counterattack. Rommel insisted that the Anglo-American forces must not be allowed to establish a secure bridgehead from which to penetrate inland. If the Germans did not repel the assault on the beaches, the Allies would quickly land large numbers of tanks, anti-tank guns, and tens of thousands of additional troops, and their air superiority would devastate German positions and disrupt the movement of reserves, as he had witnessed in North Africa. German forces would beat their heads against a much superior force and then wind up fighting a land war both in Russia and the West, that it had no hope of winning.

Rejecting this view, Field Marshal Gerd von Rundstedt, Commander-in-Chief West, would allow the Allies to land and to advance to open country beyond the range of gunfire from their battleships. Once the site of the main invasion was determined, strong mobile panzer forces would race to the front and encircle and throw the enemy back into the sea. Hitler intervened with a compromise solution: the whole coastline would be defended, but some reserve divisions were to be placed well back from the coast and others at different locations closer to the coast. Actually, Hitler's compromise diluted the mobile reserves needed for an effective counterattack at the coast, and the reserves farther inland were insufficient to deal the invaders the crushing blow that von Rundstedt intended.

In the middle of 1942, the Germans had started construction of the Atlantic Wall, defensive ramparts that ran from Holland to Brittany in northwest France.

They used French workers and Polish and Russian POWs to help with construction. Under Rommel's command, the Germans massively strengthened their defenses along the Channel coast. Millions of mines and steel stakes that could wreck landing craft were strategically placed in coastal waters, and wooden stakes topped with mines designed to stall advancement off the beach were planted in the sand. Situated on the cliffs overlooking the beaches were hundreds of strongpoints consisting of concrete bunkers and blockhouses and trenches from which mortar shells and machine-gun fire could strike the beaches below. A network of barbed wire and antitank barriers shielded the strongpoints.

But the Germans' Atlantic Wall was not as impregnable as Hitler had intended. Because it could not cover every foot of coastline, there were numerous weak spots. Also fortunate for the Allies, the Normandy coast did not have as many obstacles to impede landing craft and the movement of infantry or as many fortified bunkers as did the coast of Pas de Calais. Moreover, German divisions defending the coast were under strength and included many second-line troops. This late in the war, the Wehrmacht simply did not have enough troops to defend the entire coast.

With only a handful of destroyers and torpedo boats available to protect a long coastline, the German navy posed no threat to the invasion armada. And massive search-and-destroy missions had greatly reduced the submarine threat. On D-Day, despite the good efforts of the Allies' minesweepers, mines destroyed a U.S. destroyer and sixteen landing craft headed for the beaches with troops. Once the lanes were cleared for them, the battleships, cruisers, and destroyers began a massive shelling of fixed enemy positions that pulverized bunkers, shattering the nerves of the German defenders and, at times, burying alive their crews. However, in many cases, little damage was done to the German bunkers that were reinforced by six feet of concrete and cleverly concealed from naval gunners; only a direct hit could disable such fortified gun emplacements. Allied ground forces would have to immobilize these bunkers once on the beaches.

To protect the landings on the beachheads, the plans called for three American and Anglo-Canadian airborne divisions to land several miles behind the beachheads where they would destroy artillery batteries and secure key bridges and roads, blocking the Germans from reinforcing their forces defending the beaches. Pilots of the low-flying aircraft struggled to evade flak and machine-gun fire. Jumping in the dark, some paratroopers landed in water and swamps and, unable to disentangle themselves from their equipment, drowned. Some crashed into the ground with barely opened parachutes because the plane released them too close to the ground. Gliders carrying airborne troops groped their way through the darkness and enemy flak searching for a designated landing area. Some gliders shattered when they landed on the piling Rommel had ordered installed in the ground. In some sections, Allied officers faced a major problem of assembling units, for their men were scattered, some of them because of inaccurate drops. Also, in the dark and trying to evade flak, some gliders missed their landing zone. Adding to the problem was the loss of considerable heavy equipment. Nevertheless, the dispersed men found each other and contributed to the success of the landings by seizing bridges and crossroads and neutralizing enemy positions. In the end, the cost was less than anticipated. Of the 1,250 Allied air transports, only 29 had been destroyed.

Omaha Beach: A Near Disaster

In particular, units of the U.S. 82nd and 101st Airborne Divisions, by disrupting German attempts to reinforce their defenses, aided the American landing on Utah Beach.* On three other beaches—Juno, Sword, and Gold—British and Canadian soldiers came ashore facing comparatively light enemy resistance. On these beaches, the defense was primarily older men with little or no combat experience and Eastern European recruits who had no wish to fight and die for Germany.

At Omaha, the most heavily fortified beach, the Americans almost did not make it. Originally, the Americans thought there would be a limited number of defenders, some of them Poles and Soviet POWs forced into the German army who were waiting for an opportunity to desert. But the garrison had been reinforced with a first-line unit of combat veterans from the Eastern Front, a fact that the Americans did not learn until one day before the invasion. Soldiers who had been assured that they would face second-rate troops were not told of the reinforcements. Nevertheless, thirty-five thousand Americans were heading for the Omaha Beach. This overwhelming numerical superiority, it was thought, should guarantee victory if the soldiers could get off the beaches and neutralize the German emplacements.

Fortunately for the Americans landing at Omaha, the unexpected German reinforcements consisted of only two regiments; the rest of the German division remained miles away from the beaches. But unfortunately, British bombers sent to attack German positions just before the landing missed their targets. Cloud cover that blocked their vision and fear of hitting the assault troops led them to drop their bombs three miles from the German fortifications. Neither the air force nor the navy had destroyed the German strongholds on Omaha Beach. And American intelligence had underestimated German strength in this area.

Packed into landing craft that were tossed by waves that reached six feet, the assault troops endured a two-to three-hour journey to shore, during which they were drenched and weakened by sea sickness. On the way in, several boats capsized in the choppy sea. As they approached the beach, underwater mines and obstacles and German artillery destroyed some barges, killing and wounding their human cargo. Rough waters swept the first wave of landing craft off target, separating units from senior commanders. Many of the landing craft lowered their bow ramps too soon. Weighed down by heavy equipment, particularly those carrying radios and flame throwers, more than a few drowned as they jumped into water that was chest-deep and sometimes over their heads as

---

*Ironically, the Americans lost more troops in an exercise held in the English Channel than they did invading Utah Beach. On April 28, 1944, German torpedo boats eluded British destroyers protecting LSTs—vessels designed to transport tanks, jeeps, and men for an amphibious landing—in a dress rehearsal for the landing on Utah Beach. The torpedo boats destroyed two of the ships and damaged a third, killing and wounding 938 American soldiers.

they struggled to wade or swim ashore with waves crashing over them. As ramps were lowered, men were killed or wounded by artillery, mortar, and machine-gun fire. Bodies were floating everywhere. In one area, thirty-two amphibious tanks—they were specially equipped with dual-time transmissions, small propellers, and heavy canvas attachments that permitted them to float—were released too far from shore and twenty-seven sank; thirty-three tank crewmen could not be rescued from the doomed DD (dual-drive or duplex drive) tanks.

Exiting off the ramps in the teeth of German firepower and amid mined obstacles, men struggled to find protection on shore. The beach was soon littered with wrecked landing craft and tanks; burning equipment; and dead, mutilated, and blood-drenched wounded Americans sobbing with pain. There were dead Americans floating face up in water reddened with blood or being washed up on the sand. Boats were ablaze and sinking. Soldiers hugged the seawall and sheltered themselves behind whatever barrier they could find, including the bodies of the fallen, to escape the murderous gunfire from emplacements built into the steep cliffs from where the Germans had a perfect view of the beach. That same gunfire made it deadly for engineers to clear safe paths through the rows of mined beach obstacles; several were killed trying.

Traumatized by the ferocious German fire and surrounded by the wounded and dead, the often leaderless soldiers seemed paralyzed in what was for many their first combat experience. Their situation worsened by the minute as German artillery zeroed in on them. There was no place to retreat. Moreover, with the tide rising rapidly, the beach would narrow, squeezing thousands of men into a small space behind the three- to twelve-foot seawall. It was imperative that they move forward and take the high ground that held the German guns.

German officers were reporting to headquarters that they had repulsed the invasion on this beach. Aboard one of the cruisers, General Omar Bradley, commanding the U.S. First Army, later admitted that he was gravely worried: "As the morning lengthened, my worries deepened over alarming and fragmentary reports we picked up on the navy net. From these messages we could piece together only an incoherent account of sinkings, swampings, heavy enemy fire, and chaos on the beaches."[3] The situation seemed so bad that Bradley was contemplating diverting follow-up forces to Utah and the British beaches, virtually sacrificing the men on Omaha beach.

Amid the chaos, some intrepid officers and noncoms cajoled, coerced, and inspired the men to advance off the beach, as the official U.S. army account explained:

> At half-a-dozen or more points on the long stretch, they found the necessary drive to leave their cover and move out over the open beach flat toward the bluffs.... [T]he decisive factor was leadership. Wherever an advance was made, it depended on the presence of some few individuals, officers and noncommissioned officers, who inspired, encouraged, or bullied their men forward by making the first forward moves.... Colonel [George A.] Taylor [of the First Infantry Division] summed up the situation in a terse phrase: "Two kinds of people are

staying on this beach, the dead and those who are going to die—now let's get the hell out of here."[4]

Additionally, Brigadier General Norman D. Cota, Assistant Division Commander of the 29th Infantry Division, fearlessly walking upright and waving his pistol, calmly encouraged the troops to get off the beach.

Individual units inched their way through minefields and barbed wire and up the bluffs; others quickly followed these valiant trailblazers. The Americans outflanked German strongpoints that they neutralized with bazookas, machine guns, and grenades. Tanks continued to fire, knocking out enemy gun emplacements despite being mired on the beach, unable to maneuver and easy targets for German guns. The heavy ships had been reluctant to blast the German strongholds, fearing they would hit their own men huddling on the beach. But with the situation turning desperate, they moved into perilous shallow water infested with mines and let loose a murderous barrage on German gun emplacements, destroying and silencing them. A destroyer commander recalls:

> With a sick feeling in my stomach that we were facing a total fiasco, I left my assigned sea area and moved in as close to shore as I could without bumping the bottom. This gave us an extra mile to improve vision…. My gunnery officer in the gun director found pill boxes, machine gun nests, and other targets by telescope…. We began to bang away.[5]

Naval gunfire, which the Germans could not ward off, was a vital factor in enabling the infantry to overwhelm German positions.

By mid-morning, larger landing craft began depositing on the beach more tanks, half-tracks, and jeeps armed with machine guns, and wave after wave of Americans was coming ashore. By the end of day one, although they were still fighting cut-off German units and were being shelled by enemy artillery from inland, the Americans on Omaha Beach had secured a foothold fifteen hundred to two thousand yards deep. American casualties were considerable: three thousand killed, wounded, or missing. In tribute to American valor, General Montgomery commented a few days after D-day, "If you saw OMAHA beach, you would wonder how the Americans ever got ashore."[6]

Allied Success

The Allies were ashore on all the beaches. Although narrow, their beachheads were too strong and broad to be dislodged; they would not be driven into the sea as Rommel had hoped. Taking the Germans by surprise with overwhelming strength in men and materiel accounted for the success of the greatest amphibious operation ever undertaken. Also contributing to the Allied success was Germany's failure to launch an immediate counterattack with their panzer reserves. And because of Hitler's modification of Rommel's plan, panzer divisions were too far inland to prevent the Allies from establishing bridgeheads.

American soldiers wounded fighting at Omaha Beach.

Moreover, at this early stage, the German High Command was not convinced that the landings were the main attack. Waiting for greater clarification, they did not press Hitler—actually they were afraid to wake him from his drugged sleep—to authorize at once a counterattack by two panzer divisions one hundred miles away from the landings. Delayed for hours, the panzers entered the fray too late to hurl back the invaders. Still believing that Normandy was only a feint, that the main attack would be directed at Pas de Calais—a fiction that British double agents continued to feed the Germans—the German High Command, in what was a fatal blunder, delayed committing additional crack panzer reserves to the counterattack before the Allies could enlarge their bridgeheads. It took several weeks for the Germans to grasp that Normandy was not a diversion, that there would be no landing at Pas de Calais. Most of the exceptionally large German Fifteenth Army stationed there never did get to the Normandy front.

Adding to the Germans' woes was the destruction of the French transportation system by Allied aircraft just before the invasion. By D-Day, the French railway system was functioning at a mere 10 percent of its regular capacity. And just as Rommel feared, unopposed Allied planes wreaked havoc on German troop reinforcements moving to the front and on communications and command headquarters once the invasion began, keeping commanders and lower-level officers off balance. The sabotage of bridges and railways by the French Resistance and Allied special forces dropped behind the German lines also delayed the movement of German armored divisions sent to fortify the coastal defenses in Normandy. The SS engaged in fearful reprisals in retaliation for their men killed by the Resistance; they hanged, shot, and burned French civilians.

In some sections as many as 20 percent of the defenders of the Atlantic Wall were foreign volunteers, mainly anti-Communist Russians, Ukrainians, and other Eastern Europeans; Poles pressed into military service; and Red Army prisoners of war desperate to escape starvation and disease in the POW camps. These non-German units wanted to fight Joseph Stalin, not the Western Allies, or just stay alive. According to evidence gathered from British interrogation of prisoners, a considerable number of these non-Germans sought to surrender as quickly as possible.

With the Germans it was a different story. Possessing good morale and a heightened sense of loyalty to each other and the fatherland, many fought with skill and determination. No doubt, a significant number of defenders retained an unshakeable faith in Hitler and National Socialism that strengthened their determination, as a young officer serving at the Atlantic Wall wrote before the invasion: "1944 will see us steadfast and victorious on all fronts, although the struggle will be hard. Our faith in the Führer is boundless and we know that at the end of the struggle the only victory will be ours."[7] As the Normandy campaign progressed, the Waffen-SS (combat divisions of the SS that served alongside the Wehrmacht, the regular army) in particular would be the Allies' most dangerous opponents.

On D-Day, more than 150,000 American, British, Canadian, Free French, and Polish infantry and airborne troops had secured a foothold on the Normandy coast and hundreds of thousands more would quickly follow. Now the Allies faced the critical task of rushing in more men and supplies before a German counterattack could thwart their advance. The planners had given this problem considerable thought. They rejected an assault on a French port because the ports were too heavily fortified. A port would be seized only after the beachheads had been expanded and strengthened. Instead, two ingeniously constructed artificial harbors called Mulberries were built in Britain and, in an operation involving ten thousand men and 132 tug boats, were towed in sections across the Channel and assembled in the coastal waters off Normandy. With the Mulberries in place, the invasion force would be immediately reinforced.

D-Day was an immense success, and casualties were fewer than the Allies had feared. The dreaded second front was now a reality for the German High Command. However, the Germans had contained the bridgehead, and it was far narrower than the six miles for which the Allies had planned. Linking the bridgeheads into a continuous front, which the plans also called for, would take another six days to achieve, which was longer than anticipated. Nor did the British realize another principal objective: capturing the city of Caen, strategically important for a breakout into open country. The Allies would be fighting in Normandy for a longer period than they had expected. It would take several weeks for the Allies to expand the lodgment, and it would be costly.

STRUGGLING TO BREAK OUT

Total control of the air was a decisive factor for the success of the Allied breakout from the bridgehead. Both prior to and immediately after D-Day, the Allies made a concerted effort to raid German airfields throughout France, not just those near the invasion beaches. Allied aircraft made these airfields unserviceable and destroyed a large number of enemy planes both on the ground and in the air, greatly diminishing Germany's aerial strength, which had already been eroded by the air war over Germany. By targeting Luftwaffe factories and destroying German planes in aerial combat, the British and American raids on Germany significantly reduced the Luftwaffe's capacity to challenge their planes over Normandy. At the time of D-Day, the Luftwaffe had great trouble replacing the loss of veteran pilots. Hurriedly trained German replacements were not ready for aerial combat and were quickly shot down by superior American and British aviators. (In May 1944, flying accidents, mainly problems with landing, cost the Luftwaffe 656 planes.) Unfortunately, Allied air attacks before and after D-Day also destroyed French towns and villages, killing several thousand men, women, and children.*

Domination of the skies enabled the Allies to provide support for infantry and tank units, to reconnoiter enemy positions, to attack reinforcement units, and to bomb bridges, rail junctions, tracks, and rail cars, creating an enormous supply problem for the Germans. Carried out with impunity, these attacks also damaged the enemy's morale, for German troops could not help but notice the Luftwaffe's lack of support. A German general who commanded a panzer division noted soon after D-day that the Allies "have complete mastery of the air. They bomb and strafe every movement, even single vehicles and individuals ... and during the [bombing] barrages the effect on inexperienced troops is literally 'soul shattering.'"[8] On June 10, Rommel notified the German High Command in Berlin of the conditions.

> During the day practically our entire traffic—on roads, tracks, and in the open country—is pinned down by fighter bombers and bomber formations with the result that the movement of our troops on the battlefield is ... almost completely paralyzed, while the enemy can manoeuvre freely. [All roads] in the rear [are] under continual attack, and it is very difficult to get essential supplies, ammunition, and petrol up to the troops. Even the movement of minor formations on the battlefield—artillery going into position, tanks forming up, etc.—is instantly attacked from the air with devastating effect. During the day, fighting troops and headquarters alike are forced to seek cover ... in order to escape continual pounding from the air.[9]

---

*During the first twenty-four hours of D-Day, three thousand French civilians in Normandy died, including almost eight hundred residents of St. Lô. They were the unfortunate casualties of Allied aerial bombings. Eleven thousand more would perish by the end of August. In the five months before D-Day, Allied aerial raids killed fifteen thousand French civilians in Normandy and other parts of France. And tens of thousands of people in Normandy had their homes and farmhouses destroyed by Allied bombs and artillery shells. After the Liberation, unexploded shells, mines, and grenades killed and maimed many more people, including children. Some Normans whose daily lives had not been greatly upset by the German occupiers had ambivalent feelings about the Liberation.

Both Rommel and von Rundstedt also noted that naval artillery was instrumental in shattering German counterattacks. Rommel recorded that no operation involving tanks or infantry was possible in an area commanded by rapid-fire artillery.

Cherbourg and *Bocage* Country

On June 10, American forces drove westward intending to isolate and then seize the vital port of Cherbourg. Supported by relentless naval and air attacks, by the end of June the Americans overwhelmed the defenders of Cherbourg and took several thousand prisoners, including six generals, which greatly irked Hitler. But German engineers had masterfully demolished the port's facilities by clogging its waters with sunken ships and planting mines both on land and underwater that would take weeks to clear. Nevertheless, possessing a large deep water port was crucial for solving the supply problem, particularly given that the powerful storm that hit Normandy June 19–22 had destroyed one of the artificial harbors. Also, the capture of a major port must have caused Germans to wonder about Nazi assurances that the invader would be thrown back.

The Allies had consolidated their bridgehead and seized a key port, but strong German resistance kept them from moving inland according to schedule. The Allied forces were making very slow progress in their attempt at breakout. Shortly after the invasion, Hitler had ordered, "There can be no question of fighting a rearguard action nor of retiring to a new line of resistance. Every man shall fight or fall where he stands."[10] Rommel planned a limited tactical withdrawal that would take his troops beyond the range of Allied naval guns and then attack with his motorized armor. Hitler would not hear of it and accused Rommel's troops of cowardice. True to their Führer's orders to hold their ground at all costs, German soldiers fought ferociously. They were aided by the topographical barriers in the French countryside that provided the Germans with near perfect cover.

To break out of Normandy, the Allies had to pass through the *bocage* country—small fields and narrow roads lined with dense hedges generally six to eight feet high and as much as ten feet thick that covered the western Normandy landscape. Originally constructed by farmers as boundary markers and to contain livestock, these hedgerows, superb defensive positions, had escaped American intelligence; having no training in overcoming these natural defenses, American soldiers were entering killing zones. Concealed by vegetation and trees, Germans with rifles, *panzerfausts* (bazooka-like antitank weapons carried by hand), and machine guns ambushed infantry and disabled tanks. Infantrymen hacking their way through or scrambling over the hedges onto open ground made excellent targets for these German gunners lying in wait. A tank attempting to go through a hedgerow had to climb almost vertically thus exposing its vulnerable unarmored underside to gunners hidden in the hedges wielding panzerfausts. Nor from this position could a tanker hit an enemy target. Under these circumstances, the morale of Allied infantrymen and tank crews suffered, and they became reluctant to advance into the thicket.

American ingenuity enabled the tanks to become a weapon again. An American sergeant suggested attaching to the front of the tank two blades made from the iron salvaged from German beach defenses. Acting like a scythe, the blades effectively cut through the hedges. American tankers also experimented with explosives that blew a hole in the hedgerows that would permit a tank to pass through. Safely through the hedgerow, tanks shelled German machine-gun nests in the distance and sprayed the hedges that concealed German gunners. Then the infantry moved in and neutralized the remaining German defenders. But this was a drawn-out and costly process. In the bocage, both sides suffered heavy casualties in some of the fiercest fighting of the war.

Caen

By the beginning of July, some 900,000 men and 150,000 vehicles had come ashore, strengthening the Allies who also had overwhelming air and naval superiority. But still there was no decisive collapse of the German lines that would permit an Allied breakout into open country, where they could take advantage of their superior firepower and mobility. Caen, for example, was supposed to have fallen on D-Day, and yet one month later it remained under German control. Unforeseen by the Allies, the veteran 21st Panzer Division had been moved to Caen prior to D-Day, holding up the British advance.

The Allies feared that continued strong German resistance would produce a stalemate, that they would get bogged down in a war of attrition—a slugfest between dug-in forces reminiscent of the trench warfare of World War I—for which they would pay a high price in casualties. Allied High Command moved to carry out the preinvasion plan for capturing Caen. Taking Caen would facilitate a breakout because the city was a gateway to good roads and the Falaise plain in which tanks could maneuver; it was also the shortest way to the Seine River and Paris. Demonstrating great skill in defensive warfare, the Germans had prevented an Allied breakout, but Rommel revealed in a letter to Hitler on July 15 that his forces were taking heavy losses in men and tanks that were only being replaced on a small scale. Moreover, continued Rommel:

> Due to the destruction of the railway system and the threat of enemy air force to roads and tracks up to 90 miles behind the front, supply conditions are so bad that only the barest essentials can be brought to the front.... On the enemy's side, fresh forces and great quantities of war material are flowing into his front every day. His supplies are undisturbed by our air force.... In these circumstances we must expect that in the foreseeable future the enemy will succeed in breaking through our thin front ... and thrusting deep into France.... [W]e dispose of no mobile reserve for defence against such a break-through. Action by our air force will, as in the past, have little effect.... [T]he unequal struggle is approaching its end. It is urgently necessary for the proper conclusion to be drawn from this situation.[11]

Rommel pleaded with Hitler to allow a withdrawal of German armies in France to the Seine, a natural line of defense. The Führer, who now viewed Rommel as a "defeatist," refused. He would not deviate from his imperious demand to hold fast to every foot of land.

Prior to D-Day, Montgomery, commander of ground forces for Overlord, had said with conviction that his Anglo-Canadian forces would take Caen on the first day. But he could not deliver. In June and early July, hoping to achieve the breakout, Montgomery made several costly attempts to take the city. The British greatly out-numbered the Waffen-SS in tanks, artillery, and troops and controlled the air. Defend-ing the area with some of their best panzer divisions, the Germans fought tenaciously.

On July 7, massive bombardments first by Allied bombers and then by artil-lery completely devastated this medieval town; its great centuries-old churches were blasted into nothingness, and many civilians perished, but the German defenders suffered little damage. When the Anglo-Canadian force entered the city, they found no signs of destroyed German tanks or gun positions in the bombed sector; nor did they find many German dead. In the two days after the bombing, British and Canadian troops succeeded in taking parts of the city as the Waffen-SS units withdrew after ferocious fighting. On July 20, the Anglo-Canadian forces finally gained complete control. However, the Germans established in-depth defensive positions amid the trees, hedges, stone houses, and walls of villages surrounding Caen, stalling Montgomery's advance and tak-ing a terrible toll—four thousand Anglo-Canadian dead and 469 tanks destroyed, about one-third of the tanks that had been brought ashore in Normandy. "I saw one [tank] knock out eight of our tanks, one after another," said a Canadian veteran of Normandy, "and they didn't even know where the thing was hidden."[12] Although the Anglo-Canadian force lost far more tanks than the Germans, their losses could be almost instantly replaced. Not so for the Germans. With replacements very few, German armor was rapidly eroding.

The Western Allies had an advantage in numbers, but many of their tanks were inferior to that of the enemy. The British Churchill and Cromwell and the American Sherman, which the British widely used, stood up to the Mark IV medium that comprised half of Germany's tank force. But these tanks were no match for German Panthers and Tigers, which had greater firing power and range and thicker armor. Usually, a single shot from the Panther was sufficient to knock out a Sherman. But only by hitting their flanks could standard Allied tank guns penetrate the heavy German tanks.* Some Shermans were equipped

---

*During the Battle of the Bulge, discussed later in this chapter, an American combat veteran writing years later narrates a revealing incident regarding an encounter between a Sherman and a Panther. "A tank commander reported that he had come face-to-face with a Panther.... He fired the first round from the 76mm gun and struck the Panther square in the middle of its forward glacis plate. There was a tremendous flash of sparks like a grinding wheel hitting a piece of steel. When it was over, the tank commander realized that the round had ricocheted and not penetrated the tank. He quickly reloaded, fired the second round and struck the glacis plate again.... Before the Panther could get its gun zeroed in on the [Sherman] M4, the tank commander got off a third round, with equal results. The Panther was finally able to fire its high velocity 75mm, which penetrated the M4 tank like a sieve. Fortunately, the tank commander survived to tell the story." Belton Y. Cooper, *Death Traps: The Survival of an American Armored Division in World War II* (New York: Ballantine Books, 1998), 192–193.

with an antitank gun capable of piercing the Panther, but only a handful of these models were then available. In January 1945, several new heavy and well-armored tanks, the Pershings, that were designed to counter the Panthers and Tigers, were introduced into combat.

There was a redeeming benefit resulting from Montgomery's failure to achieve a breakout. The American attempt at breakout had stalled before the town of St. Lô. The Anglo-Canadian offensive in the Caen sector pinned down a large number of German troops and armor including six hundred tanks, which left the area where American troops were deployed near St. Lô less well defended. The Germans did not have sufficient armor and troops for both sectors. Hitler, still thinking that a second invasion was imminent, decreed that the divisions remain at Pas de Calais instead of rushing to Normandy. For the same reason the Germans did not move divisions near the Seine into Normandy.

The German panzer divisions were being worn down at Caen, and sufficient replacements for lost soldiers and destroyed armor, including tanks, were not forthcoming. Military historians dismiss Montgomery's insistence that he had planned it this way from the beginning, that he had attacked Caen in order to draw German panzer divisions away from the American sector and grind them down by constantly engaging them in battle. In this way, said Montgomery, he was easing the pressure on the Americans to enable them to break out from the bocage country into open plains. His extraordinary self-confidence and desire for the limelight had led him to claim that he would take Caen on D-Day. And when he could not do it, his obsession with his image led him to invent a cover-up.

On July 17, Rommel was being driven back to his headquarters when two British fighters attacked his staff car, causing the driver to lose control. Thrown from the car, Rommel lay in a ditch, unconscious, covered with blood, and with a fractured skull. Taken to a hospital, his life was in the balance, but he did recover. Having observed first hand the overwhelming material might of Anglo-American forces in North Africa and in Normandy, Rommel increasingly had doubts about an ultimate German victory and wanted to make peace with the Western Allies before Germany was destroyed. He also had misgivings about Hitler and was not against deposing him. Implicated in the July 20 plot, Rommel was given a choice: face trial for high treason or commit suicide. (In actuality, although he knew about the plot, he did not actively participate in it.) If he chose suicide, no harm would come to his family, the people would be told that his war injury was the cause of death, and he would receive a state funeral with full military honors befitting one of Germany's greatest generals. On October 14, he took poison. The German people knew nothing of Rommel's opposition to Hitler and of the Führer's revenge.

Rommel's duties were absorbed by Field Marshal Günther von Kluge, who had replaced von Rundstedt as Commander-in-Chief West on July 2. When Field Marshal Wilhelm Keitel, Hitler's lackey Chief of Staff, had asked von Rundstedt "What shall we do," he replied famously: "Make peace, you fools! What else can you do?" When told of von Rundstedt's remark, Hitler dismissed

© Sygma/Corbis

American forces enter an almost totally destroyed St. Lô.

him. In 1940, von Kluge had distinguished himself in France and later in the Soviet Union. He also had ties with the opposition to Hitler both before and during the war. Convinced that defeat was certain, he listened with interest to the conspirators behind the July 20 plot on Hitler's life but was not directly involved.

The Falaise Pocket

For much of July, while the British were struggling to take Caen, the Americans were bogged down in the bocage. Finally, on July 18–19, after twelve days of vicious fighting in the hedgerows and eleven thousand casualties, the Americans captured St. Lô, an important road juncture and jumping off point for a break-out. The heavy bombing had destroyed 95 percent of the city's buildings. On July 25, seven weeks after D-Day, General Bradley, commander of the

U.S. First Army, unleashed a major offensive south of St. Lô designed to escape the inhospitable bocage country in which the Allies had suffered tens of thousands of casualties and to push out into open terrain of the southern Contentin Peninsula where the Americans could take advantage of their greater number of tanks and planes. Code-named Operation Cobra, the offensive began with massive bombing raids on German positions. Tragically, two days in a row the barrage also hit Americans in front-line units, killing and wounding more than seven hundred.

The Germans continued to fight tenaciously, but with the great bulk of their tanks in the Caen sector and unable to cope with Allied tactical aircraft that punished men and machines—virtually every main road was littered with destroyed vehicles—they could not halt the powerful American ground attack. "My front lines looked like the face of the moon and at least 70 percent of my personnel were out of action—dead, wounded, crazed, or numbed," recalled a panzer commander.[13] In several places, the Americans were circling behind a disintegrating German front line. A German SS corporal recalled a scene of desperation: "I had seen the first retreat from Moscow which was terrible enough, but at least units were still intact. Here we had become a cluster of individuals. We were not a battle-worthy company any longer."[14]

Taking advantage of the gap opened up by the First Army, Patton's U.S. Third Army, which had just landed in Normandy, raced west into Brittany on August 1; his mission, which he fulfilled, was to liberate the Brittany Peninsula and seize ports. Observing an unprotected gap in German defenses, Patton, with Bradley's approval, reduced his forces in Brittany and drove east toward the Seine and Paris in a sweeping maneuver intended to envelop the Germans west of the Seine. His adrenalin racing, Patton was doing what he did best, advancing with speed and audacity, and with great success. Patton was not only an aggressive and superb tactician who earned the respect of German generals. He also relished combat. Now that he was in the thick of things, he shouted to the sky, "Compared to war, all other forms of human endeavor shrink to insignificance. God, how I love it."[15]

Like Montgomery, who was often his rival in the pursuit of glory, Patton made a point of being seen with his men and had an insatiable ego. Unlike the very cautious Montgomery who held back until he had overwhelming power and everything was in place, the daring and risk-taking Patton kept driving fast and hard, not even worrying about his flanks. Both generals had unshakeable confidence in their battle plans and leadership abilities.

At this point, seeing a unique opportunity to drive a wedge between Patton's advancing army and the forces of Bradley and Montgomery in the rear, Hitler ordered a massive concentration of German forces in the area for a counterattack that would enclose the Allied breakout and split their armies. Then, advancing to the sea, the German Seventh Army would obliterate the cut-off U.S. First Army to the south and the U.S. Third Army in Brittany, crushing the Allied Normandy invasion. Virtually every senior German general in Normandy opposed the plan, arguing that their exhausted divisions, with insufficient armor and unprotected by a virtually nonexistent Luftwaffe, would be rushing into a trap and be savaged by Allied planes that dominated the skies. The move they favored was withdrawing under the protection of mobile units their battered infantry to the Seine, a natural defensive barrier. Determined not to lose Normandy, Hitler would not hear of it. Far from being the personal triumph Hitler anticipated, his attempt at a masterstroke almost totally destroyed the German Fifth Panzer and Seventh Armies.

In the early hours of August 7, German armored divisions captured Mortain. But the German counterattack could go no farther in the drive to the coast. Lacking reserves, the Germans could not exploit their initial successes, and Bradley's skillful transfer of troops stabilized the front. A decisive battle in halting the German drive was the American defense of Hill 317, which had a superb view of the flat land south and west of Mortain. From this observation post, Americans guided artillery barrages and aerial bombardments onto German positions with devastating effect. The Germans surrounded the hill. Although suffering from lack of food and medical supplies, the American infantry battalion holding the hill refused a German offer of surrender and continued its fierce resistance. After five days of trying, the Germans failed to dislodge the seven hundred American infantrymen whose stubborn defense helped halt the German drive. But the Americans paid a heavy price: nearly three hundred killed or wounded.

In the battle for the Mortain-Avranches corridor near Falaise (see map on page 227), the Allies controlled the skies. The German planes marshaled to support the counteroffensive took off from their bases near Paris but were intercepted by British and American fighters and never did reach the battlefield. Whatever support the Luftwaffe could provide had minimal effect on the Allies. A furious Hitler went into wild tirades denouncing the Luftwaffe and Hermann Goering. Attacking in force, at will, and mercilessly, Allied pilots hunted down German tanks, artillery, and troops. General Heinrich von Lüttwitz described such an attack on August 7 against his advancing panzers: "Suddenly the Allied fighter-bombers swooped out of the sky. They came down in hundreds firing their rockets at the concentrated tanks and vehicles. We could do nothing against them, and we could make no further progress. The next day the planes came down again. We were forced to give the ground we had gained, and by 9 August the division was back where it started from north of Mortain, having lost thirty tanks and eight hundred men."[16] "This was the first time in history that an attacking force had been stopped solely by bombing," observed a German general after the war.[17]

German accounts written at the time and after the war all say that, more than any other factor, the terror from the skies and the almost total absence of the Luftwaffe devastated and demoralized the infantry and panzer units. Constant harassment from Allied planes forced German reinforcements to travel at night and off main roads, which seriously delayed their arrival at the Normandy front. And most important, the Allied air forces prevented the panzer divisions from fighting their kind of war—attacking in mass formations in open country. After the war, General Walter Warlimont told Allied interrogators, "All commanders were discouraged by your overpowering air force. They said that whatever they planned to execute was impossible to execute and control because your air force spotted and attacked every movement."[18]

On August 8, as the battle for Mortain raged, Bradley had an inspiration: if Patton's Third Army could link up with British and Canadian forces near the town of Falaise, the Germans would be encircled and trapped in a pocket, making possible the annihilation of the entire German Seventh Army, most of Germany's combat troops in Normandy. Eisenhower immediately recognized the merit of Bradley's revision of Operation Cobra and gave his approval. The plans were set in motion. That morning, Bradley told Secretary of the Treasury Henry Morgenthau, Jr., who was observing the front, that the Allies were about to surround the enemy on his open flank. "This is an opportunity that comes to a commander not more than once in a lifetime. We're about to destroy an entire hostile army."[19] Helping the Allied envelopment of the German forces were Hitler's orders to continue the counteroffensive when the situation necessitated an orderly retreat.

On August 9 and 10, counterattacking SS Panthers and Tigers, bolstered by 88mm antitank guns, littered the battlefield with the hulks of Canadian and Polish armor—the Polish First Armored Division had participated in the Normandy invasion since D-Day. But the Germans were in no position to capitalize on their success. Short of troops, armor, and fuel; exhausted by weeks of almost daily battle; constantly terrorized by Allied planes; and fighting against well-supplied and growing numbers of Allied troops, the German army in Normandy was facing inevitable defeat. What made its situation hopeless was Hitler's ill-conceived counteroffensive. Fully aware of their desperate situation, German generals in the field pleaded that they be permitted to escape from the jaws of the Allied pincers. But Hitler, determined to hold Normandy and throw the Allied invasion force back to the sea, demanded that his soldiers hold their ground, regroup, and then continue with the counterattack. As in other instances throughout the war, Hitler's "stand and die" order placed German troops in an untenable position.

On August 15, Field Marshal von Kluge arranged to meet his generals trapped in the pocket, but Allied aircraft attacked his procession. His radio destroyed, he was unable to inform his generals of his whereabouts. When Hitler heard of von Kluge's disappearance, he believed the field marshal was conspiring to surrender German forces in the West to the Allies. Already convinced on the basis of evidence supplied by the Gestapo that von Kluge was involved with the assassination plot, Hitler ordered the field marshal to report to his headquarters and replaced him with Field Marshal Walther Model, a Hitler loyalist, ardent Nazi, and master of defensive warfare. Fearing torture, von Kluge sent a letter to the Führer and then took his own life. In the letter, he stated that a sober assessment of Anglo-American strength requires an end to this hopeless struggle. He also expressed admiration for Hitler's "will and genius."

On August 16, the Canadians moved into Falaise and two days later took control of the destroyed city, which was resolutely defended largely by fanatical teenaged SS troops. In one instance, sixty teenagers held out for three days; only two wounded were taken alive. The American and Anglo-Canadian forces succeeded in smashing the German counterattack and encircling the German Seventh Army. However, in one of the most controversial decisions of the war, the Allies delayed in closing the ring until August 19. Patton begged to be allowed to seal immediately the eighteen-mile gap between Falaise and Argentan through which the Germans were escaping the noose. Fearing that in the confusion American and Canadian troops might inadvertently fire on each other, Bradley turned down Patton's pleas. The failure to seal the gap and obliterate the trapped army allowed perhaps as many as forty thousand Germans, including senior officers, to slip out of the pocket as it was about to close, cross the Seine, and get back to Germany to fight again.

Nevertheless, it was a crushing defeat for the Germans caught in the Falaise pocket. Allied artillery and tanks pounded the Germans trying desperately to flee the trap, and Allied planes relentlessly strafed and bombed them. Roads and villages were clogged with horse-drawn transports and exhausted, often leaderless men, which made them a gunner's dream. The wounded were left where they fell; horses stampeded in panic; and everywhere mutilated, unburied dead soldiers, rotting horses, and hulks of blackened, burned-out vehicles from which piercing screams could be heard added to the despair of the retreating Germans. An American officer who fought in the campaign describes the plight of the Germans trying to escape from the pocket:

> Worst of all for the Germans caught in this pocket must have been the annihilating bombing and strafing by Allied planes, then in complete control of the skies.... The dead Germans were literally stacked by the hundreds—in some places two and three feet deep. It was a real massacre. All of the roads for miles were strewn with German corpses and littered with hundreds of smoking or burning tanks, trucks, and wagons. The debris of the fleeing Germans was everywhere. Hulks of burned-out tanks, trucks, half tracks, and self-propelled and towed guns were dramatic proof of the devastating power of airplanes.... [It] must have been absolute terror and total panic for the German soldier under the deluge of destruction from our Air Force.[20]

Visiting what he called "killing grounds" forty-eight hours after the gap had been closed, General Eisenhower observed the dead and mutilated bodies and destroyed equipment everywhere. He encountered "scenes that could be described only by Dante. It was literally possible to walk for hundreds of yards at a time, stepping on nothing but dead and decayed flesh."[21] In all, some ten thousand Germans corpses littered the fields and roads and some fifty thousand were taken prisoner. Aware that the tide of battle had turned and weary of the war, German soldiers (but rarely the Waffen-SS) increasingly reasoned that their best hope for survival was surrendering to American and British forces. The Germans abandoned much of their heavy weapons and armor, including five hundred tanks, and escaped on foot, in horse-drawn wagons and in vehicles of every sort. The Allied breakthrough had succeeded: the entire German front in Normandy had collapsed. Now the Allies, with 1.5 million troops in France, could drive to the German border. The remaining German forces in France could not hope to stop them. Shattered in the Falaise pocket was Hitler's hope of retaining control over France.

The Falaise disaster again revealed Hitler's limitations as a military strategist—Bradley called it the worst mistake made during the war. Once the Allies had established beachheads that were protected by their air force, which roamed the skies virtually unopposed, Germany should have pulled its forces back behind the Seine, as Hitler's generals advised. But Hitler, who abhorred retreats, remained inflexible, insisting that his soldiers stand pat and defend every foot of occupied Normandy, an order for which they paid a heavy price in troops and arms. Then, thinking he would crush the Allied forces in a daring maneuver, Hitler ordered the counterattack in the Mortain and Avranches area, further draining German manpower and armor that would have been best used to defend the German frontier.

Liberation

On August 19, French Resistance fighters, who had been harassing retreating Germans and taking over towns, rose up against the German occupiers in Paris. The partisans placed posters on walls calling for all men from age eighteen to fifty to join the struggle against the invader. On several streets, the Parisians built barricades and snipers fired at Germans from rooftops. The German garrison controlled several strongholds and most of the city's important monuments, but it lacked the manpower to crush the Resistance. On August 24, Charles De Gaulle's Free French forces that had fought in Normandy entered Paris and battled the Germans. The following day, General Dietrich von Choltitz, military governor of Paris, knowing he lacked the troops to win a battle of urban warfare, surrendered to the Free French commanded by General Jacques Leclerc. Hitler had given strict orders that if Paris could not be held it must be reduced to a pile of ruins, including all of its architectural splendors; nothing was to be left standing. Von Choltitz disobeyed the order because he knew the war was lost and wanted to spare this great European city.*

On August 25, De Gaulle, returning to Paris in triumph, gave an emotional speech to Parisians: "Paris. Paris outraged. Paris broken, Paris martyred, but Paris liberated! Liberated by herself, liberated by her people with the help of the whole of France, that is to say of the France which fights, the true France, eternal France."[22] On the following day, the people of Paris turned out for a victory parade down the Champs Élysées. While Paris was being liberated, the Germans sent their last transport of Jews in France to Auschwitz and the gas chambers.

---

*Whereas Germans look at von Choltitz as a heroic figure, the French qualify this view. During the battle for Paris, they point out, von Choltitz ordered the execution of thirty-five captured French Resistants and the burning of the Grand Palais. He was also guilty of war crimes in the Soviet Union. While in a British prison, he was secretly taped telling other generals that when in Russia, "The worst job I ever carried out—which however I carried out with great consistency—was the liquidation of the Jews. I carried out this order down to the very last detail." Sönke Neitzel, ed., *Tapping Hitler's Generals: Transcripts of Secret Conversations, 1942–1945* (Barnsby, S. Yorkshire: Frontline Books, 2007), 192.

Frank Scherschel/Time & Life Pictures/Getty Images

Parisians celebrate their liberation.

The Allies continued their advance toward the frontiers of the Reich against battered German forces, liberating one French community after another. In all liberated towns and villages, the local population cheered, waved flags, and handed flowers to the Allied soldiers. A British tanker's description of his unit's entry into the northern city of Arras was typical of the welcome the French people extended to their liberators: "As soon as we were well into the town … every door and house was thrown open and out from every street alleyway the liberated people of Arras flooded and swarmed around the tanks. They completely abandoned themselves, rejoicing, shouting and cheering. Old men and young girls dancing down the street climbed onto my tank kissing and embracing me, shouting 'Vivre les Anglais' and 'No more Gestapo.' … The bells pealed."[23]

As the Germans were retreating to the French border and the French were celebrating their liberation, a combined American and French force was fighting its way northward from the Mediterranean coastline of southern France. Originally conceived as an amphibious landing to be conducted simultaneously with Overlord, a dire shortage of landing craft forced the postponement of the operation until August 15. Over 150,000 Allied troops invaded near St. Tropez and seized Toulon and the critically important port city of Marseilles, through which approximately 30 percent of Allied supplies for Eisenhower's forces would eventually pass. As in Normandy, the German defenders of southern France suffered considerable casualties—some one hundred thousand men killed, wounded, captured, or missing. Most of the missing were killed by the French Resistance.

After liberation, French women who slept with the hated Germans are marched through Paris; their heads are shaved and swastikas are painted on their faces.

By the end of August, the battle for France had been won, and remnants of the Wehrmacht forces in France, ragged and demoralized, limped back to German-controlled territory, often harassed by Resistance fighters. The retreat was "like running the gauntlet through a hate-filled country in an uprising," recalled a German officer.[24] A German soldier recorded his feelings in his diary: "In May 1940 I first set foot on French soil with the best-equipped and best-trained army in the world. Then the German troops overran this land with a victory march without comparison.... Today, four years later, I slip out by the dark of night toward the starting-point, back in the Reich, with a bitter feeling of shame in my soul at the way the rest of my brave division has dissolved, while troops from a continent 4,000 miles away follow close on our heels."[25]

Fleeing from the Falaise pocket, German troops headed for the Seine and joined other troops in what was a large-scale withdrawal from France. A successful river crossing would enable them to escape to occupied Belgium and to Germany. Pursuing Allied divisions attacked the withdrawing Germans who fought tenaciously to protect their crossing sites. In a superb demonstration of improvisation, coordination, and discipline, the Germans succeeded in getting 240,000 men and more than 20,000 vehicles across the Seine using every means possible: ferries, pontoon bridges, small boats, hastily constructed rafts, and even swimming. The Allies would soon have to face again these soldiers—and their senior officers—who had escaped from Normandy and other parts of France. Some military historians fault the Allies for not doing enough to cut off, entrap, and destroy the fleeing German forces as they neared and crossed the Seine. Although the pursuit could have been more aggressive, poor flying weather did hamper the Allied effort.

German casualties in France from D-Day to the end of August amounted to about four hundred thousand killed, wounded, captured, and missing, including hard-to-replace senior officers. Thousands of German tanks, guns, planes, and air defenses were either smashed or captured. In addition, the loss of France deprived the Third Reich of valuable resources needed for the war: armaments factories, a labor supply, food, iron ore, and hundreds of thousands of horses used to move artillery and supplies. German soldiers who survived the debacle in Normandy could never forget having to deal with Allied air and artillery superiority and what seemed like limitless quantities of weapons and manpower.

TEMPORARY STALEMATE ON
THE WESTERN FRONT

German Recovery

After their heady victories in France, Anglo-American military leaders believed that the Wehrmacht was a spent force; that Germany was virtually finished and the war would be over before the end of the year. Their thinking seemed logical because from June to September, Germany had suffered more than a million casualties in France and on the Eastern Front, and Allied aircraft continued their horrific raids on German towns and cities.

But the Western Allies were mistaken. They underestimated the organizational expertise of the Wehrmacht's professional staff; the imagination and daring of German generals and lower-level officers; and the resolve and tenacity of the German soldier, most of whom were still loyal to the Nazi regime and committed to defending their fatherland that was threatened with invasion. Throughout the war, German officers had shown that they knew how to exploit battlefield opportunities and their opponents' mistakes. They excelled at the offensive breakthrough, the tenacious defense, and the unexpected and resourceful counterattack. And fighting on the German frontier meant shortened supply lines. Defying all Allied expectations, the Germans displayed remarkable resilience and were able to regroup the divisions extricated from France and reinforce them with troops moved from other areas. In a short time, they had built an effective combat force on their western border.

The Allies faced difficult logistical problems that slowed down their advance. The rapid drive across northern France left their forces hundreds of miles ahead of their sources of supply in Normandy. The destruction of French railways and bridges by systematic Allied bombing in preparation for D-Day and the demolishing of port facilities by German engineers hampered the movement of supplies, ammunition, and, most important, fuel. So too did a shortage of trucks made worse by a mechanical deficiency in one model that cost the British the service of fourteen hundred three-ton trucks. The famous Red Ball Express, thousands of large trucks manned to a great extent by African Americans, did a superb job transporting supplies to the front, but the tremendous wear and tear on the trucks caused many mechanical breakdowns. The capture of the port of Marseilles in southern France also somewhat eased the supply problem. A cautious Eisenhower wanted to pause and resolve the supply problem before launching a major offensive into Germany.

The Allies' spearhead, which had the Wehrmacht reeling in August, lost momentum in September, giving the Germans time to regroup and refortify their defenses on the German border. Upon their arrival in Germany, the remnants of the German forces from France were reinforced by troops shifted from military units based in Germany and hastily organized into "fortress battalions." Hitler recalled Field Marshal von Rundstedt and directed him to organize the defense of the "West Wall," which the Allies referred to as the "Siegfried Line."

Established in the late 1930s and stretching along Germany's western border for over three hundred miles, these defenses had been largely neglected following Germany's swift defeat of France in 1940. Now they were being rapidly strengthened with the recently arrived troops and improved fortifications. Particularly troublesome for tanks were the "dragons' teeth," pyramid-shaped obstructions about three to four feet tall. Planted in the terrain along with mines and cleverly staggered, they impeded the movement of tanks, which then became targets for antitank weapons. In addition to these tank traps, the Germans constructed well-camouflaged pillboxes that were reinforced with several feet of concrete. Rows of "dragons' teeth" in front of the pillboxes protected the defenders from Allied tanks, and the Allies had to pass German tanks placed in pits with virtually only the gun barrel exposed. If Allied troops broke through one defensive line, they would immediately face a second and third line. And they had to contend with artillery bombardments from the rear.

In early September, before logistical problems had virtually halted the Allied drive, most of Luxembourg and Belgium had fallen to the Allies, including Brussels and the key port of Antwerp. Taken by surprise and blocked by Belgian resistance groups—"probably the most important contribution made by any resistance group in World War II"—the Germans were unable to destroy the port's installations.[26] However, the Germans still commanded the Scheldt estuary that connected Antwerp to the sea. Britain's failure to clear immediately the weakened German forces only fifteen miles away from this approach to Antwerp, like the hesitancy of the Americans to exploit their advantage at Falaise, was a major mistake. It permitted large numbers of German troops to escape, and while the British procrastinated in Antwerp the Germans were busy mining the waters of the estuary and strengthening their coastal batteries, barring Allied ships from using the port. Now it would require weeks of hard fighting by British and Canadian troops and eighteen thousand casualties to clear the banks of the Scheldt River. By November 8, the Scheldt estuary was in Allied hands; by November 26, the Royal Navy had removed the mines, and two days later the port was operational. That Antwerp was not in service for Allied shipping until ten weeks after its capture complicated a growing supply crisis that stalled the American and British advance.

A principal sign of German recovery was expanding armaments production. Under Albert Speer, the very capable Minister of Armaments and Munitions, German industry pulled out all stops. He was also a fervid Nazi who believed that an unfaltering national will could yet achieve victory. To protect against Allied air bombardments, factories were moved to caves, mines, and underground caverns that the Germans feverishly tunneled out of the earth and the sides of mountains. Between February 1942 and July 1944, aircraft production increased by almost 600 percent and tank production by 300 percent, despite the heavy Allied raids. In the middle of 1944, the German armaments industry was producing more than at any other time. In underground caverns in the Harz Mountains, slave laborers produced the V-weapons. Developed by German scientists and called "miracle weapons" by Joseph Goebbels' propaganda machine, these missiles served to boost the home front's morale. In particular, the Germans pinned their hopes on the V-2 rockets—missiles fired randomly at London from the coasts of Belgium, Holland, and France. The V-2 was more effective than the V-1 flying bomb because its speed and height made it invulnerable to countermeasures. Between September 1944 and March 1945, some twenty-seven hundred Londoners perished in the V-2 missile attacks. If the Allies fanning out from Normandy had not overrun key launching sites, casualties would have been significantly greater. But the Vs had no impact on the war's outcome, despite the illusions Goebbels conveyed to the nation.

To achieve his production goals, Speer utilized forced laborers, including emaciated concentration camp inmates. German industrialists treated them like draft animals. Appalling living conditions, long hours, and execution for breaking rules produced high mortality rates in these arms factories. The welfare of slave laborers was of no importance to Speer, although he later claimed to have tried to improve conditions for the workers building the rocket sites, half of whom, some thirty thousand, perished. Speer was a committed Nazi: he had a good working relationship with Heinrich Himmler, who supplied him with concentration camp slave labor; expressed his admiration for Goebbels; remained loyal to Hitler virtually to the end; and took pride in greatly increasing armaments production. His ego soared, for he relished the power and recognition his achievements brought him.*

After the war, Speer argued that Hitler had delayed too long by waiting until after Stalingrad in early 1943 to place the German economy on a total-war footing. A protracted war requiring the full mobilization of Germany's

---

*Imprisoned by the Allies after the war, Speer struggled with his conscience and expressed regrets for lending his talents to a criminal regime. He also insisted that he knew nothing about death camps and gas chambers—a claim made by many German generals and officials and virtually all civilians—which his biographers find difficult to believe. And with good reason; it seems ridiculous that one of the best informed of Nazi leaders was unaware of what was common knowledge to many officials, soldiers, and civilians, particularly given that he had dealings with Himmler and the SS.

resources seemed inconceivable to Hitler after the initial success of the blitzkrieg. Speer insisted that if he had been given authority earlier, the Wehrmacht in Russia would not have been short of tanks, planes, and other equipment and the war might have taken a different turn. Despite Speer's herculean efforts and access to the human and material resources of conquered Europe, German war production could not keep pace with that of the Allies, particularly with the American industrial giant moving ahead at full steam. For example, in 1944, Germany produced 34,100 combat airplanes and 18,300 tanks. In comparison, the United States, Britain, and the Soviet Union together produced 127,300 planes and 54,100 tanks. In addition, Germany's lack of key raw materials, especially oil, was an insuperable handicap in the last six months of the war. Also impeding the production and movement of weapons were the concentrated air attacks on Germany's transportation system.

German Military Resurgence: Market Garden, Aachen, Huertgen Forest, Metz

By mid-September 1944, the Allies had reached the German border and the Siegfried Line, which was now strengthened with new fortifications and new divisions. For the Allies, a painful indication that the German army still had plenty of life was its fierce resistance to the Allied offensive in southern Holland, the German border city of Aachen, the French city of Metz, and the Huertgen Forest on the German–Belgian border. The brutal fighting in the autumn of 1944 cost the Americans 250,000 dead, wounded, and captured, and the territorial gains were meager.

On September 17, the Allies launched Operation Market Garden. Conceived by Montgomery, who had been promoted by Churchill to field marshal after the Normandy campaign,* its objective was to outflank the Siegfried Line by crossing the Lower Rhine in Holland and then to proceed to envelop the Ruhr, Germany's industrial heartland. Deprived of its heavy industries, Germany's position would be hopeless, said Montgomery, and it would be forced to sue for peace. Intrigued by an audacious airborne assault that would establish a bridgehead across the Rhine into Germany, Eisenhower approved the plan. To get to the Rhine, the Allies first had to cross several rivers and canals. An airborne force, equipped with jeeps and artillery, was assigned the mission of seizing the bridges that spanned these waterways. More than 34,600 British, American, and Polish airborne troops either parachuted or came by glider into the battle zones in what was the largest airborne operation in World War II. They were to link up with a tank force ready to spring from the Dutch–Belgian border.

---

*There was more to the promotion than Montgomery's performance as commander of the Allied armies in France during and after the Normandy invasion, serving under Eisenhower, the Supreme Commander. In September, Eisenhower took direct charge over Allied ground forces and Montgomery reverted to commander of the 21st Army Group. Montgomery bitterly resented this change. Promotion to field marshal, the highest rank in the British army, was a form of compensation.

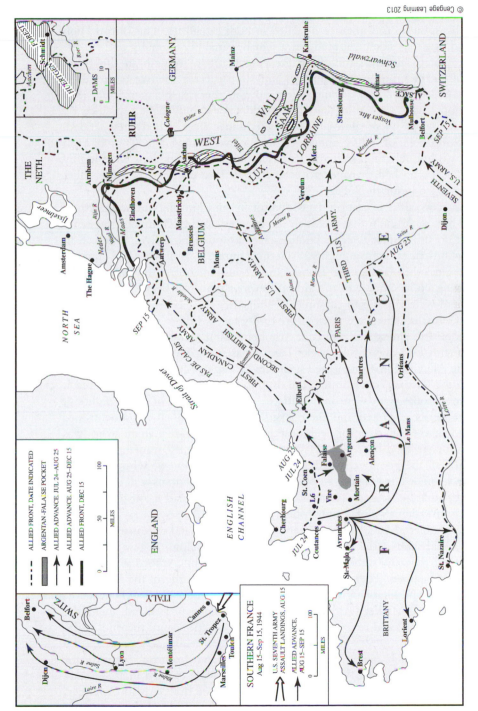

MAP 6.1 Advance to the German Border, July 24–December 15, 1944

After D-Day, the Allies moved to drive the Germans from France and the Low Countries and then advance into Germany.

Montgomery always meticulously planned an operation and was careful not to waste lives, but in this instance he failed in both categories. The British High Command brushed aside decrypted Ultra signals, aerial photographs, and reports from the Dutch resistance indicating growing German strength in the zones designated for the airborne drops and landings. In particular, the two panzer divisions that had escaped from France were now in the area being refitted. The Allied troops, who were told that they could expect only light resistance by second-rate troops, were almost everywhere under siege when they landed. There was no hope of lightly armed paratroops overcoming a tank force, even one that was not up to full strength. Ironically, the panzer divisions were led by senior officers who had managed to escape the Falaise pocket when the Allies were slow to go in for the kill.

The success of the operation depended totally on capturing the bridge crossing the Rhine at Arnhem that provided direct access to the Ruhr. But the Allies could not do this despite their success in achieving other objectives. Shielded in the forest bordering a narrow highway, German gunners, some wielding antitank weapons, ambushed advancing British armor and infantry, preventing them from moving up in support of the airborne troops who had been dropped near Arnhem and were fighting to capture the bridge.

The Germans, who were in close proximity to the bridge, responded to the Allied drop with quick and effective countermeasures, including point-blank bombardments by heavy artillery and Tiger tanks firing 88mm rounds at close range. The Allies had not anticipated such rapidly deployed and strong resistance. And with the Germans overrunning the drop locations, supplies could not reach the airborne troops who were under attack. After nine days of heavy fighting, their ammunition depleted and their position hopeless, Allied airborne troops either fled across the river or were captured. A British lieutenant who was taken prisoner recalled his feeling of "absolute fury at High Command…. I was thinking of all the people that I'd seen there, people I knew, who had been needlessly wounded or killed in an operation that was quite frankly ill conceived, ill planned, and ill executed. There was nothing to commend it and I believe it was merely megalomania of a certain field marshal."[27]

To its planners, Market Garden seemed an audacious and imaginative operation that could shorten the war, but it ended a costly failure: in just nine days, almost eleven thousand airborne and five thousand ground troops were killed, wounded, or captured. There would be no immediate crossing of the Rhine and seizing of the Ruhr. Germany was not near collapse, as the Allies had believed.

The failure of Market Garden also meant that much of Holland, including its principal cities, would remain under German occupation until the end of the war. The occupation grew more brutal. The Germans deliberately deprived the Dutch of food, which caused rampant malnutrition and death by starvation for thousands by the spring of 1945. The Dutch people were trapped in a desperate struggle for survival. At the end of April, a week before the German surrender, the German command in Holland, hoping to get reduced punishment for their crimes, worked out a truce with the Allies that allowed for massive airdrops of food to the starving Dutch.

Attempts by American forces in September to capture Aachen, a large German city close to the border of Holland and Belgium and a pathway to the Ruhr, also suffered a setback. When the SS discovered a letter by the city's commander offering to surrender the city to the attacking Americans, Hitler ordered his arrest and replaced his division with another. Ordering that this historic city, the burial place of the great medieval emperor Charlemagne, whom he revered as a heroic German, never fall into Allied hands, Hitler reinforced the defenders with a panzer division.

The battle raged from October 2 to October 21. American artillery and aircraft bombardments often did not destroy German pillboxes and bunkers that defended the towns approaching the city. Eventually, these defensive positions had to be captured pillbox by pillbox by infantry employing flamethrowers and explosives. In these towns, the Americans had to fight house-to-house, often with grenades, against defenders who turned cellars into strongpoints. Storming pillboxes and other strongpoints and staving off German counterattacks caused American casualties to climb, but relentlessly advancing Americans soon encircled Aachen. The German commander in Aachen rejected an American ultimatum to surrender in order to save the encircled city from being leveled by artillery and air bombardments. The city was soon reduced to huge mounds of rubble and skeletal ruins. The Americans entering the city were ambushed from sewers and basements and had to fight off German counterattacks. But American tanks and other guns kept hitting German strongpoints at point-blank range; their position hopeless, the Germans surrendered on October 22. American and German losses amounted each to five thousand killed and wounded. In addition, the Americans took fifty-six hundred prisoners.

That a sizable German city, which Hitler vowed would never fall, was now in Allied hands further weakened home-front morale. Germans could not help but regard Aachen's fall as a foreboding sign of what was to come. At the same time, many residents of the ruined city who had not fled the battle effusively greeted the Americans, no doubt after burning anything that could identify them as a Nazi supporter or member of the Nazi Party. Furious that Aacheners were collaborating with the Americans, who were helping to make the city function again, Himmler sent a death squad to kill the American-appointed mayor; he was murdered in March 1945.

From September to December 1944, in one of the bloodiest campaigns on the Western Front, the Americans struggled to overrun the Germans defending the dense Huertgen Forest, a fifty-square-mile region on the German-Belgian frontier that starts about five miles south and east of Aachen. The American objective was to prevent the Germans from flanking the U.S. First Army as it drove to the frontier and the Siegfried Line. Temporarily halted in December because of the German Ardennes offensive—the Battle of the Bulge—the battle for the forest was resumed in January 1945 and finally ended on February 10.

The Germans were determined to defend the region for two principal reasons: First, unknown to the Americans, the forest served as a staging area for the forthcoming Ardennes offensive. Second, the Germans wanted to retain possession of the Roer River dams, particularly the Schwammenauel Dam, because opening the dams would flood the valley downstream and delay the Allies from crossing the Roer River, thereby stalling their drive into Germany. At first, seizing the dams was not a major objective for American generals who were involved in the assault; they discounted the deleterious effects a flood would have on their armies crossing the Roer River. (In February 1945, as U.S. First Army troops were closing in on the dams, the Germans managed to destroy partially just one of them, the Schwammenauel Dam; the Americans then had to wait thirteen days for the flood to subside in order for the advance to continue.)

The misconceived American assault was a costly mistake; it would have been better simply to bypass the forest, for the dense woods provided a natural shield for German defenders holding the high ground and entrenched in pillboxes and bunkers. Minefields, tank traps, hidden pillboxes, and mortar and artillery fire devastated American infantry, and tanks could not maneuver on the heavily mined, muddy, and narrow roads. Many tanks were destroyed by Germans hidden in the forest firing antitank weapons. Artillery fire striking the tall trees caused a cascade of thick wood to maim and kill the unprotected men below. Moreover, poor weather and the dense forest that made it difficult to spot targets neutralized Allied air superiority. And, unlike the German defenders, American soldiers, some of them raw recruits sent to the front as replacements as casualties mounted, had no experience fighting in forests or in the bitter cold winter. So ferocious and unremitting was the fighting that some American infantrymen broke under the strain, throwing away their weapons and fleeing to the rear. Official U.S. Army histories estimate American dead, missing, wounded, and those treated for frostbite and trench foot at more than twenty-six thousand. Military historians view the Battle of Huertgen Forest as misconceived and the victory as fruitless because the conquered terrain, attained with staggering casualties, served no significant tactical value for future operations.

During this trying autumn of 1944, General Patton's U.S. Third Army was having a difficult time trying to take the fortress city of Metz. American intelligence was unaware of the strength of the forts that encircled the city and doubted that demoralized German soldiers would offer much resistance. Storming a strongly held fortress was not Patton's forte. The lynchpin of the fortress system was Fort Driant, built in 1902 and continually strengthened by the French and then by the Germans after their conquest of France in 1940. After pounding the fort with heavy artillery and high-explosive bombs, the Americans sent in their infantry, thinking that the German defenders could not have survived the shelling and aerial bombardment. But the sturdy German defenses held up. Firing from thick concrete pillboxes that were largely impervious to the shelling from tanks, the Germans forced the Americans to withdraw. Several days later, the Americans again assaulted Driant, but after bitter fighting within the fort they again had to withdraw.

Analysts criticize Patton for trying to take Metz at a cost of thousands of American casualties. It made more sense simply to bypass the city, but Bradley's orders to Patton made it clear that the region must be secured before attempting crossing the Saar and Moselle rivers, gateways into Germany. After a two-month siege, Patton's infantry entered Metz on November 22. After several days of street fighting, the city was in American hands.

BATTLE OF THE BULGE: HITLER'S LAST GAMBLE

In the autumn of 1944, the Germans had succeeded in stabilizing the Western Front. Although the hope of a quick end to the war—which had seemed possible after the Allies' spectacular sweep through France—had dissipated, the ultimate defeat of the Nazis still appeared certain. Time was running short for the Third Reich, which was fighting a two-front war against opponents possessing a huge advantage in troops, airpower, and industrial capacity. Most worrisome for the German military was the diminishing fuel supply, the result of Allied air raids on refineries and synthetic oil plants and the loss of Romania's oil fields; after a successful coup in August 1944, the Romanians had joined the Soviets in battling the Germans, their former ally. Deprived of fuel, German forces could only hold out for a few months. Allied bombardments also devastated transportation networks, hampering the movement of resources to factories and supplies to the front. The stalemate on the Western Front would not endure.

Hitler's Goals and Strategy

In the face of Germany's deteriorating military situation, Hitler still retained the conviction that his intuitive mastery of the art of war, fortified by an unshakeable faith in victory, would enable Germany to triumph over its enemies. And he continued to believe that the Allied coalition, an unnatural alliance between the Western democracies and Communist Russia, would eventually collapse. Hitler made one last gamble: a counteroffensive through the Ardennes to Antwerp. Capturing Antwerp would deprive the Allies of a crucial supply port needed for carrying the war to German soil. It would also drive a wedge between the British and American forces, enabling the Germans to destroy the cut-off Allied armies. And it would give Germany the time it needed to develop the new weapons that would turn the war in its favor, especially the V missiles and jet planes. For Hitler, an attack through the Ardennes and across the Meuse River would recapitulate the Wehrmacht's triumphant invasion of France in 1940. A deluded Hitler conjured up various scenarios that would follow a German victory. He thought that Britain, cut off from its bases of supply, might evacuate the Continent in a second Dunkirk. Or a battered Britain and United States, recognizing that victory was not in sight, would negotiate peace with him, allowing Germany to concentrate all its forces against the Russians. Or the Western Allies might even join with him against the common Communist enemy.

Several German generals, including Field Marshal Walther Model, a Nazi loyalist, and von Rundstedt opposed the plan as too ambitious, arguing that Germany had insufficient reserves to support an initial breakthrough and insufficient planes to counter Allied air power. To be sure, said these generals, the panzers would make headway against weak American positions, but the Allies would rush in reinforcements from France over a good network of roads and attack with force the German flanks. Without armored reserves replenishing their forces, the offensive would not be able to sustain its momentum and break through into the Allied rear. Most important, without capturing Allied fuel depots, the panzers could make it only half way to Antwerp. Von Rundstedt agreed that an attack in the Ardennes would bloody the Americans, but he wanted to halt the assault at the Meuse; the seizure of Antwerp he considered a hopelessly unrealistic goal. Hitler, fired up by a high-stakes gamble that the Allies would not anticipate, rejected this more moderate plan. The belief that the Americans would fold and flee before an unexpected onslaught of his panzers convinced Hitler that the odds were in his favor.

To prepare a powerful striking force, the Germans continued to restore their badly mauled divisions by transferring panzer divisions from the Eastern Front and Italy. They increased manpower by conscripting teenagers and transferring military office staff personnel to active duty. The troops and equipment were moved at night to escape Allied detection and concealed in forests. A thousand aircraft were also moved to the Western Front. The newly created Sixth SS Panzer Army commanded by Josef "Sepp" Dietrich, an early comrade of Hitler and committed Nazi, would lead the attack. To neutralize Allied air superiority, Hitler ordered the offensive to start in bad weather. All of these deployments were carried out in strict secrecy. Enthusiastic about the operation, the troops trusted Hitler's pledge of victory. A junior officer in an SS panzer division wrote home: "It is enough to know that … we will throw the enemy from our homeland. It is a holy task."[28] And after the war, von Rundstedt said, "The morale of the troops taking part was astonishingly high at the start of the offensive. They really believed victory was possible—unlike the higher commanders who knew the facts."[29]

That the Germans could in three months rebuild and reequip the smashed remnants of the divisions in France that had limped back to Germany and then launch a major offensive was an extraordinary feat. It was also a desperate gamble by Hitler to keep the Western Allies from invading Germany. Its failure, which cost Germany its best remaining divisions, helped decide the Third Reich's fate.

Initial Success

Not believing that the Germans were capable of a massive offensive after the enormous losses they had endured since D-Day, the Allies were totally surprised when the offensive exploded in force on December 16. Allied intelligence, including Ultra decrypts, had detected several signs indicating that the Germans were engaged in aerial reconnaissance over the Ardennes and were massing troops, armor, and supplies. But the intelligence community failed to integrate these bits and pieces of information. Consequently the Allies, in what British military historian Max Hastings calls "the most notorious intelligence disaster of the war," either ignored or did not take seriously these warnings.[30] German military commanders, the Allied High Command reasoned, had to be thinking of strengthening Germany's defenses or, at best, very limited counterattacks, not of launching an all-out offensive against superior Allied might, particularly air power. The Allied High Command also failed to factor in Hitler's past record of overruling his commanders' military advice and trusting to his own intuition, which often went against professional judgment. After the war, General Hasso von Manteuffel, who commanded the Fifth Panzer Army in the campaign, reflected on the American failure: "The enemy air force had not recognized our assembly for battle; it had thus missed the unique possibility of making use of its unlimited air superiority to deal an annihilating blow to the German forces assembled and concentrated in a small area—the last German reserves."[31]

The Germans began their all-out attack with 2.5 times as many men as the Americans (two hundred thousand to eighty thousand) and considerably more tanks (six hundred to four hundred). It was a mightier force than the divisions that had moved through the Ardennes in May 1940 but still less than Hitler had promised and the offensive required, for the Americans could immediately rush in reinforcements that would give them superiority both in numbers and armor. Meeting with considerable initial success against lightly manned American forward positions, the Germans ripped open a huge "bulge" in the Allied lines that they continued to expand. As Hitler anticipated, weather conditions prevented Allied planes from attacking the advancing Germans.

Many American soldiers, recent arrivals from the United States, had no battlefield experience; others had been sent to what seemed a quiet area to rest and recuperate after participating in the grueling combat in Huertgen Forest. After a ferocious artillery bombardment, the Germans drove through American lines that bent and broke. Some battered American units surrendered when they were cut off and surrounded; other units fought desperately as they were reeling back. In the first five days, the Germans, in their broad and deep breakthrough, destroyed three hundred tanks and seized supplies, including precious gas; secured several bridges; and captured twenty-five thousand Americans, the largest number of Americans to surrender in the war against Hitler.

To confuse the Allies, the Germans used English-speaking commandos outfitted in American uniforms and riding in captured American jeeps to cut telephone lines and misdirect traffic by changing signposts and giving wrong directions. Although they caused some confusion, many of these commandos were captured and some immediately shot.

So overwhelming was the initial German onslaught, for which the Americans were unprepared, that some units broke and fled in panic. "The Krauts are coming. They're running all over everything. No one can stop them. I'm getting the hell out," was the mood that gripped them.[32] A young American paratrooper in a truck convoy headed for the battlefield recalled the scene:

> Then we saw them. Mobs of retreating Americans—walking, running, stumbling, and riding in all sorts of vehicles—clogged the road up ahead.... On and on they came in ever-increasing numbers, a wave of human lemmings ... filling the road, the ditches, on either side, and the fields all around us. They shambled along in shock and fear.... I had never before—or since—seen such absolute terror in men.[33]

This frantic flight testifies to the power of the German offensive, but it was not characteristic of American troops, most of whom dug in and fought courageously and tenaciously in isolated units, holding their ground against superior forces until resistance was no longer possible. Their determined stand gave

Eisenhower the time needed to coordinate a counterattack. Fifty years later, an American captain recalled the determination of these infantrymen: "Everyone was aware that there would be no further withdrawal, whatever the cost. Moreover, I could sense in the demeanor of the troops at all ranks that this resolution was written in their hearts."[34]

Reports of Waffen-SS massacring both Belgian civilians as they reentered just liberated Belgian towns and American prisoners of war served to strengthen American resolve. The most notorious incident occurred near Malmedy, where American prisoners were herded into a killing area and eighty-six were shot to death. A veteran of the battle recalls the outrage of American frontline soldiers: "American feelings toward Germans hardened into vindictive hate. Chances of survival for newly caught German POWs diminished greatly."[35] (To be sure, American soldiers shot prisoners, particularly the SS after they had liberated concentration camps. Nevertheless, an individual American shooting a captured German cannot be equated to an organized massacre with machine guns and the methodical murder of 130 Belgian civilians, many of them children, in the reoccupied town of Stavelot.)

American Resistance and German Defeat

The Germans were satisfied with their early success, but several factors eventually caused the offensive to fail. Plans called for the Germans to reach the Meuse River by day four and then push as fast as possible to Antwerp; any delay would give the Americans time to reorganize and reinforce. But moving tanks and horse-drawn artillery along narrow, snow-covered roads in freezing cold slowed down the German drive, interrupting their carefully planned timetable. Other factors that delayed the German advance included the difficulty of gasoline trucks in reaching forward motorized units running dry, the skill and courage of American engineers who blew up vital bridges, bombardments by American and British artillery, and the fierce resistance of American units at strategic crossroads, despite overwhelming odds against them.

One such crossroad was the town of St. Vith, a gateway to the Meuse that the Germans planned to overrun in one day. Instead, the Germans had to battle the American defenders for six days before taking the town that the Americans had finally evacuated. The Americans' stubborn defense had tied down more troops than the Germans had foreseen, forcing them to send in additional units that were needed elsewhere and seriously delaying their drive to the Meuse.

The outnumbered and cut off 101st Airborne Division achieved legendary status for its heroic defense at the key Bastogne road junction. The Germans needed this area for their push to the Meuse and to be resupplied. Because of the dreadful weather, aircraft could not come to the aid of the besieged Americans. The 101st, however, had been reinforced with several excellent artillery and tank destroyers and a superb tank unit, Combat Command B, of the Tenth Armored Division.

For eight days, the Americans managed to repulse every German attack despite running short of ammunition, food, and medical supplies, and despite enduring debilitating cold. Their tenacious defense impeded the German advance and tied down several German divisions. When the Germans demanded that the American garrison surrender or be destroyed, their commander, Brigadier General Anthony McAuliffe, simply and famously replied, "Nuts!" The American colonel who delivered the message told the somewhat confused German emissaries that in plain English "Nuts" means "Go to Hell!" And he added that if the attack continues, "we will kill every goddamn German that tries to break into this city." With the chances of an American surrender very slim, the Germans tightened the vise around Bastogne, taking away more men and armor needed for the advance to the Meuse.

On December 19, at his headquarter at Verdun, Eisenhower explained the situation to his top commanders. But rather than present a grim picture, he told the officers that the German drive presented the Western Allies with an opportunity to destroy the enemy forces that were now miles away from their border fortifications and having supply problems. When Eisenhower asked Patton how long it would take him to counterattack, the always audacious Patton said two days. Eisenhower admonished him for his brashness in claiming to accomplish the seemingly impossible.

Patton, however, relished the opportunity to do the impossible. Moreover, anticipating what was needed, Patton had already ordered his staff to draw up a plan to reach the front. His U.S. Third Army, which had been driving eastward into the Saar and toward the Siegfried Line, immediately broke off its attack and conducted a ninety-degree pivot—an extremely difficult maneuver for some one hundred thousand troops and thousands of vehicles—and turned north. In two grueling days and nights Third Army divisions drove one hundred miles in cold, snow, sleet, rain, and fog over frozen roads intersected by hills and woods to reach their assigned destination within the time frame promised by Patton. And on the morning of December 22, they launched a counterattack. In his account of the war published in 1951, General Bradley paid tribute to Patton whom he often regarded as irascible: "Patton's brilliant shift of the 3rd Army from its bridgehead in the Saar to the snow-covered Ardennes front became one of the most astonishing feats of generalship of our campaign in the West."[36] Units of the Third Army were now only twenty miles from Bastogne, but they still had to fight the brutal weather, the awful roads, and the Germans to get there. Meeting intense enemy resistance, they took substantial losses in tanks and men.

At the outset of the offensive, foggy weather had grounded Allied planes, which, as Hitler intended, prevented aerial bombardments of the advancing Germans. But on December 23, the fog suddenly lifted, permitting American planes to strike with deadly effectiveness at German supply trucks and panzer units crowding the roads and to drop badly needed supplies to the defenders of Bastogne. An American private's recollection provides an insight into the ordeal of the defenders: "Watching those bundles of supplies and ammunition drop was a sight to behold. As we retrieved the bundles, first we cut up the bags to wrap around our [frostbitten] feet.... What a great feeling to have warm feet!"[37]

On Christmas Day, thinking that the Americans would be less alert, the Germans launched a fierce frontal attack on Bastogne that was preceded by a massive artillery barrage. Again the Americans held. Attacking a German flank from December 22 to December 26, tanks of the Fourth Armored Division of Patton's Third Army opened a corridor to the battered and beleaguered American garrison, breaking the German encirclement. At the same time, swarms of Allied planes, meeting little resistance, pulverized the German besiegers, inflicting heavy losses. Further, reacting more quickly than the German High Command anticipated, powerful American infantry and armored reserves were rapidly entering the battle zone. On December 30, reinforced German divisions attacked the corridor leading to Bastogne but were repulsed. In the bloody struggle marked by massive air battles, the Germans suffered heavy casualties.

In another area, units of the Fifth Panzer Army did manage to get within five miles of the Meuse on December 24, but they lacked the fuel to go on. With Allied fighter-bombers wrecking German supply lines, including troop convoys and gasoline carriers and pummeling German ground forces, and with American artillery hitting their targets with devastating effect, the offensive was dying. Having lost 277 planes in a desperate attempt to attack Allied air bases, the Luftwaffe was a much diminished threat. Also, Anglo-American forces with their heavy armor kept pouring into the fray. "We faced a highly motorized enemy," reflected a German general after the war. "The Western Allies could speedily and aggressively draw divisions from other fronts and commit them in depth against our flanks."[38] On January 3, 1945, Hitler confessed that the campaign had not succeeded.

The Allies had stabilized the front and in early January launched a counteroffensive. After much hard fighting in bitter cold and heavy snow, the dangerous bulge into Allied territory had been eliminated by the end of January 1945, and the German troops were forced back behind Germany's borders. Hitler's gamble had failed.

The German Ardennes offensive was a costly battle for the Americans— 10,276 killed, 47,493 wounded, and some 30,000 missing or captured.* It was also costly for Germany—12,652 killed, 38,600 wounded, and some 30,000 missing or captured. But within two weeks, the Americans had replenished their losses in soldiers and materiel. Not so the Germans; the loss of considerable military equipment, including eight hundred tanks and sixteen hundred planes, and the further depletion of fuel reserves greatly weakened the Wehrmacht. Hitler's initial insistence on his usual "no withdrawal" prevented an expeditious retreat that his generals had requested. Instead, the Germans suffered heavy losses in needlessly prolonging what was already a lost campaign. But the Allies, in what was an error by the High Command, did not exploit their advantage: they failed to pursue, cut off, and destroy the retreating Germans, allowing large numbers of troops, with tanks and artillery, to return to their lines to fight another day. In defense of the Allied High Command, atrocious weather conditions grounded their planes and impeded a hot pursuit.

---

*Several hundred Jewish-American prisoners (and those who "looked" Jewish) were sent to a Berga, a slave labor camp. There they did back-breaking work digging underground tunnels for a synthetic oil plant alongside concentration camp inmates, many of them near death. Underfed, overworked, and abused, at war's end some four months later, some 20 percent of the Jewish-American prisoners had perished. Many of the rescued emaciated prisoners would not have survived much longer.

Eisenhower made significant mistakes by not assessing German intentions prior to the offensive and not destroying the defeated German forces as they retreated back to Germany. Nevertheless, the Battle of the Bulge—this is how the German salient in the American lines appeared on maps—demonstrated Eisenhower's skill as a commander. He was quick to grasp that the attack was a major German counteroffensive and just as quickly perceived that Bastogne was the key point to hold. Recognizing that the advancing Germans had overextended their supply line and no longer had the protection of the Siegfried Line, he saw the situation as an opportunity, as he said, to turn Hitler's "great gamble into his worst defeat."[39] Instead of diluting his strength by trying to reinforce all positions, even if this permitted the Germans to advance further, he harvested his reserves and then unleashed a powerful and punishing counterattack against the weakly defended German flanks. His calmness throughout the whole operation reflected well on his leadership ability. Above all, the Battle of the Bulge showed the courage and fortitude of American soldiers who fought off repeated attacks, particularly at St. Vith and Bastogne, that slowed the German advance and gave the tactical reserves the time needed to bolster threatened positions and to stage a counterattack.

The Battle of the Bulge was Germany's last major offensive on the Western Front. Its power gravely diminished, after the battle the Wehrmacht could think only of fighting defensively. Although difficult fighting and more suffering lay ahead, the outcome of the war was certain. With its reserve strength now depleted beyond restitution and its industrial capacity eroded by Allied bombings and the loss of Romanian oil fields, Germany lacked the troops, tanks, planes, and fuel to forestall an Allied assault into its heartland from the west or to turn back the Red Army's winter offensive that began on January 12, 1945.

Believing Hitler's assurances of victory, German soldiers and civilians had pinned great hopes on the Ardennes offensive. One participant had written to his wife in the early days of the offensive: "Victory never seemed as close as it does now. The decisive moment is at hand. We shall throw these arrogant big-mouthed apes from the New World into the sea. They will not get into our Germany.... If we are to save everything that is sweet and lovely in our lives, we must be ruthless at this decisive hour of the struggle."[40] Hitler's failed Ardennes offensive no doubt led more Germans to question the inevitability of a German victory. But to vocalize sentiments like this was a death sentence at the hands of the security police and special courts established to stifle defeatism.

CHRONOLOGY

January 1944	Rommel given command of defending the Channel coast
June 6, 1944	D-Day
June 27, 1944	Port of Cherbourg falls to the Americans

July 7, 1944	Caen virtually destroyed by Allied bombers
July 17, 1944	Rommel severely wounded when two British fighters attack his staff car
July 20, 1944	Anglo–Canadian forces gain complete control of Caen
July 20, 1944	Attempt to assassinate Hitler fails
July 25, 1944	Operation Cobra launched
August 18, 1944	Allies take control of Falaise
August 25, 1944	The liberation of Paris
Early September 1944	Allies liberate Brussels and Antwerp
September 14, 1944– February 10, 1945	Huertgen Forest campaign
September 17, 1944	Launching of Operation Market Garden
November 26, 1944	Port of Antwerp is operational
December 16, 1944	Start of Hitler's Ardennes offensive
December 26, 1944	Lifting of siege of Bastogne
Late January 1945	The bulge in American lines is eliminated and German troops are forced back to Germany's borders

NOTES

1. Joseph Balkoski, *Omaha Beach: D-Day* (Mechanicsburg, PA: Stackpole Books, 2004), 10.

2. Johannes Steinhoff et al., eds., *Voices from the Third Reich: An Oral History* (Washington, D.C.: Regnery Gateway, 1989), 254.

3. Robert J. Kershaw, *D-Day: Piercing the Atlantic Wall* (Annapolis, MD: Naval Institute Press, 1994), 158.

4. *Omaha Beachhead*, prepared by the War Department Historical Division (Washington, D.C.: 1945), 58, 71.

5. Kershaw, *D-Day*, 155.

6. Nigel Hamilton, *Master of the Battlefield: Monty's War Years 1942–1944* (New York: McGraw-Hill, 1983), 667.

7. Richard Hargreaves, *The Germans in Normandy* (Mechanicsburg, PA: Stackpole Books, 2006), 10–11.

8. Alan Wilt, "The Air Campaign," in *D-Day 1944*, ed. Theodore A. Wilson (Lawrence: University of Kansas Press, 1994), 134.

9. B. H. Liddell-Hart, ed., *The Rommel Papers*, trans. Paul Findlay (New York: Da Capo Press, 1982), 476–477.

10. Carlo D'Este, *Decision in Normandy* (New York: HarperPerennial, 1994), 152.

11. Liddell-Hart, *The Rommel Papers*, 487.

12. Kershaw, *D-Day*, 234.

13. Charles B. MacDonald, *The Mighty Endeavor: The American War in Europe* (New York: William Morrow, 1986), 334.

14. Hargreaves, *The Germans in Normandy*, 170.

15. Ladislas Farago, *Patton: Ordeal and Triumph* (New York: Dell, 1970), 469.

16. Excerpted in Desmond Flower and James Reeves, eds, *The War, 1939–1945* (New York: De Capo Press, 1997), 911–912.

17. Bodo Zimmerman, "France, 1944," in *Fatal Decisions*, ed. Seymour Freidin and William Richardson, trans. Contantine Fitzgibbon (New York: Berkley Publishing, 1958), 208.

18. John Ellis, *Brute Force: Allied Strategy and Tactics in the Second World War* (New York: Viking, 1990), 368.

19. Omar N. Bradley, *A Soldier's Story* (New York: Modern Library, 1999), 375.

20. George Wilson, *If You Survive* (New York: Ivy Books, 1987), 57–58.

21. Dwight Eisenhower, *Crusade in Europe* (Garden City, NY: Doubleday, 1948), 314.

22. Antony Beevor, *D-Day: The Battle for Normandy* (New York: Viking, 2009), 512.

23. Lloyd Clark, *Crossing the Rhine: Breaking into Nazi Germany 1944–1945* (New York: Atlantic Monthly Press, 2008), 7.

24. Hargreaves, *The Germans in Normandy*, 237.

25. Ibid., 237–238.

26. Alan J. Levine, *D-Day to Berlin: The Northwest Europe Campaign, 1944–1945* (Mechanicsburg, PA: Stackpole Books, 2000), 99.

27. Andrew Williams, *D-Day to Berlin* (London: Hodder and Stoughton, 2004), 243.

28. Stanley Weintraub, *11 Days in December: Christmas at the Bulge, 1944* (New York: NAL Caliber, 2007), 8.

29. B. H. Liddell-Hart, *The German Generals Talk* (New York: William Morrow, 1979), 278–279.

30. Max Hastings, *Armageddon: The Battle for Germany, 1944–1945* (New York: Alfred A. Knopf, 2004), 199.

31. Hasso von Manteuffel, "The Fifth Panzer Army During the Ardennes Offensive," in *Hitler's Ardennes Offensive: The German View of the Battle of the Bulge*, ed. Danny S. Parker (London: Greenhill Books, 1997), 137.

32. Donald R. Burgett, *Seven Roads to Hell: A Screaming Eagle at Bastogne* (New York: Dell, 1999), 50.

33. Ibid., 46.

34. Stephen W. Ambrose, *The Victors: Eisenhower and His Boys—The Men of World War II* (New York: Simon & Schuster, 1998), 283.

35. William L. Hitchcock, *The Bitter Road to Freedom: A New History of the Liberation of Europe* (New York: Free Press, 2008), 80.

36. Bradley, *A Soldier's Story*, 472.

37. George E. Koskimaki, *The Battered Bastards of Bastogne: The 101st Airborne in the Battle of the Bulge, December 19, 1944–January 17, 1945* (New York: Ballantine Books, 2007), 257.

38. Günther Blumentritt, "The Ardennes Offensive: A Critique," in *Hitler's Ardennes Offensive: The German View of the Battle of the Bulge*, ed. Danny S. Parker (Mechanicsburg, PA: Stackpole Books, 1997). 254–255.

39. Ambrose, *The Victors*, 284.

40. Hastings, *Armageddon*, 211.

Chapter 7

✳

The End of the Third Reich

The large number of civilian deaths from British and American bombings had brought the war home to the German people, and by early 1945 Soviet and Anglo–American armies were invading the German homeland. This was a monumental turn of events from the blissful days of battlefield victories that had so electrified nationalist sentiments and cemented devotion to the Führer and from the good life that the plundered resources of German Jews and occupied Europe had brought to millions of civilians. The Third Reich was in its death throes; its demise would cause much suffering for soldiers at the front and increasingly German civilians. And the Nazis in a murderous frenzy brutalized forced laborers, prisoners of war, concentration camp inmates, and political prisoners, hundreds of thousands of whom perished in the closing months of the war.

GERMAN MORALE: AMBIVALENT, FANATIC, FATALIST

Even before the landings in Normandy, the lure of conquest had lost its appeal for many Germans, who only wanted the war to end. Several months after the start of Operation Barbarossa, it became apparent that there would be no quick and painless victory, that the Wehrmacht could be embroiled in a long war in the vast Russian space. In succeeding months and years, letters home and soldiers on leave informed the home front of the cruel life-and-death struggle taking place on the Eastern Front that was in marked contrast to the exaggerated optimism Joseph Goebbels' bogus propaganda propagated. Also contributing to the growing revulsion to the war were the long lists of death notices in newspapers, the sight of numerous painfully wounded young men, and women wearing mourning black. Virtually every German family either had lost a loved one in battle or knew a neighbor or relative who had. The rain of misery from the sky was making the war unbearable—burned, asphyxiated, and crushed corpses, heaps of rubble, shells of buildings, and hundreds of thousands of people with their homes destroyed. From July 1944 until Germany's surrender on May 8, 1945, between three hundred thousand and four hundred thousand German soldiers and civilians perished each month; the total number of fatalities in these months was significantly greater than in the preceding five years combined. The hours of waiting in long lines to buy rationed necessities that were decreasing in availability also heightened civilian distress.

No simple generalization satisfactorily explains what impact the death, destruction, deprivation, continued battlefield setbacks, and prospects of fighting on German soil had on German morale as the war dragged on. Reactions to these conditions were variable and changeable. Doubtless, the collapse of the Western Front in France, the relentless aerial terror across the Reich, the defeat of the winter offensive in the Ardennes, and the mounting death toll on the Eastern Front had caused many Germans to question the Nazi Party's leadership, to regard the Nazi Party's promise of ultimate victory as a cruel fantasy, and to flatly reject Goebbels' propaganda. In the summer of 1944, the SD (Security Service) cautioned that there was a growing feeling on the home front that the war could not be won and reported voices critical of Adolf Hitler. Fewer people were giving the "Heil Hitler" greeting, and death notices simply read that a loved one died serving the fatherland—references to dying for the Führer were now noticeably absent. Jokes disparaging the Party hierarchy and even Hitler were circulating widely. One refrain asked contemptuously if drafting granny was the promised new miracle weapon. Additionally, criticism of the Party big-wigs grew more acute in succeeding months as conditions worsened. In March 1945, the Propaganda Ministry reported: "Trust in the leadership shrinks ever more because the proclaimed counter-blow to liberate our occupied eastern provinces did not take place and because the manifold promises of an imminent shift in fortunes have proven incapable of fulfillment.... Criticism of the upper leadership ranks of the Party and of the military leadership is especially bitter."[1] As the struggle for personal survival became the dominant concern, the Hitler mystique weakened for an increasing number of Germans.

However, despite growing pessimism about victory, revulsion for Nazi Party bigwigs, Hitler's diminishing popularity, and overwhelming war-weariness, German civilians continued to perform their duties for the Third Reich. Many no doubt feared the police and security forces that were on the alert for conspiracies and enforced ruthless discipline in the workplace. The police, the Party, and the legal system collaborated in terrorizing and executing those who expressed defeatist sentiments and shirked the Führer's command to fight to the finish. The inhabitants of a house displaying a white flag as the enemy approached faced execution. Thus, for several reasons there was no repetition of the popular uprising that Germany had experienced in the last weeks of World War I.

Amid the deepening gloom, there were still plenty of ardent Nazis. More than a decade of perverse but clever propaganda had conditioned Germans to believe in Hitler, his mission, and Goebbels' lies. These diehards were outraged by the July 20 conspiracy—as were most Germans—and were relieved that

Hitler had survived. They also opposed surrender and still clung to a belief in a victorious outcome or, at least, a satisfactory compromise peace made possible by the "miracle weapons" Hitler promised—an outlook many ordinary Germans also shared. Still under Hitler's dark spell, true believers remained faithful to their Führer even in early 1945, when the military situation was hopeless. For many Nazi Party loyalists and careerists who owed their positions, power, and financial standing to the Nazi regime, loyalty to Hitler and faith in him as Germany's redeemer remained unshakeable until the end of the war and even after. To lose trust in their leader and his National Socialist vision, especially after all the sacrifices the German people were enduring, required a painful change of heart and mind that they were unable to face. Moreover, if the enemy occupied Germany, particularly the Russians, Party members feared for their lives, for they knew of the atrocities committed on Soviet soil. True, in the regime's dying days many Nazi Party functionaries thought only of saving their own skin. But others continued to serve the regime, often with dedication. In many cities and towns, the Party apparatus continued to function until Allied armies approached.

Nor did the Nazi state collapse. With varying degrees of enthusiasm, government bureaucrats coped with administrative routines. Seeing no alternative and ever fearful of the Gestapo, they dealt with the enormous problems afflicting a battered nation—refugees fleeing combat zones, food shortages, putting out the fires, clearing the rubble, removing the dead, and providing for the injured and homeless after Allied aerial bombardments.

In early 1945, Germany's military position was hopeless. The skill the Germans demonstrated in battlefield tactics and improvisations could not offset the great preponderance of Allied armaments and reserve strength. By early January, some 3,725,000 Allied soldiers had landed in Western Europe, and Anglo-American superiority in artillery, tanks, and aircraft was overwhelming. Securing Antwerp and the ports of southern France enabled the Allies to rush armaments to the front in quantities that astonished the Germans. Furthermore, the Soviet menace on the Eastern Front had worsened. Germans were attempting to fill their depleted units with barely trained young recruits, and desertion was on the rise. Fuel shortages hampered the effectiveness of aircraft and tanks, and the destroyed transportation system—a result of Allied bombings—impeded the movement of ammunition and weapons from the factory to the front. The Wehrmacht lost the mobility that had brought it great success in the early years of the war.

But despite its huge losses and the disproportionate strength of its enemies, the German army was still a formidable foe, especially the Waffen-SS divisions. Massive mobilization of German manpower, including older men and teenaged boys, replenished somewhat the ranks of the Wehrmacht. To be sure, many soldiers and their commanders no longer believed in victory and longed for an end to the war. Nevertheless, as Soviet troops moved closer to Germany—and particularly once they were on German soil—German generals displayed a great talent for fighting a defensive war, and many German soldiers fought with remarkable skill and determination, inflicting proportionately more casualties than they suffered, as they had done throughout the war. There is little doubt that the Wehrmacht was the finest fighting force in the European war.

Undoubtedly, too, many soldiers, particularly the SS, remained driven by a fanatical dedication to their supreme commander and Nazi ideology that stressed self-sacrifice for racial comrades and for the national-racial community and mental toughness—themes constantly repeated by Nazi propaganda. Earlier in the war, General Lothar Rendulic had expressed the SS creed that now inspired determined resistance: "When things look blackest and you don't know what to do, beat your chest and say, 'I'm a National Socialist!' that moves mountains."[2] During the Battle of the Bulge, the Americans executed some members of an elite German unit of saboteurs wearing American uniforms behind American lines. One of the condemned's last words, "Long live our leader, Adolf Hitler," show the persistence of Hitler's eerie magnetism and the capacity of Nazi ideology to fortify morale.[3] Surveys of captured German prisoners of war conducted by American intelligence revealed that through March 1945,

> faith in Hitler was expressed by well over fifty percent of the Wehrmacht.... Many a German soldier although personally despairing in ultimate victory continued to resist vigorously, in part because of devotion to Hitler ... [the] man who had done so much good for Germany.... It was only in March 1945, when the German armies were cut up and at the verge of disintegration that the figure dropped below fifty percent.... About half of a sample of November prisoners of war professed their faith in secret weapons.[4]

Other soldiers, however, gave Hitler little thought. These men were motivated by self-preservation, loyalty to their comrades, and devotion to the endangered fatherland—defeat, they feared, would mean the end of Germany's existence, with millions of their people enslaved by the Bolsheviks. They were also well disciplined, trained to do their duty, obey orders, and take pride in the tradition of German arms. Knowing that their armies had committed great crimes in Soviet territory, German soldiers feared a moral reckoning if Germany fell into the hands of vengeful Russians—directed by Jews, they were repeatedly told. What we did to them they will do to us if we lose the war—this was a common perception. Increasingly on the Western Front, German soldiers sought to surrender to the Americans and British. This was not the case on the Eastern Front, where capitulation could mean deportation to the Gulag. The SS in particular were very much aware that falling into Russian hands most likely meant an instant shot in the head. To those concerned only about surviving, surrendering to the Soviets did not seem a viable option. They also feared the ruthless SS and other special units that were hunting down and executing deserters and "defeatists." Even soldiers fleeing Soviet tanks faced immediate execution. In this climate of fear and repression, particularly on the Eastern Front, mass desertion was unlikely; also unlikely were organized insurrections against the regime. Those battling the Red Army had become fatalistic, believing that they had no choice but to continue fighting and hope that mercifully the war would end before they died in battle.

Whatever their motivation, never did soldiers perform so capably for so reprehensible a cause. And only rarely in the history of warfare did so prostrate a nation continue to sacrifice its people, both soldiers and civilians, in a lost cause. From January to April 1945, the number of German military dead soared to about 1.3 million. Scores of thousands of civilians also perished, many of them victims of Allied bombings. Although Wehrmacht leaders knew that the war was lost and that further fighting only increased the senseless butchery and the destruction of German cities and towns, they continued to feed their men into the inferno, some with Goebbels-like ideological motivation. With their questionable, if not perverted, sense of honor, generals remained committed to the oath they had sworn to a leader whose evilness was now beyond any doubt. On November 6, 1944, General Heinz Guderian told an assembly of civilians recruited into the Home Guard that "85 million National Socialists ... stand behind Adolf Hitler. We took our oath voluntarily, and after centuries they will speak of the invincibility of our generation which protected justice against our enemies."[5] Moreover, interpreting the Allied demand for unconditional surrender as the death of Germany, many generals felt that they had no other recourse but to fight to the bitter end. And there was the popular fantasy that fear of the Soviets would soon lead Britain and the United States to join with Germany against the Soviet Union, the real enemy of European civilization.

The misery of Nazi victims remained unabated. In the months, weeks, and even days before Germany's surrender, when everything was lost, the Nazis continued to kill in staggering numbers concentration camp inmates, slave laborers, prisoners of war, and German political prisoners who had resisted Hitler: They remained committed to Nazi racial ideology even when the regime was near death and engaged in further slaughter of helpless people whom they continued to perceive as enemies of the Volk.

RED ARMY ON THE OFFENSIVE

After the battle of Kursk in July 1943, the advantage was with the Soviets, who were producing more tanks and planes than the Germans and benefiting from the huge quantities of Lend-Lease aid provided by the United States, particularly trucks that could handle the Russian terrain even under the worst conditions. Many German replacements for the huge losses suffered were rushed to the front with insufficient training. The high casualty rate among these poorly trained infantry recruits necessitated pouring ever more raw conscripts into battle. Also, the mechanized units could not maintain their high level of tactical proficiency with the loss of well-trained and experienced combat veterans and shortages of armor and fuel. Hurriedly assembled tanks, newly arrived from factories that were trying mightily to keep up with the demand for replacements, were often disabled due to mechanical problems and a severe shortage of spare parts.* With a diminishing number of trained pilots and lacking fuel to send aircraft into combat,

---

*Overworked and stressed out by constant bombings that often drove them from their homes, there is no doubt that German workers suffered a decline in efficiency. Similarly, tired and overwhelmed foremen could not prevent slave laborers from engaging in "hostile carelessness.... [I]ncreasing number of panzers were coming on line with screws poorly tightened, hoses poorly connected—and an occasional handful of shop grit or steel filings deposited where it might do some damage." Dennis Showalter, *Hitler's Panzers: The Lightning Attacks That Revolutionized Warfare* (New York: Penguin Books, 2009), 345.

the Luftwaffe could not compete with the Soviet Union's massively augmented air force. And yet, despite this disparity in troops and weaponry, the German Army still proved a formidable opponent.

A pivotal reason for the Soviet Union's ability to seize the strategic initiative was the significant improvement in the Red Army's High Command, which had become considerably more professional. Soviet generals studied every campaign; learning from mistakes and successes, they became increasingly more adept at mechanized warfare—deception, concentration of forces, lightning armored thrusts, breakthroughs, encirclements, coordinated air and artillery bombardments, and deep antitank defenses. In 1944, the Red Army was far more capable than the forces that had confronted the Wehrmacht in the debacle of 1941, a development that worried the German High Command and boosted confidence in all ranks of the Soviet military. To be sure, because of superior tactical skills, in individual battles the Wehrmacht continued to suffer fewer casualties than did the Red Army. But the combination of improved generalship, massive numbers of troops, and an abundance of weapons gave the Red Army a decisive advantage in their offensives that started in late 1943 and early 1944. By March 1944, the Red Army had broken the siege at Leningrad, liberated key areas of the Ukraine, and driven the Germans and their Romanian satellite out of the Crimea. Hitler's refusal to evacuate the Crimea while there was still a chance ended in a crushing defeat for the Axis powers in April and May; most of the 120,000 German and Romanian soldiers trapped there did not escape the Russian net.

Operation Bagration

On June 22, 1944, coincidentally the third anniversary of Operation Barbarossa, the Red Army began a summer offensive called Operation Bagration,* which demolished German armies, drove the Germans out of the Soviet Union, and advanced into German-controlled countries. Attacking with overwhelming strength—1.25 million men, 4,000 armored vehicles, and some 6,500 planes—the Red Army broke through German lines, struck the enemy in the rear, and cut off the retreat of bottled-up German forces. As in the past, Hitler's determination not to surrender a yard of conquered ground meant certain death or capture for vast numbers of German troops. The Soviets took huge numbers of prisoners when they forced the collapse in Belorussia (now Belarus) of Army Group Center, Germany's strongest army unit. Unlike the overly cautious or simply neglectful Anglo-American commanders at Falaise (see page 215), at the Scheldt (see page 224), and at the German retreat from the Ardennes (see page 236), Soviet generals did not hesitate to exploit immediately a German weakness with the specific aim of destroying the enemy. In what was a significantly larger operation than Overlord and a greater victory than Stalingrad, the Red Army inflicted huge casualties on the retreating Germans, whom they drove all

---

*Pyotr Bagration was a famous Russian general in the late eighteenth and early nineteenth centuries in whose honor Tsar Nicholas I had a monument erected at Borodino, where he was mortally wounded fighting Napoleon Bonaparte.

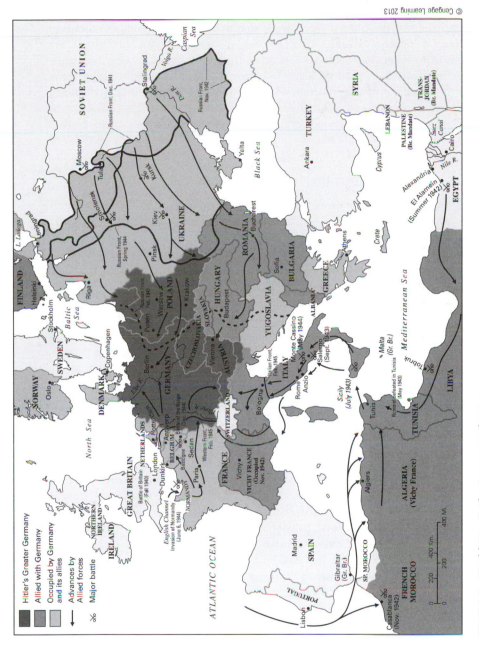

MAP 7.1 World War II: The European Theatre

By 1942, Germany ruled virtually all of Europe from the Atlantic to deep into Russia. Germany's defeat at Stalingrad in Russia and El Alamein in North Africa were decisive turning points.

the way back to the outskirts of Warsaw. Mass surrenders, something unusual for the Wehrmacht on the Eastern Front, were signs that generals would not command their troops to fight to the death as Hitler often demanded. These surrenders were also signs that soldiers were losing heart. More than fifty thousand Germans taken prisoner at Minsk, the capital of Belorussia, were paraded through Red Square in Moscow. Marching in the procession were more than one thousand officers, including nineteen generals in full uniform, medals and all. The Muscovites watching the spectacle comprehended its meaning: the Soviet Union had broken German power.

Beyond the Soviet Union's Borders

Moving with breathtaking speed, massive Red Army spearheads liberated additional areas of the Ukraine and outflanked German forces in the Baltic area. By August 1, 1944, the Red Army had cleared all Soviet territory of German troops. A successful attack against Finland, Germany's ally, forced the Finns to conclude an armistice in September. The Red Army moved into Poland and was encamped by the Vistula River, a few miles from Warsaw, where they remained while the Germans crushed the Warsaw Uprising in August-September 1944. Stalin wanted the Germans to eliminate the Polish Home Army, making it easier for a Communist-controlled government to rule postwar Poland. Soviet troops were also at the border of East Prussia and in striking distance of Hungary and Romania, Germany's allies. Determined to extend Soviet power into Eastern Europe, Stalin, who had learned to allow his commanders significant autonomy now because of political considerations, increasingly asserted his authority over military decisions.

Romanian armies had been badly mauled at Stalingrad in 1943 and in the Crimea in early 1944. Realizing that its soldiers had no will to fight and hope for a German victory was gone, Romania sought to withdraw from the war. In late August, Soviet forces attacked German and Romanian armies on the Romanian frontier. The Red Army drove through the Romanian forces, which speedily collapsed, and captured the Ploesti oilfields on which Germany was heavily dependent. The Red Army destroyed sixteen retreating German divisions that were unable to cross the Danube to safety. Three days after the Soviet onslaught, Marshal Ion Antonescu, the pro-German premier, was ousted in a coup. The new government broke with the Axis, declared war on Germany, and agreed to fight alongside the Red Army in Hungary. The Germans were quickly driven from Romania with substantial losses.

In October 1944, Josip Tito's partisans (see page 146), with some help from the Red Army, annihilated the German forces in Belgrade, the capital of Yugoslavia. Several thousand German soldiers died in the vicious fighting. Soon Tito's forces drove the Germans from other Yugoslav cities and liberated the country.

When Miklós Horthy, leader of Hungary, sent peace overtures to Moscow in October 1944, the Germans set up a new government under Ferenc Szálasi. Szálasi was head of the Arrow Cross, an extremist right-wing party that shared the Nazis hatred of Jews. Arrow Cross gangs killed thousands of Jews, often torturing them first; the Danube was littered with Jewish dead and reddened with Jewish blood.

So too were hospitals and old people's homes, where the Arrow Cross searched for Jewish victims. One Arrow Cross commander, Father Kun, a Catholic priest who later admitted to directing mass killings of five hundred Jews, ordered his subordinates: "In the name of Christ—fire."[6] For seven or eight days, the Arrow Cross marched eighty thousand Jews to the border of Austria where they would do forced labor. They marched with virtually no food, water, or shelter, and many died of exhaustion or were murdered by the guards en route.

The Soviet steamroller rolled across Hungary. At the year's end, the Red Army surrounded German and Hungarian forces in Budapest. The fighting caused great hardship for the trapped civilians who were short of food; deprived of water, gas, and electricity; and subjected to aerial and artillery bombardment. But it would take weeks of brutal fighting and heavy casualties, both military and civilian, until Budapest finally fell on February 14, 1945. The victorious Soviet soldiers went on a rampage of rape and looting that a Hungarian official equated with the invasion by Genghis Khan's Mongolian hordes in the thirteenth century.

THE DRIVE INTO GERMANY FROM THE WEST

After the defeat of the Germans in the Battle of the Bulge, Germany's position on the Western Front rapidly deteriorated. The production of armaments, which had greatly expanded under Albert Speer in 1944, dropped drastically. German armored units were desperately short of tanks and gas; woefully undermanned infantry units were reduced to conscripting teenagers and the infirm; and there were not enough trained pilots to fly or enough fuel to propel what was left of the German air force. The Anglo–American forces had overwhelming manpower and firepower, especially heavy artillery and fighters and bombers.

The Rhineland

Relations between Bernard Montgomery and Dwight D. Eisenhower, never very good, soured even more after Montgomery's unfortunate and widely publicized remark made at a press conference that the counteroffensive he had directed during the Battle of the Bulge had rescued the Americans. He gave the impression that the Americans could not have succeeded without his leadership, even though both his role and British troop commitment in the battle were limited. Often insufferably vain and haughty, Montgomery was not beyond displaying an arrogant attitude toward the Americans. Eisenhower also regretted endorsing Montgomery's plan to seize a bridgehead at Arnhem, which led to the disastrous Market Garden campaign. The British field marshal's quarrel with Eisenhower on how to proceed in the endgame approached insubordination.

Montgomery pressed Eisenhower for a bold, powerful drive into the Ruhr, a "dagger-thrust" by his army; the capture of Germany's industrial center, he argued, would bring a quick end to the war. After the Ruhr fell, the Allies would march across the north German plain directly to Berlin, with Montgomery commanding the drive and Americans providing support. Eisenhower feared that Montgomery's strategy would leave the Allies vulnerable to a German counterattack against a weak section of the front, a repetition of the Battle of the Bulge. And having suffered through Montgomery's calamitous "dagger-thrust" in Market Garden, a reflective Eisenhower rejected the British field marshal's narrow front plan, opting instead for relentlessly attacking on a broad front. Unable to cope with Allied numerical strength and air superiority at all points, a battered Germany, he believed, would suffer irreplaceable losses and soon collapse. Both Churchill and Montgomery resisted Eisenhower. Attacking on a broad front, they argued, would diffuse and dilute Allied strength and draw its forces into a costly war of attrition reminiscent of World War I, but Eisenhower prevailed. Montgomery and other members of British High Command generally did not have a favorable opinion of Eisenhower. "Ike's ignorance of how to run a war is absolute," said Montgomery.[7] And on July 27, 1944, Field Marshal Alan Francis Brooke (later First Viscount Alanbrooke) recorded in his diary: "Ike knows nothing about strategy and is quite unsuited to the post of Supreme Commander as far as running the strategy of the war is concerned!"[8]

To implement his broad front strategy, Eisenhower first planned to clear German troops from the Rhineland, the region of Germany west of the Rhine River, as a prelude to crossing the Rhine and moving deep into Germany. Unable to bear the thought of Allied troops invading and occupying German territory, Hitler overruled the advice of his generals and decided to fight on the west bank rather than to retreat to the east bank of the Rhine, a natural line of defense. This was still another costly blunder because German forces in the Rhineland were vulnerable to overwhelming Allied might.

Supported by aerial and artillery bombardments, the offensive began in early February in dreadful weather. Determined German resistance, including flooding the terrain by opening the gates of the Schwammenauel Dam on the Roer River, held back the Allied advance for almost two weeks. But short of fuel and ammunition and unable to counter Allied planes that fired on anything that moved, German commanders pleaded with Hitler for permission to pull back. As in the past, Hitler commanded that they hold their ground. Particularly after the attempt on his life, Hitler interpreted withdrawals as signs of defeatism or even treason. By March 21, German forces west of the Rhine were trapped, and a few days later resistance collapsed. Some 250,000 were taken prisoners, with an additional 60,000 killed or wounded. These enormous losses left Germany without sufficient forces to defend large areas of the east bank of the Rhine.

Everywhere retreating German troops had detonated bridges spanning the Rhine, but on March 7, 1945, American soldiers spotted a bridge at Remagen that the Germans had not yet destroyed. As the Americans charged the bridge, the Germans struggled frantically to blow it up but failed. The Americans could see a German engineer pushing a plunger but there was no explosion; apparently, a shell had severed the wire leading to the demolition charges. The platoon rushed across and captured the German squad. American infantry and armor quickly crossed and set up a defense line on the east side of the Rhine. An infuriated Hitler ordered several officers considered responsible for the bridge falling into American hands to be court-martialed and executed and replaced Field Marshal von Rundstedt with Field Marshal Kesselring, who had led German troops in Italy, as commander in the West.

Immediately, engineers built heavy pontoon bridges in other areas, enabling more Americans to cross the river almost unopposed and establish additional bridge-heads on its east side. Meanwhile George Patton's U.S. Third Army, constantly on the attack, battered German forces west of the Rhine, bagging a large number of prisoners, and reached the river near Oppenheim. Totally surprising the Germans, Patton's army crossed the Rhine on March 22 in assault boats and advanced rapidly.

Montgomery's Crossing of the Rhine

Montgomery, so different from Patton, hesitated to move beyond the Rhine barrier until his elaborate set-piece plan was in place. Always concerned with casualties and achieving overwhelming superiority over the enemy, he was determined to leave nothing to chance. His staff took the time to check every detail of the operation. Montgomery wanted no repetition of Operation Market Garden, where his usual meticulous operational planning had been faulty and costly.

After much delay, which angered the Americans, on March 23, following a ferocious military barrage, Montgomery's forces crossed the Rhine at Wesel, north of Patton's crossing, in the largest amphibious operation since D-Day. After waves of assault troops overwhelmed German defenses on the east bank, RAF bombers dropped eleven hundred tons of explosives on Wesel, setting it ablaze. Moving into the town, British forces crushed German resistance. Additional troops under Montgomery's command, including American divisions, crossed the Rhine in large numbers meeting little resistance. The Allies had secured and expanded their bridgehead.

To protect against a German counterattack, Montgomery ordered British and American airborne units to seize bridges, neutralize strongpoints, and link up with the ground troops advancing from the lodgment. The transport planes had to fly through a hail of antiaircraft and machine-gun fire that hit descending paratroops and planes, especially the slow gliders approaching landing zones. Nevertheless, the airborne forces accomplished their mission. Because the Germans were forced to deploy much of their mobile armored reserves against the airborne troops, pressure on the ground forces eased. With German resistance crumbling and Allied armor advancing from the bridgehead, British and American divisions were in a position to drive deeper into Germany. Other crossings by American and French forces established a 250-mile front, which was in compliance with Eisenhower's broad front strategy. Allied armies with a gigantic concentration of men and armor were now poised to advance from the Rhineland into the heart of Hitler's Third Reich.

Saturation Bombing

While Allied ground forces were pressing their offensive in February and March, American and British bombers continued striking high-value targets vital to the

German war machine and carpet-bombing German cities in terror raids that day and night relentlessly rained bombs on civilians. With the Luftwaffe now a spent force short of pilots and fuel and offering only feeble resistance, the raids increased in intensity and destructiveness. German cities and towns were being demolished as Churchill had advocated, although toward the end of the war the enormous loss of civilian life caused him to have misgivings. From January 1945 until Germany's surrender, 130,000 Germans, most of them civilians, perished in Allied raids. The German people lost all confidence in the Luftwaffe, which was unable to protect the homeland, and mocked Hermann Goering, the head of the Luftwaffe. Conditioned by Goebbels' propaganda, many Germans believed that Jews controlled Britain and the United States and ordered the bombings in order to wreak havoc on Germany. Some religious Germans viewed the destruction as biblical retribution for what had been done to the Jews, particularly when churches were destroyed. Nazi propaganda claimed the bombings only united the people and strengthened their determination to fight their enemies.

Although the bombings did not lead to a total collapse of German morale, Nazi studies of public opinion concluded that the heavy bombardments did contribute to feelings of hopelessness and apathy and diminished confidence in both final victory and the Third Reich's leadership, including Hitler. Many civilians, desperate to end the ceaseless torment from the skies, eagerly awaited the arrival of American and British troops. Goebbels recorded in his diary that by early 1945, the air war had eroded Germany's "armaments potential … quite beyond repair"; devastated its transportation system, preventing supplies from reaching the fronts; and caused civilian morale to plummet.

> During the last 24 hours the air war has again raged over Reich territory with devastating effect…. The greater part of Dessau is a sheet of flame and totally destroyed; yet another German city which has been largely flattened…. Evidence of demoralization is now to be seen…. Desertions have reached a considerable level…. Again and again one hears that the enemy air bombardment is at the bottom of it all. It is understandable that a people which has been subjected for years to the fire-effect of a weapon against which it has no defence, should gradually lose its courage…. The necessary transport and communications are no longer available to us. Not only our cities but also our industry have largely been demolished. The result is a deep dent in German war morale.[9]

Morale may have weakened somewhat, but the German people did not alter their behavior toward the Nazi regime. After a night of horrific bombing, people emerged from their basements and bomb shelters located in subways and beneath government buildings to report to work—no doubt some out of fear of the Gestapo and the police, who hunted down absentee workers. And there were no mass protests against the state, no armed resistance to the Nazis. Most German people complied with the regime until the end.

To support the Soviets who were advancing west into Germany and in a continuing attempt to shatter German morale, the Allies mass-bombed cities in east Germany in early 1945. They believed that such attacks, particularly if they destroyed rail yards, would hinder the movement of German men and supplies to the Eastern Front. On February 3, one thousand bombers from the U.S. Eighth Air Force plastered railway installations and administrative buildings in Berlin, causing enormous destruction and the deaths of twenty-five thousand Berliners, according to the Nazi authorities.

On February 13 and 14, Allied planes dropped tons of high-explosive bombs and incendiaries packed with highly combustible chemicals on Dresden, which was now crammed with refugees fleeing the Red Army and virtually defenseless. The bombings created a firestorm that turned the city into an inferno. A landmark cultural center famous for its splendid architecture, Dresden was totally devastated and between twenty thousand and thirty thousand inhabitants perished. Those caught outdoors were engulfed in a sea of flames; those seeking shelter in basements were frequently asphyxiated by the inhalation of carbon monoxide gas. When reached by fire, these shelters were turned into crematoriums. Shriveled and blackened corpses could not be identified. Thousands of survivors suffered horrific wounds. So catastrophic was the destruction that Churchill, who had strongly supported the air campaign, now had doubts about mass terror raids; he called instead for concentrated attacks on military objectives.

Some British and American, along with German, commentators have called the bombing a criminal act. Dresden, they argue, was of no military importance and with the war nearly won its destruction was totally unnecessary. Defenders of the raid point out that Dresden was a major railway junction that could be used for transporting troops to fight the Soviets; its factories produced military gunsights, radar equipment, gas masks, parts for the German air force, and fuses for antiaircraft shells; and that with the Germans offering strong resistance on both fronts, there was no certainty that the war would end shortly. (The debate over area bombing is treated in Chapter 5, pages 188.)

The chaos caused by area bombing in Dresden and other cities did enable a few surviving German Jews, either in hiding or married to gentiles, to remove the Star of David with the word Jude inscribed that they were required to wear on their clothes and to blend in with the population. This saved their lives, for otherwise they were likely to be rounded up in the last act of genocide. Slave laborers, Jews and non-Jews, regarded the fires as beacons of hope that the war would soon end. Some took advantage of the destruction to escape from servitude.

The Ruhr and Beyond

After advancing across the Rhine, Eisenhower now focused on the Ruhr Basin, Germany's industrial heartland. Given that the industrial regions of Silesia had been captured by the Red Army, the loss of the Ruhr, the principal supplier of coal and steel and a key producer of armaments, would mean the death of the German war machine. Virtually unopposed, British and American bombers relentlessly pounded numerous towns in the Ruhr Basin, and the east bank of the Rhine.

On April 1, 1945, two U.S. armies converged on the Ruhr, one commanded by Lieutenant General William Simpson moving north and the other commanded by Lieutenant General Courtney Hodges moving south. In a brilliantly executed double envelopment, by April 4 the German armies were effectively surrounded in a pocket measuring some thirty miles by seventy-five miles that the Allies were methodically tightening. Their ammunition depleted, their vehicles including tanks idle for lack of fuel, and their morale breaking, German units were disbanding and taking to the woods. Field Marshal Walther Model's order to attempt a breakout was resisted by his generals who knew the situation was hopeless; increasingly, commanders were capitulating to the Americans.

Model, who had always been an ardent Nazi and Hitler loyalist, refused to carry out the Führer's orders to destroy the Ruhr's industrial and communication installations. Realizing that his army was facing total destruction but considering it disgraceful for a German field marshal to surrender and be taken prisoner, Model discharged the very young and old—many of his soldiers were untrained and uneager recruits—and sent them home. The remaining soldiers could choose either to surrender to the advancing Americans or to try to break out of the pocket. German resistance in the Ruhr ended on April 18 and another 325,000 German soldiers were taken prisoner, the greatest mass surrender of German troops in the war. On April 20, Hitler's birthday, Model told his officers, "I sincerely believe that I have served a criminal. I led my soldiers in good conscience ... but for a criminal government."[10] Then he took his own life. No doubt this decision was also prompted by reports that the Soviets intended to try him for war crimes, including the deportation of 175,000 slave laborers to Germany and the death of 575,000 people in concentration camps in Latvia.

Model's army, now gone, had been the Third Reich's last major combat force on the Western Front. The encirclement of the Ruhr, perhaps America's most outstanding victory in the war, showed that American commanders had mastered the tactic of breakthrough and envelopment, and unlike the endgame at Falaise and the Bulge, this time the Germans did not escape the pocket.

It is often said that only an overwhelming supply of weapons—brute strength—enabled the Americans to emerge victorious on the Western Front. Based largely on poor American performance in the early days of the campaign in North Africa, this interpretation overlooks the American army's deliberate move to improve battlefield performance by weeding out unfit commanders and improving training. In the campaigns in Normandy, the Bulge, the Rhineland, and the Ruhr, the American army on all levels, front-line soldiers, officers, and general staff, had become an effective fighting force. In 1944–1945, American citizen-soldiers and their commanders—despite some miscalculations and some units' failure to accomplish missions—were up to the challenge of defeating Germany's vaunted Wehrmacht.

Had the Germans decided to fight to the end in the Ruhr as Hitler ordered, they could not have changed the outcome of the war. But if they dispersed in advantageous places—city ruins and thick forests provided near perfect cover for a determined resistance—they could have inflicted huge casualties on the Allies. Was it the horrific attacks from the air, now unopposed by the Luftwaffe, that broke the fighting spirit of all but the most diehard? Was the massive destruction all around them a clear sign that no miracle weapon or miracle strategy devised by Hitler could save the Third Reich, that further resistance would only invite more destruction, that surrender was the only option? If so, then strategic bombing did contribute to shortening the war and reducing Allied casualties.

At the same time that Germans were being trapped in the Ruhr, other Allied armies were forging ahead to the Elbe River, which was reached on April 11. Choosing not to advance to Berlin only seventy miles away, Eisenhower had already shifted the offensive to the Ruhr. Eisenhower has been criticized for not driving all the way to Berlin before the Russians could take the city. But several factors, both military and political, entered into his decision. First, the Americans at the Elbe were only an advance force of fifty thousand men with limited artillery; they would have to wait for the bulk of their forces to catch up. The Soviets, on the other hand, only thirty-three miles from Berlin, had amassed a huge army in preparation for the attack on the heart of the Nazi Reich. Rather than allowing the Americans to capture the prize that they had been savoring for so long, they would have increased the tempo of their offensive. Stalin would not be denied the glory of conquering the capital of Hitler's Third Reich. Second, Eisenhower wanted to concentrate on destroying the German armed forces not diverting troops to capture a city that had little military value. Moreover, concerned about casualties, Eisenhower knew that the Americans would pay a steep price fighting in Berlin's approaches and streets against zealous Nazis. He did not want tens of thousands of his men to die for a political objective just as the war was nearing its end. Third, at the Yalta Conference in February 1944, Churchill, Stalin, and Roosevelt had agreed to divide Berlin into occupation zones. If the Americans had taken the city, how could they retain the area designated for the Soviet Union? A fourth factor entered into Eisenhower's decision not to take Berlin. Intelligence reports suggested that Waffen-SS troops were setting up a "redoubt" in Bavaria and the Austrian Alps to make a suicidal stand against the Allies. Heeding these reports, which turned out to be totally false, Eisenhower moved a substantial number of troops south into the region. Eisenhower's decision to allow the Soviets to take Berlin greatly distressed Churchill, who was thinking about postwar Europe.

American, British, Canadian, and De Gaulle's Free French forces fanned out in all directions, moving deeper and deeper into Germany. In rapid succession, villages, towns, and cities fell into Allied hands. In his diary entry for March 4, Goebbels lamented that "the population of the western districts conquered by the Anglo-Americans is giving them a comparatively good reception. This I had really not expected."[11] Desperate to end the war and to avoid falling into Russian hands, many of these civilians welcomed the arrival of American and British soldiers, at times greeting them with white flags and flowers. By the end of March, Aachen, Cologne, Bonn, Bad Godsberg, Mainz, Frankfurt, and Mannheim had fallen. In late April, the Western Allies captured two cities venerated by the Nazis: Munich, the birthplace of Nazism, and Nuremberg, where the Nazis held their giant rallies. On April 25, 1945, at the Elbe, some seventy-five miles south of Berlin, an American patrol met vanguards of a Soviet division. The soldiers embraced and a joyful celebration followed.

After playing a key role in the encirclement of German forces in the Ruhr pocket, Patton's U.S. Third Army, facing limited German resistance, drove across southern Germany into Czechoslovakia and Austria. In early May, the Third Army took Linz, where Hitler had spent his boyhood, and was prepared to liberate Prague. However, strong objections by the Soviet Union, which had its own plans for Czechoslovakia, compelled Eisenhower to hold Patton back.

By the last days of April, German resistance was rapidly collapsing. Large numbers of German soldiers on the Western Front, recognizing the futility of further fighting, reasoned that it was more prudent to surrender to the Western Allies than to fall into Russian hands. Joining them were German troops desperately rushing west to escape the Red Army. Indeed, by this time many German soldiers wanted the Americans and British to overrun as much of Germany as possible in order to keep these areas from being occupied by the Russians. Many soldiers were discarding their arms, medals, and military IDs and exchanging their uniforms for civilian clothes in order to wipe away any complicity with the Nazis and war crimes.

Another act of prudence was for civilians to rid their homes of anything incriminating—photographs of Hitler, Nazi banners, emblems, and literature, especially *Mein Kampf*, and anything that identified them as Nazi Party members. Most of the time, German civilians in the West opted not to resist when the Allies entered their towns and villages, ignoring the commands of Nazi Party officials to engage in a last-ditch stand against the enemy. Villagers learned quickly that if they did offer resistance, even if slight, American artillery would rain destruction on the entire village. And often the townspeople and villagers had rehearsed what they would tell their conquerors: there were no Nazis in their community, only innocent victims of a criminal regime and a cruel war; and they knew nothing of concentration camps and atrocities.

Victory in Italy

In Italy, too, the Germans were going down to defeat, but it continued to be a grueling process for the Allies. After Rome fell in June 1944, the Germans retreated to new defensive positions that crossed the peninsula. Again, the two Western Allies quarreled over the same issue. Churchill wanted to devote more resources to the Italian campaign. After the German forces were defeated, he maintained, the Allies would move from Italy into Vienna before the Red Army reached the Austrian capital, and then into Germany. Eisenhower, the American Joint Chiefs of Staff, and President Roosevelt would countenance no diversion of men and materiel away from the battle being waged in France after D-Day. They were emphatic that Italy would remain a secondary consideration and that some divisions would be moved from Italy to France, a decision with which the British had to live.

Meanwhile, Germany was reinforcing its forces in Italy with divisions that had been earmarked for the Eastern Front. As British and American forces moved north, they had to make their way through mountains, across what seemed like an endless succession of rivers, and over muddy roads in the face of tough German resistance that used the terrain to its advantage. Although the Allies had greater firepower and dominated the skies, the Germans had the advantage of a terrain that favored the defense and could choose where they would fight. As in the earlier stages of the Italian campaign, the German strategy was to stand and fight when appropriate, fall back to a new defensive position as Allied strength mounted, and counterattack when conditions were suitable. This elastic defense enabled the Germans very effectively to trade space for time, limiting the Allies' advance to a snail's pace and driving up casualties.

Italian partisans engaged in guerrilla actions against the Germans, who retaliated by conducting antipartisan sweeps and massacring hostages. One of the worst massacres took place on August 12, 1944, when the Germans rounded up villagers and herded them into barns. The Germans then hurled grenades into the barns, opened up with machine-gun fire, and set the sheds on fire. Some five hundred men, women, and children perished. Maintaining that the partisans depended on the support of locals, the Germans also resorted to mass evacuations from areas thought to be centers of partisan resistance. Many of the partisans were young men escaping German dragnets for forced laborers sent to build fortifications or, worse, for deportation to toil in Germany.

The slogging match continued until April 1945, when the Allies achieved a major breakthrough, cutting off the Germans who were in retreat. By the end of the month, Bologna and Venice were in Allied hands and the number of Germans surrendering was increasing. Tens of thousands of Italian partisans were liberating towns and villages and taking revenge on Fascists in authority. Mussolini tried to escape to Switzerland but was captured by Italian partisans and executed on April 28; his corpse, and that of his long-time mistress, were both hung upside down for public display. With their armies collapsing, on May 3, German commanders formally surrendered all Axis forces in Italy to General Clark, the Allied commander.

Unconditional Surrender: Prolonging the War?

Some analysts argue that the war might have ended earlier had not the Allies insisted on Germany's unconditional surrender. They maintain that when the Red Army drove the Wehrmacht from Soviet soil and the Allies were not thrown back at Normandy, Hitler, in his more lucid moments, knew that he could no longer win the war. (Indeed, after the war some German generals who had contact with Hitler said that reverses in the Soviet Union early in the war had already caused Hitler to have doubts about a German victory.) According to this view, Hitler was hoping for one resounding battlefield victory that might convince the Anglo-Americans that subduing a resolute and still powerful Germany was too costly, that a negotiated settlement on the Western Front was preferable to endless bloodshed. Hitler continued to believe that the unnatural alliance between the Soviet Union and the Western Allies could not endure, that Britain and the United States would eventually recognize the need to join with him against the Bolshevik threat. He also thought of the possibility of striking a deal with Stalin who, unlike Churchill and Roosevelt, did not have to answer to public opinion. "The only hope for a successful end to the war," Goebbels entered in his diary for March 4, "is that the split in the enemy camp becomes irreparable before we are flat on the floor.... But before we can start talks either with one side or the other, it is essential that we score some military success. Even Stalin must lose a few tail feathers before he will have anything to do with us."[12]

However, American and British determination to rid Europe of Hitler, the Third Reich, and National Socialism overrode ideological differences between East and West; Hitler would not be able to drive a wedge between them. It was out of the question that they would negotiate with the leader of a regime that had dragged Europe into a war of unprecedented savagery and made genocide and slavery state policy. And Stalin, who had his eye on Soviet expansion and a prostrate Germany, would never let a beaten Hitler off the ropes regardless of the human cost.

Most importantly, with a vivid memory of Germany's resurrection after World War I, the United States and Britain were determined that never again would Germany be in a position to threaten the Continent. In November 1918, the overthrow of the Kaiser and the signing of an armistice kept Britain, France, and the United States from invading a defeated Germany, giving rise to the legend that the German army had not been beaten in the battlefield but was betrayed, "stabbed in the back," by socialists and Jews. This time the German people had to know unequivocally in their hearts and minds that they had lost the war and that there was no possibility of Germany ever waging a third world war. This meant totally crushing the German army and, if necessary, destroying much of the country. Although costly in fatalities for all the combatants and for German civilians, the policy of unconditional surrender did contribute to a changed German mindset, making possible the emergence of a peaceful and democratic Germany after the war.

Doubtless some Germans felt that unconditional surrender gave them no alternative but to continue fighting, particularly when it was identified with the plan proposed by U.S. Treasury Secretary Henry Morgenthau, Jr. The Morgenthau Plan called for stripping Germany of its industrial machinery and converting it into two agricultural states. But the plan was quickly shelved. It did, however, provide Goebbels with ammunition for his propaganda mill, particularly given that Morgenthau was Jewish. Nevertheless, despite the appeals of local Party officials, Goebbels' hyperbole, and Hitler's orders, the German masses did not spontaneously organize local militias to battle the Allied armies with National Socialist zeal.

LIBERATING CONCENTRATION CAMPS

The retreating SS evacuated inmates from concentration and slave labor camps so that they would not be liberated by Allies. Sometimes, before closing a camp down, they simply killed the inmates; for example, at Mielec in southern Poland they massacred three thousand Jews on August 24, 1944, and another three thousand at Klooga in Estonia on September 19. Alarmed that the Allies would make them answer for their crimes, the SS tried to destroy as much evidence as possible. Earlier, they had established special squads of Jewish slave laborers, who would later be executed, to exhume and cremate the corpses in the numerous killing fields in the Soviet Union.

But the SS could not destroy all the concentration camps that were still filled with people. When the advancing Soviets and Western Allies reached these camps, even battle-hardened veterans were sickened by what they found. The Red Army liberated the first camp, Maidanek, near Lublin in eastern Poland, in July 1944; it was a death camp in which more than three hundred thousand people had been murdered. The horrified Soviet soldiers found gas chambers, crematoriums that the fleeing Germans did not have time to dismantle, mounds of bodies, and storage rooms filled with mountains of shoes, clothes, children's toys, and human hair shorn from inmates. The Soviets publicized their findings, describing those who perished as "victims of Fascism," never as Jews, the same policy they had employed with the massacres committed by the Einsatzgruppen in the Ukraine, Belorussia, the Crimea, and other areas of the Soviet Union. Soviet authorities deliberately tried to conceal the Holocaust. They wanted their people to remember the suffering the Germans inflicted on Mother Russia; mentioning the Jewish tragedy would detract from this objective.

In April 1945, as American and British armies penetrated deeper into Germany, they came across numerous concentration camps, including Buchenwald, Nordhausen, Bergen-Belsen, and Dachau. (American and British troops, though, never saw the extermination centers in Poland where millions were gassed.) Unprepared for what they experienced, they recoiled in horror and revulsion at the torture chambers, the gallows, and the crematoria. At Nordhausen, which supplied slave labor for the production of V-2 rockets, an American soldier remembers "seeing the mounds of dead bodies, naked and piled so high. I remember the stench. We all vomited."[13] A sergeant in a medical unit saw men "too weak to move dead comrades from their side.... There were others, in dark cellar rooms, lying in disease and filth, being eaten away by diarrhea and malnutrition. It was like stepping into the Dark Ages."[14] At Buchenwald, the corpses were stacked like firewood. At Bergen-Belsen, the British found emaciated victims in their own filth dying of dysentery, barely distinguishable from the thousands of corpses strewn all over. Bulldozers were needed to move the bodies into huge pits. British officers forced German civilians from neighboring towns to view what their countrymen had done and to assist with the mass burials. Within a short time after liberation, almost fourteen thousand more inmates of the camp perished.

Many of the prisoners in the liberated camps had been moved west from Auschwitz and other evacuated camps. When the Soviets liberated Auschwitz on January 27, 1945, still remaining were six thousand survivors, pitiful skeletons near death, and one thousand corpses. The Germans had set fire to twenty-nine huge storehouses; in the six storehouses still standing, the Soviets found an enormous number of shoes, spectacles, and dentures, more than a million men's suits

© Topham Picturepoint/The Image Works

Thousands of emaciated and diseased inmates of German concentration camps died in the weeks after liberation by the Allies. These camps will forever remain a monument to the capacity of human beings for inhumanity.

and women's coats and dresses, and thousands of bundles of human hair. In an attempt to cover up their crimes, the SS had destroyed documents and installations, including the gas chambers. To prevent the prisoners from being liberated by the enemy, on January 18, 1945, the SS evacuated about fifty-eight thousand inmates who were marched into the German interior in brutal cold weather. Some fifteen thousand perished in still another ordeal of torment and terror inflicted on them by sadistic SS guards.

In total, the Germans, principally SS but also Wehrmacht and home guard, transferred in midwinter some 750,000 concentration camp inmates, Jews and non-Jews, to other camps in areas still under German control. Sometimes they were transported in open rail cars. One such car carrying evacuees from Poland arrived at a camp in Germany. A prisoner at that camp ordered to unload the corpses and the dying from the rail car described the horror: "These people ... were transported from Poland to central Germany in open goods wagons for 20 days without food. On the way they froze, starved, or were shot. Men women and children of all ages were among them. When we took hold of the dead, arms, legs, or heads often came off in our hands, as the corpses were frozen."[15]

Most inmates simply trudged, sometimes for weeks, in what the survivors called "death marches." Marching for miles in the dead of winter wearing thin striped rags, already emaciated by their ordeal in the camps, given little food or water, and repeatedly beaten, many simply collapsed and were clubbed to death or shot by Nazi and Ukrainian guards. A British prisoner of war doing forced labor observed with white hot anger a typical death march.

> I have seen today the filthiest foulest and most cruel sight of my life. God damn Germany with an everlasting punishment. At 9 a.m., this morning a column straggled down the road towards Danzig—a column far beyond the words of which I am capable to describe. I was struck dumb with a miserable rage a blind coldness which nearly resulted in my being shot.... They came straggling through the bitter cold about 300 of them limping, dragging footsteps, slipping and falling, to rise and stagger under the blows of the guards, SS swine. Crying loudly for bread, screaming for food, 300 matted haired, filthy objects that had once been—Jewesses! A rush into a nearby house for bread resulted in being clubbed down with a rifle butt, but even as she fell in a desperate movement she shoved the bread she'd got into her blouse.[16]

The documented atrocities committed on these death marches included driving prisoners into the sea, murdering them with machine-gun fire, and herding them into barns that were then set ablaze. On April 20, in a Hamburg concentration camp, the SS hanged twenty-two Jewish children between four and twelve years who had been transferred from Auschwitz to be used for medical experiments. In the march from Malthausen in Austria, while some bystanders expressed sympathy for the half-dead prisoners, "not just the SS guards got involved in killing stragglers,"[17] notes Robert Gelately, but so did soldiers, members of the Nazi Party, and ordinary citizens as well. Some locals took part in the massacres of Jews, and others shot Jews who happened to survive when they were left behind. It is estimated that in this killing frenzy, 250,000 to 350,000 concentration camp prisoners perished in the last months of the war.

At the end of April, American forces liberated Dachau concentration camp with all its horrors; there were corpses everywhere, torture chambers, and thousands of living skeletons near death. The Americans found more than fifty cattle cars filled with deportees from Auschwitz-Birkenau. A Turkish Catholic journalist, who had been imprisoned at Dachau for his reports about the Warsaw Ghetto and his prediction that the German armies would be defeated in Russia, later described what the Americans encountered:

> The train was full of corpses, piled one on the other, 2,310 of them, to be exact. The train had come from Birkenau and the dead were Hungarian and Polish Jews. Their journey had lasted perhaps thirty or forty days. They had died of hunger, of thirst, of suffocation, of being crushed, or of being beaten by the guards. There was evidence of cannibalism.... They were all practically dead when they arrived at Dachau Station. The SS men did not take the trouble to unload them. They simply decided to stand guard and shoot down any with the strength left to emerge from the cattle cars. The corpses were strewn

When the Bergen-Belsen concentration camp was liberated in April 1945, British officials ordered local residents to view the atrocities and to join captured SS, including female guards, to bury the corpses that littered the camp.

everywhere—on the rails, the steps, the platforms…. One soldier … pointed to something in motion among the cadavers. A louse-infested prisoner was crawling like a worm, trying to attract attention. He was the only survivor.[18]

The enraged American soldiers then hunted down and killed numerous SS guards—the exact number is unknown—and inmates, with the Americans' approval, beat to death other guards, some of whom attempted to hide their identity by changing into prison garb. The inmates also hunted down the kapos—prisoners, often criminals, given authority by the SS—who had brutalized them. Virtually to a man, the British and American troops that liberated the camps evidenced a grim determination to defeat and destroy an evil enemy.

THE DRIVE INTO GERMANY FROM THE EAST

The Red Army's summer offensive of 1944 had shattered the German military, which suffered more than nine hundred thousand casualties from June 1 to November 30. And Bulgaria, Finland, and Romania, whose oilfields Germany badly needed, were no longer allied to the Third Reich. The Red Army had moved into Yugoslavia to fight alongside Tito's partisans and was positioned to overrun Poland and Hungary. In October 1944, the Soviets had temporarily occupied some villages on the East Prussian border, where they committed dreadful atrocities against the villagers that Goebbels widely publicized. In some cases, the reaction of Germans to Goebbels' depiction of Soviet crimes was not anticipated. According to the Security Services of the SS, these graphic portrayals of the behavior of Russian soldiers reminded the civilian population "of the atrocities we have committed in enemy territory, even in Germany itself. Have we not murdered thousands of Jews? Don't soldiers again and again report that Jews have had to dig their own graves? ... By doing all this we have shown the enemy what they can do to us if they win."[19]

The Vistula Offensive: Poland and the Reich

After these grueling campaigns, in the last weeks of 1944 the Red Army temporarily halted its drive in order to resupply and reorganize. Now in January 1945, the Soviets had amassed a huge array of power—some four million men, ninety-eight hundred tanks, and over forty thousand pieces of artillery, a larger force than the Germans had assembled for Operation Barbarossa. Guderian's department, Foreign Armies East, calculated that the Red Army had a superiority of 15 to 1 on the ground and 20 to 1 in the air. On December 24, 1944, Guderian informed Hitler of these figures; the Führer, more and more reluctant to confront reality, responded that the reports "were based on an enemy bluff.... It's the greatest imposture since Genghis Khan. Who's responsible for producing all this rubbish."[20]

The new Vistula offensive, in which Stalin himself coordinated the various armies, called for driving the Germans from Poland and invading the German homeland, the "lair of the Fascist beast." On January 12, 1945, Soviet artillery pulverized German positions. Then swarms of infantry and tanks rolled westward toward Krakow through the enormous gap that had opened in the German lines. On January 14, the Red Army began another offensive north and south of Warsaw that ripped through the German front, stripped of reserves. When the Red Army and the Polish First Army serving with it entered Warsaw on January 17, 1945, they found only ruin and rubble. During and after the Polish uprising several months earlier (see Chapter 4, page 145), the Germans had methodically destroyed street after street; they resumed this wanton destruction as they now evacuated the city.

In Polish towns and concentration camps, the retreating Germans massacred captured Polish partisans, Soviet prisoners of war, and Jews. When the Soviet soldiers entered Polish villages and towns, they searched for German inhabitants who had not fled because they trusted the propaganda of Goebbels and local officials assuring victory. These hapless Germans fell victim to a wave of murder, rape, and looting. By January 20, the Red Army had taken Krakow and Lodz; on January 25, it surrounded Poznan, whose German population had streamed out of the city in panic. The German defenders fought ferociously and had to be driven from every house. A month later the city capitulated. A Soviet camera-man filmed the wretched soldiers marching through the town, some of them barefoot, as Poles pelted them with stones.

The evacuation of Warsaw infuriated Hitler, who had given orders to hold the city to the last man. Four days later, he issued an order stipulating that any withdrawal from a position required his authorization. In effect, this order forced a commander to order his men to fight and die for every foot of ground, an inflexible approach to tactics beloved by Hitler that had hurt the Wehrmacht several times in the past. Nor would Hitler permit his field commanders to offer an objective analysis of Germany's military position. On January 24, when told that Guderian thought the war was lost, Hitler, in a fit of rage, warned his generals that "anyone who tells anyone that the war is lost will be treated as a traitor, with all the consequences for him and his family. I will take action without regard to rank and prestige."[21]

Despite some temporary tactical successes, the German forces could not halt the Red Army's momentum as it rolled into Germany. By the end of January, the Red Army had overrun Upper Silesia, whose factories and mines Germany could not afford to lose, and was surging into East Prussia. German propaganda demanded that all citizens and soldiers resist this invasion of the fatherland by Soviet hordes. Old men and boys as young as fourteen were called to serve in the *Volkssturm*,* local militia units organized to defend the homeland. They received virtually no training and were issued whatever weapons were available, some of them obsolete rifles. Also called to serve with the Volkssturm were hospitalized soldiers who appeared fit enough to handle a weapon. The most fervent desire for many of those dragooned from their homes into the Volkssturm was simply to survive. Casualty rates for the five hundred thousand men serving in the Volkssturm were horrendous.

Soviet Retribution and German Flight

Designed to arouse hatred of the enemy, Soviet propaganda in inflammatory language reminded soldiers of the death and destruction the Nazis had inflicted on their villages, homes, and families in the years of occupation. A prominent journalist wrote: "Not only divisions and armies are advancing on Berlin. All the trenches, graves, and ravines, with the corpses of the innocents are advancing

---

*Heinrich Himmler, on orders from Hitler, introduced the Volkssturm, or people's militia, in October 1944. Like soldiers in the regular army, the men in the Volkssturm had to swear unconditional loyalty to Hitler. Required to supply their own clothing and eating utensils and inadequately armed because weapons were in short supply, many conscripts recognized the Volkssturm for what it was: a pointless sacrifice for a war that was already lost. Some 175,000 of these conscripts perished in the closing months of the war.

on Berlin.... As we advance through Pomerania, we have before our eyes the devastated blood-drenched countryside in Belorussia.... Germany, you can whirl around in circles, and howl in your deathly agony. The hour of revenge has struck."[22] The Soviet soldiers' craving for vengeance was condoned, even encouraged, by their commanders. In January 1945, included in an order from Marshal Zhukov was a call for "terrible revenge" against the "land of murderers." And the hatred of Germans was intensified even more as Soviet soldiers entered concentration camps and execution sites like that outside of Tallinn, Estonia, where they came across large numbers of slaughtered Jewish inmates. Their corpses were stacked in piles among gasoline-soaked logs ready to be set afire like kindling. Years after the war, a Russian officer at the time, and later a career general, reflected on the mood of Soviet soldiers as they neared the German frontier:

> When we got [to the concentration camp], most prisoners were dead; the Germans had machine-gunned them down before retreating.... When we entered [another] camp, ... [the inmates] could barely stand on their legs, merely skin and bones.... You can imagine what kind of hatred our soldiers felt.... I recall coming across the body of a German officer.... I found a photograph in [his] wallet. Apparently, this photo came from home. It showed six Soviets harnessed like oxen to a cart, and two German boys, about twelve years of age, were driving them with whips. Besides them stood adult Germans, making sure the poor bastards couldn't do anything.... How could such a thing not evoke hatred? Yes, we took it out on the Germans; we made them pay for what they did to us.[23]

When they entered German territory, Soviet soldiers were driven by hate fueled by almost unendurably painful experiences and memories; they wanted not just victory but revenge that often translated into looting and brutal and sadistic acts against civilians. A Soviet veteran recalls the mood of his comrades as they moved into East Prussia:

> I witnessed this scene. It was the first death of a German civilian that I saw in Germany. Catching up to the man who had crushed the German's skull with his rifle butt, I asked him: "Why did you kill him? He plainly was not a soldier and there was no way this [old man] could have harmed us." The soldier gruffly answered me. "To me ... they are all the same—just scum. I won't find any peace until I kill a hundred of them." ... It was not difficult to understand either his hatred or that of the soldiers who spat on the Germans. But how many more Germans would they have to kill, humiliate, and tear to pieces in order to soothe their grief, dull their hatred, thaw their icy soul, and find inner peace? ... Soldiers, literally rabid with fury, burst into badly damaged homes and shattered or destroyed everything they could find....

> The elements of hatred and revenge had by the end of January 1945 become a raging inundating river ... brutality, sadism, cynical cruel acts, unbridled lust, and, at times, even murders. In this raging storm of

retribution the primary instigators of the violence became the commanders and political workers.... Individual commanders and political workers who openly protested over the outrages against the civilian population suffered for it.[24]

Serial rape by drunken soldiers until women became unconscious was not an uncommon atrocity. Most of the civilians the Soviets encountered were women because men were in the military, in hospitals wounded, or deceased, so sexual violence became a routine way of expressing hatred of Germans and seeking vengeance for their racial arrogance and the suffering they had inflicted on the Soviet people, including the soldiers' immediate families. Victims of rape reported that the soldiers often told them "of a German soldier swinging a baby, torn from its mother's arms, against a wall—the mother screams, the baby's brains splatter against the wall, the soldiers laugh."[25] Such images of German brutality, often more than lust, triggered the barbaric behavior of these Soviet soldiers. Thousands of German women committed suicide. Whereas some Soviet troops lost all discipline, others were repelled by their comrades' barbaric behavior, which they felt dishonored the Red Army. At times, these soldiers protected German civilians from out-of-control troops.

Political officers who spoke for the Soviet government at first did not interfere with the rapes and looting. Soon, however, unhappy with the breakdown of discipline that could affect battlefield performance, Soviet authorities issued orders calling for proper treatment of civilians and cracked down on marauding soldiers, imprisoning and occasionally executing rapists. Moreover, they recognized that brutalizing the civilian population strengthened German resistance and after the war would make more difficult Soviet occupation of German lands. They were also concerned with the wanton destruction of property, particularly factories that could be of value after the war. Under orders from the Kremlin, Soviet authorities were already systematically plundering occupied regions, transporting to the Soviet Union industrial machinery, trains, weapons, works of art, and anything else of value. Uranium and heavy water needed for atomic research were high on their list of priorities.*

The efforts of Nazi officials to prevent citizens from fleeing the advancing Red Army did not succeed and was quickly abandoned. From January 12, just before the invasion, to mid-February several million Germans, including Nazi Party bigwigs and functionaries fled west to escape the Russians, some driving their luxurious official cars. In midwinter, the panic-stricken evacuees traveled in farm carts, on foot, and, if fortunate, by rail. At times, Soviet planes strafed and tanks crushed these refugee caravans, killing thousands; many more perished in

---

*British and American forces were also removing valuable industrial and scientific equipment from the Ruhr. Americans, in particular, were rounding up leading scientists and technicians to be transported back to the United States to continue their work in rocket science. Several of these luminaries had helped set up the rocket launching facilities in the Harz Mountains, where thirty thousand slave laborers perished. The suffering of these missile slave laborers, which may not have been exceeded by any other slave laborers, was a matter of indifference to these scientists and technicians. The U.S. authorities, wanting to avoid war crime trials for these valuable assets, conveniently ignored their past and even removed damaging evidence from their security files.

the bitter cold. Most of the fleeing Germans were women and children because men, even older ones, were forced to serve with the Volkssturm. The Soviets were also rounding up German men and deporting them east for slave labor. Very few refugees and deportees would ever return to their homes.

Many evacuees tried to reach Baltic ports, particularly Danzig, which could handle large ships. A Soviet submarine torpedoed a cruise ship packed with refugees, killing between fifty-three hundred and seventy-four hundred people, many of them children, in what still is the worst sea catastrophe on record. In a desperate herculean effort, the German navy succeeded in evacuating more than two million refugees congregating in ports along the Baltic coast. As Soviet troops moved deeper into Prussia, the refugee problem grew more severe.

TO THE BITTER END

Soviet Advance and Goebbels' Desperate Appeals

By early February 1945, the Red Army stood within forty miles of Berlin. In March and April, vicious fighting took place in key German cities, including Köningsberg, Danzig, and Vienna, before they were subdued by the Soviets. Despite heavy military and civilian casualties, Breslau held out until virtually the end of the war; apparently the civilian population that did not flee westward believed Goebbels' propaganda that from their city a victorious offensive would be launched.

In February and March, the fiery Guderian quarreled bitterly with Hitler. With Berlin threatened, Guderian wanted to transfer the twenty-two divisions stationed in the Courland, a region in Latvia, to reinforce battered German troops in East Prussia and to strengthen the approaches to Berlin, but Hitler permitted the evacuation of only one division, perhaps fantasizing that the other divisions would soon join with Britain and America against the common Soviet enemy. Still hoping to retain part of the Reich's empire. Hitler also refused Guderian's appeal to withdraw German forces from other countries still under German control in order to provide him with the troops needed to wage an effective counterattack against the Red Army advancing on Berlin. Guderian was infuriated with Hitler's plan for transferring SS panzer divisions to Hungary to recapture Budapest and to protect the Hungarian oilfields, which Speer had deemed absolutely essential for the German war effort, when these troops were needed to counter Georgy Zhukov's drive on Berlin. He also infuriated the Führer when he bluntly stated that Heinrich Himmler, whom Hitler had just given command of the newly activated Army Group Vistula, lacked both the military experience and ability to lead a counterattack designed to check the formidable Zhukov. (Himmler knew that he was in over his head and in mid-March authorized Guderian to inform Hitler that because of overwork he should be replaced. Hitler agreed.) These encounters, often heated, plus Guderian's intimations that the war could not be won, led Hitler to place him on sick leave at the end of March.

Meanwhile, Goebbels was struggling to bolster a deteriorating morale. On March 23, he recorded: "Among most sections of the German people faith in victory has totally vanished." To rally the people, Nazi propaganda stressed continued faith in the Führer, defiant resistance to the last, and the nobility of making heroic sacrifices for the fatherland. Germans were told that their heroism would inspire future generations to renew the struggle against Germany's enemies. They were also warned that the ruthless Allies sought the annihilation of the German people. In early April, Goebbels ordered the press "to make clear to the German people that ... Churchill and Roosevelt are just as merciless as Stalin and will ruthlessly carry out their plans for annihilation should the German people ever give way and submit to the enemy yoke." By turning every German city into a Stalingrad defended by people fanatically devoted to Hitler and National Socialism, Goebbels hoped to break the will of the invaders; shattered by the bloody stalemate, the Allied armies would then accept a negotiated settlement. But this did not happen. Goebbels continued to receive reports, which "makes one sick," of demoralization among civilians and soldiers deserting with the watchword "Home to mother."[26] Although German civilians did not engage in armed resistance against the regime, their disillusionment with the Nazi Party, disgust with the war, and desire to survive led the overwhelming majority to disregard the doomsday commands of Party officials to fight the invaders to the death.

If the terror from the sky and enemy advances on both fronts did not shatter morale, the sight of hordes of retreating soldiers did for many. The swagger gone, these beaten and dispirited German soldiers shocked villagers. The feelings of one villager on April 6 observing troops retreating from the Western Allies were typical:

> The whole day one saw retreating German soldiers. Some were bandaged, some were not. Others limped as their feet had swollen. Only a few had weapons. Some came on farm wagons, a few still on military vehicles, we saw two on unsaddled ponies. A deadly seriousness lay on all their faces, the height of despondency.... My wife was shocked by the misery of these German soldiers. She cried. She also asked the question that concerned all of us: "why are we still fighting when we can no longer fight?" But one could only ask this question in a soft voice, and only then to close relatives, otherwise one would inevitably be brought before a flying court-martial.[27]

At times, retreating units pillaged stores in villages and towns and engaged in drinking bouts that outraged and frightened the locals. As the predatory behavior of dispirited soldiers worsened, civilians came to fear them more than the Western Allies. Moreover, the generally correct behavior of Allied soldiers—not abusing civilians and passing out chocolate to children and food and cigarettes to adults—made nonsense of Goebbels' propaganda that the Western Allies, like the Russians, were seeking to annihilate Germans. It also undermined Nazi Party officials' command to resist to the death.

By mid-April, the war was careening to an end. American, British, and Soviet troops were penetrating deeper into Germany. On the brutal Eastern Front, Germany was suffering huge losses, thousands every day. On the Western Front, resistance was collapsing; Wehrmacht troops were surrendering to the

Allies in large numbers and most towns and key cities fell without significant opposition, although in several places, the Germans did fight tenaciously, particularly the SS and Hitler Youth.

Nazi Terror

The crumbling of Germany's military position led the Nazis to lash out in a killing frenzy against so-called defeatists—those who expressed doubts about a German victory or criticized Hitler or the Nazi regime. The following memorandum, issued by the Reich Ministry of Justice on June 26, 1944, less than three weeks after D-Day, illustrates Nazi concerns with the home front as the tide of battle was turning.

> The following types of utterances shall no longer be tolerated and are fundamentally deserving of the death penalty: The war is a lost cause; Germany or the Führer senselessly or frivolously started the war and must lose; the NSDP [Nazi party] should or will step down and like the Italian example make way for a negotiable peace; a military dictatorship must be established, which will be able to make peace; we have to work slower so the end will come; Bolshevist infiltration is not as bad as the propaganda paints it and will hurt only the leading National Socialists; British and Americans would bring Bolshevism to a halt at the German borders; word-of-mouth propaganda and letters to the front calling upon soldiers to throw away their weapons or turn around; the Führer is sick, inept, a human butcher, etc.[28]

In 1944, there were 13,986 people denounced for voicing defeatist sentiments. Court records indicate that complaints were filed against coworkers, siblings, spouses, old friends, and employees, most of whom were executed. The butchery continued until virtually the last day of the war. Special drumhead courts established on Hitler's orders sentenced to death civilians whose words, such as "the war is lost," or deeds, such as displaying a white flag or sheet in their window as the Anglo-American forces approached their village or town or listening to Allied broadcasts, conveyed defeatism and betrayal. Even as the Third Reich was collapsing, Party officials and local police executed villagers and townspeople for lapses in performing their duty for the Third Reich. German civilians were often more fearful of fanatic Nazis than they were of the approaching American and British forces.

The SS and Gestapo hunted down deserters and defeatists and hung them from lampposts, telephone poles, and trees with signs pinned to their clothes: "I was too cowardly to defend my fatherland." "I am a deserter." "All traitors die like this one." "I had no faith in the Führer." In early February 1945, the Soviets found the bodies of eighty German soldiers in a railway station. Above them was a sign that read, "They were cowards but died just the same." Between January and May 1945, roving military courts sentenced some four thousand soldiers to death; squads searching for deserters and shirkers killed thousands more. These executions were widely publicized as a warning to soldiers in the field.

To prevent opponents of the Nazi regime, many of them prominent, who were in prison or in concentration camps, from being liberated by the Western Allies and the Soviet Union, the Nazis tried and executed them; many of those killed by the SS and Gestapo were political prisoners arrested after the July 20 assassination attempt on Hitler. Driven by a compulsion to kill more of their racial enemies while there was still time, particularly Jewish slave laborers, or simply seeking to lash out in frustration and anger at their deteriorating situation, the SS and Gestapo butchered prisoners of war, captured underground resistance fighters who had aided the Allies, and foreign workers. As authority broke down, gangs of desperately hungry foreign laborers survived by looting homes destroyed by bombings. Fearing violent acts of revenge and a surge in crime, local Nazi authorities tracked the laborers down and summarily executed them. In March 1945, the Nazis publicly hanged some two hundred foreign laborers, most of them Italians, for having taken food from bombed-out ruins. Nor was it uncommon for civilian lynch mobs to kill foreign workers whom they found scavenging for food.

The Bunker: A Delusional Hitler

In his rise to power and later during the war, Hitler maintained his belief in the paramount importance of the will and in the power of beliefs to shape and strengthen the will. As the military situation deteriorated, he insisted that German soldiers, fortified by an all-consuming commitment to National Socialist ideology, would have the strength of will to prevail over their less resolute enemies. In the closing months of the war, these two core principles coalesced with greater urgency in both Goebbels' propaganda and Hitler's pronouncements. Holding to his ideological conviction that racially superior Germans, although outnumbered and outgunned, would defeat primitive Russian-Mongol hordes if their will remained unbroken and their leadership determined, Hitler declared German cities fortresses to be defended to the death by their inhabitants.

Holed up with his staff in a sealed underground bunker complex fifty feet beneath the Reich Chancellery in Berlin, Hitler retained absolute authority over military operations, and he could still mesmerize subordinates and bend them to his will. Even some generals who knew the situation was hopeless gained confidence after an audience with Hitler in the bunker and remained loyal to him. At the same time, people raised concerns about his physical deterioration: trembling left hand, stooped body, halting and shuffling gait, chalk-white complexion, and glazed eyes. These same people also commented on his mental state: he often seemed apathetic, depressed, and detached from reality. Suffering from insomnia, he was constantly medicated with sedatives and to stay alert he took heavy doses of amphetamines. At military briefings and in conversation, a paranoid Hitler frequently engaged in tirades of uncontrollable fury against subordinates and army commanders whom he castigated as spineless and fools and accused of treachery and betrayal. He had bizarre fantasies about new German victories and spent hours reminiscing about the glory days of his movement. To several intimates and visitors, the rapidly aging fifty-five-year-old Hitler was a mere shadow of his former self and showed signs of senility. And yet, several people who had encounters with Hitler in these last weeks noted that he was usually mentally alert and lucid during briefings.

When President Roosevelt died on April 12, Hitler and Goebbels clung to their hope that Harry Truman, now president, would negotiate peace and unite with Germany against Communist Russia. An exhilarated Hitler went from person to person telling each one that the Allied coalition will now break apart and the United States and Britain will realize that he had been defending Western civilization against Asiatic-Bolshevik barbarians. Hitler grasped on to this delusion virtually to the end. As late as April 25, when the Red Army was already moving into Berlin, he told Goebbels, "If I strike here successfully and hold the capital, then the hope might grow among the British and Americans that they might possibly be able to oppose [the Bolshevik "colossus" and "Devil"] with a Nazi Germany after all. And I am the only man for this.... [T]here is only one who is in a position to stop the Bolshevik colossus, and that is I and the party and today's German state."[29] One wonders if the Führer and his propaganda minister just could not comprehend how hateful they and their New Order were to the Western Allies.

Also almost to the end, Hitler retained an irrational faith in his destiny: having brought him triumphs in the past, it would not fail him. And if victory could not be achieved—something he might have sensed since the turning of the tide in the Soviet Union—he was adamant that there must be no repetition of the humiliating surrender of 1918. By fighting for every building and street in every town and city, the Germans would bleed the Allies to death even if they perished and the nation were destroyed. He wanted future generations to marvel at this epic last stand in defense of the nation and his heroic leadership, for one day a revived National Socialist Reich would rise from the ashes.

Hitler was driven by cruel destructive impulses that he had demonstrated in the war of annihilation waged against the Soviet Union and the liquidation of European Jewry. Early in the war, he planned with great relish to obliterate Leningrad, Moscow, and Stalingrad; after the Warsaw Uprising in 1944, he called for the complete destruction of the historic Polish capital; and when German forces were retreating from Paris, he ordered that they leave behind nothing but ruin and rubble.

As the end of the Third Reich neared, Hitler's obsession with carnage intensified, and he vented his dark instincts against his own people, whose suffering did not move him—he never visited field hospitals or bombed cities and did not want to hear about the agony of German civilians as the war closed in on them. Hitler ordered the destruction of Germany's factories, sewage systems, power stations, telephone lines, railways, bridges, farms, even theaters and opera houses—everything needed to reconstruct the country after the war. His racist and Social Darwinist worldview buttressed this mania for destruction. A totally devastated country is what the German people deserved, for they had proven unworthy in the racial struggle for existence with Slavs. A supreme egomaniac, Hitler also believed that the German people had failed him. It was only fitting that they should go down in ruin with him; once he was gone, the German nation deserved to sink into oblivion. The great loss of life that Germans continued to suffer in a losing cause meant nothing to him. In March 1945, Hitler told Speer:

> If the war is lost, the people will be lost also. It is not necessary to worry about what the German people will need for elemental survival. On the contrary, it is best for us to destroy even these things. For the nation has proved to be the weaker, and the future belongs solely to the stronger eastern nations. In any case only those who are inferior will remain after this struggle, for the good have already been killed.[30]

Disobeying Hitler, Speer urged Nazi officials and generals not to execute Hitler's death wish for the nation; although SS demolition squads did do some damage, Hitler's command was not implemented. Ironically, it was Allied bombings and artillery barrages that carried out, to a considerable extent, Hitler's scorched earth order.

The destruction of the country's infrastructure was not the only command that was disobeyed. In the last days of the war, General Gotthard Heinrici (discussed in the next section), recognizing that Germany's position was hopeless and not wanting to see his men die needlessly, disobeyed Hitler's orders to march into Berlin. Instead, he battled to preserve escape routes to the west and advised his troops to surrender to the Americans or British.

The Storming of Berlin: The Last Battle

By mid-April, three Soviet Fronts were poised to attack Berlin: Marshal Ivan Konev from the south, Marshal Konstantin Rokossovskii* from the north, and Marshal Zhukov from the east. For the final kill, the Soviets assembled two and a half million men, sixty-two hundred tanks, forty thousand field guns and mortars, and seventy-five hundred airplanes. Arrayed against this huge force, were one million Germans, with eight hundred eighty tanks, and an incapacitated Luftwaffe. Before dawn on April 16, 1945, Zhukov mounted one of the heaviest artillery barrages of the war against German forward positions in the area of the Seelow Heights; located west of the Oder River, the heights were the most direct approach to Berlin. But General Henrici, who had replaced Himmler as commander of Army Group Vistula, constructed a three-layered defense, each with formidable obstacles to bog down the enemy and to which the defenders could retreat, reorganize, and prepare to counterattack. Anticipating a heavy artillery attack that typically preceded a Soviet assault, Henrici pulled back frontline troops to a rear defensive position, a move that significantly reduced the number of casualties.

---

*A former political commissar and trusted Communist, Konev was given training as an officer and in 1939 was promoted to the rank of army commander. He successfully commanded a large strike force at Kursk that included over four thousand tanks. Stalin used Konev to counterbalance Zukhov, whose growing popularity the ever-suspicious dictator perceived as a threat to his rule. Polish born, Rokossovoskii was imprisoned and tortured in Stalin's purge of army officers, but released before the war and given a command. Serving under Zhukov, he distinguished himself in the battles of Moscow, Stalingrad, and Kursk.

When Russian infantry and tanks moved forward, they came into range of well-situated German artillery and machine guns. In scenes that resembled the massacres of World War I, concentrated German fire destroyed wave after wave of attacking Soviet infantry attempting to cross "no man's land." The usually astute Zhukov then made a serious mistake when he ordered his powerful T-34 tanks, held in reserve and waiting to exploit a breach in the German lines, to attack too early. Tanks, other vehicles, and infantry were caught in a horrific traffic snarl on soggy, mine-infested roads. Entire columns of T-34s were ambushed and picked off one by one by German tanks and flak batteries. Mobile Russian artillery could not get through to pound German strongpoints that were slaughtering front-line infantry. Zhukov had severely underestimated German strength in the area of the Seelow Heights. For four days, the Soviets suffered staggering losses. But possessing what seemed like an inexhaustible number of artillery pieces, tanks, and men, whom Zhukov was willing to sacrifice in mass attacks in order to achieve a military objective, and benefiting from massive aerial bombardments, the Red Army forced the Germans to retreat. Although the Soviets hoped to secure the Seelow Heights in one day, the capture took several days and cost Zhukov thirty thousand dead compared to twelve thousand Germans. The last natural barrier into Berlin had fallen, and German units were running short of ammunition and artillery rounds, and the limited supply of aviation gas forced the curtailment of combat missions.

While Zhukov was meeting fierce resistance in his efforts to take the Seelow Heights, his rival for the honor of reaching Berlin first, Marshal Konev, successfully crossed the Neisse and Spree rivers and was driving toward Berlin. As their front collapsed, German soldiers retreated to the capital; so too did refugees from nearby villages, clogging the roads. On April 20, while Hitler was celebrating his fifty-sixth birthday, Zhukov's artillery blasted Berlin's suburbs. The next day, Soviet shells hit the German capital.

Out of touch with reality, Hitler ordered counterattacks by decimated or nonexistent divisions and threatened officers with execution if they did not obey his commands. When SS General Felix Steiner told Hitler on April 21 that the few inexperienced troops at his disposal could not possibly halt Zhukov, Hitler lectured him and closed with these words: "You will see Steiner. You will see. The Russians will suffer their greatest defeat before the gates of Berlin."[31] In the written order signed by Hitler that he received, Steiner was told: "It is expressly forbidden to fall back to the west. Officers who do not comply unconditionally with this order are to be arrested and shot right away. You, Steiner, are liable with your head for the execution of this order."[32]

Soviet commanders, eager for the historic honor, pressed their tank forces to race to Berlin, which was completely encircled on April 24–25. After an intense artillery barrage, Soviet troops moved into the city from all sides. Berlin's bridges, streets, and buildings now became the battlefield.

On March 9, Lieutenant-General Helmuth Reymann, appointed commander of the defense of Berlin a few days earlier—and soon to be removed—had issued a thirty-three page document calling for Berlin to be defended "to the last man and the last shot.... Every block, every house, every storey, every hedge, every shell hole" had to be defended by Germans "filled with a fanatical desire to fight, ... for Berlin can decide the war."[33] (Although Reymann signed the document, judging from the grandiose prose, Goebbels may well have written it.) And on April 14, in his order of the day, Hitler, whose depression and rages were interspersed with blind hope, reassured the German people that the Bolsheviks would meet a bloody defeat in Berlin: "Colossal artillery forces are welcoming the enemy. Countless new units are replacing our losses.... Once again, Bolshevism will suffer Asia's old fate—it will founder on the capital of the German Reich.... Asia's final onslaught will come to naught—just as the invasion of our Western enemies will in the end fail."[34] Meanwhile, Berliners desperately trying to flee the city before the jaws of the Russian vise tightened had to contend with roadblocks manned by security forces that turned them back. Most Berliners went on with their routines with a resigned stoicism, at least until Soviet artillery barrages and the fighting in the streets forced them to retreat into underground shelters.

Berlin's defenders were made up of exhausted remnants of several panzer and Wehrmacht units and SS, including thousands of volunteers from France, Belgium, Spain, Norway, the Netherlands, and Lithuania—Nazi sympathizers, anti-Communists, and adventurers who had joined the SS earlier. (By 1945, less than half of Himmler's Waffen-SS consisted of Germans.) Fearing capture by the Russians and facing dire retribution if they ever managed to return home, these non-German units had little alternative other than to fight and die. The defenders also consisted of police units, some of whom had been hunting down deserters and defeatists; battalions of elderly conscripts in the Volkssturm, many of them reluctant warriors; and teenaged Hitler Youth, often zealous Nazis but poorly trained. Reared in Nazi ideology, many of these heavily indoctrinated young idealists were completely devoted to the Führer and wanted to prove their loyalty in battle—the Hitler Youth had already fought in Normandy, the Battle of the Bulge, Hungary, and East Prussia. Other conscripted Hitler Youth were just scared, whimpering boys who wanted to go home. Tens of thousands of old men and boys in the Volkssturm perished in the closing months of the war.

The main fighting for Berlin had taken place in the approaches to the capital. Before the Soviets had penetrated the city, the outcome had already been decided. Now the Soviets were deployed in a fierce mopping-up operation against pockets of resistance within the capital. The German defenders, numbering about two hundred thousand, had little chance of holding off the Red Army closing in on Berlin on three fronts. They were short of tanks, artillery, rifles, and ammunition, and the hurriedly prepared antitank ditches, barricades, minefields, and other defensive fortifications were few and inadequate to stop the Soviets. Never expecting that one day enemy forces would threaten their capital, earlier in the war Nazis had given no thought to fortifying Berlin. Now it was too late.

Although their position was hopeless, diehard Germans fought tenaciously, motivated by a fierce duty to protect the fatherland from the Russians. Exhausted and outnumbered veterans knew that continued fighting was futile, but for many surrender was not an option. Aware of the crimes Germany had committed in the Soviet Union, they feared that falling into the Red Army's hands meant death or Siberia. On a crowded train filled with terrified and angry Berliners, a much-decorated soldier got their attention: "I've got something to tell you.... We have to win this war. We must not lose our courage. If others win the war, and if they do to us only a fraction of what we have done in the occupied countries, there won't be a single German left in a few weeks."[35]

The accounts of Soviet atrocities circulated by refugees from Silesia and East Prussia confirmed the defenders' worst fears about Russian barbaric vengeance and gave them the impetus to go on fighting, many of them knowing that the end was near. Reluctant soldiers who did not want to die for a lost cause had to contend with SS and Gestapo who were hunting down and lynching deserters and ordinary soldiers for the flimsiest of reasons. An eyewitness recalled:

> Panic had reached its peak in the city. Hordes of soldiers ... deserted and were shot on the spot or hanged on the nearest tree. A few clad only in underclothes were dangling on a tree quite near our house. On their chests they had placards reading: "We betrayed the Führer." The [Nazi diehards] pasted leaflets on the houses:

> Dirty cowards and defeatists
> We've got them all on our lists.[36]

Indoctrinated for years to believe in the superiority of Aryan Germans and in the Führer's mission, true believers remained unshaken in their conviction that defeat was not possible for National Socialist Germany led by the Führer, a man of destiny. Alternately, they felt they were participants in an epic fight to the death against the Mongol—or, at other times, Judeo-Bolshevik—hordes from the East that would earn them the admiration of future generations. For their Führer, who symbolized the fatherland, they were willing to sacrifice themselves. A wounded veteran of the Russian campaign who had long since become disillusioned with Hitler and the war and was being sent to Berlin where he would be killed told a family member:

> If you had seen those hollow-eyed men in the hospital today, you would feel as I do. We were all mustered out like sheep to stand in front of an SS officer telling us about the Führer's plans. How we would beat the Russians with the secret weapon. How the Russians would turn and run; and do you know some of these poor sick devils still fell for it! They still believed in the Führer; they had to. They would have gone mad if they had faced the truth. The truth is that Hitler is mad himself, so mad he is going to hurl all of us to destruction, himself as well. By the way, the SS officer finished his speech with the words: "Never before have we been so near to victory! Sieg Heil!"[37]

To encourage the defenders of Berlin to hold on, Goebbels' propaganda ministry preached final victory. They were told that thousands of reserves, tanks, and guns were on their way; that miracle weapons were forcing Britain and America to come to terms; that the Western Allies were about to join Hitler to fight the Communist peril; that they were noble idealists defending European civilization against invading Asiatic-Russian barbarians manipulated by sinister Jews; and that repulsing the Russians in Berlin would bring about a decisive turn in the war and save Germany and Europe.

Berliners who remained committed Nazis continued to swallow Goebbels' propaganda. Some formerly ardent Nazis, however, now had doubts; they expressed anger if only in their diaries and to their trusted friends and relatives that Nazi leaders and officials were sacrificing the German people just to retain their power a little longer. Increasingly, non-Nazi Berliners were contemptuous of Goebbels' repeated lies and believed that it was criminal to continue fighting—in the 1930s, Berlin, with a cosmopolitan and liberal tradition, was less a center of Nazism than other German cities. In a show of resistance, they painted the word "Nein!" on walls and store windows, indicating their disapproval of Hitler and rejection of his order to fight to the death, and they posted leaflets denouncing "the lunatic Hitler and his bloodhound Himmler…. Throw all pictures of Hitler and his accomplices out into the gutter! Organize armed resistance!"[38]

Most Berliners were too war weary and fearful to give Goebbels and Hitler much thought, even dropping the "Heil Hitler" greeting. Survival was their only concern. Some hoped desperately but futilely that the Anglo-American forces, moving rapidly across western Germany, would take Berlin before the Red Army did. But as atrocity stories of Soviet behavior against civilians spread, thousands of Germans obtained cyanide capsules, particularly women terrified of being raped.

When the Soviets overran German positions in the last days of the battle of Stalingrad, a Soviet colonel, pointing to the devastation all around, angrily told a group of German prisoners, "That's how Berlin is going to look!"[39] This turned out to be an accurate prophecy. Starting on April 21, Soviet artillery methodically pounded the city, adding to the death and wreckage caused by American and British round-the-clock saturation bombing of the capital. Heaps of rubble, abandoned and destroyed military vehicles, deep craters, and streets strewn with bodies were everywhere, and fires continued to rage in the endless miles of ruin.

Urban warfare is onerous and costly. Concealed amid the ruins and from basements, balconies, upper floors, and rooftops, German defenders wielding machine guns and rifles fired on the Soviets who were storming through the city. From high ambush sites, they hurled inflammable Molotov cocktails or knocked out with their hand-held panzerfausts—many of them fired by fifteen- and sixteen-year-old boys—vulnerable tanks moving down streets in columns. The Soviets overcame the problem by dispersing their tanks and having them work in close cooperation with small storm units. Additionally, lashing sandbags to the tanks sides and turrets greatly reduced the antitank gun's power to penetrate armor. Proving particularly troublesome to the Soviets were the high flak towers from which antiaircraft guns had fired on American and British bombers. Now the guns were directed at the Soviets advancing on the streets below.

After Soviet assault weapons destroyed barricades and buildings harboring defenders, infantry moved in, which often meant fighting house to house with machine guns, grenades, and flame throwers. General Vasily I. Chuikov, who had distinguished himself in Stalingrad's urban warfare, instructed his men not to take chances. First, toss a grenade before entering a room, he ordered, and follow up with machine-gun fire. Sappers laid heavy charges that blew down walls and doors, which cleared passages for Soviet assault squads at times armed with lethal flame-throwers that turned soldiers and civilians into flailing and screaming torches. The Soviets used flame throwers to burn out Nazis holed up in basements and sewers who were determined not to surrender. Soviet airmen targeted movement in the streets, which were littered with dead soldiers and civilians, dead horses, and wrecked vehicles. As the fighting intensified, numerous German soldiers rid themselves of their weapons and uniforms and hid with the civilians. SS squads scoured the city for these deserters and for houses unfurling white flags. With cold fury they shot any man there.

Berliners retreated to cellars, air raid shelters, and underground railway stations. There, they huddled together with the unattended wounded, often without electricity and gas due to the bombardments, desperate for food and water, revolted by the overpowering stench of human waste, and terrified by the incessant shellfire and the nightmare of falling into Russian hands. Some went mad and suicides were common. SS squads dragged men out of cellars and public shelters, gave them rifles, and ordered them to the forward positions; those who hesitated were immediately shot. To prevent the Soviets from getting through tunnels, on April 26, engineers blasted the locks of a canal; water flooded the tunnels where civilians and wounded were seeking shelter. A German officer described the harrowing scene: "People are fighting around the ladders that run through air shafts up to the street. Water comes rushing through the tunnels. The crowds get panicky, stumble and fall over rails and sleepers. Children and wounded are deserted, people are trampled to death. The water covers them.... The panic lasts for hours. Many are drowned."[40]

The End of Hitler and His Third Reich

On April 28, General Karl Wiedling, the commander of the Berlin garrison, asked Hitler in his bunker, now ringed by Soviet tanks and shelled by Soviet artillery, what the defenders should do once their depleted ammunition ran out. The Führer's instructions were for them to break out in small groups and continue the fight, but under no circumstances should Berlin be surrendered to the Russians. Steadfast German defense did persist. It was particularly ferocious in the Reichstag, the shell of the old parliament. On April 30, while still battling often hand to hand the German defenders in the building, principally SS and Hitler Youth, Soviet soldiers hoisted the Red flag atop the building, a visible sign of Soviet victory and German defeat.

The determined resistance of German fighters and the skilled tactics employed by German commanders for a doomed criminal cause only produced more suffering, death, and destruction. The Soviets suffered 274,184 dead and wounded in the twenty-three-day battle for Berlin (including the approach to the city)—some estimates are as high as 400,000. This was an indication of the

The Soviet flag is planted on top of the Reichstag in Berlin, a symbol of the Red Army's victory over Nazi Germany.

price the Western Allies would have paid had Eisenhower attempted to preempt the Red Army. About 292,000 thousand German combatants and civilians were killed and wounded and 479,295 were captured, many of them fated for deportation to the Soviet Union. In April and May, more than 5,000 civilians and soldiers in Berlin chose suicide, and hundreds of thousands fled west to escape Soviet soldiers, who in indiscriminate acts of rage and vengeance burned, pillaged, murdered, mutilated, and raped. The number of rape victims in Berlin is estimated at more than 100,000: some 90,000 sought medical assistance in the capital's hospitals. Counting all the regions of Germany invaded by the Red Army, the number of women raped is as many as 1.4 million, many brutalized countless times. Thousands of these women committed suicide. Red Army authorities, who felt no mercy for Germans, eventually tried to end the mayhem, even taking severe measures against soldiers who abused civilians. Along with these outrages, there are also accounts of Soviet soldiers dispensing food to desperate Berliners, including rape victims.

On April 29, with the Soviets in the center of the city just blocks from the bunker and with artillery fire falling above it, Hitler married his longtime companion, Eva Braun. As part of the simple ceremony, they both swore they were of pure Aryan descent. On April 30, 1945, the Führer took his own life by shooting himself in the mouth rather than risk capture. Eva Braun killed herself by biting down on a cyanide capsule. Following Hitler's instructions, his aides burned the bodies outside the bunker—Hitler did not want the Russians to find and display his corpse. To preserve the Hitler myth, the German people

Vast numbers of Londoners congregate in Trafalgar Square to mark the Allied triumph in Europe.

were not told of Hitler's suicide; instead, they were told of his heroic death "fighting Bolshevism to the last breath."

In his last will and political testament, Hitler again resorted to his malignant delusions and vile obsessions, blaming the war on a sinister Jewish cabal: "It is untrue that I or anybody else in Germany wanted the war in 1939. It was desired and instigated exclusively by those international statesmen who either were of Jewish descent or worked for Jewish interests." And he commanded the new "leaders of the nation and those under them to scrupulous observance of the laws of race and to merciless opposition to the universal poisoner of all people, International Jewry." He chose suicide to avoid falling "into the hands of an enemy who requires a new spectacle organized by the Jews for the amusement of their hysterical masses."[41] He expelled Himmler from the Nazi Party for trying on his own to negotiate Germany's surrender to the Allies with Swedish diplomat Count Folke Bernadotte; he expelled Goering for suggesting that he assume the leadership of the Reich while Hitler was sequestered in his bunker; and he appointed Admiral Karl Dönitz to succeed him.

Two days later, the Berlin garrison capitulated, although some units and individuals continued to fight with suicidal fanaticism. Tens of thousands of surrounded German troops in Berlin managed to slip out of the ring and surrender to the British and Americans. Additional thousands of soldiers and civilians from other parts of Germany struggled desperately to reach the Western Allies' lines in order to escape the Red Army.

Hitler's death touched off a chain reaction of suicides among Nazi officials, generals, and ordinary Germans who saw no future without the Führer and Nazism or feared Soviet retaliation and subjugation. Included among the suicides were Goebbels and his wife, Magda, now residing in Hitler's bunker. Just prior to taking her own life, Magda arranged for an SS doctor to give her six young children lethal injections in the belief that they had no future without Hitler and the Third Reich.

The Western Allies rejected Dönitz's efforts to negotiate a separate peace with them so that Germans could continue fleeing from the Soviets. On May 7, 1945, a demoralized and devastated Germany surrendered unconditionally. Hitler's "Thousand Year Reich" was buried in the ruins of Berlin along with the Führer's charred remains. The wreckage of once great German cities symbolized what the Nazis had achieved for the German people. Their enduring legacy would always be unredeemable evil. And Auschwitz, the symbol of civilization's collapse, would sadly join Beethoven and Goethe as an indelible component of Germany's heritage.

CHRONOLOGY

June 22, 1944	Start of Operation Bagration, Red Army's summer offensive
August 1, 1944	Last of German troops driven from the Soviet Union
August–September 1939	Uprising in Warsaw by Polish Home Army
October 20, 1944	Tito's partisans and Red Army liberate Belgrade
January 12, 1945	Start of Red Army's Vistula Offensive
January 17, 1945	Germans evacuate Warsaw
January 27, 1945	Soviets enter Auschwitz
February 13–14, 1939	Terror bombing of Dresden
February 14, 1945	Budapest falls to Red Army
March 7, 1945	Americans seize Rhine bridge at Remagen
March 22, 1945	Patton's U.S. Third Army crosses the Rhine in assault boats
March 23, 1945	Montgomery's forces cross the Rhine at Wesel
April 12, 1945	Death of President Roosevelt
April 16–19, 1945	Battle of Seelow Heights
April 18, 1945	End of German resistance in the Ruhr

April 24, 1945	Berlin encircled by Soviet forces
April 25, 1945	Americans and Soviets meet at the Elbe
April 28, 1945	Mussolini slain by Italian partisans
April 30, 1945	Hitler takes his own life
May 3, 1945	Surrender of Axis forces in Italy
May 7, 1945	Germany surrenders unconditionally

NOTES

1. Ian Kershaw, *Hitler: 1936–1945 Nemesis* (New York: W. W. Norton, 2000), 765.

2. Quoted in Robert Kirchubel, *Hitler's Panzer Armies on the Eastern Front* (South Yorkshire: Pen & Sword, 2009), 90.

3. Gerald Astor, *A Blood-Dimmed Tide: The Battle of the Bulge: By the Men Who Fought It* (New York; Donald I. Fine, 1992), 247.

4. M. I. Gurfein and Morris Janowitz, "Trends in Wehrmacht Morale," *The Public Opinion Quarterly*, 10, no. 1 (Spring 1946): 82–83.

5. Geoffrey P. Megargee, *Inside Hitler's High Command* (Lawrence: University Press of Kansas, 2000), 223.

6. Krisztián Ungváry, *The Siege of Budapest: One Hundred Days in World War II* (New Haven, CT: Yale University Press, 2005), 293.

7. Terry Brighton, *Montgomery, Patton, Rommel: Masters of War* (New York: Crown Publishers), 326.

8. *Field Marshal Lord Alanbrooke, War Diaries, 1939–1944*, ed. Alex Daniches and Daniel Todman (London: Phoenix Press, 2001), 575.

9. *Final Entries 1945: The Diaries of Joseph Goebbels*, ed. and anno. Hugh Trevor-Roper, trans. Richard Barry (New York: G. P. Putnam's Sons, 1978), 39, 78–79, 196.

10. Derek S. Zumbro, *Battle of the Ruhr: The German Army's Final Defeat in the West* (Lawrence: University of Kansas Press, 2006), 378.

11. *Final Entries 1945*, 38.

12. Ibid., 42–43.

13. Martin Gilbert, *The Day the War Ended: May 8, 1945—Victory in Europe* (New York: Henry Holt, 1995), 10.

14. Charles B. MacDonald, *The Mighty Endeavor: The American War in Europe* (New York: William Morrow, 1986), 529.

15. Richard Bessel, *Germany 1945: From War to Peace* (New York: HarperCollins, 2009), 51.

16. Martin Gilbert, *The Second World War: A Complete History* (New York: Henry Holt, 1989), 633–634.

17. Robert Gellately, *Backing Hitler: Consent and Coercion in Nazi Germany* (New York: Oxford University Press, 2001), 251.

18. Nerin Gun, *The Day of the Americans* (New York: Fleet, 1966), 62.

19. Richard J. Evans, *The Third Reich at War* (New York: Penguin, 2009), 562.

20. Heinz Guderian, *Panzer Leader*, trans. Constantine Fitzgibbon (New York: Da Capo Press, 1996), 383

21. Albert Speer, *Inside the Third Reich*, trans. Richard and Clara Winston (New York: Macmillan, 1970), 423.

22. Catherine Merridale, *Ivan's War: Life and Death in the Red Army, 1939–1945* (New York: Henry Holt, 2006), 302.

23. Helene Keyssar and Vladimir Pozner, *Remembering: A U.S.–Soviet Dialogue* (New York: Oxford University Press, 1990), 73.

24. Boris Gorbachevsky, *Through the Malestrom: A Red Army Soldier's War on the Eastern Front, 1842–1945,* trans. and ed. Stuart Britton (Lawrence: University of Kansas Press, 2008), 359, 363.

25. Evans, *The Third Reich at War*, 710.

26. *Final Entries, 1945*, 212, 304, 306–307.

27. Stephen G. Fritz, *Endkampf: Soldiers, Civilians, and the Death of the Third Reich* (Lexington: The University Press of Kentucky, 2004), 41.

28. Jörg Friedrich, *The Fire: The Bombing of Germany 1940–1945*, trans. Allison Brown (New York: Columbia University Press, 2006), 397.

29. *Hitler and his Generals: Military Conferences 1942–1945,* ed. Helmut Heiber and David M. Glantz (New York: Enigma Books, 2003), 723–724.

30. Speer, *Inside the Third Reich*, 440.

31. Cornelius Ryan, *The Last Battle* (New York: Simon and Schuster, 1966), 426.

32. Ibid., 426.

33. Earl F. Ziemke, *Stalingrad to Berlin: The German Defeat in the East* (New York: Barnes and Noble, 1996), 462.

34. Excerpted in Juergen Thorwald, *Defeat in the East: Russia Conquers—January to May 1945*, trans. and ed. Fred Wieck (New York: Bantam Books, 1980), 198.

35. Antony Beevor, *The Fall of Berlin 1945* (New York: Viking, 2003), 189.

36. Louis Hagen, *Follow My Leader* (London: Allan Wingate, 1951), 315.

37. Else Wendel, *Hausfrau at War: A German Woman's Account of Life in Hitler's Reich* (Long Acre, London: Odhams, 1957), 214–215.

38. Anthony Read and David Fisher, *The Fall of Berlin* (New York: W.W. Norton, 1992), 330.

39. Beevor, *The Fall of Berlin 1945*, xxxiii.

40. Excerpted in Jon E. Lewis, ed., *World War II: The Autobiography* (Philadelphia: Running Press Books, 2009), 504.

41. *U.S. Chief Counsel for the Prosecution of Axis Criminality, Nazi Conspiracy and Aggression* (Washington, D.C.: U.S. Government Printing Office, 1946), vol. 6, doc. no. 3569-PS, 260, 263.

Chapter 8

✳

The Aftermath, Legacy, and Meaning of the War

World War II was total war, pitting people against people in a life-and-death struggle.* Greatly expanding central authority and organization, the warring states mobilized their populations and economies in a massive effort to defeat the enemy that threatened the nation's survival; they also utilized the press, radio, film, and public demonstrations to promote ideological commitment and sacrifice from both soldiers and civilians. The belligerents wanted a totally beaten enemy. For Nazi Germany, this meant the destruction and subjugation of the Soviet Union; for the Allies, it meant Germany's unconditional surrender. The course of the war eroded the boundary between soldier and civilian. Aerial bombardments alone killed well more than one million civilians, and the Third Reich's policy of genocide, enslavement, and punitive executions of noncombatants, which totally disregarded international law and civilized moral standards, led to the killing of many millions more. In choosing to fight a war without limits and restraints, the Nazis demonstrated the total savagery that total war could generate.

World War II was the most destructive, murderous, and dehumanizing war in history. At the end of the war, Winston Churchill lamented, "What is Europe now? A rubble heap, a charnel house, a breeding ground for pestilence and

---

*Some scholars do point to limitations of the total-war paradigm when applied to World War II. For example, although the Soviet Union totally mobilized immediately after the German invasion, Hitler hesitated to place his country on a total-war footing until after the defeat at Stalingrad. Despite its impressive production achievement, the United States did not fully exploit all its material resources, and vast numbers of American men did not serve in the armed forces. Moreover, only in the Soviet Union did women fight as front-line combatants. But one wonders what these exceptions prove. The concept of total war provides clarity and meaning as to how World War II was waged. It is not intended to encompass every facet of combat and mobilization. See Roger Chickering, Stig Förster, and Bern Greiner, eds., *A World At Total War: Global Conflict and the Politics of Destruction, 1937–1945* (Cambridge: Cambridge University Press, 2005).

Thousands of homeless Berliners and German refugees uprooted by the war were to be seen in Berlin in 1945.

hate."[1] George Orwell, reporting from Germany, wrote, "To walk through the ruined cities of Germany is to feel an actual doubt about the continuity of civilization."[2] Almost everywhere the magnitude of human suffering was staggering. Members of families searched for each other, hoping their loved ones were still alive. Millions of Germans were homeless, some victims of Allied bombings and others in flight from the Russians. Homeless and semi-starving liberated forced laborers, principally Poles, Russians, Ukrainians, and other East Europeans, wandered German roads and streets; they terrified Germans by looting stores and homes, raping, and murdering in retaliation against their former oppressors. Medical staff worked desperately to keep alive emaciated and disease-ridden concentration camp survivors—at the former Bergen-Belsen alone, some three hundred to four hundred a day were dying immediately after liberation. In all, some fourteen thousand survivors perished after the British had liberated Bergen-Belsen. Traumatized Jews from concentration camps or from hiding places, almost all having lost their families, returned to open life or were harbored in displaced-persons (DP) camps. Throughout Europe, destroyed transportation systems and the devastation of arable land, machinery, and livestock caused rampant food shortages, and a lack of coal in a particularly bitter winter added to the misery of Europeans. Amid the rubble of cities, people bartered for food, the black market was ubiquitous, and juvenile crime soared.

Then there was the plight of some thirteen million orphaned children and hundreds of thousands of others separated from their parents, as Nicholas Stargardt notes:

> There were the children of forced labourers and children brought for "Germanisation," children from concentration camps and children whose parents had been sent to concentration camps. There were those who had survived the liquidation of the ghettos and those who had fled from villages where the whole population had been locked into barns or wooden churches before they were set alight. There were also German children who had been stranded ... at the end of the war.[3]

And there was the special problem of some 250,000 Eastern European children, most of them Poles, kidnapped by the Nazis because they appeared to possess "racially valuable" qualities and then sent to live with German families. Their adoptive parents were told that the children were orphans whose birth parents had been ethnic Germans living in the newly conquered lands. Their real parents, those still alive, were desperately trying to reclaim them. Abducted at a very young age, many of these "Germanized" children had little or no memory of their birth parents and had grown attached to their second German parents who had given them a loving home; they did not want to be repatriated back to Poland. In the end, of the estimated 200,000 missing Polish children, some 40,000 were returned.* Thousands were never located. Many of the returned children taken from their foster parents were not reunited with their family but were sent to Polish orphanages.

In an extraordinary turn of events, popular support for the Nazi regime, which had plummeted in the mayhem that marked the last weeks of the war on German soil, virtually disappeared under the Allied occupation. To be sure, many Germans still found much to admire in Hitler and Nazi ideology, but they would make no effort to resurrect the Third Reich. Many Nazi officials committed suicide; others tried to change their identities or flee Europe. Numerous former Party members were still unregenerate Nazis and would remain so until their last breath, but many others now sought to hide their past and work with the occupying powers. At the war's end, the Allies feared that diehard Nazis would organize bands, code-named Werewolf, to wage guerrilla warfare. But the Allies found the Germans remarkably docile. Lacking leadership, organization, and, most important, popular support from

---

*There is no agreement on the figure of 200,000 provided by the Poles. Recently, Isabel Heinemann, a German scholar, has maintained that this figure is grossly inflated, that no more than 50,000 from all over Europe were kidnapped. Other sources provide different numbers.

the physically and emotionally exhausted, beaten, and humbled German people, the Werewolf movement never represented a threat, although a few fanatics did attack Allied soldiers, Germans cooperating with the occupation authorities, and women who fraternized with American and British soldiers.

DEATH TOLL

The total war waged by the combatants killed millions of soldiers; millions of civilians, who were victims of reprisals, genocide, slave labor, and aerial terror also perished. Everywhere the survivors counted their dead. (Estimates of the number of dead for different countries vary, often considerably. For both the United States and Britain and its Commonwealth, the following figures include the war with Japan.) The Soviet Union sacrificed more than the other participants in both population and material resources: 25 million Soviet citizens died, including 8.6 million military deaths. One of three Soviets lost a father. In comparison, the United States suffered about 418,000 military fatalities. British military deaths are estimated at 305,000, and more than 60,000 civilians perished in bombing raids on British cities. In addition, Britain's Commonwealth—Canada, Australia, New Zealand, South Africa—suffered a total of 110,000 fatalities. Germany lost about 3.25 million military men, the great bulk on the Eastern Front. German civilian deaths reached some 2 million civilians, approximately 500,000 to 600,000 of whom were victims of Allied bombing. More than 5 million Poles, 3 million of them Jews, and more than 1 million Yugoslavs perished. And the wounded, some of whom suffered disfigurement and amputation, numbered in the tens of millions.

MATERIAL DAMAGE

The material destruction had been unprecedented in the battle zones, particularly in Eastern Europe, where Hitler's and Stalin's armies had fought without mercy to people, animals, or the environment. Material costs were staggering: some 1,700 towns and 70,000 Soviet villages demolished, leaving millions of people homeless; once-great cities, including Warsaw, Berlin, Dresden, Vienna, Belgrade, and Budapest, ruined; bridges, railway systems, waterways, and harbors destroyed; farmland wasted; livestock killed; and coal mines and factories wrecked. In Italian, French, German, and other European cities, architectural splendors dating back to the Middle Ages and Renaissance were reduced to rubble. The countries occupied by Nazi Germany had been plundered of their resources, wealth, and art treasures. Europe faced the gigantic task of rebuilding. Yet West Europe did recover from this material blight, and with astonishing speed. Instrumental in West Europe's recovery was the massive amount of aid the United States provided between 1948 and 1951 in the European Recovery program, or Marshall Plan, that was proposed by Secretary of State George C. Marshall, formerly U.S. Chief of Staff.

After the end of hostilities, women in Berlin clear rubble from a destroyed factory. With so many men lost in the war and German infrastructure in ruins, women were responsible for much of the reconstruction work.

POPULATION TRANSFERS AND ETHNIC CLEANSING

The war produced a vast transfer of peoples unparalleled in modern European history. During the war, millions of people were uprooted from their homes. The Soviets forcibly deported to Central Asia and Siberia more than one million people accused of collaborating with the Nazis; these consisted chiefly of Soviet citizens of German descent living in the Volga region, Crimean Tartars, and several nationality groups residing in the Caucasus. In accordance with an agreement made with the Soviet Union at the Yalta Conference in February 1945, Britain and America compelled some two million Soviet prisoners of war, whom Stalin regarded as traitors, slave laborers, and those who had either volunteered or were pressured to serve in the German army, to return to the Soviet Union, many against their will, a callous act for which Churchill and Roosevelt have been roundly criticized. Of these deportees, 10 percent were executed—including generals who were rehabilitated posthumously after Stalin's death—and 70 percent were sent to the Gulag. The Soviet Union annexed the Baltic lands of Latvia, Lithuania, and Estonia, forcibly deporting several hundred thousand of the native inhabitants to distant regions of the Soviet Union. Many of these deportees perished.

The bulk of East Prussia was taken over by Poland, and the Soviet Union annexed the eastern portion—also approved at Yalta. Some four hundred thousand Germans from this region were deported to the Soviet Union, generally to labor camps. In the closing months of the war, some six million Germans fled west to escape the invading Red Army. From late 1944 to 1946, Germans were expelled or fled from Poland, Czechoslovakia, Yugoslavia, Romania, and Hungary, places where their ancestors had lived for centuries. Tens of thousands were deported to labor camps in the Soviet Union. Leaders in these countries, driven by nationalist aspirations, welcomed an opportunity to rid their nations of an ethnic minority, particularly given that many of these Germans had aided the Nazi occupiers. In all, some twelve million Germans fled or were driven from their homes, victims of a massive campaign of ethnic cleansing, and several hundred thousand died from malnutrition, disease, exposure, and mistreatment; thousands took their own lives.

Often forced out in midwinter with only a warning of hours or minutes, the expellees had to leave their property and possessions behind, replicating what the Nazis had done to Poles and Jews in the opening stage of the war. Fleeing on foot pushing handcarts, sleeping outdoors, scavenging for food, and robbed by police and paramilitary groups, many died en route to Germany. Some were even shot by guards. German refugees were also herded into internment camps, some of them former Nazi labor and concentration camps, where they were mercilessly brutalized by Polish and Czech guards who relished the opportunity to torment the German "master race." Rape was common. In what is historical irony, some Germans from Czechoslovakia were placed in Theresienstadt, which the Nazis had used as a temporary camp for German Jews before sending them to the gas chambers at Auschwitz. A Jewish physician who had been interned at Theresienstadt by the Nazis described what was now an internment camp for Germans, many of them children and adolescents. "The rags given to the Germans as clothes were smeared with swastikas. They were miserably undernourished, abused, and generally subjected to much the same treatment one was used to in the German-run camps…. The camp was run by Czechs, yet they did nothing to stop the Russians from going in to rape the captive women."[4]

RETRIBUTION FOR COLLABORATORS

Immediately after liberation—and even before—throughout Europe members of resistance movements, many of them Communists, took their revenge on collaborators in their own country. In September 1943, after Italy had switched to the Allies, Italian partisans hunted down Fascists who had collaborated with the Germans and summarily executed thousands. In several places, Fascists were thrown into prison and then brought before hastily formed tribunals that often handed out death sentences.

As the Germans abandoned French towns and cities, members of the French Resistance and other anti-Nazis shaved the heads of women who had consorted with German soldiers and paraded them through the streets to publicly humiliate them. Almost 10,000 collaborators—no doubt some of them on a flimsy charge—were killed out of hand by Resistance fighters determined to settle old scores. Resistance fighters had painful memories of French collaborators turning in their colleagues to authorities who tortured and executed many of them. After the war, French courts imprisoned 38,000 French men and women for their wartime collaboration with the Nazi occupiers. Another 6,763 (3,910 in absentia) were condemned to death, of which 791 sentences were carried out. Marshal Philippe Pétain was sentenced to die, but the sentence was transmuted to life imprisonment because of his advanced age. Pierre Laval, a high Vichy official who had authorized the conscription and deportation of French workers to Germany, assisted the Nazis in the roundup of foreign Jews for the death camps, and approved the formation of the Milice, the paramilitary police force that had collaborated with the Nazis in hunting down Resistance fighters and Jews, was sentenced to die by firing squad. As the government became more concerned with preserving civil peace and national unity, the French parliament started to grant amnesty to jailed collaborators. By 1951, only 4,000 were still in jail; five years later, only 62 of those jailed immediately after the war (or liberation, which was several months earlier) remained in custody.

Several French collaborators involved in major war crimes managed to escape justice for decades; apparently the government did not pursue them because it feared that opening old wounds would divide the country. But when Nazi hunters called attention to them, the resultant publicity demanded that something be done. Thus René Bousquet, who headed the French police under the Vichy regime and ordered the roundup and deliverance of thousands of Jews to the SS even before the Germans asked, was set to stand trial in 1993. But he fell victim to an assassin. Paul Touvier, an official of the Milice, had been sheltered for years by Catholic institutions. Discovered and placed on trial in 1994, he was sentenced to life imprisonment. After the war, Maurice Papon, a Vichy official who led the Bordeaux area police and had signed the arrest warrants of 1,650 Jews, served as a government official for many years. Following his retirement, he won a seat in parliament. He became head of the finance committee and in 1968 was named budget minister. Three years later, his complicity in the deportation of Jews was discovered by Nazi hunters. After years of delay, the ninety-two-year-old Papon was tried and sentenced to ten years imprisonment in 1998; in 2002, the aging Papon was released from prison for reasons of health. The arrests and trials of these war criminals aroused considerable furor in France. Not all agreed with the verdicts, and many thought this episode in French history, with its painful and divisive memories, should be buried forever.

Historian Tony Judt summarizes the treatment of collaborators in other Western lands:

> In Norway, a country with a population of just 3 million, the entire membership of the Nasjonal Sammlung, the main organization of pro-Nazi collaborators, was tried, all 55,000 of them, along with nearly 40,000

others; 17,000 men and women received prison terms and thirty death sentences were handed down, of which twenty-five were carried out.... In the Netherlands 200,000 people were investigated, of whom nearly half were imprisoned, some of them for the crime of giving the Nazi salute; 17,500 civil servants lost their jobs (but hardly anyone in business, education, or the professions); 154 people were condemned to death, forty of them executed. In neighboring Belgium many more death sentences were passed (2,940), but a smaller percentage (just 242) carried out. Roughly the same number of collaborators were sent to prison but whereas the Dutch amnestied most of those convicted, the Belgian state kept them in prison longer and former collaborators convicted of serious crimes never recovered their full civil rights.[5]

WAR CRIMES TRIALS

After the war, many German war criminals went into hiding, changed their identity, lied about their wartime record, or fled to other countries, particularly in South America.* In what has been called "one of the most shameful episodes in the history of the Vatican," a substantial number of the escapees, including major war criminals involved in mass murder, were aided by Austrian, German, and Croatian clerics, some of them important figures at the Vatican.[6] Vatican prelates provided war criminals with safe houses, money, and forged documents. Only a small percentage of Nazi war criminals were prosecuted, and many of the convicted served ridiculously short sentences. Thousands of Germans who shot hostages, rounded up Jews for deportation to the gas chambers, staffed the concentration camps, were part of units that massacred Jews, and brutalized slave laborers never faced punishment. With the Cold War looming, Nazi war criminals escaped justice by working for British, American, and Soviet intelligence services that protected them. For example, Britain recruited Friedrich Buchardt, an Einsatzgruppen commander who oversaw the murder of some one hundred thousand Jews. Using a pseudonym or hiding their past, some Nazis criminals launched successful careers in postwar

---

*The two most famous escapees to South America were Adolf Eichmann, the meticulous and ideologically committed bureaucrat who arranged the deportation of millions of Jews to death camps, and Josef Mengele, the notorious SS doctor at Auschwitz who selected which Jewish arrivals would be immediately gassed and performed cruel medical experiments on children. Abducted in Argentina by Israeli agents in 1960, Eichmann was tried in Israel and executed in 1962. Mengele, who managed to escape his pursuers, died in Brazil in 1979 by drowning, which might have been precipitated by a stroke. There were numerous lesser figures who participated in mass murder who found refuge in Latin America, including Josef Schwammberger, an SS officer responsible for ordering the shooting of two hundred slave laborers when Kommandant of a labor camp and engaging in many sadistic acts when serving as ruler of the Jewish ghetto in Przemysl, Poland. Extradited from Argentina in 1990, Schwammberger was tried in Germany and sentenced to life imprisonment. In 1979, the United States established the Office of Special Investigation (OSI), which was empowered to investigate American citizens or residents suspected of complicity in Nazi war crimes. As of 2008, OSI had successfully won cases against 107 people for their wartime actions; some were deported and others denaturalized. With varying degrees of success, Canada, Britain, and Australia have participated in the hunt for Nazi war criminals. With surviving criminals in their nineties, the hunt is coming to an end.

Leading Nazis were put on trial before the International Military Tribunal at Nuremberg, where the Nazis had staged their giant rallies.

Germany.* Thousands of East European collaborators, including a number who had participated in mass murder, hid their past and found asylum in the United States, Australia, Canada, and Britain, where they established new lives for themselves and their families. Many who remained in their homelands continued with their lives without facing punishment.

Nevertheless, a significant number of German war criminals were indicted, and their trials provided a detailed record of the Nazi regime and its criminal behavior. In 1945–1946, twenty-two leading Nazis stood trial before the International Military Tribunal (IMT), comprised of representatives of the United States, Great Britain, the Soviet Union, and France, for conspiracy to wage war and crimes against humanity. They were tried at Nuremberg, the scene of Hitler's giant rallies prior to the war. The IMT amassed a wealth of documents that proved crucial for historical research into the Nazi era. And the interrogations of defendants, as well as their testimonies, continue to provide historians (and psychologists) with valuable insights into the motivations and personalities of prominent Nazis.

---

*For example, Hans Heinrich Eggebrecht, who became one of Germany's leading musicologists, was part of a unit that slaughtered fourteen thousand Jews in the Crimea in just a few days. After the war, he lied about his past in all the forms he filled out first as a student then as an academic. Not until after his death in 1999 was his past exposed.

The accused were shown horrifying documentaries of German atrocities, including the concentration camps when American, British, and Soviet troops entered them. A few of the defendants whimpered; Hermann Goering declared that the films were fakes. They also heard equally horrifying accounts from survivors. Particularly distressing for the war criminals were pictures of young children with skulls bashed in and descriptions of Jewish children thrown alive into the furnaces. In denying responsibility for war crimes, the defendants offered a variety of specious defenses: they were not anti-Semitic and had no knowledge of the murder of Jews: they tried to save Jews; they did not personally kill anyone; they were obeying orders. In response to these claims, the newly founded anti-Nazi *Berliner Zeitung* commented sarcastically:

> Having now heard the testimony of more than half of the defendants, one could get the impression from their words that the inmates of the concentration camp had themselves carried out the selections for the gas chambers, ordered themselves to march into the chambers, themselves turned on the gas and obediently choked to death or had … beaten and bestially mistreated themselves, … and shot themselves. All these villainous organizers of mass extermination claim to not have been there at all, in fact they were practically benefactors of the inmates.[7]

Rejecting the defendants' arguments that they did not personally participate in the atrocities committed against Jews and others or that they were obeying orders forced on them in wartime against their will, the court sentenced twelve to death by hanging and one in absentia; seven were given jail sentences from ten years to life; and three were acquitted. Among those condemned were Hans Frank, Governor General of the General Government in Poland; Arthur Seyss-Inquart, Frank's deputy and Reich Commissioner of the Netherlands; Goering, Commander of the Luftwaffe and head of branches of the SS (swallowing poison smuggled into his cell, he managed to commit suicide the night before he was to be hanged);* Ernst Kaltenbrunner, a high official in the SS; Fritz Sauckel, head of the Nazi slave labor program; and Field Marshal Wilhelm Keitel, Hitler's lackey, who signed orders calling for the execution of captured Soviet officials and French pilots serving in the Soviet Union and gave Heinrich Himmler's SS a free hand to impose terror and mass murder in the Soviet Union. Martin Bormann, Hitler's personal secretary and an enormously powerful bureaucrat who pressed for the liquidation of the Jews, was sentenced to death in absentia—most likely, he perished fleeing Hitler's bunker after the Führer's suicide. Noticeably absent were Goebbels, who killed himself in Hitler's bunker, and Himmler, who swallowed poison after being captured and identified. Frank, who embraced Christ in his cell, showed contrition: "A thousand years will pass and still the guilt of Germany will not have been erased."[8] (He later claimed that the expulsions of Germans from Poland and Czechoslovakia had erased German guilt.)

---

*With his well-tailored uniforms, vast store of elegant velvet robes, and magnificently furnished castle decorated with art plundered from conquered Europe, the self-indulgent Goering thoroughly enjoyed the high life that came with power. During the trial, he remained arrogant and defiant.

Struggling to survive amid the devastation surrounding them and the debilitating food shortages, Germans took little interest in the trial; some denounced it as a poor example of justice—the victors' justice they exclaimed. How could Soviet jurists judge Germans, they asked, when their government either executed or deported millions to death in their war against the kulaks, the more prosperous farmers, and in the purges of so-called enemies of the people? Were the Soviets not guilty of war crimes by deporting in 1939–1941 hundreds of thousands of Poles deep into the Soviet Union, where many perished, and again in the massacre of Polish officers in 1941? And was the Anglo-American air campaign against German cities that killed six hundred thousand civilians not a war crime?

Nevertheless, in a survey taken by Office of the Military Government, United States (OMGUS) after the trial ended, 55 percent of Germans considered the verdicts to be just. In their eyes, these high Nazis were responsible for the immense misery that now afflicted the German people. Moreover, they interpreted the verdict to mean that a handful of Nazi bigwigs, and not the German people as a whole, were to blame for wartime atrocities.

Between December 1946 and April 1949, American, British, and French military courts held trials of other German war criminals, including the murderers of downed American pilots; judges who sentenced dissenters to death; doctors accused of performing medical experiments on concentration camp inmates; commanders of the murderous Einsatzgruppen; and concentration camp administrators and guards. Also indicted were senior army officers involved in the rounding up and executing of Jewish and non-Jewish hostages and industrialists who had employed both Jewish and non-Jewish slave labor. In total, the three occupying powers convicted 5,025 people of war crimes or crimes against humanity and condemned 806 to death, of which 486 sentences were carried out. Most Germans, although eager to distance themselves from the Nazi past, viewed these lesser trials with disfavor.

With the development of the Cold War, which made the new Federal Republic of Germany a valued ally, U.S. and British authorities had other priorities than bringing Nazi criminals to justice. Consequently, they commuted death sentences and reduced jail terms. By 1958, all the Nazis convicted in American courts between 1945 and 1955 were released from prison. In 1948, Britain ended the trials in its zone of occupation, and by 1956 it had released all but a handful of Nazi war criminals in its custody. Some of those released had been convicted of mass murder. For example, in the trial of the commanders of the Einsatzgruppen (1947–1948), the mobile death units that killed more than one million Jews in the Soviet Union, fourteen defendants received the death penalty, three received life imprisonment, six were sentenced to serve twenty years, and three were sentenced to serve ten years. Four were actually executed, and between 1951 and 1958 all the others were released from prison, free to reenter German society.

For more than a decade, West German officials made little attempt to investigate German war crimes committed in the concentration camps and in occupied lands. Indeed, German officials protected former Nazis from prosecution and punishment. Because so many Europeans had actively or passively collaborated with the Nazis, they too wanted the whole matter to just go away; it was past history that had no bearing on the present. Thus, according to evidence recently uncovered, it appears that West German intelligence knew where Adolf Eichmann was almost a decade before his capture by Israeli agents in 1960, but made no move to apprehend him.

In the 1960s, West Germans began to confront their past more openly and honestly. A precipitating event was the trial in 1958 of a member of the Einsatzgruppen who had been restored to his position as a high police official after the war. He was given a stiff sentence for participating in the murder of four thousand Jews. The details of his crimes, which were widely publicized, stirred liberal journalists, politicians, lawyers, and intellectuals to demand a systematic investigation and prosecution of Nazi war criminals. That same year, the Central Office of the State Justice Ministries for the Investigation of National Socialist Crimes (ZS) was established. In succeeding years, the details emerging from the trials of Eichmann in Israel in 1961 and of Auschwitz guards in Frankfurt in 1963 awakened a younger generation to the crimes of the Nazi era and led to greater reflection on the Nazi past. David Cesarani summarizes the war crimes trials in Germany:

> From 1945 to 1992 West German courts indicted more than 100,000 persons for Nazi crimes. More than 13,000 cases were tried, and 6,487 persons were convicted; 6,197 were sentenced to prison terms, including 163 to life imprisonment; 12 were sentenced to death. From 1958 to 1993 the ZS instigated 4,853 prosecutions.... These included the Treblinka guards' case (1959–65), the Majdanek and Auschwitz SS personnel trials (1960–1979 and 1963–64), the trial of Franz Stangl, commandant of Sobibor and later Treblinka (1974–75) [both death camps], and the trial of Joseph Schwammberger, who ran and eventually liquidated the Przemysl ghetto (1991–92). In addition, from 1949 German courts arraigned with mixed success the Gestapo staffs responsible for the deportation of Jews from the major German cities and the members of several German police battalions implicated in mass murder in Poland and Russia. For all their failures, the German courts enabled a confrontation with the Nazi past, documented Nazi crimes, kept the plight of their victims from being forgotten, and sustained the principle of seeking justice.[9]*

---

*Many Nazi criminals were never put on trial or finally faced justice decades after the war had ended. Often, there were shocking miscarriages of justice. Coached by defense attorneys, perpetrators presented themselves as powerless victims who were only following legal orders. They denied any racist beliefs in Aryan supremacy or any hatred of Jews—confessing to anti-Semitism would lead to a certain guilty verdict—and even declared that they tried to alleviate Jewish suffering. To support his claim that he did not enjoy the shootings, one perpetrator said he refrained from the common practice of throwing children into the air and shooting them for sport. Judges sentenced mass murderers to one, two, or three years in jail, ruling that they were victims of an unscrupulous regime; sometimes judges allowed them to escape punishment entirely as in the case of Walther Becker. From 1941 to 1945, Becker headed the Security Police in a Polish district. When the war ended, he served as a policeman in Hamburg, retiring in 1957. In 1971, he was tried for his participation in the liquidation of the Polish ghetto in Wierzbnik. Numerous Jewish survivors testified that Becker assisted in the ghetto-clearing operation on October 27, 1942, that sent sixteen hundred Jews to slave-labor camps and four thousand to the gas chambers at Treblinka. During the *Aktion*, said the survivors, Becker personally beat and killed Jews, and he ordered his subordinates to kill others. Becker claimed that he merely observed the roundup of Jews and their loading into the trains; he neither participated nor gave orders. Christopher R. Browning describes the presiding judge's verdict given on February 8, 1972: "[H]e proceeded methodically to discredit the testimony of each key Jewish witness individually, often with techniques of systematic doubt and tortuous reasoning that demanded perfect consistency within and between testimonies nowhere to be found in the real world. Additionally, whole categories of testimony were deemed intrinsically flawed for one reason or another and dismissed as well. The judge then concluded that since Becker's account was not contradicted by any 'reliable' evidence before the court, the defendant was acquitted." The verdict, said Browning, shamed the German judicial system. *Remembering Survival: Inside a Nazi Slave-Labor Camp* (New York: W. W. Norton, 2010), 2.

War crimes trials were also held in every land occupied by Germany. Among the major war criminals sentenced to death by Polish courts were Jürgen Stroop, commander of the SS troops that suppressed the Warsaw Ghetto Uprising, and Rudolf Höss, commandant of Auschwitz. By 1977, Poland had tried 5,358 German war criminals, including concentration camp guards. By 1950, more than 10,000 war criminals were incarcerated in Soviet prisons. Many people convicted of war crimes insisted on their innocence, claiming they knew nothing of atrocities, never killed innocents, or were only doing their duty and following orders; they labeled their sentence as a victor's revenge not justice. Few showed genuine contrition.

JEWISH SURVIVORS

Two-thirds of Europe's Jews, some six million men, women, and children, perished in the Holocaust—the liquidation of European Jewry was the only major objective of the Third Reich that was largely realized. The end of the war did not end Jewish misery. Of the Jewish concentration camp survivors, 40 percent died within a month or two after liberation, so dreadful was their physical condition. The survivors, many of them in camps for displaced persons (DPs) tended by American and British authorities, were being nurtured back to health, both physically and mentally. An American army rabbi described these hapless people: "Almost without exception each is the last remaining member of his entire family.... Their stories are like terrible nightmares which make one's brain reel and one's heart bleed."[10]

It was hoped that Jews would go back to their native lands, but European countries were often not eager for the return of Jewish survivors, ghosts who made too many people uncomfortable.* They did not recognize the torment Jews had endured and often made it difficult or impossible for survivors to regain stolen property. During the war, anti-Semitism was on the rise throughout the Continent. It appears that the Nazis' characterization of the Jew had found a receptive audience among wide segments of the European population, as Goebbels had intended: "At present about 70 to 80 percent of our broadcasts are devoted to [anti-Semitic propaganda]. The anti-Semitic bacilli naturally exist everywhere in all Europe; we must merely make them virulent."[11] And in much of Europe, traditional anti-Semitism remained undiminished after the war.

For many who came from Eastern Europe, going back to their native land would be returning to a vast Jewish graveyard and traumatic memories. Could they return to Poland, where the Nazis had slaughtered their families and destroyed their villages and synagogues, where Jews were fleeing west from

---

*Certainly Swiss bankers had no desire to see Jewish survivors. When surviving Jews went to Swiss banks to claim the deposits of relatives murdered in the camps, the bankers demanded the death certificate of the depositor as if the SS at Auschwitz and Treblinka issued such documents before herding them into gas chambers. The bankers simply intended to keep—"steal" is not too inaccurate a word—the assets of murdered Jews. Fifty years later, after considerable pressure from Jewish organizations and the United States, the Swiss banks, uncomfortable with the disparaging publicity, searched their records for these dormant accounts and made restitution.

violent pogroms by anti-Semitic Poles? Some fifteen hundred to two thousand Jews were murdered in Poland just after the war,* and many Poles, some of them living in former Jewish homes, made it clear they did not want Jews to return. In a three-month period in 1946, more than sixty-three thousand Jews fled Poland, seeking the protection of Allied occupation forces in Germany.† Or could they return to the Ukraine, where nationalists continued to murder Jewish survivors after the Germans had retreated? Or to Hungary, Romania, Lithuania, and other lands, where the authorities and elements of the population had assisted the Nazis in brutalizing, killing, and deporting Jews to death camps? Immediately after the war, Jews trying to escape these lands sought sanctuary in occupied Germany, Austria, and Italy. Of course, some Jewish DPs, many searching for family members who might have survived, returned to their native lands and started life anew either there or in new European surroundings. But most of the Jews languishing in DP camps in hated Germany wanted to leave Europe, which was soaked with Jewish blood.

Since their emancipation in the nineteenth century, Jews had striven to assimilate into European society, often with considerable success; their contributions to science, medicine, and intellectual life were unmatched by any other ethnic minority. But the lesson they drew from the Hitler years was that no matter how much they contributed to European society and culture, they were not wanted and would never be treated decently and equally. With their faith in European civilization shattered, many of these now stateless Jews longed to start a new life in the United States or Canada if immigration restrictions in these countries were eased. Others turned to Palestine, the ancient Jewish homeland. Zionism, previously the ideology of an ardent minority, became the desperate hope of the survivors languishing in DP camps, as one observer noted:

> They are on the verge of moral collapse. The only substance on which they exist is Palestine. It dominates their every waking moment. The word itself is incandescent with meaning to them. One is appalled even to contemplate what might now be taking place among them if there were no Palestine on which to fasten their hopes and with which to identify their future.[12]

---

*A particularly horrific anti-Semitic episode took place in the town of Kielce in early July 1946, when a young boy concocted a tale that he had been kidnapped by Jews and placed in the cellar of a Jewish house. When the father reported the boy's story to the police, rumors quickly spread that the Jews used the house—which incidentally had no cellar—in order to murder Polish children and obtain their blood for making matzo for Passover. This bizarre and cruel myth, which had caused the death of thousands of Jews in the Middle Ages, survived into the twentieth century in much of Eastern Europe. Polish police and soldiers entered the building shooting and turned Jewish inhabitants over to a frenzied mob that beat them unmercifully. Later, steelworkers, wielding iron bars, joined in the pogrom. Neither the soldiers nor the police intervened as more than forty Jews were killed and scores severely wounded. The pogrom spread to Kielce's main railway station where Jews were shot, thrown out of trains, and beaten, which added to the death and injured toll. Identifying Polish patriotism with hatred of Jews, most Poles expressed no displeasure with the pogrom. The clergy, traditionally anti-Semitic, remained largely indifferent to the massacre.

†In 1968, the Communist government launched an anti-Semitic purge, whose aim was the expulsion of Jews. Most of Poland's remaining Jewish population immigrated to Israel. Only a few thousand Jews dwell in Poland today. In recent years, Polish–Jewish relations have improved considerably (see Chapter 4, footnote on page 134).

Jews living in the British mandate of Palestine attempted to smuggle their compatriots in Europe (many living in DP camps) into Palestine, which was in violation of British quotas. The British intercepted the *Exodus*, which had set sail from France in July 1947, and returned the approximately 4,550 refugee Jews back to Europe in prison ships. A world-wide storm of protest followed, which influenced the UN decision to partition Palestine into Jewish and Arab states.

But Palestine was still a British mandate, and not wanting to antagonize the Arabs as war loomed, Britain had greatly restricted Jewish immigration to Palestine in 1939 and seized ships trying to smuggle in Jews after the war. In November 1947, the UN partitioned Palestine into a Jewish state and an Arab state, and in May 1948 the State of Israel was born. Amid the war waged by Arab countries to destroy the infant Jewish state, Jews left the DP camps to start a new life. The murder of two-thirds of European Jews and the exodus of survivors meant that in no country in Europe did Jews constitute more than 1 percent of the population; nevertheless anti-Semitism still persisted in varying degrees among the general population.

World War II and its immediate aftermath shattered, or should have shattered, several pernicious myths about Jews that had been staples of European and Nazi anti-Semitism. The Holocaust demonstrated the absurdity of the myth of an international Jewish conspiracy, with its paranoid fantasy that the Jews had gained control over international finance, governments, and the press as part of a plot to dominate the world. So prevalent was this belief that many Germans had been convinced that Jews had started the war, had created the Allied alliance in order to destroy Germany, and had ordered the carpet-bombing of their cities as an act of revenge. The war years showed how weak and without influence Jews really were. After the war, an SS general, himself guilty of war crimes in the Soviet Union, confessed:

> I must say the truth. Contrary to the opinion of the National Socialists that the Jews were a highly organized group, the appalling fact was that they had no organization whatsoever.... It gives the lie to the old slogan that the Jews are conspiring to dominate the world and that they are so highly orga-nized.... If they had some sort of organization, these people could have been saved by the millions; but instead they were taken completely by surprise.[13]

The Soviets, the Americans, and the British did not give serious thought to employing military operations to rescue Jews. With all the power anti-Semites attribute to Jews, said Gerhard L. Weinberg, "in the hour of supreme agony, all the Jewish organizations on earth could not get one country to send one plane to drop one bomb [on Auschwitz]."[14] Nor could they get countries to allow more than a trickle of Jewish immigrants to find sanctuary when there was still a chance to escape the Nazis. (The myth of an international Jewish conspiracy and the *Protocols of the Elders of Zion*, that notorious forgery that buttresses this myth, continue to be widely circulated and believed in the Muslim world.)

Crucial to the Nazi worldview, which many people in other lands shared, was the myth that the Soviet Union was ruled by Jews who used Communism to spread their tentacles over Europe. Many of Hitler's generals subscribed to this myth. "I can see quite clearly that all this Bolshevism is nothing but a colossal Jewish plot," stated one German general. And another: "One day history will say the Führer was right in recognizing this great Jewish danger threatening all nations and in realizing the Jewish communist threat to Europe from the east."[15] Dutch historian André Gerrits comments on the historical significance of this linkage of Jews and Communism:

> Few historians would deny that "Jewish Communism," a variant of the "Jewish World Conspiracy," has been one of the most powerful and destructive myths in early-20th century Europe.... The identification of Jews with communism coloured the perceptions of Jews in general.... It turned traditional, often religiously inspired anti-Jewish sentiments into a murderous, politically motivated rampage. Apart from Nazi Germany, where Judaeo-Bolshevism became the centerpiece of state ideology, the myth of Jewish communism achieved its greatest poignancy in the countries of East Central Europe.[16]*

Although individual Jews served in the rank and file of the Soviet bureau-cracy, collectively Jews exercised zero power in the Soviet Union, and, at the time of World War II, there were virtually no Jews holding senior positions in the Communist Party and the government (see footnote in Chapter 3, page 57). The Soviet Union officially condemned anti-Semitism, but many Soviet leaders,

---

*Only a small percentage of the European Jewish population participated in revolutionary Communist movements, but a disproportionate number of revolutionaries were Jews. Why this was so is a subject of historical inquiry. Gerrits provides a good account of this and related issues dealing with Jews and Communism.

including Stalin, and Soviet citizens, particularly in the Ukraine and Belorussia, harbored a crude anti-Semitism.

During the war, Soviet authorities barred any mention of the Nazi genocide of Jews and prohibited the publication of a book of documents compiled by two prominent Jewish journalists illustrating the Nazi treatment of Jews in Poland and the Soviet Union: in the eyes of the authorities, such documentation was an expression of Jewish nationalism not Russian patriotism. When the Red Army liberated death camps, the gas chambers were described, but the victims were never identified as Jews. After the war, at ceremonies commemorating the two-day massacre of 33,771 Jews in a ravine at Babi Yar at the outskirts of Kiev, it could only be said that the victims were Soviet citizens, not Jews. Soviet authorities were uncomfortably aware that any serious discussion of the Holocaust would reveal the complicity of numerous Soviet citizens who assisted the Germans in rounding up and murdering Jews and staffed the death camps.

From the end of the war until his death in 1953, Stalin, himself a pathological Jew-hater, embarked on an anti-Semitic campaign that included murdering prominent Jewish writers and members of the Jewish Anti-Fascist Committee, stamping out Yiddish culture, and denouncing Jews as "criminal nationalists" engaged in a "Judeo-Zionist" plot against the Soviet Union. Many Jews were arrested; fired from their positions in the arts, journalism, and medicine; and executed. In 1953, several Jewish physicians, "saboteur doctors" they were labeled, were accused of plotting to poison high Kremlin officials. In preparation for the trial, an intense press campaign castigated Jews, and there is some evidence that this was only the beginning of a campaign to round up Jews for deportation to the Gulag or worse. Stalin's death ended the affair, and the doctors were released.

Following Israel's victory in the Six Day War in 1967, Soviet propaganda used Nazi-like language and caricatures to increasingly demonize the Jewish people by condemning Zionism as Fascist, Judaism as a wicked religion, and Jews as a criminal and conspiratorial people. These and numerous other examples of Soviet anti-Semitism show that the accusation that Jews controlled the Soviet Union was another in a long list of irrational myths that people have believed about Jews.

THE NEW (WEST) GERMANY: OVERCOMING THE PAST*

The Reality of Total Defeat

Since Germany had not been invaded during World War I, after the war many Germans had believed the myth that they had not lost the war but rather had been betrayed—"stabbed in the back"—by democrats, socialists, and Jews. No stab-in-the-back legend could emerge after World War II, however, for the

---

*Much of what is said about the "New Germany" in this section is confined to West Germany. In East Germany, the Communist government imposed an official line regarding the nature and meaning of Nazism and, in accord with Moscow's anti-Israel policy and purging of Jewish Communist officials in its satellites, treatment of the Holocaust was suppressed or marginalized.

German people knew they were beaten. The evidence of Germany's total defeat and impotence was everywhere and unambiguous: the all-too-common sight of the shattered Wehrmacht as the war neared its end; foreign armies on German soil; massive destruction of towns and cities, including the infrastructure that supplied fuel, water, electricity, public transportation, and postal service; millions of German refugees driven from their homes; pervasive hunger; and the ubiquitous presence of death—decomposing corpses in streets and in the ruins of buildings and the loss of loved ones who had perished in the military or were victims of aerial bombardments and the fighting on German soil. Buried in the rubble was the lure of militarism and aggressive nationalism that had fueled two world wars. Unlike after World War I, a demolished, traumatized, occupied, and cowed Germany wanted nothing to do with wars of revenge and wars of expansion. Buried also was National Socialism, which could not survive defeat, Hitler's death, and identification with mass murder. Hitler's hope that a heroic last stand by a population fanatically committed to National Socialism would inspire the German people in a future struggle proved to be another evil fantasy. The millions of German dead, the gargantuan task of reconstruction, and the widely publicized incomprehensible and shameful crimes committed by the Nazi regime—even if many purged them from memory—provided the impetus for the German people to break with their immediate Nazi past and haltingly confront the historic militaristic, authoritarian, chauvinistic, and racist traditions that had helped spawn Nazism.

To be sure, there were plenty of confirmed Nazis, including veterans. They formed organizations and political parties that preserved National Socialist doctrines. (They were, however, careful to distance themselves from the atrocities of the Nazi regime.) And National Socialist ideas continued to be propagated in newspapers, periodicals, and books. But as economic conditions improved and political stability was established, a revived German Right that tried to keep National Socialism alive had little impact on the shaping of a new Germany and little future. Viewing the irrational ideology and murderous deeds of the Nazi dictatorship as a betrayal of civilization and a reversion to barbarism, the new leadership wanted to fashion a democratic and peaceful Germany, one that endorsed the values of Western civilization and sought reconciliation with neighboring states. Fostering the creation of a democratic Germany were anti-Nazis who had been liberals and democratic socialists in the Weimar Republic and returning émigrés who were committed to the Western and German humanistic traditions. Over the years, the unprecedented evil of the Nazi tyranny and its mad biological racism that culminated in the crime of genocide led the German people to appreciate the virtues of liberal democracy and human rights. Ironically, while citizens of defeated Germany quickly enjoyed both freedom and prosperity, Soviet citizens, who had sacrificed so much, continued to be tyrannized and regimented by Stalin. And to this day, they have a much lower standard of living than Germans.

Divided among the four occupying powers—the United States, Britain, France, and the Soviet Union—the German nation was politically extinct. By 1949, two new and chastened German states had emerged. West Germany (the Federal Republic of Germany), formed from the three Western zones of occupation, faced hostile Soviet-dominated East Germany (the German Democratic Republic). At first, the occupying powers tried to keep former Nazi Party members and ardent supporters of the Third Reich from retaining or obtaining positions in the civil service, business, and industry, a policy that was soon abandoned in both West and East Germany. There were just too many ex-party members, and their services were needed to rebuild the two Germanys. For example, many school teachers, university instructors, judges, and other judicial officials had been enthusiastic Nazi party members. Purging them would paralyze education and the courts. And should the large number of doctors who had joined the Nazi party be barred from practicing medicine at a time when their skills were much in demand?

It would take time for the German people, who had been indoctrinated for twelve years with Nazi propaganda, to distance themselves completely from Nazi ideology and to undergo a moral reckoning with their past. Based on OMGUS surveys conducted in West Germany from 1945 to 1947, between 47 and 55 percent of Germans still believed that National Socialism was a good idea that was not well implemented—a figure that would endure for a generation; only 20 percent believed that Germany was responsible for the war; 33 percent opposed equal rights for Jews; and 39 percent could be classified as anti-Semitic. Other surveys showed that the majority of Germans, still under the spell, did not consider Hitler a criminal; as late as 1954, only a minority of Germans had an unfavorable impression of Hitler. Retaining admiration for the Führer, many Germans remained convinced that Hitler knew nothing about the brutal crimes committed by the SS. Nevertheless, the mass of German people, even those who had once embraced and fondly remembered Hitler and Nazism, showed no inclination to support once more an extremist political movement, especially one that glorified war and sought territorial aggrandizement; very few, whatever their private feelings, openly endorsed Nazi racist teachings, including anti-Semitism, although anti-Semitic acts—the desecration of cemeteries—and bigoted attacks on Jewish DPs as black marketers and speculators did occur. Returning to normal life was everyone's overwhelming concern.

Konrad Adenauer: Architect of the New West Germany

Konrad Adenauer, the architect of the new West Germany and its chancellor from 1949 to 1963, placed the country on a sound democratic path, shouldered responsibility for the crimes of the Nazi regime, and assumed the payment of indemnifications to the Jewish victims and survivors of the Nazi era, as well as the payment of reparations to the newly created Jewish state of Israel, which was absorbing the survivors of genocide. Although two-thirds of the population interpreted these reparations as extortion, seeking reconciliation with world Jewry was politically expedient: it was intended as another sign to the Western powers that the new Germany should be treated as an equal partner and ally. It was also intended to cement ties with the United States, where Jews constituted a vocal minority.

Seeking to promote public harmony, Adenauer restored to public service many Nazis, whom Allied occupation authorities had dismissed from their positions in accordance with their denazification program; brought the prosecution of war criminals to a virtual halt; and fought for amnesty for convicted war criminals. Concerned with West German support in an era of Cold War, the United States and Britain reduced sentences, released war criminals from jail, and shielded others from indictment. With the emergence of the Cold War, the issue of Nazi crimes faded, and it was claimed that the expertise of former Nazis—many of whom opportunistically became democrats—was needed in the reconstruction of the country. In 1951, it was reported that of the one hundred members of the West German diplomatic corps, forty-three had served in the SS and seventeen with the Gestapo. Many former Nazis advanced their careers as bureaucrats, teachers, police, judges, lawyers, physicians, and industrialists. Nevertheless, the presence of former Nazis in government and society and the emergence of small radical Right parties did not threaten the new German democracy, which Germans overwhelmingly— even ex-Nazis—wanted to succeed. Those who had participated in mass murder now tried to be good citizens in the new democratic Germany.

Facing Responsibility

The new Germany had to come to terms with its past, a painful process that would persist into the twenty-first century. Immediately after the war, German intellectuals dealt with several pressing questions: Was National Socialism an aberration, a deviation from the course of German history that a gang of criminals forced on the German people? Were Germans the first victims of a barbarian ideology that was a perversion of German tradition? Or was Nazism deeply rooted in German history, the terrible and logical fulfillment of cultural and political trends that comprised a flawed national character? To what extent did ordinary Germans share the burden of guilt? The dominant approach of West German historians and cultural critics in the postwar decade, says Mary Fulbrook, was "to condemn Nazism and Hitler as evil, while at the same time asserting that Nazism neither arose from long-stem trends in German history, nor had any intrinsic relationship with the German people, who appear simply to have bumped into it and been blown off their proper course."[17] Germans looked back at Nazism as an accident or aberration in their historical development and attributed Nazi crimes largely to Hitler, an Austrian fanatic who imposed un-German ideas on the country. Commentators in other lands and the Allied occupation authorities were much more skeptical. Pointing to Germany's strong tradition of authoritarianism, militarism, extreme nationalism, and racism, and the enthusiasm with which both the elite and ordinary people had embraced Hitler, they insisted that Germans required reeducation. They had to be taught the failings of their nation's "special path"— the much admired nationalist and militarist political culture that had culminated in world wars and Nazi barbarism. They must also be made aware of their own failings, their personal complicity as participants or followers in great evil. The Allied authorities maintained that denazification and reeducation were necessary for building a viable democracy in the new Germany.

In 1945, most Germans did not believe that they bore responsibility for supporting, serving, and obeying without protest a criminal regime whose crimes were without parallel in human history. At first, many Germans dismissed the British documentary films showing the liberation of Bergen-Belsen with the piles of corpses and the sick and emaciated survivors as staged, a propaganda ploy similar to what the Nazis had employed. Germans could never have done such things was the initial reaction. Further, they viewed the scale of Jewish suffering as vastly exaggerated, no worse than what they themselves had endured. It would take time for the truth to sink in.

As Tony Judt observes, a comforting myth emerged: "Throughout the fifties West German officialdom encouraged a comfortable view of the German past in which the Wehrmacht was heroic, while the Nazis were in a minority and had been properly punished."[18] This, of course, was a self-serving myth. It would take a generation and longer for most West Germans to treat honestly and objectively the suffering they had brought to Europe. In the war's immediate aftermath, numbed by their country's defeat and the carnage around them, Germans were concerned with sheer survival; they wanted to forget about Hitler and the Third Reich, particularly the great number of Germans who had believed in Hitler and supported his regime, and devote all their energies to rebuilding their lives and reconstructing their country. When confronted with the Nazi past, they were reluctant to talk about it, especially with their children. When pressed, they often displayed either historical amnesia or a selective memory, claiming to have been unaware of the extermination of the Jews and vehemently denying any involvement with or personal responsibility for Nazi crimes. This denial was shared by many Europeans who forgot completely their empathy with certain Nazi doctrines and their collaboration with the German occupation authorities.

Although some Germans, especially those who had never embraced Hitler and his ideology, confronted the truth of the Nazi regime, most did not recognize their nation's moral collapse and their own moral failure; they felt little compulsion to make amends for the suffering and misery the Third Reich had brought to millions of people. They were also filled with self-pity. When they spoke of victims, survivors, suffering, and war crimes, often they were referring to Allied carpet-bombing of German cities; the barbaric behavior of invading Russian soldiers; the death, abuse, and loss of land and homes endured by Germans expelled from Eastern European countries; the struggle for survival in the closing months of the war and immediately after it ended; and the plight of German prisoners of war still languishing in Soviet camps. Many Germans saw themselves not as perpetrators and collaborators but as the primary victims of the war, and they drew no distinction between the suffering the Nazis had inflicted on Jews—and they often minimized the extent of the Jewish tragedy—and the suffering the war had caused them. In their eyes, they were as much victims as Jews, the Allied commanders who ordered the bombing of their cities were war criminals morally equivalent to the Nazi leadership, and the plane crews that rained death and destruction were no better than the SS.

These Germans also saw themselves as innocent victims of a handful of Nazi criminals who had deceived and betrayed the German people's patriotism and idealism by dragging them into a war that they did not want and committing evil acts of which they were unaware and would never have approved. It was psychologically comforting to believe that a small coterie of Nazi leaders was solely responsible for war crimes and that the German people as a whole were free of shame and guilt and neither as individuals nor as a nation owed a moral debt to the Nazis' victims. In this all-inclusive interpretation of victimization, even the SS could be seen not as perpetrators of inhuman acts but as victims of criminal leadership and a cruel war.

It was also common for Germans, even former Nazi Party members and officials, to declare that they never were truly committed to National Socialism and to reject any notion of personal accountability or guilt, and they vociferously rejected the notion of collective guilt and the need for collective remorse. Indeed, Germany was a land without Nazis after the war. Virtually no one openly confessed to having supported the Nazi regime and its policies, and virtually everyone sought to escape responsibility for the crimes of the Third Reich. A week after the war had ended, the astute Victor Klemperer* noted that "the 3rd Reich is already almost as good as forgotten, everyone was opposed to it, 'always' opposed to it."[19] To an American major, the Germans acted "as though the Nazis were a strange race of Eskimos who came down from the North Pole and somehow invaded Germany."[20]

In pinning sole responsibility for war crimes on a small group of Nazi leaders, the Germans erased from memory the popularity of the Nazi regime with the German people, the profound devotion and loyalty that much of the nation had given to Hitler, and the hysterical adulation shown the Führer at mass rallies and parades. Many Germans had regarded Hitler as a savior who had united and revived the sacred fatherland and removed the shame of the Versailles Treaty. This admiration discouraged resistance and made it easier for Hitler to impose his will on the nation, a task promoted by enthusiastic intellectuals whose nationalistic, racist and anti-Semitic treatises endorsed Hitler and the Third Reich. The ideas found in these treatises were popularized and propagated by journalists, school teachers, artists, and filmmakers. Germans also forgot their embracing of National Socialist principles, their dedicated service to the Third Reich during the war, their euphoria over the Wehrmacht's victories, and their initial gratitude to the Nazi regime for the economic benefits they derived from the Wehrmacht's early conquests.

---

*A professor of literature and decorated veteran of World War I, Victor Klemperer was stripped of his academic position by the Nazis despite his conversion to Protestantism in 1912 and his strong attachment to German culture. Previously addressed as "Herr Professor Klemperer," he was now referred to as "the Jew Klemperer" and forced to do factory work. Because his wife was not Jewish, he was able to escape deportation, but he was routinely beaten, humiliated, and robbed by the Gestapo, who frequently searched the dwellings where Jews were rehoused after being forced out of their homes. Surviving the bombing of Dresden but fearful of being deported to a death camp along with the few surviving Jews married to gentiles or of being beaten to death by enraged civilians who attributed the bombings to Jewish power in the United States and Britain, he removed the yellow Star of David that Jews were required to display on their clothing and together with his wife made his way to the part of Germany occupied by the Americans. Published in 1995, thirty-five years after his death, Klemperer's diary provides astute insights into daily life in the Third Reich, particularly for a persecuted Jew.

These Germans also repressed their indifference and passive response to the ordeal of Jews—persecution before the war and deportation to the camps during the war—all before their eyes and their indifference to the millions of slave laborers from all over Europe whose often barbaric treatment they also observed. Many of these self-proclaimed innocents lived in the apartments of German Jews deported to concentration camps and enjoyed the furniture, tableware, linens, toys, jewelry, and furs stolen from these Jews and Jews from other lands that they had purchased at bargain prices at public auctions. More than a few had benefited from the expropriation of Jewish-owned businesses. Martin Dean, who has done extensive research in the despoiling of the Jews in Germany and other countries, concludes:

> The deportations left a very large economic footprint. Many contractors and private individuals became involved; among those were property assessors, auction houses, trustees, estate agents, notaries, and transport companies. Hundreds of thousands of individuals benefited from the sale of cheap household items or the availability of apartments. The Nazis attempted to maintain a hierarchy of beneficiaries ranked according to the Party's racial and social priorities. However, rampant corruption ensured that Nazi potentates and hangers on, as well as police and finance personnel, secured the best items for themselves. The processing of property became a pivotal act in the destruction process, involving hundreds of thousands of ordinary Germans who thereby became complicit in the destruction of their Jewish neighbors.[21]*

Into the 1950s, West Germans continued to see themselves as victims, not as perpetrators; it was German suffering, particularly at the hands of Soviet Communists, not the suffering that Germany had inflicted on Europe that was the main topic of concern in parliament, the press, and public discourse. Moreover, they maintained that focusing on the dark past would undermine efforts at economic recovery and building a viable democracy. Both the leaders of the newly created Federal Republic of Germany and the population at large fought against the German justice system investigating Nazi war crimes (which included judges who had served under the Nazis), and the number of convictions fell from 1,523 in 1949 to 21 in 1955. They also pressured the Allies to grant amnesty to convicted Nazis.

Nazis who had participated in murder, bureaucrats who did the paperwork that sent tens of thousands to their death, and bystanders who taunted the hapless deportees or showed no moral concern all tried to suppress or sanitize the criminal past. Until the 1960s, West German secondary school history courses generally ended with the beginning of the twentieth century, and university historians

---

*Knowledge of the mass murder of Jews was also widespread throughout the Continent. Martin Dean also concludes: "One important consequence of recent research on Holocaust-era assets has been to dispel the myth that few people in Europe were aware of the disappearance of the Jews and their likely fate. The vast number of institutions, organizations, companies, and individuals mentioned in this book makes this point abundantly clear." Martin Dean, *Robbing the Jews: The Confiscation of Jewish Property in the Holocaust, 1933–1945* (New York: Cambridge University Press, 2008), 391.

paid little attention to World War II. Few teachers discussed the Nazi regime, and appropriate books about Nazism and the Holocaust were lacking. It is understandable that teachers found the subject uncomfortable because only a few years earlier many had faithfully served the Third Reich, some by indoctrinating youth with Nazi doctrines.

New generations of government officials, teachers, students, intellectuals, historians, and clergy have made vast strides in confronting the past and reaching out to Jews (and other victims of Nazism), developments that the West German republic had generally approved. Starting in the 1960s, a younger generation of West Germans, activated by the trial of Adolf Eichmann in Jerusalem and the Auschwitz trials in Germany that included the chilling testimony of victims and led to a huge amount of published documentation, challenged the previous generation's oversights and cover-ups of the Nazi era. Two decades after the end of the war, these trials revealed the horror and magnitude of Nazi atrocities and awakened West Germans, particularly the young, and others to the immense suffering that Germans had inflicted on Jews. Henceforth, the Holocaust became embedded in German and Western consciousness. West German novelists and playwrights wrote perceptively about the guilt of Nazi criminals and the many Germans who were committed followers or passive bystanders. Scholars showed the connecting links between Nazism and German militarist, authoritarian, and anti-Semitic traditions. Also during the decade of the 1960s, a more strenuous effort was made to bring Nazi war criminals to trial, and the proceedings, which detailed the extermination process, elicited horror and introspection particularly in the younger generation. In 1979, the televising in Germany of *The Holocaust*, an American made-for-television miniseries revolving around fictional Jewish and Nazi families, stunned and moved the huge German audience. Laying bare the insensitivity and cruelty of ordinary Germans—not just the Nazi elite—and the immense pain inflicted on innocent Jews, the broadcasts stirred deep feelings and did more than scholarly treatises and thousands of documents to focus attention on the moral breakdown of German society and the Jewish catastrophe. The series jolted West German lawmakers to repeal the statute of limitations for war crimes, which decreed that after 1965 crimes committed before 1946 were no longer subject to prosecution.

German scholars have contributed significantly to our understanding of the Nazi era, including the Holocaust, which is now prominently featured in books and the media and is taught in the schools. More than any other European country, Germany has struggled to confront openly and honestly the Nazi years in general and the Holocaust in particular.* Today, an overwhelming number of

---

*It took longer for Austrians to come to terms with their past. After the war, although Austrians welcomed ex-Nazis into government service, they made it quite clear that they did not want Jewish survivors to return to the country. For years, anti-Semitic discourse was tolerated, and the Austrian authorities fought Jews' efforts to regain their stolen property or to receive compensation. In a poll taken as late as 1991, over 50 percent of those queried wanted an end both to the prosecution of Nazi war criminals and discussion of the Holocaust. However, in recent years clergy, educators, and government officials have confronted the carefully propagated historical fiction that Austrians were victims not collaborators and that they bore no responsibility for Nazi crimes. Today, as in Germany, the Holocaust is taught in the schools and survivors are invited to address students. Also, as in Germany, denying the Holocaust is regarded as a crime that promulgates ethnic hatred and is subject to imprisonment. The openly racist Austrian Freedom Party is seeking to repeal this law.

Germans regard the Nazi era with horror, shame, and remorse and seek friendly relations with the nations they had plundered and persecuted. Germany continues to be a leader in promoting peaceful European integration and guards its democracy against the resurgence of Nazism. They have no plans to regain lands lost after the war or to revenge the mass expulsion of millions of Germans from Eastern Europe. In all levels of education, it is compulsory to teach about the Nazi era including the Holocaust. The painful awareness of Nazi crimes and the public remembrance of the victims in monuments, museums, and ceremonies have strengthened the German people's commitment to democracy and human rights.

Enduring Myths: A Defensive War
and the Wehrmacht's Clean Hands

Despite this, some myths still persist in Germany about the Nazi era. One such myth held by some conservative historians and extreme Right groups, which German scholars have debunked, is that the German invasion of the Soviet Union—as Heinz Trettner, the former inspector general of the West German army, declared in 1997—"was first and foremost a preventive war, begun by force of necessity and with a heavy heart. From the first day, inhuman behaviour was introduced by overheated Soviet soldiers, who murdered prisoners of war."[22] For those who take this position, the invasion was a moral and justifiable act of self-defense to thwart the Soviet Union's design to attack and destroy Germany as a first step in Stalin's plan to dominate all of Europe; that in reality the German soldier was fighting to save his country and European civilization from Communism. An overwhelming number of scholars, including leading German historians, hold that this interpretation, which coincides with Goebbels' propaganda, is without substance; according to German historian Gerd R. Ueberschär, it "is part of a tendency that continually resurfaces in Germany to twist the historical facts about the Second World War in order to escape responsibility for the Soviet-German war of 1941–1945 and present a nationalistic, anti-Communist view of German history.... [It is an attempt] to deny or justify what happened."[23]

Another myth that had gone unchallenged for decades and to which some Germans, particularly some conservative circles, still cling, is the belief that the Wehrmacht was untainted by war crimes; that its behavior, unlike that of the criminal SS, was morally correct; that Wehrmacht generals knew nothing of or had no control over the special units that committed atrocities and genocide. Those who have espoused this view argue that the conduct of German soldiers and officers was honorable, that their loyalty was not to Hitler but to their comrades in arms and to the fatherland. To associate the Wehrmacht with the SS and the Security Police, the instruments of terror and extermination, and to treat it as a willing agent of Hitler's genocidal racial war, claim the Wehrmacht's defenders, besmirches the dignity of the German soldier who was not a Nazi fighting for Hitler and his ideology, but a patriot valiantly defending his country against the Soviets who were intent on destroying it.

When not proclaiming the Wehrmacht's innocence, apologists have insisted that German soldiers were themselves victims of Hitler's criminal leadership. As soldiers, they could not disobey the military commands issued by the Nazi regime; to do so would be committing treason in wartime. The loyal, patriotic, and dedicated German soldier had been betrayed by Hitler and his Nazi criminals.

Identifying the Wehrmacht with war crimes had disconcerting implications for Germans. Given that the millions of men who served in the Wehrmacht represented a cross-section of the nation, associating them with criminal behavior, including genocide, meant that much of the German nation was also indicted, a powerful reason why for decades Germans fought to preserve the myth of the Wehrmacht's innocence.

At the Nuremberg trials, considerable evidence was provided that the generals on the Eastern Front not only knew of the extermination of the Jews but also cooperated with SS murder units in their genocidal actions, and that Wehrmacht troops were deeply involved, both actively and passively, in atrocities committed against Soviet prisoners of war and civilian populations in occupied Europe. This evidence sometimes came out in the testimony of high-ranking German officers. Nevertheless, within a few years after the war the criminal behavior of the Wehrmacht was ignored or repressed and the myth of the Wehrmacht's "clean hands" emerged.

The myth was manufactured and propagated first in the numerous memoirs and autobiographies written by Hitler's generals, lower officers, and ordinary soldiers. Common themes ran through all these sanitized versions of the war: the German soldier was an honorable warrior who fought courageously and competently to defend his fatherland and family; he was not fighting to implement Hitler's ideology and was neither involved with concentration camps and mass murder nor knew anything about such atrocities. Responsibility for these crimes rested solely with Hitler and Himmler's SS. Indeed, when these war memoirs treated atrocities, they focused on those the Soviets committed against Germans.

The cinema and popular literature perpetuated uncritically this romanticized and heroic image of the Wehrmacht. Military historian Gerhard L. Weinberg concludes that, when it came to war crimes, close examination of the World War II memoirs, "especially that of the generals like Heinz Guderian and Erich von Manstein, ... has shown the memoirs to be almost invariably inaccurate, distorted, and in some instances simply faked."[24] For example, it is difficult to give any credence to Guderian's assertion that he knew nothing about German war crimes, for Hitler and Himmler succeeded in keeping "strictly secret" their racial policies. The atrocities carried out in the concentration camps "were made known to most people, as to myself, only after the collapse. The way the concentration camp methods were kept secret can only be described as masterly."[25]

A telling illustration of Wehrmacht generals' forgetfulness, evasiveness, and lies is seen in the memoirs and trial testimony of Field Marshal von Manstein. To the end of his life, he insisted that he was a professional soldier doing his duty and uninvolved with political matters and Nazi ideology. Yet his staff in the Crimea provided transport and supplies for the Einsatzgruppen, which massacred some ninety thousand Jews in the region under his command. It is incontrovertible that his commanders were fully briefed by the leaders of these death squads and that they reported the mass executions to him, but at his trial von Manstein insisted that he knew nothing about such developments. He also claimed not to know of the secret army order that he issued in November 1941 in which he told his soldiers, "The German soldier ... marches also as the carrier of a racial idea and the avenger for all the cruelties that have been inflicted on him and the German people.... The soldier must summon understanding for the necessity of a harsh atonement on Judaism, which is the spiritual carrier of the Bolshevik terror."[26]

In 1949, von Manstein was found guilty, among other charges, of allowing the Einsatzgruppen murder squads to operate in his area, deporting civilians, ordering the killing of Soviet prisoners of war, and having civilians shot in reprisal for partisan attacks. Sentenced to eighteen years in prison, he was released in 1953. Afterward, he served the Adenauer government and in his memoirs and other writings diligently strove to preserve the Wehrmacht's honor.

"The greatest victory of the German army," writes Omer Bartov, "was won on the field of politics, where it managed to return from the most murderous military actions in German history all but unscathed."[27] In recent years, researchers, many of them German, have demolished the myth of the Wehrmacht's innocence. "Backed by overwhelming evidence," says German historian Hannes Heer, "historical research has proved that the Wehrmacht participated and shared responsibility for the Nazi genocide."[28]* And the evidence they supply is overwhelming: At the very start of the conflict with the Soviet Union, several senior German officers instructed their soldiers that this was to be a war of annihilation in order to achieve National Socialism's racial goals, and junior officers, many of them Nazi Party members, constantly indoctrinated their troops in Nazi racial doctrines; because of a deliberate policy of liquidation, more than three million Russian POWs died of starvation, exposure, abuse, and indiscriminate shootings in camps run not by the SS but by the Wehrmacht; German military leaders agreed with and helped to implement the policy of confiscating food from the agriculturally rich Ukraine in order to feed the Wehrmacht and civilians back home, knowing that this would mean starvation and death for large numbers of Soviet citizens; the Wehrmacht assisted the Einsatzgruppen, the mobile killing squads, in rounding up Jews, cordoning off ghettos, and, at times, in the actual massacre of Soviet Jews; senior Wehrmacht generals were fully cognizant of the mass slaughter of Jews in the territories they had just conquered, and, at times, groups of curious enlisted men managed to see the sites where Jews were being annihilated and took pictures that they brought back home when on leave; in the war against Soviet partisans, the Wehrmacht executed thousands of hostages and burned to the ground tens of thousands of villages; and in Serbia, the Wehrmacht rounded up and slaughtered Jews, Roma, nationalists, and Communists in retaliation for partisan attacks. The pithy observation of German historian Jürgen Förster says it all: "Between 1939 and 1945, the military followed its supreme ideological and military commander [Hitler] ... and moved—as Christopher

---

*With the publication of *The Ministry and the Past* in 2010, four historians commissioned by the German government dispelled another Third Reich myth. Contrary to the long held view that Nazi Germany's Foreign Ministry opposed the Nazi regime, the book proves conclusively that German diplomats were criminally involved in the liquidation of Europe's Jews.

Browning has said—from 'abdication of responsibility to outright complicity.' With regard to the Holocaust, the Wehrmacht acted in many roles. It was perpetrator, collaborator, and bystander. Only after the war did it claim to be a victim."[29]

In the 1990s, the "Crimes of the Wehrmacht" exhibit, which included graphic photographs of atrocities, toured Germany. Seen by nearly a million people including many school children, the exhibit created a public furor. Despite opposition from the German Right—neo-Nazis staged marches—and the protests of some veterans, the exhibit and the publicity that it generated, including the commentary by knowledgeable historians and interviews with veterans who wanted to unburden themselves, helped to dispel the myth of the Wehrmacht's "clean hands."

It is true that the overwhelming majority of ordinary German soldiers did not actively participate in the murder of Jews and Soviet prisoners of war. But there is little doubt that, inspired by Hitler and Nazi ideology, they either tolerated or justified the criminal behavior of those who did. And certainly many ordinary soldiers participated in the looting and burning of Russian villages and in the expelling and deporting of villagers. Despite efforts to salvage the reputation of the Wehrmacht, the army brought no honor to Germany. The German soldier's skill, courage, and devotion to his fatherland served only to keep in power an evil ideology and evil men and to lead him to participate or assist in evil acts.

The German Clergy in the Confession Booth

For the most part, the German clergy also did not bring honor to their faith (there were, of course, a few notable exceptions; see Chapter 4, page 150). Both the German Evangelical (Lutheran) and German Catholic churches supported the Nazi regime, and with long histories of anti-Semitism they turned a blind eye to Nazi persecution of the Jews. Even before World War II and the implementation of genocide, many Evangelical churches approved of the Nazis' anti-Jewish legislation, banned baptized Jews from entering their temples, and dismissed pastors with Jewish ancestry. The complacency of the churches was graphically illustrated on November 8, 1938, Kristallnacht, when the Nazis orchestrated a massive pogrom in Germany. In a ruthless display of organized violence, the SS, at times aided by ordinary citizens, destroyed two hundred synagogues, wrecked more than seventy-five hundred Jewish-owned businesses, killed ninety-one Jews, and arrested almost thirty thousand others who were then sent to concentration camps. Harboring both a theological and nationalist contempt for Jews—the Jews were infamous enemies of Christ and dangerous aliens subverting the German nation—Catholic and Protestant clergy, with some rare exceptions, offered no formal protest. When the deportation of German Jews began in 1941, the churches continued to remain conspicuously silent. That the German churches complied with and backed the Third Reich and showed no public sympathy for the persecuted Jews—admittedly such protests could have meant arrest and the concentration camp—constitutes a depressing chapter in their history, which in recent decades they have publicly recognized and lamented.

Immediately after the war, however, the churches, in which many of the same clergy who had endorsed the Nazi regime still had considerable influence, gave little thought to their silent response to the brutalization, degradation, and mass murder of European Jewry. Despite objections from many clergy and laymen, Protestant leaders did issue in October 1945 the Stuttgart "Declaration of Guilt" in which they repented their lack of Christian resistance to Nazi evil, but they made no mention of the fate of the Jews. Or, still holding to a traditional Christian anti-Judaism, some German clergy interpreted the Holocaust as punishment from God for the crucifixion. Only gradually did German clergy confront their complacency to Jewish suffering during the war, condemn anti-Semitism forcefully, and seek interfaith dialogue with Jews. And increasingly they recognized—some with great reluctance—the uncomfortable truth that, in the words of Father John T. Pawlikowski, "many Catholics acquiesced or even collaborated with the Nazis because of the history of Christian anti-Semitism.... [C]lassical Christian anti-Semitism provided an indispensable seedbed for the growth of Nazism, especially on the popular level."[30] In 1950, an Evangelical church synod issued a declaration of guilt regarding the church's behavior toward the Jews: "We state that by omission and silence we became implicated before the God of mercy in the outrage which has been perpetrated against the Jews by the people of our nation."[31]

For nearly two millennia, the Roman Catholic Church had borne a hateful antipathy for Jews and Judaism based largely on the Gospel accounts of the crucifixion, but the Holocaust compelled the church to rethink its attitudes and teachings. In 1965, the Second Vatican Council promulgated *Nostra Aetate* (In Our Time), the first document in the church's history to speak affirmatively of Jews that is doctrinally binding. Although there was no recognition of Christian guilt for the baleful historic effects of its religious anti-Semitism, it did state that the crucifixion "cannot be charged against all Jews, without distinction, then alive, nor against the Jews of today." *Nostra Aetate* was a theological breakthrough that inaugurated a revolution in Catholic-Jewish relations. In 1973, the Catholic Church of Germany regretted its failings during the war and, in the spirit of Vatican II, proclaimed its responsibility to the Jewish people to dispel centuries-old hatred and disparagement:

> We are the country whose recent political history was darkened by the attempt to systematically exterminate the Jewish people. And in this period of National Socialism—despite the exemplary behavior of some individuals and groups—we were nevertheless as a whole a Church community who kept on living their life in turning their back too often on the fate of the persecuted Jewish people, ... who remained silent about the crimes committed against the Jews and Judaism.... We feel particularly distressed about the fact that Christians even took active part in these persecutions. The practical sincerity of our will of renewal is also linked to the confession of this guilt and the willingness to painfully learn from this history of guilt of our country and even our Church: to the extent that our German Church in particular ... is bound to accept special responsibility in respect of the encumbered relationship of the Church as a whole with the Jewish people and its religion.[32]

EMERGENCE OF THE COLD WAR

The Cold War (the American financier Bernard Baruch coined the phrase in 1947) stemmed from the divergent historical experiences and the incompatible political ambitions of the United States and the Soviet Union. The war produced a shift in power arrangements. The United States and the Soviet Union emerged as the two most powerful states in the world. The traditional Great Powers—Britain, France, and Germany—were now dwarfed by these superpowers. The United States had the atomic bomb and immense industrial might—its economy, previously suffering from the Great Depression, boomed during the war; the Soviet Union had the largest army in the world and was extending its dominion over Eastern Europe. With Germany defeated, the principal incentive for Soviet-American cooperation evaporated. The wartime coalition of the United States, Britain, and the Soviet Union was based solely on temporary political expediency—the need to defeat the common enemy. Both the United States and Britain had long disdained the Communist system and feared its spread to Western Europe, and the Soviet Union had a profound distrust for Western capitalist states, particularly Germany, which in both world wars had invaded Russia, leaving behind death and destruction. Fearing a revival of German power, Stalin was determined to protect Soviet security by annexing border regions and establishing subservient Communist governments throughout Eastern Europe.

Protecting the Soviet Union from its capitalist enemies was one major concern for Stalin. The other was to retain his absolute rule. The epic struggle against the Nazi invaders had further hardened Stalin. The liberation from terror and dictatorship, which many soldiers had hoped for as a reward for their heroism, never occurred. Sixty-six years old in 1945, Stalin displayed in his last years an unrelenting ruthlessness and paranoid suspiciousness. And as leader in the victorious war against Nazi Germany, his authority was unquestioned and his stature had grown immensely. The cult of the great leader was shaped and propagated by a vast propaganda machine that included the state-controlled media and educational institutions.

As the Red Army fought its way west in 1944–1945, Eastern European Communists, trained in the Soviet Union, followed. The Baltic states (Lithuania, Latvia, and Estonia), seized after the Nazi-Soviet Pact of 1939 and then lost to Hitler, were reincorporated into the Soviet Union. The Soviet Union also annexed part of East Prussia; Ruthenia in eastern Czechoslovakia, whose population was predominantly Ukrainian; parts of Romania; and eastern Poland, for which the Poles were compensated with German territory, including much of East Prussia. Elsewhere, Stalin respected, at least outwardly, the national sovereignty of the occupied countries by ruling through returning native Communists and whatever sympathizers he could find. In the Soviet-occupied zone of Germany, Stalin arranged for the establishment of Communist rule. Stalin knew that in free elections, Communists had little chance of winning and that left to their own devices these countries would return to their traditional anti-Russian orientation.

In what became Soviet client states, Stalin retained a morbid fear of nationalist and anti-Communist insurgencies backed by the capitalist West. Poles, for example, had bitter historical memories of being under Russian rule until after World War I. Strongly Catholic, they also hated the atheistic Communist ideology and resented the Soviet Union for invading eastern Poland in 1939 and deporting hundreds of thousands of Poles to desolate regions of the Soviet Union, for massacring thousands of Polish officers during the war, and for not helping the Polish insurrection against the Nazis in 1944. It would also be extremely difficult to win the hearts of Czechs and Hungarians, who were passionately patriotic and identified with Western Europe, and of the Baltic nations, which hated Russian domination.

Local populations and their supporters in Western European lands viewed the Soviet occupation of Eastern Europe as a calamity that replaced Nazi totalitarianism with Communist totalitarianism. But unwilling to risk another war, Western countries were powerless to intervene. By the end of 1948, the lands of Eastern Europe had become Soviet satellites. Wartime cooperation between the former allies, admittedly tenuous and forced, was replaced by suspicion and hostility, initiating the era of the Cold War. For the next forty-five years, the two parts of the Continent would be known as East Europe and West Europe: two camps of opposing ideologies. In Churchill's famous words, "From Stettin in the Baltic to Trieste in the Adriatic, an iron curtain has descended across the Continent."[33]

Profoundly concerned, American leaders undertook the responsibility of rallying Western Europe, and possibly the world, against universal Communism, another form of totalitarianism that threatened both freedom and the free market. And, in what is a significant consequence of the war, the three Axis powers—(West) Germany, Italy, and Japan—embraced democratic principles and sided with the United States and its allies in their hostility to Communism and Soviet expansion. At the same time, the United States was concerned about the rapid growth of Communist parties throughout non-Soviet occupied Europe. The specter of these countries ruled by Communist parties with allegiance to the Soviet Union was a gnawing worry for American policy makers.

EUROPEAN UNITY

Whereas after World War I nationalist passions intensified, the Hitler years convinced many Europeans of the dangers inherent in extreme nationalism. After two ruinous world wars, most people felt the price of violent conflict had become excessive; war no longer served any national interest, and fear of the Soviet Union prodded West Europeans toward greater cooperation and integration. A major step in this direction was taken in 1951 when the chief continental consumers and producers of coal and steel, the two items most essential for the rebuilding of Western Europe, created the European Coal and Steel Community, the foundation of today's European Union.

THE DEMISE OF EUROPEAN IMPERIALISM

World War II accelerated the disintegration of Europe's overseas empires. The war had stirred up non-Western peoples living under colonial rule to liberate themselves. The European states could hardly justify ruling over Africans and Asians after they had fought to liberate European lands from German imperialism. Nor could they ask their people, exhausted by the Hitler years and concentrating all their energies on reconstruction, to fight new wars against Africans and Asians pressing for independence. In this setting, a mighty groundswell of decolonization eventually abolished all overseas empires. In the years just after the war, Great Britain surrendered India, France lost Lebanon and Syria, and the Dutch departed from Indonesia. In the 1950s and 1960s, virtually every colonial territory gained independence. In those instances where the colonial power resisted independence for the colony, as in Algeria and Indochina (Vietnam), both ruled by the French, the price was bloodshed.

THE WAR AND WESTERN CONSCIOUSNESS

The Nazi era, which repudiated the core ideals of the Enlightenment, had a profound impact on Western consciousness. It showed the fragility of the Enlightenment tradition of reason, freedom, and human dignity. The popularity of Fascism in many European lands demonstrated that liberty is not appealing to many people—that, at any rate, there are many things they consider more important. It seems that without much reluctance, people will trade freedom for security, a feeling of solidarity with their fellows, or national grandeur. And the Nazis' criminal behavior demonstrated that in an age of heightened national feeling, a determination to further the interests of the nation could precipitate and justify horrendous crimes against other ethnic groups.

A painful lesson of the Nazi era is how easily the rational mind can be made to surrender to dangerous political myths and how important it is to comprehend the impact of the irrational on political life. Nazism's idolization of the leader, the race, the party, and the state and its core belief in a Jewish conspiracy to destroy Germany and dominate the world were striking examples of human irrationality, the triumph of mythical thinking over reason. The wide acceptance of these myths shows how easily people can be indoctrinated to believe what is absurd and, dominated by these beliefs, to demonstrate an astonishing capacity for inhumanity that elevates barbarism to an accepted norm. In his trial after the war, a member of a police battalion involved in the extermination of Jews told the court: "I would like to say that it did not at all occur to me that these orders could be unjust.... I was then of the conviction that the Jews were ... guilty. I believed the propaganda that all Jews were criminals and subhumans and that they were the cause of Germany's decline after the First World War. The thought that one should disobey or evade the order to participate in the extermination of the Jews did not therefore enter my mind at all."[34]

The Nazi vision of a regenerated nation—a New Order led by a determined and heroic elite arising from the ruins of a decadent Old Order—also had the appeal of a great myth. The myth of rebirth—of a nation cured of evil and building a new and vigorous society—had a profound impact on people angered at the aftermath of World War I and dissatisfied with liberal society and searching for new beliefs. The myth of the nation reborn, suffused with a racial spirit that united all Germans in the hope of constructing an ethnic utopia, answered a metaphysical yearning to give meaning to life and history. National Socialist ideology provided an emotionally gratifying worldview at a time when many people had lost confidence in liberal-democratic ideals and institutions, and it evoked commitment and loyalty. That many Germans, including many of the intellectual elite, succumbed to Hitler's charisma and an irrational Nazi ideology unnerved Western liberals who were heirs to the Enlightenment tradition of reason.

Nazi racial theories showed that even in an age of sophisticated science, the mind remains attracted to irrational beliefs that are fraught with danger. Committed to these beliefs, people will annihilate all traditional moral precepts and torture and kill with religious-like zeal and machine-like indifference. This regression to mythical thinking and savagery bears out Walter Lippmann's contention that "men have been barbarians much longer than they have been civilized. They are only precariously civilized, and within us there is the propensity, persistent as the force of gravity, to revert under stress and strain, or under temptation, to our first natures."[35]

Many German intellectuals avidly served the Nazi cause, helping to seduce a nation into believing that National Socialism represented a new and higher morality, that Hitler was leading the German people into a new and glorious age, and that they were participants in a noble patriotic mission. The behavior of these intellectuals contains a distressing warning, says German historian Karl Dietrich Bracher: "The intellectuals who supported the Nazis in one way or another all document that the mind can be temporarily seduced, that people can be bribed with careers and fame, that thinking people, especially, are tempted by an irrational cult of action and are peculiarly susceptible to 'one-dimensional' answers and promises of salvation."[36] One might add another limitation of thinking people: a propensity for rationalization and self-justification. In every land, intellectuals and other elites who embraced Nazi ideology and colluded with Nazi policies spun a web of rationalizations to justify their support, even claiming to be defenders of European civilization.

The Holocaust was heightened irrationality and organized evil on an unprecedented scale. Auschwitz, Treblinka, Sobibor, and the other death factories represent the triumph of human irrationality over reason—the surrender of the mind to a bizarre racial mythology that provided a metaphysical and pseudo-scientific justification for mass murder. They also represent the ultimate perversion of reason. A calculating reason divorced from human values manufactured and organized lies and demented beliefs into a structured system with its own inner logic and employed sophisticated technology to meticulously destroy human beings spiritually and physically. Science and technology, venerated as

the great achievement of the Western mind, had made industrialized mass murder possible.

So too did modern rationalized bureaucratic techniques. In the late nineteenth century, prominent German sociologist Max Weber had warned that
the secular rationality that characterizes the modern world produces bureaucracies that, in their relentless pursuit of efficiency, depersonalize the individual.
Modern bureaucrats, said Weber, are emotionally detached; concerned only
with the efficient execution of tasks, they employ reason in a cold and calculating way. Treating people impersonally, as mere objects, these bureaucrats rule
out human feelings such as compassion and affection as hindrances to expediency, efficiency, and effectiveness. Weber's warning proved to be an apt description of the professional bureaucrats who, from their desks, diligently and
meticulously served as functionaries of genocide, organizing the deportations to
the death camps and processing the confiscation of Jewish property. And it
described as well the SS, who systematically disposed of the "freight" in gas
chambers and systematically harvested the victims' jewelry, clothing, and body
remains—hair (for industrial use) and gold teeth (for currency). To the SS, Jews
had ceased to be human. After the war, the incarcerated Franz Stangl, commandant of the Treblinka killing center in which 870,000 Jews were exterminated,
told an interviewer that he had viewed his victims as cattle in a slaughterhouse.

The thinkers of the Enlightenment had not foreseen the destructive power
inherent in reason. Historian Omer Bartov poses this disturbing question about
the failure of reason and the Western humanist tradition:

> What was it that induced Nobel Prize-winning scientists, internationally
> respected legal scholars, physicians known throughout the world for
> their research into the human body and their desire to ameliorate the lot
> of humanity, to become not merely opportunist accomplices, but in
> many ways the initiators and promoters of this attempt to subject the
> human race to a vast surgical operation by means of mass extermination
> of whole categories of human beings? What was there (or is there) in
> our culture that made the concept of transforming humanity by means
> of eugenic and racial cleansing seem so practical and rational?[37]

Related questions might be added to Bartov's list: Why did so many ordinary Germans living in a modern and civilized society embrace the Nazi racial
state and willingly carry out its criminal policies? How much responsibility do
ordinary Germans bear for atrocities committed by a government they supported
and that acted in their name? Why were so many members of the clergy supporters of the Nazi regime? Why were these bearers of a message of humanity so
uncaring regarding the dehumanizing, despoiling, deportation, and eventually
the mass murder of Jews?

Both the Christian and the Enlightenment traditions had failed the German
nation and its many collaborators and sympathizers throughout Europe. And the
millions of people who backed Hitler had betrayed Western civilization's core
principles, as Joachim Wieder, a German officer and veteran of Stalingrad, concluded after the war:

> By means of a destructive battle against the universal educational and cultural powers of classic antiquity, humanism, and Christianity, an anti-intellectual political religion of power had successively extracted the German people from the best of the commonly-held European body of human thought and thereby also out of any commitment to the objective concepts of truth, compassion and justice.[38]

And this has implications for our own day. "[W]hat is both historically unique and persistently disturbing about the Holocaust" notes Bernhard Schlink, a prominent German novelist, "is that Germany, with its cultural heritage and place among civilised nations, was capable of those kinds of atrocities. It elicits troubling questions: if the ice of a culturally-advanced civilisation upon which one fancied oneself safely standing, was in fact so thin at that time, then how safe is the ice we live upon today?"[39]

For many intellectuals, Auschwitz marked a breach in the progressive advancement of European civilization. It demonstrated that against the forces of mythical thinking, fanaticism, and the human being's limitless capacity for committing and justifying evil, our rational faculties that were so admired by the philosophes of the Enlightenment and their liberal heirs have limited power. It demonstrated also that reason, harnessed and perverted by these dark forces, can extinguish Western civilization's core values. It would forever cast doubt on the Enlightenment's conception of human goodness, secular rationality, and the progress of civilization through advances in science and technology.

Christian thinkers drew a different conclusion. They saw Nazism, and its horrors, as a consequence of modern Europe's growing secularization and turning away from God, both developments advanced by the Enlightenment. They insisted that reason without God degenerates into an overriding concern for technical efficiency without regard for human concerns, and the self without God degenerates into the domination and exploitation of others—the mentality that conceived and administered Auschwitz. Human dignity conceived purely in secular terms does not permit us to recognize the *thou* of another human being, to see another person as someone who has been dignified by God. Without reorienting thinking around God and transcendent moral absolutes, argued Christian thinkers, liberal democracy cannot resist the totalitarian temptation or overcome human wickedness.

In 1945, only the naive could have faith in continuous progress or believe in the essential goodness of the individual—the questions of evil and fanaticism would become principal areas of philosophical inquiry. Many intellectuals shocked by the irrationality and radical evil of the Hitler era drifted into despair. To these thinkers, life was absurd, without meaning; human beings could neither comprehend nor control it. The Enlightenment philosophes' hopes for a free and rational society seemed illusory.

Nevertheless, this profound disillusionment was tempered by hope. Democracy had, in fact, prevailed over Nazi totalitarianism and terror. In the post–World War I era, it was common for intellectuals to pour scorn on liberal democracy as weak and ineffective. Some even praised Fascist movements for their dynamism and virility and provided ideological justification for these movements. After the Nazi experience, fewer European intellectuals were attracted to the anti-democratic thought of the radical Right. The full disclosure of Nazi barbarism convinced many of them, even some who had wavered in previous decades, that reason, freedom, and human dignity—the legacy of the Enlightenment—were precious ideals and that liberal constitutional government, despite its imperfections, was the best means of preserving these ideals. To be sure, immediately after the war, many Europeans gravitated to the Left, believing that the Communists, who had been very active in resistance movements against the Nazis and Fascists, would overcome social injustice. However, in the decades to come, more disclosures of Communist oppression and ineptitude would greatly weaken Marxism's appeal. The future for Western civilization belonged to liberal (and social) democracy, its institutions and values, for which the West had fought and sacrificed in World War II. A year before he perished at Normandy, a young British soldier wrote to a friend in words that would aptly describe the sentiments of many skeptical liberal-democrats immediately after the war: "To … admit any hope of a better world is criminally foolish, as foolish as it is to stop working for it."[40]

NOTES

1. Walter Laqueur, *Europe Since Hitler* (Baltimore: Penguin Books, 1970), 118.

2. A. C. Grayling, *Among the Dead Cities: The History and Moral Legacy of the WWII Bombing of Civilians in Germany and Japan* (New York: Walker & Company, 2006), 205.

3. Nicholas Stargardt, *Witnesses of War: Children's Lives Under the Nazis* (New York: Alfred A. Knopf, 2005), 351.

4. Alfred-Maurice de Zayas, *A Terrible Revenge: The Ethnic Cleansing of the East European Germans* (New York: Palgrave Macmillan, 2006), 97.

5. Tony Judt, *Postwar: A History of Europe Since 1945* (New York: Penguin Press, 2005), 45–46.

6. Istvan Deak, *Essays on Hitler's Europe* (Lincoln: University of Nebraska Press, 2001), 182.

7. Atina Grossmann, *Jews, Germans, and Allies: Close Encounters in Occupied Europe* (Princeton, NJ: Princeton University Press, 2007), 39.

8. Robert E. Conot, *Justice at Nuremberg* (New York: Harper & Row, 1983), 380.

9. David Cesarani, "War Crimes," in *The Holocaust Encyclopedia*, ed. Walter Laqueur (New Haven, CT: Yale University Press, 2001), 680.

10. Atina Grossman, "Trauma, Memory, and Motherhood: Germans and Jewish Displaced Persons in Post-Nazi Germany, 1945–1949," in *Life After Death: Approaches to a Cultural and Social History of Europe During the 1940s and 1950s*, ed. Richard Bessel and Dirk Schumann (New York: Cambridge University Press: 2003), 113.

11. *The Goebbels Diaries 1942–1943*, ed. and trans. Louis P. Lochner (Garden City, NY: Doubleday, 1948), 366.

12. Gerold Frank, "The Tragedy of the DPs," *The New Republic* (April 1, 1946), 436.

13. Norman Cohn, *Warrant for Genocide* (New York: Harper Torchbooks, 1967), 253.

14. Gerhard L. Weinberg, "The Allies and the Holocaust," in *The Holocaust and History,* ed. Michael Berenbaum and Abraham J. Peck (Bloomington: Indiana University Press, 1998), 489.

15. Sönke Neitzel, ed., *Tapping Hitler's Generals: Transcripts of Secret Conversations, 1942–45* (Barnsley, S. Yorkshire: Frontline Books, 2007), 130.

16. André Gerrits, *The Myth of Jewish Communism: A Historical Interpretation* (Brussels: Peter Lang, 2009), 9–10.

17. Quoted in Jeffrey K. Olich, *In the House of the Hangman: The Agonies of German Defeat, 1943–1949* (Chicago: University of Chicago Press, 2005), 170.

18. Judt, *Postwar,* 271.

19. Victor Klemperer, *I Will Bear Witness: A Diary of the Nazi Years,* trans. Martin Chalmers (New York: Random House, 1999), vol. 2, 478.

20. Grossmann, *Jews, Germans, and Allies,* 38.

21. Martin Dean, *Robbing the Jews: The Confiscation of Jewish Property in the Holocaust, 1933–1945* (New York: Cambridge University Press, 2008), 385–386.

22. Walter Seinsch, "Afterword," in Götz Aly, *Into the Tunnel, The Brief Life Of Marion Samuel 1931–1943,* trans. Ann Millin (New York: Henry Holt, 2007), 111.

23. Rolf-Dieter Müller, "The Results of the War," in *Hitler's War in the East: A Critical Assessment,* ed. Rolf-Dieter Müller and Gerd R. Ueberschär (New York: Berghahn Books, 2002), 373.

24. Gerhard L. Weinberg, *Germany Hitler and World War II: Essays in Modern German and World History* (Cambridge: Cambridge University Press, 1995), 307.

25. Hans Guderian, *Panzer Leader,* trans. Constantine Fitzgibbon (New York: Da Capo Press, 1996), 446.

26. Stephen G. Fritz, *Frontsoldaten: The German Soldier in World War II* (Lexington: The University Press of Kentucky, 1995), 199.

27. Hannes Heer and Klaus Naumann, eds., *War of Extermination: The German Military in World War II 1941–1944* (New York: Berghahn Books, 2004), 8.

28. Hannes Heer, "How Amorality Became Normality: Reflections on the Mentality of German Soldiers on the Eastern Front," in *War of Extermination: The German Military in World War II 1941–1944,* ed. Hannes Heer and Klaus Naumann (New York: Berghahn Books, 2004), 329.

29. Jürgen Förster, "Complicity or Entanglement: Wehrmacht, War and Holocaust," in *The Holocaust and History: The Known, the Unknown, the Disputed, and the Reexamined,* ed. Michael Berenbum and Abraham J. Peck (Bloomington: Indiana University Press, 2002), 280.

30. John T. Pawlikowski, "Divine and Human Responsibility in the Light of the Holocaust," in *Humanity at the Limit: The Impact of the Holocaust Experience on Jews and Christians,* ed. Michael A. Signer (Bloomington: Indiana University Press, 2000), 24.

31. Excerpted in Marvin Perry and Fredrick M. Schweitzwer, eds., *Antisemitic Myths: A Historical and Contemporary Anthology* (Bloomington: Indiana University Press, 2008), 241.

32. Hans Hermann Henrix, "In the Shadow of the Shoah: Being a Theologian in Germany Today," in *Humanity at the Limit: The Impact of the Holocaust Experience on*

Jews and Christians, ed. Michael A. Singer (Bloomington: Indiana University Press, 2000), 71.

33. Winston S. Churchill, "Sinews of Peace: Address, March 5, 1946," *Vital Speeches of the Day*, March 15, 1946, 3.

34. Ernst Klee, Willi Dressen, and Volker Ries, eds., *"The Good Old Days," The Holocaust as Seen by Its Perpetrators and Bystanders*, trans. Deborah Burnstone (New York: The Free Press, 1991), 220–221.

35. Walter Lippmann, *The Public Philosophy* (Boston: Little, Brown, 1955), 86.

36. Karl Dietrich Bracher, *Turning Points in Modern Times*, trans. Thomas Dunlap (Cambridge, MA: Harvard University Press, 1995), 198.

37. Omer Bartov, *Germany's War and the Holocaust: Disputed Histories* (Ithaca, NY: Cornell University Press, 2003), 136.

38. Joachim Wieder, *Stalingrad: Memories and Assessments*, trans. Helmut Bogler (London: Arms and Armour, 1993), 87.

39. Bernhard Schlink, *Guilt about the Past* (Toronto: House of Anansi, 2009), 29.

40. Paul Fussell, ed., *The Norton Book of Modern War* (New York: W. W. Norton, 1991), 381.

Selected Bibliography

Atkinson, Rick. *The Day of Battle: The War in Sicily and Italy 1943–1944*. New York: Henry Holt, 2007.

Bastable, Jonathan. *Voices from Stalingrad: Nemesis on the Volga*. Newton Abbot, UK: David and Charles, 2006.

Bartov, Omer. *Hitler's Army: Soldiers, Nazis, and War in the Third Reich*. New York: Oxford University Press, 1991.

Beevor, Antony. *Stalingrad: The Fateful Siege: 1942–1943*. New York: Viking, 1998.

———. *The Fall of Berlin 1945*. New York: Viking, 2002.

———. *D-Day: The Battle for Normandy*. New York: Viking, 2009.

Bellamy, Chris. *Absolute War: Soviet Russia in the Second World War*. New York: Alfred A. Knopf, 2007.

Berenbaum, Michael, ed. *A Mosaic of Victims: Non-Jews Persecuted and Murdered by the Nazis*. New York: New York University Press, 1990.

Bessel, Richard. *Germany 1945: From War to Peace*. New York: HarperCollins, 2009.

Braithwaite, Rodric. *Moscow 1941: A City and Its People at War*. London: Profile Books, 2006.

Brighton, Terry. *Patton, Montgomery, Rommel: Masters of War*. New York: Crown, 2009.

Burrin, Philippe. *France Under the Germans: Collaboration and Compromise*. New York: New Press, 1996.

Churchill, Winston, S. *The Second World War*. 6 vols. Boston: Houghton Mifflin, 1948.

Citino, Robert M. *Death of the Wehrmacht: The German Campaigns of 1942*. Lawrence: University Press of Kansas, 2007.

Clark, Lloyd. *Crossing the Rhine: Breaking into Nazi Germany 1944 and 1945; The Greatest Airborne Battles in History*. New York: Atlantic Monthly Press, 2008.

Cowley, Robert, ed. *No End Save Victory: Perspectives on World War II*. New York: G. P. Putnam's, 2001.

Dallas, Gregor. *1945: The War That Never Ended*. New Haven, CT: Yale University Press, 2005.

Dear, I. C. B., ed. *The Oxford Companion to the Second World War*. New York: Oxford University Press, 1995.

Eisenhower, Dwight. *Crusade in Europe*. Garden City, NY: Garden City Books, 1948.

Ellis, John. *Brute Force: Allied Strategy and Tactics in the Second World War*. New York: Viking, 1990.

Evans, Richard J. *The Third Reich at War*. New York: Penguin, 2009.

Flower, Desmond, and James Reeves, eds. *The War 1939–1945: A Documentary History*. New York: Da Capo Press, 1997.

Friedländer, Saul. *The Years of Extermination: Nazi Germany and the Jews, 1939–1945*. New York: HarperCollins, 2007.

Friedrich, Jörg. *The Fire: The Bombing of Germany 1940–1945*. New York: Columbia University Press, 2006.

Fritz, Stephen G. *Frontsoldaten: The German Soldier in World War II*. Lexington: The University Press of Kentucky, 1995.

——————. *Endkampf: Soldiers, Civilians, and the Death of the Third Reich*. Lexington: The University Press of Kentucky, 2004.

Gilbert, Martin. *The Day the War Ended: May 8, 1945—Victory in Europe*. New York: H. Holt, 1995.

Glantz, David M. *Barbarossa: Hitler's Invasion of Russia, 1941*. Stroud, UK: Tempus, 2001.

Glantz, David M., and Jonathan M. House. *The Battle of Kursk*. Lawrence: University Press of Kansas, 1999.

Goebbels, Joseph. *Final Entries 1945: The Diaries of Joseph Goebbels*. Edited and annotated by Hugh Trevor-Roper. New York: Putnam, 1978.

Grayling, A. C. *Among the Dead Cities: The History and Moral Legacy of the WWII Bombing of Civilians in Germany and Japan*. New York: Walker and Co., 2006.

Guderian, Heinz. *Panzer Leader*. New York: Da Capo Press, 1996.

Halder, Franz. *The Halder War Diary, 1932–1942*. Edited by Charles Burdick and Hans-Adolf Jacobsen. Novato, CA: Presidio, 1988.

Hastings, Max. *Armageddon: The Battle for Germany, 1944–1945*. New York: A. A. Knopf, 2004.

Heer, Hannes, and Klaus Naumann, eds. *War of Extermination: The German Military in World War II 1941–1944*. New York: Berghahn, 2004.

Hitchcock, William I. *The Bitter Road to Freedom: A New History of the Liberation of Europe*. New York: Free Press, 2009.

Hitler's Table Talk, 1941–1944. Edited with preface and essay by H. R. Trevor-Roper. New York: EnigmaBooks, 2008.

Hoyt, Edward P. *Backwater War: The Allied Campaign in Italy, 1943–1945*. Westport, CT: Praeger, 2002.

Jackson, Julian. *The Fall of France: The Nazi Invasion of 1940*. New York: Oxford University Press, 2003.

Jones, Michael. *The Retreat: Hitler's First Defeat*. New York: Thomas Dunne, 2010.

——————. *Leningrad: State of Siege*. New York: Basic Books, 2008.

——————. *Stalingrad: How the Red Army Survived the German Onslaught*. Philadelphia: Casemate, 2007.

Kershaw, Ian. *The End: The Defiance and Destruction of Hitler's Germany, 1944–1945*. New York: Penguin, 2011.

Kershaw, Robert J. *D-Day: Piercing the Atlantic Wall*. Annapolis, MD: Naval Institute Press, 1994.

Klemperer, Victor. *I Will Bear Witness: A Diary of the Nazi Years*. New York: Modern Library, 2001.

Korda Michael. *With Wings Like Eagles: A History of the Battle of Britain*. New York: Harper, 2009.

Laqueur, Walter, ed. *The Holocaust Encyclopedia*. New Haven, CT: Yale University Press, 2001.

Liddell-Hart, Basil Henry, ed. *The German Generals Talk*. New York: W. Morrow, 1979.

————, ed. *The Rommel Papers*. New York: Da Capo Press, 1982.

Lukas, Richard C. *Forgotten Holocaust: The Poles Under German Occupation 1939–1944*. New York: Hippocrene, 2001.

Mazower, Mark. *Hitler's Empire: How the Nazis Ruled Europe*. New York: Penguin, 2008.

Merridale, Catherine, *Ivan's War: Life and Death in the Red Army, 1939–1945*. New York: Metropolitan, 2006.

Moorhouse, Robert. *Berlin at War*. New York: Basic Books, 2010.

Morison, Samuel Eliot. *History of United States Naval Operations in World War II*. Vol. 1, *The Battle of the Atlantic 1939–1943*. Boston: Little, Brown, 1947.

Müller, Rolf-Dieter, and G. R. Ueberschär, eds. *Hitler's War in the East: A Critical Assessment*. New York: Berghahn, 2002.

Nagorski, Andrew. *The Greatest Battle: Stalin, Hitler, and the Desperate Struggle for Moscow that Changed the Course of World War II*. New York: Simon and Schuster, 2007.

Overy, Richard. *Russia's War: Blood upon the Snow*. New York: TV Books, 1997.

————. *Why the Allies Won*. New York: W. W. Norton, 1995.

Parker, Danny S., ed. *Hitler's Ardennes Offensive: The German View of the Battle of the Bulge*. Mechanicsburg, PA: Stackpole, 1997.

Porch, Douglas. *The Path to Victory: The Mediterranean Theater in World War II*. New York: Farrar, Straus, and Giroux, 2004.

Read, Anthony, and David Fisher. *The Fall of Berlin*. London: Hutchinson, 1992.

Roberts, Andrew. *The Storm of War: A New History of the Second World War*. New York: Allen Lane, 2009.

Snyder, Timothy. *Bloodlands: Europe Between Hitler and Stalin*. New York: Basic Books, 2010.

Tucker-Jones, Anthony. *Falaise: The Flawed Victory; The Destruction of Panzergruppe West, August, 1944*. Barnsley, South Yorkshire: Pen and Sword Military, 2008.

Weinberg, Gerald L. *A World at Arms: A Global History of World War II*. New York: Cambridge University Press, 2005.

Werner, Herbert A. *Iron Coffins: A Personal Account of the German U-Boat Battles of World War II*. New York: Bantam Books, 1978.

Wieder, Joachim. *Stalingrad: Memories and Reassessments*. London: Arms and Armour, 1995.

Wilson, Theodore A., ed. *D-Day 1944*. Lawrence: University Press of Kansas, 1994.

Zayas, Alfred-Maurice de. *A Terrible Revenge: The Ethnic Cleansing of the East European Germans, 1944–1950*. 2nd rev. ed. New York: Palgrave Macmillan, 2006.

Index